THE SIGNIFYING MONKEY

THE SIGNIFYING MONKEY

MONKEY

*A Theory of Afro-American
Literary Criticism*

Henry Louis Gates, Jr.

New York   Oxford
OXFORD UNIVERSITY PRESS
1988

OXFORD UNIVERSITY PRESS

Oxford   New York   Toronto
Delhi   Bombay   Calcutta   Madras   Karachi
Petaling Jaya   Singapore   Hong Kong   Tokyo
Nairobi   Dar es Salaam   Cape Town
Melbourne   Auckland

and associated companies in
Berlin   Ibadan

Published by Oxford University Press, Inc.
200 Madison Avenue, New York, New York 10016

Oxford is a registered trademark of Oxford University Press

Library of Congress Cataloging-in-Publication Data
Gates, Henry Louis, Jr.
The signifying monkey.
Bibliography: p.   Includes index.
1. American literature—Afro-American authors—History
and criticism—Theory, etc.   2. Afro-Americans—Intellectual life.
3. Afro-Americans in literature.   4. Criticism—United States.
5. Oral tradition—United States.   6. Mythology, African, in literature.
7. Afro-Americans—Folklore.   8. American literature—African influences.
I. Title.
PS153.N5G28   1988   810'.9'896073   88–14005
ISBN 0–19–503463–5

3 5 7 9 8 6 4 2

Printed in the United States of America
on acid-free paper

For Sharon Adams

There is a cruel contradiction implicit in the art form itself. For true jazz is an art of individual assertion within and against the group. Each true jazz moment (as distinct from the uninspired commercial performance) springs from a contest in which each artist challenges all the rest, each solo flight, or improvisation, represents (like the successive canvases of a painter) a definition of his identity: as individual, as member of the collectivity and as link in the chain of tradition. Thus, because jazz finds its very life in an endless improvisation upon traditional materials, the jazzman must lose his identity even as he finds it.

Ralph Ellison

Improvisation is the play of black differences.   Kimberly W. Benston

Slowly but steadily, in the following years, a new vision began gradually to replace the dream of political power,—a powerful movement, the rise of another ideal to guide the unguided, another pillar of fire by night after a clouded day. It was the ideal of "book-learning"; the curiosity, born of compulsory ignorance, to know and test the power of the cabalistic letters of the white man, the longing to know. Here at last seemed to have been discovered the mountain path to Canaan; longer than the highway of Emancipation and law, steep and rugged, but straight, leading to heights high enough to overlook life.

*   *   *

The would-be black *savant* was confronted by the paradox that the knowledge his people needed was a twice-told tale to his white neighbors, while the knowledge which would teach the white world was Greek to his own flesh and blood. The innate love of harmony and beauty that set the ruder souls of his people a-dancing and a-singing raised but confusion and doubt in the soul of the black artist; for the beauty revealed to him was the soul-beauty of a race which his larger audience despised, and he could not articulate the message of another people. This waste of double aims, this seeking to satisfy two unreconciled ideals, has wrought sad havoc with the courage and faith and deeds of ten thousand thousand people,—has sent them often wooing false gods and invoking false means of salvation, and at times has even seemed about to make them ashamed of themselves.   W. E. B. Du Bois

Look like to me only a fool would want you to talk in a way that feel peculiar to your mind.   Alice Walker

Preface

The Signifying Monkey, even more than is usual, has been shaped with the help of my friends. The central idea of this book assumed its initial form in a paper that I delivered at a Yale English Department seminar on Parody, conducted by James A. Snead, an old friend since our undergraduate days at Yale College. Snead's enthusiastic response, and that of his students, confirmed my hope that I had at last located within the African and Afro-American traditions a system of rhetoric and interpretation that could be drawn upon both as *figures* for a genuinely "black" criticism and as *frames* through which I could interpret, or "read," theories of contemporary literary criticism.

After several active years of work applying literary theory to African and Afro-American literatures, I realized that what had early on seemed to me to be the fulfillment of my project as a would-be theorist of black literature was, in fact, only a moment in a progression. The challenge of my project, if not exactly to invent a black theory, was to locate and identify how the "black tradition" had theorized about itself. It was Geoffrey H. Hartman, shortly after my return to Yale from graduate school at Cambridge, who issued this challenge to me, accompanied by what has proven to be his unflagging support for this project.

✳ [Ralph Ellison's example of a thoroughly integrated critical discourse, informed by the black vernacular tradition and Western criticism, provided the model for my work.] Ishmael Reed's formal revision and critique of the Afro-American literary tradition, a project that had arrested my attention since graduate school, helped to generate this theory, especially as Reed manifested his critique in his third novel, *Mumbo Jumbo.* It seemed to me that the relation of Reed's text to those of Ralph Ellison and Richard Wright, Jean Toomer and Sterling A. Brown, and Zora Neale Hurston, was a "Signifyin(g)" relation, as the Afro-American tradition would have it. Through Reed's character, Papa La Bas, I was able to construct a myth of origins for Signifyin(g) and its sign, the Signifying Monkey. Slowly and surely, my search for a chart of descent for the Monkey ended with that Pan-African repository of figuration and interpretation, Esu-Elegbara, the Yoruba trickster figure, by way of Nigeria, Benin, Brazil, Cuba, Haiti, and New Orleans. In a curious way, which I was to realize only much later, my discovery of Esu was a rediscovery; for my supervisor at Cambridge, John Holloway, had forced me to read Frobenius's *The Voice of Africa* a decade ago, and it was there that I first met Esu-Elegbara. But it was the Afro-American tradition that generated the concept of Signifyin(g).

A close reading of two texts has led to a theory of criticism. Ellison's critical practice and Reed's revisionary techniques of parody and pastiche generated the ideas that I develop in this book. Needless to say, neither Ellison nor Reed is in any way responsible for the extended interpretations suggested to me by *Shadow and Act* and *Mumbo Jumbo*.

Wole Soyinka's works of literature and criticism provide the African model to be strived for. Soyinka is one of the few black authors who assumes his propositions rather than claims them. This simple rhetorical gesture is devastatingly effective. Moreover, no matter how particular his subject matter appears to be, Soyinka always makes of his materials a statement about the human condition. My love of Yoruba culture and language was awakened by my friendship with Soyinka. I only hope that my analysis of his Yoruba metaphysics does that remarkable system of thought justice.

One marvelous advantage of teaching literature at Yale was the bountiful advice that one's colleagues provide. In addition to James Snead's early encouragement, I benefited from initial critical readings of parts of this manuscript generously undertaken by Fredric Jameson, Thomas R. Whitaker, Robert F. Thompson, John W. Blassingame, and Gerald Jaynes. J. Hillis Miller encouraged me to submit a first draft of what became the blueprint for this book to *Critical Inquiry*. The enthusiastic response from W. J. T. Mitchell and his board of editors gave me the energy necessary to develop my ideas into a book. Anthony Appiah's remarkable analytic abilities, and his sustaining goodwill, made the writing of this book a pleasure shared with one of the most fertile minds in the academy.

Michael G. Cooke and Robert B. Stepto's searching criticisms forced me to clarify much of my argument. Kimberly Benston's generous advice, marginalia, and encouragement at each step in the development of the drafts that led to this book provided a certain sense of direction that determined the nature and tone of my arguments.

Houston A. Baker, Jr., whose subtle and insightful book, *Blues, Ideology, and Afro-American Literature: A Vernacular Theory,* accomplishes with the blues what I try to accomplish here with Signifyin(g), deserves a special expression of gratitude. Baker, in so many senses, serves as my ideal reader, as the critical voice that I trust and respect and to which I address my work. Baker's use of the black vernacular inspired my own approach to theory by assuring me that I was on the right path. My reading of his manuscript convinced me that in the blues and in Signifyin(g) were to be found the black tradition's two great repositories of its theory of itself, encoded in musical and linguistic forms. This book, in so many ways, was written out of my deep regard for Houston Baker's critical presence.

Mary Helen Washington and Barbara Johnson, colleagues and kindred spirits with whom I correspond regularly about our field, also helped me to shape this book and complete it. To be privileged to receive such generous criticism while a book exists as but vaguely defined intuitions—that is the true benefit of being a member of a community. My debt to these friends is difficult to repay, or even to acknowledge appropriately.

The opportunity to deliver long sections of this book at the Modern Language Association (1981), the Yale English Department Faculty Colloquium (1982, 1983), the Whitney Humanities Center (1982, 1984), and John Szwed's National Endowment for the Humanities summer seminar (1984) yielded helpful suggestions for expansion, elaboration, and revision, as did lectures at the University of Pennsylvania, Princeton, the University of California at Los Angeles, Louisiana State University, and the University of Chicago. Peter Demetz's invitation to lecture in his regular course on contemporary criticism and his perceptive reading of an early draft of one chapter helped me to develop certain aspects of this theory that earlier versions merely implied. Subsequent readings by Margaret Homans, Susan Willis, R. W. B. Lewis, José Piedra, Jacques Derrida, James Olney, Ronald Rassner, Robert O'Meally, Ishmael Reed, and Wole Soyinka helped me to complete this book. Wole Soyinka, Olufemi Euba, and Dejo Afolayan made it possible for me to master difficult Yoruba concepts and texts. It is difficult to express adequately the important role that these friends and colleagues have played in the development of the ideas expressed in this book.

In addition to these literary critics, I would like to thank Roger D. Abrahams, Claudia Mitchell-Kernan, Geneva Smitherman, John Szwed, and Bruce Jackson for their strong support, comments, criticisms, and suggestions as I attempted to extract the implicit from the Monkey tales. These five highly regarded anthropologists and linguists—the truly expert theorists of the Monkey and the language of Signifyin(g)—never once wondered what in the world I was up to with "their" tales and only encouraged my attempt to lift the discourse of Signifyin(g) from the vernacular to the discourse of literary criticism. Their cooperation is a testament to the love of our common subject, the black tradition. Unlike some of their less imaginative colleagues, who collect folklore in order to imprison it, to delimit its potential implication, these scholars recognize that the import of collection is to make possible interpretation, which expands on the possibilities inherent in the primary texts themselves.

Let me expand on this idea a bit. For as long as I can remember, I have been fascinated with the inner workings of black culture, its linguistic and musical resources. My fascination with black language stems from my father's enjoyment of absolute control over its manipulation. My father has mastered black language rituals, certainly; he also has the ability to analyze them, to tell you what he is doing, why, and how. He is a very self-conscious language user. He is not atypical. It is amazing how much black people, in ritual settings such as barbershops and pool halls, street corners and family reunions, talk about talking. Why do they do this? I think they do it to pass these rituals along from one generation to the next. They do it to preserve the traditions of "the race."

Very few black people are not conscious, at some level, of peculiarly black texts of being. These are *our* texts, to be delighted in, enjoyed, contemplated, explicated, and willed through repetition to our daughters and to our sons. I acknowledge my father's capacities, not only to pay him homage but because I learned to read the tradition by thinking intensely about one of its most salient aspects. This is my father's book, even if cast in a language he does not use.

The image of the black tradition has suffered from the lack of sophisticated scholarly attention to it. I would hope that decades of careful collection and establishment of texts will be followed by decades of close readings, interpretation, and speculation. This book can be seen as a scholarly return to the relationship between black vernacular and formal traditions, a return to the forms of black criticism undertaken in the thirties by Sterling A. Brown and Zora Neale Hurston, two of the truly great minds of "the race." Brown's and Hurston's reverence for the black vernacular and their use of it as the touchstone for rhetorical excellence provide critical models that I have tried to imitate, even if the critical language that I employ might seem to be a different language from theirs. Hurston's and Brown's work informed the direction that this book has taken and provided the material cause of my speculation.

David Curtis, José Piedra, Frank Tirro, Dwight Andrews, and Anthony Davis each contributed to this book's completion in several ways—Curtis as a splendid research assistant; Piedra as translator of Spanish texts; Andrews, Davis, and Tirro as interpreters of the wonders of nonverbal black music, especially jazz. Candace Ruck cheerfully typed draft after draft of the manuscript. Count Basie graciously helped me to understand his composition entitled "Signifying," and Little Willie Dixon generously shared with me the words to his composition, "The Jungle King." David Romine at Rhymes Records and Lisa Cortes helped me to locate dozens of musical compositions about Signifyin(g) and the Signifying Monkey. Richard Smith of Keyser, West Virginia, allowed me to record several versions of the Monkey's exploits previously unrecorded in the literature.

The editors at Oxford University Press, especially Curtis Church, William Sisler, and Susan Rabiner, patiently awaited the delivery of this manuscript. Carl Brandt, as always, offered acute advice about the book's publication. Carolyn Williams and especially Mary Caraway carefully edited the excerpt printed in *Critical Inquiry*, helping me to understand what I was trying to say. A MacArthur Prize Fellowship made it feasible for me to pursue one vague intuition to a conclusion. Eva Boesenberg and Henry Finder read and criticized the final version of my manuscript.

My wife, Sharon Adams, discussed aspects of this work with me almost daily for two years. My daughters, Maude and Elizabeth, tolerated my daily and mysterious disappearances into my library. Finally, it is fair to say that my brother, Paul, is the inspiration for this book, because it was he who once asked pointedly just when I was going to write a book that our parents (and he, an oral surgeon) could understand! If I have once again failed to do so, then once again I apologize. My brother's strictures remind me of Montaigne's, who wrote that

> clever people observe more things and more curiously, but they interpret them; and to lend weight and conviction to their interpretation, they cannot help altering history a little. They never show you things as they are, but bend and disguise them according to the way they have seen them; and to give credence to their judgment and attract you to it, they are prone to add something to their matter, to stretch it out and amplify it. We need a man either very honest, or so simple that he has not the stuff to build up false inventions and give them plausibility, and wedded to no theory.

While only others are qualified to judge my honesty and simplicity, I must confess being wedded to the study of theory generally, if not to one theory over all others. My biases and presuppositions no doubt shine forth clearly in my text and need no further elaboration here.

Montaigne continues, in the well-known essay, "Of Cannibals," from which I have extracted the quotation above (a citation oddly appropriate in a book entitled *The Signifying Monkey*), to protest against verbose pontification and idle pretense:

> We ought to have topographers who would give us an exact account of the places where they have been. But because they have over us the advantage of having seen Palestine, they want to enjoy the privilege of telling us news about all the rest of the world. I would like everyone to write what he knows, and as much as he knows, not only in this, but in all other subjects; for a man may have some special knowledge and experience of the nature of a river or fountains, who in other matters knows only what everybody knows. However, to circulate this little scrap of knowledge, he will undertake to write the whole of physics. From this vice spring many great abuses. Now, to return to my subject . . .

I have diligently attempted to circulate my little scrap(s) of knowledge without rewriting the whole of black metaphysics. So remarkably much about the black literary tradition remains to be written that no scholar can claim to have had the final word. The traditions of African, Caribbean, and Afro-American literature remain intact, to be explicated and theorized about again and again. The remnants of prejudice that manifest themselves against even the academic study of these subjects can only be confronted by the scholar's patient labors. This task I have tried to fulfill here.

The Signifying Monkey literally begins where my first book, *Figures in Black: Words, Signs, and the "Racial" Self,* concludes. The final chapter of *Figures in Black* relates to this book as a blueprint relates to a fully constructed work of architecture. I chose to "end" the text of *Figures* in this way to suggest an end point of ten years' experimentation with contemporary criticism and its uses in analyzing black literature. Using that chapter as a blueprint, I have here tried to develop one idea to what I believe to be its fullest extent.

These books, along with *Black Letters in the Enlightenment,* comprise three elements in a larger literary enterprise. In the essays published in *Figures in Black,* I sought not to popularize theory or to vulgarize it by reduction or one-to-one application. On the contrary, I sought to revise contemporary literary theories, as well as our notions of appropriate ways in which one can go about reading black texts. That book of hypothesis and experimentation is here followed by a book concerned to register a theory of criticism and, more precisely, a theory of literary history.

Signifyin(g) is not the only theory appropriate to the texts of our tradition. But it is one that I would like to think arises from the black tradition itself. I have drawn upon Signifyin(g) to analyze its several levels of meaning, then used these to interpret the Afro-American literary tradition. I have tried to do what all theorists must. There is no escape either from confronting one's own textual tradition on its own terms or from relating these terms, fully explicated, to related aspects of a more general critical discourse. This book explores one specific if multifaceted principle of interpretation, whereas *Figures in Black* explores several in a much more abbreviated form.

The third book in this trilogy is *Black Letters in the Enlightenment: On Race, Writing, and Difference. Black Letters* is a history of the critical reception of our tradition's first authors. In that book, I attempt to analyze the presuppositions found in early European criticism of black literature. I assign a value to these presuppositions, but I also try to demonstrate how the criticism of black literature by Europeans between 1730 and 1830 has informed the ways in which black writers have subsequently undertaken the creation of literature, and the ways in which critics have interpreted black texts, even beyond the New Negro Renaissance of the 1920s. *Black Letters,* then, is a study of the history of reception.

I have attempted here to show how the black tradition has inscribed its own theories of its nature and function within elaborate hermeneutical and rhetorical systems. As I wrote earlier, I have liberally borrowed related examples from Western critical arguments to compare aspects of the workings of these black structures of meaning, to ground my analysis in referents familiar to my readers, but also to argue, implicitly, that the central questions asked in Western critical discourse have been asked, and answered, in other textual traditions as well. The Eurocentric bias presupposed in the ways terms such as *canon, literary theory,* or *comparative literature* have been utilized is a culturally hegemonic bias, a bias that the study of literature could best do without. Europeans and Americans neither invented literature and its theory nor have a monopoly on its development. Let us hope that the gradual erosion of those nationalistic presuppositions that are amply evident in traditional schemes of categorization of the academic study of literature will serve as a model for the aboli-

tionalistic presuppositions that are amply evident in traditional schemes of categorization of the academic study of literature will serve as a model for the abolition of racist and sexist presuppositions in literary studies as well. I would like to think that this book is one contribution to these ends.

Ithaca, NY   H.L.G.
June 1986

Contents

Introduction

I

Black English vernacular, according to William Labov's three-year National Science Foundation study released in 1985, "is a healthy, living form of language," one which "shows the signs of people developing their own grammar" and one which manifests various linguistic signs of "separate development." Labov's extensive research leads him to conclude that "There is evidence that, far from getting more similar [to standard English], the black vernacular is going its own way." The black vernacular, he continues, "is reflecting [a larger social] picture [of segregated speech communities]. The blacks' own grammar, which is very rich and complicated, is developing its own way. It looks as if new things are happening in black grammar." The black vernacular, in other words, is thriving despite predictions during the civil rights era that it would soon be a necessary casualty of school desegregation and the larger socioeconomic integration of black people into mainstream American institutions. Because de facto segregation of black and white schoolchildren has replaced de jure segregation, and because black unemployment in 1988 is much higher than it was in 1968, it is impossible for us to determine if black vernacular English would have disappeared under certain ideal social conditions. It has not, however, disappeared; as Labov's study shows, the black vernacular has assumed the singular role as the black person's ultimate sign of difference, a blackness of the tongue. It is in the vernacular that, since slavery, the black person has encoded private yet communal cultural rituals.

The Signifying Monkey explores the relation of the black vernacular tradition to the Afro-American literary tradition. The book attempts to identify a theory of criticism that is inscribed within the black vernacular tradition and that in turn informs the shape of the Afro-American literary tradition. My desire has been to allow the black tradition to speak for itself about its nature and various functions, rather than to read it, or analyze it, in terms of literary theories borrowed whole from other traditions, appropriated from without. While this latter mode of literary analysis can be a revealing and rewarding exercise, each literary tradition, at least implicitly, contains within it an argument for how it can be read. It is one such implicit argument or theory about the black tradition that I wish to discuss in this book.

At a time when the study of literature is characterized by what many scholars feel to be an undue concern with literary theory, why bother to elaborate more theory, risking further distance from the primary texts that should be, indeed must be, the critic's primary concern? This question is not idle, because theorizing can take us rather far afield from the literature that a tradition comprises. Theory can serve to mystify what strike some readers as fairly straightforward matters of taste and application, of representation and reference, of denotation and meaning. I have tried to define a theory of Afro-American criticism not to mystify black literature, or to obscure its several delightful modes of creating meaning, but to begin to suggest how richly textured and layered that black literary artistry indeed is. By discussing explicitly that which is implicit in what we might think of as the logic of the tradition, I hope to enhance the reader's experience of black texts by identifying levels of meaning and expression that might otherwise remain mediated, or buried beneath the surface. If anything, my desire here has been to demystify the curious notion that theory is the province of the Western tradition, something alien or removed from a so-called noncanonical tradition such as that of the Afro-American.

I have also taken to heart Paulin J. Hountondji's perceptive admonition that "if theoretical discourse is to be meaningful in modern Africa, it must promote within African society itself a theoretical debate of its own that is capable of developing its themes and problems autonomously instead of remaining a remote appendix to European theoretical and scientific debates." The same caution about the uses and abuses of critical discourse in philosophy applies to literature. Our goal must not be to embed, as it were, Europe within Africa or Africa within Europe, which Anthony Appiah has called "the Naipaul fallacy": "the post-colonial legacy which requires us to show that African literature is worthy of study precisely (but only) because it is fundamentally the same as European literature." Nor, Appiah continues, does African literature need "justification" to Western readers in order to overcome their tendency to ignore it. Moreover, the turn to theory is not intended, as Hountondji rightly says, "to prove that blacks could sometimes be as intelligent, moral and artistic as whites," or "to persuade people that blacks can be good philosophers too," or to "try to win certificates of humanity from whites or to display the splendours of African civilizations to them." Rather, I have written this book to analyze a theory of reading that is there, that has been generated from within the black tradition itself, autonomously. At the very least, certainly, theoretical traditions are related by analogy, but it seemed to me that an ideal way to confound a Eurocentric bias in this project was to explore the black vernacular.

To do so, I have turned to two signal trickster figures, Esu-Elegbara and the Signifying Monkey, in whose myths are registered certain principles of both formal language use and its interpretation. These two separate but related trickster figures serve in their respective traditions as points of conscious articulation of language traditions aware of themselves as traditions, complete with a history, patterns of development and revision, and internal principles of patterning and organization. Theirs is a meta-discourse, a discourse about itself. These admittedly complex matters are addressed, in the black tradition, in the vernacular, far away from the eyes and ears of outsiders, those who do not speak the language of tradition. While I shall suggest reasons for this penchant of the black tradition to theorize about itself in the vernacular, it should be apparent that this protective tendency is not generally remarked upon in studies of the literary theory of sustained literate traditions such as the European or American. My attempt to disclose the closed black vernacular tradition is meant to enrich the reader's experience of reference and representation, of connotation and denotation, of truth and understanding, as these configure in the black formal literary traditions and in the antics of two tricksters found in black myths.

At first glance, these two tricksters would seem to have little in common. Esu, both a trickster and the messenger of the gods, figures prominently in the mythologies of Yoruba cultures found in Nigeria, Benin, Brazil, Cuba, and Haiti, among others. The Signifying Monkey, it seems, is distinctly Afro-American. Nevertheless, the central place of both figures in their traditions is determined by their curious tendency to reflect on the uses of formal language. The theory of Signifyin(g) arises from these moments of self-reflexiveness.

Whereas Esu serves as a figure for the nature and function of interpretation and double-voiced utterance, the Signifying Monkey serves as the figure-of-figures, as the trope in which are encoded several other peculiarly black rhetorical tropes. While both tricksters stand for certain principles of verbal expression, I am concerned to explore the place each accords forms of language use in the production of meaning in literature. I am equally concerned to demonstrate that the Monkey's language of Signifyin(g) functions as a metaphor for formal revision, or intertextuality, within the Afro-American literary tradition. Finally, I attempt to show through their functional equivalency that the two figures are related historically and are distinct aspects of a larger, unified phenomenon. Together, the two tricksters articulate the black tradition's theory of its literature.

This book is not an attempt to chart through practical criticism the precise relations that obtain among our canonical texts. That sort of detailed account most properly should occupy a book of its own, as a sequel to this book of theory. To illustrate my initial three theoretical chapters, however, I have selected a fair sample of canonical texts to read closely. Four chapters of close readings follow, then, to explain different modes of Signifyin(g) revisions at work in the Afro-American literary tradition. I make no claim for inclusiveness in the selection of these texts; rather, they were settled on primarily for the range of concerns they demonstrate about this book's theoretical assumptions. My triangles of influence and my tracings of the intricacies of metaphors of voice from antecedent text to revised text are illustrative; other texts could just as easily have been chosen. Rather than a selective history of Afro-American literature, then, *The Signifying Monkey* is an attempt to arrive at a theory of this tradition. Precisely because I could have selected numerous other texts as exempla, I hope to draw on the premises of this book to write a detailed account of the Afro-American literary tradition. *The Signifying Monkey* is a theoretical prologue to that work.

A vernacular tradition's relation to a formal literary tradition is that of a parallel discursive universe. By explicating two seemingly distinct bodies of myths, one common to several black traditions and the other an American phenomenon, I have tried to show how the vernacular informs and becomes the foundation for formal black literature. While the history of the criticism of black texts is a subject of considerable interest to me, a truly indigenous black literary criticism is to be found in the vernacular. What's more, I believe that black writers, both explicitly and implicitly, turn to the vernacular in various formal ways to inform their creation of written fictions. To do so, it seems to me, is to ground one's literary practice outside the Western tradition. Whereas black writers most certainly revise texts in the Western tradition, they often seek to do so "authentically," with a black difference, a compelling sense of difference based on the black vernacular.

Black writers also read each other, and seem intent on refiguring what we might think of as key canonical topoi and tropes received from the black tradition itself. The editors of *The Negro Caravan*—Sterling A. Brown, Arthur P. Davis, and Ulysses Lee—noted this fact as early as 1941, when discussing the formal relation of Frances E. W. Harper's novel, *Iola Leroy* (1892), to William Wells Brown's novel, *Clotel* (1853): "There are repetitions of situations from Brown's *Clotel*, something of a forecast of a sort of literary inbreeding which causes Negro writers to be influenced by other Negroes more than should ordinarily be expected." Regardless of what should obtain in a tradition, by 1941 it was apparent to these seminal scholars that black writers read, repeated, imitated, and revised each other's texts to a remarkable extent. This web of filiation makes theorizing about black principles of interpretation and revision an obvious project for critics who have undertaken close readings of black canonical texts. This I attempt to do in *The Signifying Monkey*.

It is probably true that critics of African and Afro-American literature were trained to think of the institution of literature essentially as a set of Western texts. The methods devised to read these texts are culture-specific and temporal-specific, and they are text-specific as well. We learn to read the text at hand. And texts have a curious habit of generating other texts that resemble themselves.

Black writers, like critics of black literature, learn to write by reading literature, especially the canonical texts of the Western tradition. Consequently, black texts resemble other, Western texts. These black texts employ many of the conventions of literacy form that comprise the Western tradition. Black literature shares much with, far more than it differs from, the Western textual tradition, primarily as registered in English, Spanish, Portuguese, and French. But black formal repetition always repeats with a difference, a black difference that manifests itself in specific language use. And the repository that contains the language that is the source—and the reflection—of black difference is the black English vernacular tradition.

A novelist such as Ralph Ellison or Ishmael Reed creates texts that are double-voiced in the sense that their literary antecedents are both white and black novels, but also modes of figuration lifted from the black vernacular tradition. One can readily agree with Susan Willis that black texts are "mulattoes" (or "mulatas"), with a two-toned heritage: these texts speak in standard Romance or Germanic languages and literary structures, but almost always speak with a distinct and resonant accent, an accent that Signifies (upon) the various black vernacular literary traditions, which are still being written down. To locate, and then to theorize about, this formal difference is to utilize certain tools of close reading that facilitate explication. It is also to explain what we might think of as the discrete black difference, and to reveal its workings. It is not to be expected that we shall reinvent literature; nor shall we reinvent criticism. We shall, however, have to name the discrete seemingly disparate elements that compose the structures of which our vernacular literary traditions consist.

The black tradition has theorized about itself, explicitly. Melville Herskovits was quick to point out that the Fon of Dahomey named and could specify their philosophical system; he did not need to read into its parts metaphorical meanings analogous to Western philosophy. The tradition named its own assumptions. "[In] no sense," Herskovits contends, is the metaphysical system of the Fon "to be regarded as a kind of synthesis arrived at by the ethnographer from however implicit manifestations of the religious life he has observed in the field." Rather, the Fon themselves are characterized by "long and considered speculation," by "the systematisation of belief," by "the development of a complex philosophy of the Universe." Moreover, Herskovits concludes, "The upper-class Dahomean does not need to restrict himself to describing concrete instances when discussing the larger concepts underlying his everyday religious practice; he is not at a loss when questioned of the nature of the world as a whole, or abstract principles such as justice, or destiny, or accident are asked him." For the Yoruba, the several myths of Esu stand as the tradition's repository of its own theory of interpretation. The Fon, once removed from the Yoruba antecedent, even more extensively employ the figure of writing to name the nature and function of interpretation, of both secular and sacred interpretation.

Naming the black tradition's own theory of itself is to echo and rename other theories of literary criticism. Our task is not to reinvent our traditions as if they bore no relation to that tradition created and borne, in the main, by white men. Our writers used that impressive tradition to define themselves, both with and against their concept of received order. We must do the same, with or against the Western critical canon. To name our tradition is to rename each of its antecedents, no matter how pale they might seem. To rename is to revise, and to revise is to Signify.

The black tradition has inscribed within it the very principles by which it can be read. Ours is an extraordinarily self-reflexive tradition, a tradition exceptionally conscious of its history and of the simultaneity of its canonical texts, which tend to be taken as verbal models of the Afro-American social condition, to be revised. Because of the experience of diaspora, the fragments that contain the traces of a coherent system of order must be reassembled. These fragments embody aspects of a theory of critical principles around which the discrete texts of the tradition configure, in the critic's reading of the textual past. To reassemble fragments, of course, is to engage in an act of speculation, to attempt to weave a fiction of origins and subgeneration. It is to render the implicit as explicit, and at times to imagine the whole from the part.

Literary theory has rarely been as widely discussed in literature departments as it is today. Like every other critic of black literature, I have been trained to read using one or several of the generally accepted theories of criticism. In my first book of criticism, *Figures in Black: Words, Signs, and the "Racial" Self,* I sought to chart one noncanonical critic's experiments with these theories of criticism, which I drew on to read black texts, as if on safari through the jungle of criticism. This gesture has been crucial to the development of my thinking about the "proper work" for a black criticism: to define itself with—and against—other theoretical activities. While this sort of criticism has helped to demonstrate that distinct literary canons need not necessarily segregate critics—indeed, that shared critical approaches can define a canon of criticism—I believe it necessary to draw on the black tradition itself to define a theory of its nature and function.

Whereas various poststructural theories provide points of departure for the chapters of *Figures in Black,* in this book they surface primarily as analogies. Analogies, of course, serve to suggest moments of similarity, identity, and even difference within a shared framework of presupposition. My use of this sort of analogy is designed to show the many-faceted nature of contemporary criticism, and not to suggest limitations or lacunae in black theory. While I delight in the sense of difference that our literary tradition yields upon careful explication, I also delight in the sense of similarity that discrete literary traditions yield in comparative literary criticism. Anyone who analyzes black literature must do so as a comparativist, by definition, because our canonical texts have complex double formal antecedents, the Western and the black.

Free of the white person's gaze, black people created their own unique vernacular structures and relished in the double play that these forms bore to white forms. Repetition and revision are fundamental to black artistic forms, from painting and sculpture to music and language use. I decided to analyze the nature and function of Signifyin(g) precisely because it *is* repetition and revision, or repetition with a signal difference. Whatever is black about black American literature is to be found in this identifiable black Signifyin(g) difference. That, most succinctly if ambiguously, describes the premise of this book. Lest this theory of criticism, however, be thought of as only black, let me admit that the implicit premise of this study is that all texts Signify upon other texts, in motivated and unmotivated ways. Perhaps critics of other literatures will find this theory useful as they attempt to account for the configuration of the texts in their traditions. Comparative literature, ultimately, embraces a vastly richer field than the study of French, German, and English literature, no matter how fertile these fields admittedly are. That the myths of black slaves and ex-slaves embody theories of their own status within a tradition is only one of the more striking instances of what Ralph Ellison calls the "complexity" of the Negro's existence in Western culture.

II

The black tradition is double-voiced. The trope of the Talking Book, of double-voiced texts that talk to other texts, is the unifying metaphor within this book. Signifyin(g) is the figure of the double-voiced, epitomized by Esu's depictions in sculpture as possessing two mouths. There are four sorts of double-voiced textual relations that I wish to define.

Tropological Revision

By tropological revision I mean the manner in which a specific trope is repeated, with differences, between two or more texts. The revision of specific tropes recurs with surprising frequency in the Afro-American literary tradition. The descent underground, the vertical "ascent" from South to North, myriad figures of the double, and especially double consciousness all come readily to mind. But there are other tropes that would seem to preoccupy the texts of the black tradition. The first trope shared in the black narrative tradition is what I shall call the Talking Book. This compelling trope appears in James Gronniosaw's 1770 slave narrative, and then is revised in at least four other texts published between 1785 and 1815. We might think of this as the ur-trope of the tradition. The form that repetition and difference take among these texts is the first example of Signifyin(g) as repetition and difference in the Anglo-African narrative tradition.

The Speakerly Text

The second mode of Signifyin(g) that I have chosen to represent in this text is exemplified in the peculiar play of "voices" at work in the use of "free indirect discourse" in Zora Neale Hurston's *Their Eyes Were Watching God*. Above all else, Hurston's narrative strategy seems to concern itself with the possibilities of representation of the speaking black voice in writing. Hurston's text, I shall claim, seems to aspire to the status of what she and, later, Ishmael Reed call the Talking Book. It is striking that this figure echoes the first figure repeated and revised in the tradition. Hurston's use is remarkably complex, and accomplished. Free indirect discourse is represented in this canonical text as if it were a dynamic character, with shifts in its level of diction drawn upon to reflect a certain development of self-consciousness in a hybrid character, a character who is neither the novel's protagonist nor the text's disembodied narrator, but a blend of both, an emergent and merging moment of consciousness. The direct discourse of the novel's black speech community and the initial standard English of the narrator come together to form a third term, a truly double-voiced narrative mode. That element of narration that the Russian Formalists called *skaz*—when a text seems to be aspiring to the status of oral narration—is most clearly the closest analogue of Hurston's rhetorical strategy. The attendant ramifications of this device upon received modes of mimesis and diegesis occupy my attention in this chapter. Finally, I shall use Hurston's own theory of Signifyin(g) to analyze her narrative strategy, including the identification of Signifyin(g) rituals in the body of her text.

Talking Texts

Chapter 5 explores one instance of a black form of intertextuality. Within the limits of the metaphor of the double-voiced that I am tracing from Esu-Elegbara to Alice Walker's novel *The Color Purple,* I have chosen to explicate Reed's novel *Mumbo Jumbo* to show how black texts "talk" to other black texts. Since *Mumbo Jumbo* would seem to be a signal text of revision and critique, cast in a so-called postmodern narrative, the implicit relation among modernism, realism, and postmodernism comes to bear here in the texts of *Invisible Man, Native Son, Black Boy,* and *Mumbo Jumbo.* Again, the relation of mimesis to diegesis shall occupy my attention in *Mumbo Jumbo*'s foregrounded double voices.

Rewriting the Speakerly

If Hurston's novel seems to have been designed to declare that, indeed, a text could be written in black dialect, then it seems to me that Walker's *The Color Purple* aims to do just that, as a direct revision of Hurston's explicit and implicit strategies of narration. Walker, whose preoccupation with Hurston as a deeply admired antecedent has been the subject of several of her critical comments, revises and echoes Hurston in a number of ways. Her use of the epistolary form to write a novel in the language seemingly spoken by Hurston's protagonist is perhaps the most stunning instance of revision in the tradition of the black novel. Here, let me introduce a distinction: Reed's use of parody would seem to be fittingly described as motivated Signifyin(g), in which the text Signifies upon other black texts, in the manner of the vernacular ritual of "close reading." Walker's use of pastiche, on the other hand, corresponds to unmotivated Signifyin(g), by which I mean to suggest not the absence of a profound intention but the absence of a negative critique. The relation between parody and pastiche is that between motivated and unmotivated Signifyin(g).

Whereas Reed seems to be about the clearing of a space of narration, Walker seems to be intent on underscoring the relation of her text to Hurston's, in a joyous proclamation of antecedent and descendant texts. The most salient analogue for this unmotivated mode of revision in the broader black cultural tradition might be that between black jazz musicians who perform each other's standards on a joint album, not to critique these but to engage in refiguration as an act of homage. Such an instance, one of hundreds, is the relationship between two jazz greats on the album they made together, *Duke Ellington and John Coltrane*. This form of the double-voiced implies unity and resemblance rather than critique and difference.

The premise of this book is that the literary discourse that is most consistently "black," as read against our tradition's own theory of itself, is the most figurative, and that the modes of interpretation most in accord with the vernacular tradition's theory of criticism are those that direct attention to the manner in which language is used. Black texts Signify upon other black texts in the tradition by engaging in what Ellison has defined as implicit formal critiques of language use, of rhetorical strategy. Literary Signification, then, is similar to parody and pastiche, wherein parody corresponds to what I am calling motivated Signification while pastiche would correspond roughly to unmotivated Signification. By motivation I do not mean to suggest the lack of intention, for parody and pastiche imply intention, ranging from severe critique to acknowledgment and placement within a literary tradition. Pastiche can imply either homage to an antecedent text or futility in the face of a seemingly indomitable mode of representation. Black writers Signify on each other's texts for all of these reasons, and the relations of Signification that obtain between and among black texts serve as a basis for a theory of formal revision in the Afro-American tradition. Literary echoes, or pastiche, as found in Ellison's *Invisible Man,* of signal tropes found in Emerson, Eliot, Joyce, Crane, or Melville (among others) constitute one mode of Signifyin(g).

But so does Ellison's implicit rhetorical critique of the conventions of realism found in Richard Wright's *Native Son, The Man Who Lived Underground,* and *Black Boy.* Reed's parodies of Wright and Ellison constitute a Signification of a profoundly motivated order, especially as found in the text of *Mumbo Jumbo.* Hurston's multileveled use of voice in *Their Eyes Were Watching God* represents a Signification upon the entire tradition of dialect poetry as well as a brilliant and subtle critique of received notions of voice in the realistic novel, amounting to a remarkably novel critique and extension of Henry James's use of point-of-view as point-of-consciousness. Hurston's novel, like Sterling A. Brown's *Southern Road,* amounts to a refutation of critics such as James Welson Johnson who argued just six years before the publication of *Their Eyes* that the passing of dialect as a literary device among black authors was complete. Moreover, by representing her protagonist as a mulatto, who eschews the bourgeois life and marries a dark-complexioned migrant worker, Hurston Signifies upon the female novel of passing, an ironic form of fantasy that she inherited from Nella Larsen and Jessie Fauset. Finally, Walker's decision to place *The Color Purple* in a line of descent that runs directly from *Their Eyes* by engaging in a narrative strategy that tropes Hurston's concept of voice (by shifting it into the form of the epistolary novel and a written rather than a spoken vernacular) both extends dramatically the modes of revision available to writers in the tradition and reveals that acts of formal revision can be loving acts of bonding rather than ritual slayings at Esu's crossroads.

ONE

A Theory of the Tradition

I then commenced and continued copying the Italics in Webster's Spelling Book, until I could make them all without looking on the book. By this time, my little Master Thomas had gone to school, and learned how to write, and had written over a number of copy-books. These had been brought home, and shown to some of our near neighbors, and then laid aside. My mistress used to go to class meeting at the Wilk Street meetinghouse every Monday afternoon, and leave me to take care of the house. When left thus, I used to spend the time in writing in the spaces left in Master Thomas's copy-book, copying what he had written. I continued to do this until I could write a hand very similar to that of Master Thomas. Thus, after a long, tedious effort for years, I finally succeeded in learning how to write.   Frederick Douglass

. . . language, for the individual consciousness, lies on the borderline between oneself and the other. The word in language is half someone else's. It becomes "one's own" only when the speaker populates it with his own intention, his own accent, when he appropriates the word, adapting it to his own semantic and expressive intention. Prior to this moment of appropriation, the word does not exist in a neutral and impersonal language (it is not, after all, out of a dictionary that the speaker gets his words!), but rather it exists in other people's mouths, in other people's contexts, serving other people's intentions: it is from there that one must take the word, and make it one's own.
                                                        Mikhail Bakhtin

1

A Myth of Origins:
Esu-Elegbara and the Signifying Monkey

> Esu, do not undo me,
> Do not falsify the words of my mouth,
> Do not misguide the movements of my feet,
> You who translates yesterday's words
> Into novel utterances,
> Do not undo me,
> I bear you sacrifice.
> > Traditional *Oriki Esu*[1]

> Ah yes!
> Edju played many tricks
> Edju made kindred people go to war;
> Edju pawned the moon and carried off the sun:
> Edju made the Gods strive against themselves.
> But Edju is not evil.
> He brought us the best there is;
> He gave us the Ifa oracle;
> He brought the sun.
> But for Edju, the fields would be barren.
> > Traditional *Oriki Esu*[2]

> through Harlem smoke of beer and whiskey, I
> understand the mystery of the signifying monkey
> in a blue haze of inspiration, I reach to the
> totality of Being.
> > Larry Neal, "Malcolm X—An Autobiography"[3]

I

The black Africans who survived the dreaded "Middle Passage" from the
west coast of Africa to the New World did not sail alone. Violently and
radically abstracted from their civilizations, these Africans nevertheless
carried within them to the Western hemisphere aspects of their cultures that
were meaningful, that could not be obliterated, and that they chose, by acts

3

of will, not to forget: their music (a mnemonic device for Bantu and Kwa tonal languages), their myths, their expressive institutional structures, their metaphysical systems of order, and their forms of performance. If "the Dixie Pike," as Jean Toomer put the matter in *Cane,* "has grown from a goat path in Africa," then the black vernacular tradition stands as its signpost, at that liminal crossroads of culture contact and ensuing difference at which Africa meets Afro-America.

Common sense, in retrospect, argues that these retained elements of culture should have survived, that their complete annihilation would have been far more remarkable than their preservation. The African, after all, was a traveler, albeit an abrupt, ironic traveler, through space and time; and like every traveler, the African "read" a new environment within a received framework of meaning and belief. The notion that the Middle Passage was so traumatic that it functioned to create in the African a tabula rasa of consciousness is as odd as it is a fiction, a fiction that has served several economic orders and their attendant ideologies. The full erasure of traces of cultures as splendid, as ancient, and as shared by the slave traveler as the classic cultures of traditional West Africa would have been extraordinarily difficult. Slavery in the New World, a veritable seething cauldron of cross-cultural contact, however, did serve to create a dynamic of exchange and revision among numerous previously isolated Black African cultures on a scale unprecedented in African history. Inadvertently, African slavery in the New World satisfied the preconditions for the emergence of a new African culture, a truly Pan-African culture fashioned as a colorful weave of linguistic, institutional, metaphysical, and formal threads. What survived this fascinating process was the most useful and the most compelling of the fragments at hand. Afro-American culture is an African culture with a difference as signified by the catalysts of English, Dutch, French, Portuguese, or Spanish languages and cultures, which informed the precise structures that each discrete New World Pan-African culture assumed.[4]

Of the music, myths, and forms of performance that the African brought to the Western Hemisphere, I wish to discuss one specific trickster figure that recurs with startling frequency in black mythology in Africa, the Caribbean, and South America. This figure appears in black cultures with such frequency that we can think of it as a repeated theme or topos. Indeed, this trickster topos not only seems to have survived the bumpy passage to the New World, but it appears even today in Nigeria, Benin, Brazil, Cuba, Haiti, and the United States. Within New World African-informed cultures, the presence of this topos, repeated with variations as circumstances apparently dictated, attests to shared belief systems maintained for well over three centuries, remarkably, by sustained vernacular traditions. We can trace this particular topos ultimately to the Fon and Yoruba cultures of Benin and Nigeria. Its particular configurations in Western black cultures separated by vast distances of space and time, and isolated by the linguistic barriers of the Germanic and the Romance languages, testify to the fragmented unity of these black cultures in the Western Hemisphere. There can be little doubt that certain funda-

Figure 1. Esu-Elegbara. From the author's collection. *Photos by Sarah Whitaker.*

mental terms for order that the black enslaved brought with them from Africa, and maintained through the mnemonic devices peculiar to oral literature, continued to function both as meaningful units of New World belief systems and as traces of their origins. We lack written documents to answer the historical questions of how this occurred, questions about the means of transmission, translation, and recuperation of the ensuing difference. Nevertheless, this topos functions as a sign of the disrupted wholeness of an African system of meaning and belief that black slaves recreated from memory, preserved by oral narration, improvised upon in ritual—especially in the rituals of the repeated oral narrative—and willed to their own subsequent generations, as hermetically sealed and encoded charts of cultural descent. If the existence of such traceable topoi seems remarkable, it also seems remarkable that scholars have only begun to explicate them systematically in this century.

This topos that recurs throughout black oral narrative traditions and contains a primal scene of instruction for the act of interpretation is that of the divine trickster figure of Yoruba mythology, Esu-Elegbara. This curious figure is called Esu-Elegbara in Nigeria and Legba among the Fon in Benin. His New World figurations include Exú in Brazil, Echu-Elegua in Cuba, Papa Legba (pronounced La-Bas) in the pantheon of the loa of Vaudou of Haiti, and Papa La Bas in the loa of Hoodoo in the United States. Because I see these individual tricksters as related parts of a larger, unified figure, I shall refer to them collectively as Esu, or as Esu-Elegbara. These variations on Esu-Elegbara speak eloquently of an unbroken arc of metaphysical pre-supposition and a pattern of figuration shared through time and space among certain black cultures in West Africa, South America, the Caribbean, and the United States. These trickster figures, all aspects or topoi of Esu, are funda-mental, divine terms of mediation: as tricksters they are mediators, and their mediations are tricks. If the Dixie Pike leads straight to Guinea, then Esu-Elegbara presides over its liminal crossroads, a sensory threshold barely per-ceptible without access to the vernacular, a word taken from the Latin *ver-naculus* ("native"), taken in turn from *verna* ("slave born in his master's house").[5]

Each version of Esu is the sole messenger of the gods (in Yoruba, *iranse*), he who interprets the will of the gods to man; he who carries the desires of man to the gods. Esu is the guardian of the crossroads, master of style and of stylus, the phallic god of generation and fecundity, master of that elusive, mystical barrier that separates the divine world from the profane. Frequently characterized as an inveterate copulator possessed by his enor-mous penis, linguistically Esu is the ultimate copula, connecting truth with understanding, the sacred with the profane, text with interpretation, the word (as a form of the verb *to be*) that links a subject with its predicate. He connects the grammar of divination with its rhetorical structures. In Yoruba mythology, Esu is said to limp as he walks precisely because of his mediating function: his legs are of different lengths because he keeps one anchored in the realm of the gods while the other rests in this, our human world.

Scholars have studied these figures of Esu, and each has found one or two characteristics of this mutable figure upon which to dwell, true to the nature of the trickster.[6] A partial list of these qualities might include indi-viduality, satire, parody, irony, magic, indeterminacy, open-endedness, ambi-guity, sexuality, chance, uncertainty, disruption and reconciliation, betrayal and loyalty, closure and disclosure, encasement and rupture. But it is a mis-take to focus on one of these qualities as predominant. Esu possesses all of these characteristics, plus a plethora of others which, taken together, only begin to present an idea of the complexity of this classic figure of mediation and of the unity of opposed forces.

Esu's various characteristics are gleaned from several sources: what the Yoruba call the *Oriki Esu,* the narrative praise poems, or panegyrics, of Esu-Elegbara; the *Odu Ifa,* the Ifa divination verses; the lyrics of "Esu songs"; and the traditional prose narratives in which are encoded the myths of origin of the universe, of the gods, and of human beings' relation to the gods and their place within the cosmic order. Much of Esu's literature concerns the origin, the nature, and the function of interpretation and language use "above" that of ordinary language. For Esu is the Yoruba figure of the meta-level of formal language use, of the ontological and epistemological status of figura-tive language and its interpretation. The literature of Esu consists to a re-markable degree of direct assertions about the levels of linguistic ascent that separate literal from figurative modes of language use.[7]

Figure 2. Esu-Elegbara. From the author's collection. *Photo by Sarah Whitaker.*

The Fon call Legba "the divine linguist," he who speaks all languages, he who interprets the alphabet of Mawu to man and to the other gods. Yoruba sculptures of Esu almost always include a calabash that he holds in his hands. In this calabash he keeps *ase,* the very *ase* with which Olodumare, the supreme deity of the Yoruba, created the universe. We can translate *ase* in many ways, but the *ase* used to create the universe I translate as "logos," as the word as understanding, the word as the audible, and later the visible, sign of reason. *Ase* is more weighty, forceful, and action-packed than the ordinary word. It is the word with irrevocability, reinforced with double assuredness and undaunted authenticity. This probably explains why Esu's mouth, from which the audible word proceeds, sometimes appears double; Esu's discourse, metaphorically, is double-voiced. Esu's mastery of *ase* gives him an immense amount of power; *ase* makes Esu "he who says so and does so," as inscribed in a canonical *Oriki Esu.*[8] [See Figures 9, 10, 11.]

Ase is an elusive concept, and thus its translations vary. Part of one of the canonical *Odu,* "The Story of Osetua," informs us that *ase* is power:

> *Ase* spread and expanded on earth:
> Semen became child,
> Men on sick bed got up,
> All the world became pleasant,
> It became powerful.[9]

Figure 3. Esu-Elegbara. From the author's collection. *Photo by Sarah Whitaker.*

But *power* somehow lacks the force to convey the multiple significations of *ase.* The calabash that Esu carries (*Ado-iran*), presented to him by Olorun, contains "the power which propagates itself." In this calabash Esu carries *ase.* It is this *ase,* "controlled and represented by Esu, which mobilizes each and every element in the system," as Juana and Deoscoredes dos Santos conclude. *Ase,* in other words, is the force of coherence of process itself, that which makes a system a system. My translation of *ase* as "logos" is, I think, the closest analogue through which *ase* can be rendered in English, and in English we have merely borrowed the word from the Greek. As one *baba-lawo* put it, *ase* is "the light that crosses through the tray of the earth, the firmament from one side to the other, forward and backward." It was this *ase* that Olodumare used to create the universe. When the *babalawo* say that Orunmila acts with the *ase* of Esu, it is the logos that is implied.[10]

Esu's most direct Western kinsman is Hermes. Just as Hermes' role as messenger and interpreter for the gods lent his name readily to *hermeneu-tics,* our word for the study of methodological principles of interpretation of

Figure 4. Esu-Elegbara. From the author's collection. *Photo by Sarah Whitaker.*

a text, so too is it appropriate for the literary critic to name the methodological principles of the interpretation of black texts *Esu-'tufunaalo,* literally "one who unravels the knots of Esu."[11] Esu is the indigenous black metaphor for the literary critic, and *Esu-'tufunaalo* is the study of methodological principles of interpretation itself, or what the literary critic does. *Esu-'tufunaalo* is the secular analogue of Ifa divination, the richly lyrical and densely metaphorical system of sacred interpretation that the Yoruba in Nigeria have consulted for centuries, and which they continue to consult. Whereas the god Ifa is the next of divine will, Esu is the text's interpreter (*Onitumo*), "the one who translates, who explains, or 'who loosens knowledge.' " Indeed, Esu would seem to have a priority over Ifa in the process of interpretation. Esu not only taught his friend the system; Esu also confirms or condemns the "message" of Ifa. For this reason, it is often said in Ifa poetry that

O tase Esu bonu.
(He [Ifa] borrowed Esu's *ase* and put it in his own mouth to give a message to the supplicant.)[12]

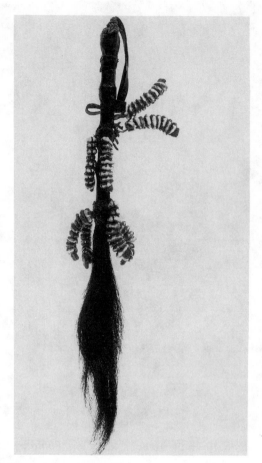

Figure 5. Esu-Elegbara. From the author's collection. *Photo by Sarah Whitaker.*

Esu, as the Yoruba say, is the path to Ifa, and his image often appears at
the center of the upper perimeter of the Ifa divining board. [See Figure 6.]

Ifa consists of the sacred texts of the Yoruba people, as does the Bible
for Christians, but it also contains the commentaries on these fixed texts, as
does the Midrash. Its system of interpretation turns upon a marvelous combination of geomancy and textual exegesis, in which sixteen palm nuts are
"dialed" sixteen times, and their configurations or signs then read and translated into the appropriate, fixed literary verse that the numerical signs signify. These visual signs are known in the Yoruba as "signatures of an *Odu,*"
and each signature the *babalawo,* or priest, translates by reading or reciting
the fixed verse text that the signature signifies. These verse texts, whose
meanings are lushly metaphorical, ambiguous, and enigmatic, function as
riddles, which the propitiate must decipher and apply as is appropriate to his
or her own quandary.

Figure 6. Opon Ifa. From the collection of Robert Farris Thompson. *Photo by Sarah Whitaker.*

Although this is not the place for a full explication of the inner principles of interpretation shared by these systems of divination from West Africa to Latin America, precisely because of Esu's role in this African myth of origins of interpretation it is instructive to explain, albeit painfully briefly, the system that Esu created and taught to his friend, the god Ifa. In African and Latin American mythology, Esu, as I have suggested, is said to have taught Ifa how to read the signs formed by the sixteen sacred palmnuts. The *Opon Ifa,* the carved wooden divination tray used in the art of interpretation, represents a trace of this priority of Esu in the process of interpretation by containing at the center of its upper perimeter a carved image of Esu himself, meant to signify his relation to the act of interpretation, which we can translate either as *itumo* (literally "to untie or unknot knowledge") or as *iyipada* (literally "to turn around" or "to translate"). That which we call close reading, moreover, the Yoruba call *Didafa* (literally "reading the signs"). Above all else, Esu, as the originator of this uniquely African mode of reading, is the Yoruba figure of indeterminacy itself, *ayese ayewi,* or *ailemo,* literally "that which we cannot know." If Esu is a repeated topos, for my purposes he is also a trope, a word that has come to be used in Yoruba discourse in figurative senses far removed from its literal denotations. If we examine some of the primal myths of origins in which Esu defines his metaphoric uses for black literary criticism, we shall be able to speculate on Esu's relation to his functional equivalent in Afro-American mythic discourse: that oxymoron, the Signifying Monkey.

Before examining myths of the origin of Ifa divination, it will be useful to consider the figures the Yoruba employ to account for this system of oral

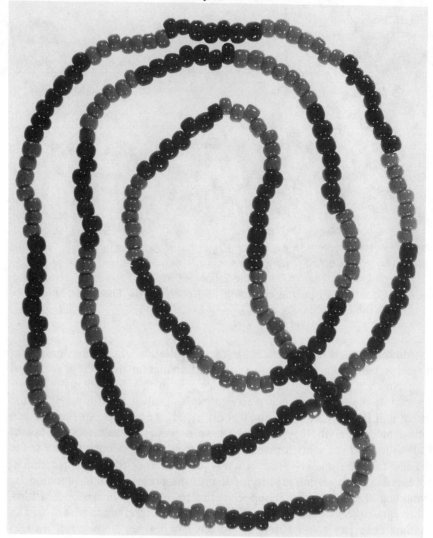

Figure 7. Opele. From the author's collection. *Photo by Sarah Whitaker.*

interpretation. Figures of writing recur in descriptions of Ifa. Ifa is frequently called "scribe" or "clerk," or "one who writes books" (*akowe, a-ko-iwe*). Ifa wrote for his fellow gods, and taught each *babalawo* to write the figures of Ifa on his tray of divination. Ifa speaks or interprets on behalf of all the gods through the act of divination. Ifa, however, can only speak to human beings by inscribing the language of the gods onto the divining tray in visual signs that the *babalawo* reads aloud in the language of the lyrical poetry called *ese*. Curiously enough, the oral literature is described in chirographic metaphors: Ifa's process of oral narration is likened to writing. This quirk of representation gives Ifa a richness that suggests a central hermeneutical principle of the system itself. The voice of Ifa, the text, writes itself as a cryptogram. Esu then assumes his role of interpreter and implicitly governs the process of translation of these written signs into the oral verse of the *Odu*.

One myth of Ifa accounts for the invention of writing and helps to explain the priority that metaphors of written language seem to have among the Yoruba:

> Olorun was the eldest of the deities, and the first child of the King of the Air (Oba Orufi). Some forty years afterward the King of the Air had a second son, Ela, who was the father of the diviners. In the *morning* all the *Whitemen* used to come to Ela to learn how to read and write, and in the *evening* his *African* children, the babalawo, gathered around him to memorize the Ifa verses and learn divination. Ifa taught them to write on their divining trays, which the Muslims copied as their wooden writing boards (wala), and the Christians copied as the slates used by school children and as books.[13] (emphasis added)

The oppositions here—morning/evening, Whitemen/Africans, reading and writing/memorizing and reciting, cryptographic/phonetic script—reveal that the Yoruba themselves felt it necessary to account for the differences between traditional African forms of writing and those practiced by "Muslims" and "Whitemen." Significantly, the myth explains phonetic scripts as copies of the oral tradition, encoded in the cryptograms formed by the sixteen sacred palm nuts of Ifa.

Another myth, which Willem Bosman claims to have recorded in the latter decades of the seventeenth century in Asante, offers a radically different account of the absence of writing among the Africans and its presence among the Europeans. While we shall return to Bosman's myth in Chapter 4, it is instructive to consider how writing figures as an opposition within its structure. God created the races of man but created the African first. Because of his priority, the African had first election between knowledge of the arts and sciences, or writing, and all the gold in the earth. The African, because of his avarice, chose the gold; precisely because of his avarice, the African was punished by a curse: never would Africans master the fine art of reading and writing. This myth, oddly enough, is remarkably compatible with seventeenth- and eighteenth-century European speculations on the absence of writing among Africans and its significance. For, without the presence of writing as the visible sign of reason, the Africans could not demonstrate their "innate" mental equality with the European and hence were doomed to a perpetual sort of slavery until such mastery was demonstrated. For the Yoruba, nevertheless, if not the Asante of the Gold Coast, phonetic scripts were derivative, shadow imitations of the prior form of inscription that is manifested in Ifa.

The Yoruba myth of the origins of interpretation is relevant to the use of Esu as the figure of the critic and is helpful in explaining the presence of a monkey in Latin American versions of this primal myth. It is the presence of the monkey in the Yoruba myth, repeated with a difference in Cuban versions, which stands as the trace of Esu in Afro-American myth, a trace that enables us to speculate freely on the functional equivalence of Esu and his Afro-American descendant, the Signifying Monkey.[14]

Frobenius's account of the myth, "given to me," he tells us, "by a dweller on the border of Kukurukuland," is one of the fullest. Frobenius translates *Esu* as "Edshu" or "Edju." His text follows:

> Once upon a time the Gods were very hungry. They did not get enough to eat from their wandering sons on the face of the earth. They were discontented with each other and quarreled. Some of them went forth to hunt. Other Gods, the Olokun in particular, wanted to go fishing; yet, although one antelope and one fish were caught, these did not last long. Now their descendants had forgotten them, and they asked themselves how they were to get their sustenance from men again. Men no longer made them burnt offerings, and the Gods wanted meat. So Edju set out. He asked Yemaya for something with which to regain man's goodwill. Yemaya said: "You will have no success. Shankpanna has scourged them with pestilence, but they do not come and make sacrifice to him; he will kill them all, but they will not bring him food. Shango struck them dead with the lightning which he sent upon them, but they do not trouble themselves about him or bring him things to eat. Better turn your thought to something else. Men do not fear death. Give them something so good that they will yearn for it and, therefore, want to go on living." Edju went further on. He said to himself: "What I cannot get from Yemaya, Orungan will give me." He went to him. Orungan said: "I know why you are come. The sixteen Gods are ahungered. They must now have something which shall be good. I know of such a thing. It is a big thing made of sixteen palm-nuts. If you get them and learn their meaning, you will once more gain the goodwill of mankind." Edju went to where the palm-trees were. The monkeys gave him sixteen nuts. Edju looked at these, but did not know what to do with them. The monkeys said to him: "Edju, do you know what to do with the nuts? We will counsel you. You got the sixteen nuts by guile. Now go round the world and ask for their meaning everywhere. You will hear sixteen sayings in each of the sixteen places. Then go back to the Gods. Tell men what you yourself have learned, and then men will also learn once more to fear you."
>
> Edju did as he was told. He went to the sixteen places round the world. He went back into the sky.
>
> Edju told the Gods what he had learned himself. The Gods spake: "It is well." Then the Gods imparted their knowledge to their descendants, and now men can know the will of the Gods every day, and what will come to pass in the future. When men saw that all evil things would happen in the days to come, and what they would be able to escape by offering sacrifices, they began to slaughter animals again and burn them for the Gods. This was the way in which Edju brought the Ifa (palmnuts) down to men. When he went back, he stayed with Ogun, Shango and Obatalla, and these four watched to see what men would do with the kernels.[15]

Esu clearly has priority in the art of interpretation. In other myths of the origins of Ifa, Esu both teaches and wills the system to his friend. This explains why the Yoruba say that "Esu is the path (or route) to Ifa." A canonical narrative, "Esu Taught Orunmila How to Divine," also stresses Esu's importance:

> Esu had taught Ifa how to divine with *ikin*. In this way, Ifa became very important as the communication link between men and the Orisas. The Irunmoles [earth spirits], who numbered two hundred and one, were jealous of Ifa, but they could not harm him because Esu was always on hand to fight on Ifa's behalf.[16]

Legba retains this priority in the Fon myths.

Melville Herskovits suggests that this is so primarily to allow human beings " 'a way out' of a supernaturally willed dilemma." And that way out

> is offered by a celestial trickster, who is the youngest son of the Creator. In Dahomey, as in most of West Africa, the youngest son is held to be the most astute in the family. Though Fa, who is destiny, is of the greatest importance, the trickster, Legba, comes even before Fa, . . . [In] dealing with the supernatural officialdom, a man can, by winning the favor of Legba, mollify an angered deity and set aside his vengeance.[17]

While Herskovits gives a practical, or functional, explanation for Legba's role in interpretation, both Ifa and Fa systems have inscribed this hierarchy within their myths of origin, and they have done so for hermeneutical reasons.

The roles of Esu and of the Monkey, in several accounts of the myth, are crucial. For reasons extremely difficult to reconstruct, the monkey became, through a displacement in African myths in the New World, a central character in this crucial scene of instruction. In the curious manner repeated throughout this transmission process from Africa to the Western Hemisphere, one structural element that appears to be minor—to judge from subsequent versions taken from Yoruba *babalawo*—became a major character in the surviving oral variation in a New World black culture. Lydia Cabrera's account of this myth within Afro-Cuban mythology makes the central role of the Monkey apparent:

> In some of the Elegua [Elegbara] tales, he is portrayed as the first interpreter, responsible for teaching or uncovering the art of divination to Oruba [Ifa] while accompanied by Moedun [the Monkey] and the tree— a palm tree growing in the garden of Orungan [the midday sun]—as well as being the messenger of Odu, the divination seeds. The reference is to the cowry shells, the means of interpretation of the babalochas and the iyaloches. Bake Elegua is associated with this orisha: "he controls the largest number of cowry shells."[18]

While *Moedun* could possibly derive from the Yoruba *omo* ("child of") *edun* ("a type of monkey"), more probably it derives from the Yoruba

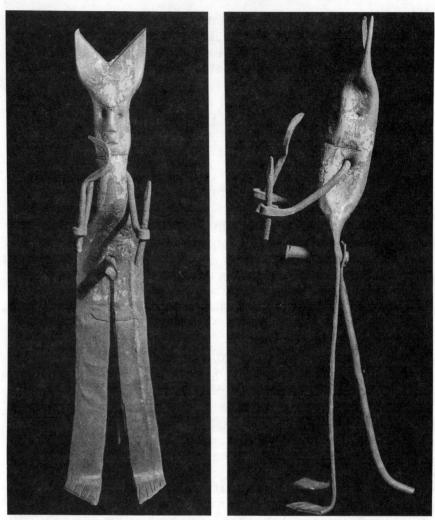

Figure 8. Ileke Exu. From the author's collection. *Photos by Sarah Whitaker.*

mo, the first person singular pronoun ("I"), used with past and continuous tenses. *Moedun,* then, can be translated as "I who was/am the Monkey." In Yoruba, furthermore, "monkey" (*òwè*) and proverb or riddle (*òwe*) are virtual homonyms. What is clear is that Esu's role as the first interpreter survived the Middle Passage accompanied by both the Monkey and the tree in which the monkeys lived and from which they selected the sixteen palm nuts that became the sacred characters of Ifa divination. Many contemporary statues of Exu in Brazil depict him with both a large erect penis and a long tail.

To be sure, the Monkey appears in other African narratives and even appears with the Lion and the Elephant (as in the Signifying Monkey narrative poems) in a well-known Fon narrative entitled "Why Monkey Did Not Become Man." The Monkey also surfaces in relation to divination in a second canonical Fon narrative, "Monkey's Ingratitude: Why One Does Not Deceive the Diviner."[19] But the direct conjunction of the Monkey and Esu seems to be confined to this myth of origins of the process of interpretation itself. The Monkey, furthermore, is one of Esu's bynames, as in the following *Oriki Esu:*

> King of Ketu,
> The Monkey has no lamp at Akesan,
> My mother's money its eyes serve as lamps all over the farm,
> Product of today's hustle and bustle
> Offshoot of tomorrow's hustle and bustle
> The evil eye has stunted Monkey's growth
> They call him child of no means and position
> Let him not consort with people on Alaketu's street
> Let him not bring about the curse more effective than poison.[20]

(Two of Esu's physical characteristics are his extraordinarily dark color and his tiny size.) Perhaps even more telling is the Fon myth, "The First Humans." Legba, acting without knowledge of Mawu, the creator, transforms two of the earth's four primal beings into monkeys. It is from these two monkeys that all monkeys descended. Legba, therefore, is the father of the Monkey.[21]

There is a fascinating conflation of the Monkey and Esu in Afro-Cuban mythology. This occurs in the figure of the *guije* or *jigue,* a black trickster topos whose identity has not yet, to my knowledge, been satisfactorily defined. The literature of the *guije* or *jigue* consists of two types. In the first, the *guije* is depicted as a small black man, as in the oral narrative, "El guije de la Bajada," collected by Salvador Bueno in his *Leyendas cubanas.* The two signal physical characteristics of Esu, as I have said above, are his extremely dark color and his tiny size. The other form that the *guije* assumes, generally in poetry rather than in narrative, is the *jigue,* or monkey. Teofilo Radillo's poem, "The Song of the Jigue," helps us to resolve the mystery of this conflated trickster's origins.[22]

"The jigue," Radillo informs us, "was born in Oriente" province, that curious Cuban site, or cauldron, at which Yoruba culture met European Hispanic culture to produce a novel mixture:

> The jigue was born in Oriente.
> The jigue came from the waters . . .
> By the edge of the lagoon,
> while the children bathe.

His emergence from the waters suggests his African origins. Among the *jigue*'s physical characteristics are his dark color, his pointed teeth, and his long hair, the color and sort of hair that are characteristic descriptions of Esu:

> A dark jigue is watching
> with a great length of hair . . .
> His teeth are pointed
> and his intentions are sharp.

The *jigue*'s eyes, in addition, are large and penetrating, as are Esu's eyes:

> Mother, I have seen a jigue
> yesterday, when I was bathing
> in the still waters:
> He was black . . . and glared at me
> with what . . . I could not tell,
> may have been eyes of live coals.

Most important, the *jigue* underwent a transformation of the most profound sort in his passage from Africa to the New World. Where once he was a monkey, he emerged from the rite of passage—or, more truly, a rite de marges (as we might think of the Middle Passage)—as Esu, or Echu:

> The jigue was born in Oriente
> and brought there from Africa,
> where he had been a monkey: the last
> monkey who fell into the water;
> the monkey who drowned
> for the sake of the nganga—
> the nganga forever floating
> over the waves of water—

The *jigue*'s connection with a monkey is clear etymologically. *Guije* and *jigue* are derived from the Efik-Ejagham word for "monkey," *jiwe*.[23]

The etymology of *nganga* is also suggestive. In Kikongo, *nganga* means one expert in medicine or magic, a doctor of various sorts, in other words. *Nganga* means action, work, or arrangement. And *nganga* means to experience an attack of wrath, to cause pain, to reflect or to question. In Kiswahili, *ng'ang'ama* means to clutch hold of, as of a swinging branch or tree, while *ng'ang'ania* means to beg earnestly, beseech, until one attains a desired end. In a study of "Langue Congo" in Cuba, Germain de Granada defines *nganga* as a magical object. Most suggestively of all, however, Tulu Kia Mpansu Buakasa defines *nganga* as "interpreter."[24]

As used in Teofilo Radillo's "The Song of the Jigue," *nganga* could connote any number of these meanings:

> the monkey who drowned
> for the sake of the nganga—
> the nganga forever floating
> over the waves of water—

It could refer to a magic object, or an interpreter (doctor) of the traditional sort; or, more suggestively, *nganga* could imply the victim of an attack of wrath or one insistent on questioning the received, or the imposed, order. In a more literal sense, the Kiswahili root of *ng'ang'ama* suggests one clutching a swinging branch of a tree (as a monkey would) to escape torrential waters, only to lose one's grip and to tumble into the water, "drowning," as the poem states, "for the sake of nganga." The poem reads:

> jigue who frightens children
> who hangs by the white girl
> by the edge of the river
> where night is bathing
> at the tune of the moon
> curling around the silver light.

The significance of *nganga* suggests a multiplicity of meanings, each of which informs the KiKongo-Cuban survival. Most dramatically of all, Rodillo figures the *nganga* "forever floating over the waves of water" like a wandering signifier, suggesting perpetually its range of meanings from its Bantu roots, even—or especially—in its New World setting. We may take this sort of perpetual, or wandering, signification as an emblem of the process of cultural transmission and translation that recurred with startling frequency when African cultures encountered New World–European cultures and yielded a novel blend.

The poem's last stanza comes to bear directly on the relationship among Esu, the monkey, and the interpreter that I am attempting to establish:

> Jigue-monkey,
> monkey-jigue,
> nganga-jigue,
> jigue-nganga;

These are represented as terms of equivalence: "Jigue-monkey / monkey-jigue" echoes the Cuban neologism *moedun,* from the Yoruba, meaning "I-monkey" and "I who am / was the monkey." "Nganga-Jigue" here suggests the identity between the monkey and the interpreter figure, clearly an interpreter of the traditional sort, a trickster figure of the order of Esu.

This conflated set of figures, now rendered equivalent semantically and functionally, represents one who has come from Africa to Cuba:

> you have come from very far,
> gallopping over the waters
> in dreams which arrived
> muzzled to these shores.

The last two lines of this wonderful image form a marvelous figure of the initiate who emerged at the Western pole of the Middle Passage; the initiate survived, dreams intact, but the dreams are "muzzled to these shores."

But what, or who, can emerge intact from such traumatic crossings, in response to the passionate call of the originary language, figured by the drum? Only the black trickster:

> One playful jigue emerges
> as the drum calls;

> as the drum bursts it is said
> that many jigues dance.

Esu is also a highly accomplished dancer, a mask-in-motion, who signifies in
ritual by his phallic dance of generation, of creation, of translation.

    Who, ultimately, is the jigue?

> The jigue while there, in the forest,
> was a monkey, the last monkey. . . .
> and drowned . . . to float today
> in the sleeping waters of legends
> which cradled a whole race.

Drowning, in Africa when the slavers stole our people, the trickster figure can
"float today / in the sleeping waters of legends," legends in which are inscribed the New World African's metaphysical origins, legends whose meanings and perpetuation "cradled a whole race." Who, finally, is the jigue?

> Monkey-jigue,
> jigue-monkey,
> nganga-jigue,
> jigue-nganga!

The jigue is the monkey, and the monkey is Esu, and both are doctors of
interpretation. The three are trickster figures of the same order, the hermeneutical order.

    While we lack archeological and historical evidence to explain the valo-
rized presence of the Monkey in Cuban mythology, in the textual evidence,
on the other hand, we commonly encounter Esu with his companion, as depicted even in visual representations of Esu. As Alberto del Pozo writes,
"Echu Elegua frequently has a monkey . . . by his side."[25] If we examine
the general characteristics of Esu, as derived from the *Oriki Esu* and as
classed together under the rubric of "rhetorical principles," the Signifying
Monkey emerges from his mysteriously beclouded Afro-American origins as
Esu's first cousin, if not his American heir. It is as if Esu's friend, the Monkey, left his side at Havana and swam to New Orleans. The Signifying Monkey remains as the trace of Esu, the sole survivor of a disrupted partnership.
Both are tropes that serve as transferences in a system aware of the nature
of language and its interpretation.

    What is the importance of these apparently related tricksters and their
myths to literary criticism? Perhaps this will be clearer if we return briefly to
Ifa divination and to a fuller discussion of Esu's role. It is convenient to think
of the Yoruba god Ifa as the text of divination, who gave to divination not
only his name but the 256 *Odu* as well as the thousands of poems that comprise these *Odu*. This extensive, highly structured body of lyrical poetry
stands as the verbal, literary, or textual analogue of 256 cryptograms that
can be formed by the *babalawo* as he manipulates the sixteen sacred palm
nuts. This vast array of poetry exists as the separate stanzas of one extensive
text, which we might think of profitably as the text of Ifa. Human beings con-

sult this text in attempts to decipher their destiny, or fate. What the supplicant hears read to him, in "the signature of Odu," is neither a literal revelation of his fate nor a set of commands that can be put into practice to appease, or redress, the human being's curse of the indeterminacy or uncertainty of fate. Rather, the supplicant hears read by the *babalawo* a series of lyrical poems that are so metaphorical and so ambiguous that they may be classified as enigmas, or riddles, which must be read or interpreted, but which, nevertheless, have no single determinate meaning. The supplicant, the reader as it were, must produce meaning by stopping the *babalawo* as he chants an *ese,* which in some way strikes the supplicant as being relevant to his dilemma. Then, the *babalawo* interprets the poem for his client and prescribes the appropriate sacrifices. Fairly frequently, the client cannot recognize his situation in the metaphorical language of the poem, despite the fact that Ifa has inscribed the person's fate into the appropriate *Odu,* signified by the patterns formed by the palm nuts.

Ifa is the god of determinate meanings, but his meaning must be rendered by analogy. Esu, god of indeterminacy, rules this interpretive process; he is the god of interpretation because he embodies the ambiguity of figurative language. Although he allowed his friend Ifa to rule and name the texts of the tradition, it is Esu who retains dominance over the act of interpretation precisely because he signifies the very divinity of the figurative. For Ifa, one's sought meaning is patently obvious; it need only be read. Esu decodes the figures.

If Ifa, then, is our metaphor for the text itself, then Esu is our metaphor for the uncertainties of explication, for the open-endedness of every literary text. Whereas Ifa represents closure, Esu rules the process of disclosure, a process that is never-ending, that is dominated by multiplicity. Esu is discourse upon a text; it is the process of interpretation that he rules. This is the message of his primal scene of instruction with his friend Ifa. If Esu stands for discourse upon a text, then his Pan-African kinsman, the Signifying Monkey, stands for the rhetorical strategies of which each literary text consists. For the Signifying Monkey exists as the great trope of Afro-American discourse, and the trope of tropes, his language of Signifyin(g), is his verbal sign in the Afro-American tradition.

We can summarize the importance of these tricksters to theory in three related ways. First, they and the myths in which they are characters function as focal points for black theories about formal language use. The figure of writing appears to be peculiar to the myth of Esu, while the figure of speaking, of oral discourse densely structured rhetorically, is peculiar to the myth of the Signifying Monkey. Here, the vernacular tradition names the great opposition of its formal literary counterpart, the tension between the oral and the written modes of narration that is represented as finding a voice in writing. As figures of the duality of the voice within the tradition, Esu and his friend the Monkey manifest themselves in the search for a voice that is depicted in so very many black texts. The tension between them surfaces in the double-voiced discourse so commonly found here. This tension between the oral and the written plays itself out in one form as the two dominant narrative voices that serve as counterpoint in texts such as Jean Toomer's *Cane*. In another form, it surfaces as the free indirect discourse of what I am calling the speakerly text, in which third and first person, oral and written voices, oscillate freely within one structure, as in Zora Neale Hurston's *Their Eyes Were Watching God*. These tensions are figured in the myths of Esu and the Monkey.

Second, in the myths of Esu and the Monkey the tradition defines the role of the figurative. Polemical traditions seem to valorize the literal. Pragmatics argues that it cannot be otherwise; the vernacular tradition, however, undercuts this penchant at its deepest level, that of underlying rhetorical principle. The myths of origins of the tradition privilege both the figurative and the ambiguous. The determinate meanings often sought in criticism run counter to the most fundamental values of the tradition as encased in myth. In this sense, the literal and the figurative are locked in a Signifyin(g) relation, the myths and the figurative Signified upon by the real and literal, just as the vernacular tradition Signifies upon the tradition of letters, and as figures of writing and inscription are registered, paradoxically, in an oral literature. This is another example of the presence of the dual voice. The notion of double-voiced discourse, related to Mikhail Bakhtin's theory of narrative but also indigenously African, comprises the crux of the method I use for the close readings of Afro-American texts in this book's final four chapters. The Afro-American concept of Signifyin(g) can be conveniently introduced here as formal revision that is at all points double-voiced.

The third conclusion that we can draw from the myths of Esu and the Monkey concerns the indeterminacy of interpretation. Esu is a principle of language, of written discourse particularly. He is "all metaphor, all ambiguous oracle," as Robert Pelton has said.[26] The most famous myth about him is read as a story about indeterminacy. It is inscribed in the well-known canonical tale of "The Two Friends," which I shall discuss below. Indeterminacy, then, is accounted for by the vernacular tradition, as an unavoidable aspect of acts of interpretation. These three general observations summarize, in the broadest sense, the self-reflexive functions that Esu serves in Yoruba discourse. In the second section of this chapter, I wish to show in some detail how the Yoruba vernacular underscores these functions and then to suggest the relationship of this theory of criticism to some common assumptions of poststructural literary theory. I am concerned in this half of the chapter to reveal the grammar of the tradition before proceeding to discuss the rhetorical forms of which the tradition consists.

II

Akinfemia, man with many names.
                    Oriki Esu.[27]

I will write Arabic and say Muslim prayers
I will write Arabic and say Muslim prayers
When the festival comes, I'll worship my deity [Esu]
I will write Arabic and say Muslim prayers.
                    Oriki Esu.[28]

The *Oriki Esu,* the *Odu, ese,* and the numerous myths in which Esu figures consist of a densely lyrical poetic diction that commands the attention of the practical critic. By explicating these vernacular literary forms, I wish to underscore the linguistic self-reflexiveness that inscribes, in what we might think of as the literature of Esu, this trickster god's preserve as the architect of interpretation, as the keeper of *ase,* the logos, as the "divine linguist of Mawu," as Herskovits put it.

Of the topoi of Esu, the Yoruba myths of Esu-Elegbara and the Fon myths of Legba contain the most explicit assertions about nature and functions of formal language use. To identify and analyze these assertions is to begin to account for a black theory of literature and its interpretation, on levels of linguistic meta-ascent, as inscribed in the black vernacular traditions. Let us descend, once again, into the shadowy realm of myth, to ascertain the black tradition's fundamental idea of itself, buried or encoded in its primal myths—ambiguous, enigmatic, profoundly figurative, complex rhetorical structures—which seem to have been scattered through several concealed fragments, as if to protect its own code from (mis)appropriation.

As I stated earlier in this chapter, the trickster figure's relation to destiny, and indeed his priority over destiny, is inscribed in his role as the guiding force of interpretation itself. The primal god of the Fon is a Janus figure; one side of its body is female and is called Mawu, while the other side is male and is called Lisa. Mawu's eyes form the moon; Lisa's eyes form the sun. Accordingly, Lisa rules the day and Mawu rules the night. The seventh son of Mawu-Lisa is Legba. Legba is the wild card of Fon metaphysics, the wandering signifier. While Legba's six siblings preside over the six domains of heaven and earth, Legba rules over all. As the earth priests' creation myth concludes, "Hence Legba was chosen to represent Mawu everywhere in the world of men and gods."[29]

This mode of subtle domination and omnipresent, simultaneous representation, curiously enough, the Fon reinforce by attributing to Legba the role of linguist. The Fon earth priests' myth of origins describes Legba's linguistic function in the following manner:

To Legba was assigned the role of linguist between the kingdoms of gods and gods, and gods and men. Whereupon, in addition to the knowledge of the "language" of Mawu-Lisa, he was given the knowledge of all the "languages" spoken by the other gods in their separate dominions. Therefore if any of the children of Mawu-Lisa, on earth or elsewhere, wish to address their parents or each other, they must transmit their messages through Legba, for they can no longer communicate directly. Thus Legba is everywhere; he is found even before the houses of *vodu* themselves, and this is because all living creatures must address themselves to him before they can be understood by the gods.[30]

That which the Fon call "the Book of Fa," or "the System of Writing of the Creator," in other words, can be read only by Legba, the sole agent of interpretation and hence mediation between man, on one hand, and the Book of Fate *(Fa)*, on the other. Only Legba is able to read this text because of the several stages of mediation and translation that occur in rapid succession in Fa divination. A supplicant's query is answered by a cryptogram, the markings made in powder on the divination tray. The priest next translates this coded sign into its appropriate *Odu* and recites the *Odu*'s several parts until the supplicant asks him to halt. The supplicant then attempts to read his dilemma into, or out of, the jungle of ambiguity that is the language of the *Odu*. R. E. Dennett, writing in *At the Back of the Black Man's Mind,* quotes the Yoruba scholar James Johnson as saying that each *Odu* is comprised of "roads," or "pathways," or "courses" (*ese* and their derivative narratives), which lead the supplicant through the maze of figuration that is Esu's kingdom.[31]

Esu rules over this kingdom, this process of interpretation, from the toss of the dice through each successive translation from one semiotic system to the next: from cryptogram, to *Odu*, to its reading, both in a literal sense of speaking aloud and in a metaphorical sense of analysis. As Peter Morton-Williams rightly concludes, "the oracle replaces a dilemma with an enigma; it was the duty of the diviners at the king's court to resolve the enigma after they had produced it, the king needing information and not riddles." The *Odu,* of course, are the oracle's riddles, the translations of the visual signs made in the sacred dust on the Ifa tray of divination. Bernard Maupoil, in his seminal work, *La Geomancie à l'ancienne Côte des Esclaves,* describes this process as "an abstract, indirect, and deductive mode of interpreting or revealing the past or the future." Because Legba's role as messenger, as lord of exchange, inscribes his role as interpreter, these abstract, indirect utterances or riddles are his domain, from which some sort of analogous meaning must be derived. Legba, then, stands as the discursive, or textual, principle itself; as Robert Pelton concludes, Legba "is a creator of discourse, for his every movement is, in T. S. Eliot's phrase, a 'raid on the inarticulate,' a foray into the formless, which simultaneously gives shape to the dark and fearsome and new life to structure always in danger of becoming a skeleton." Legba is discourse and, as we shall see, discourse upon a text.[32]

Legba, like Esu, is the divine reader, whose interpretation of the Book of Fate determines precisely what this book says. The interpreter governs meaning because he determines our understanding of the text, which in this instance is the Text of Fa. The Fon render this complex and sophisticated system of text and its determination in the following way, as spoken by a *bokono,* a priest of Fa, to Melville Herskovits:

> We *bokono* take three things for our Mawu. We take Mawu, or Fa, as the author of man and his destiny. We take Legba as the son, the brother, and the power of Mawu and as Mawu herself. . . . Fa is the writing of Mawu, which was turned over to Legba to make man. Therefore, we say Fa is Mawu and Mawu is Fa.[33]

Fa, we recall, is "a personification of the formulae of Mawu," as Herskovits puts it, or "Fa is the writing of Mawu," as the Fon themselves put it. Legba is the linguist-messenger who reads the text of Fa, a text that remains unread and unreadable without the agency of Legba. Because Legba can, indeed must, be propitiated with the most splendid sacrifices before he can be beseeched, it seems clear that even one's very fate is not inscribed in indelible ink. Indeed, Legba's reading of the crucial texts of fate can be profoundly informed by the quality and nature of one's sacrifice.

The text, in other words, is not fixed in any determinate sense; in one sense, it consists of the dynamic and indeterminate relationship between truth on one hand and understanding on the other. Fa, as the writing of Mawu, can be thought of conveniently as the truth of a text, whereas Legba's role is to effect and affect its understanding. The relationship between truth and understanding yields our sense of meaning. Meanings, in the Yoruba and Fon systems of hermeneutics, can be both multiple and indeterminate, as underscored by the densely ambiguous and figurative language of which the entire system consists. Legba governs the indeterminacy of meaning for the Fon. If, as Geoffrey Hartman has argued, "Indeterminacy functions as a bar separating understanding and truth," then we can, at last, posit a site over which Legba rules and in which he dwells. Legba dwells in this bar; indeed, he, like indeterminacy, is this bar. So, whereas the Fon say that Fa is the writing of Mawu, we can say that Legba is the indeterminacy of the interpretation of writing, and his traditional dwelling place at the crossroads, for the critic, is the crossroads of understanding and truth. And of what sort can closure be, which dwells at such a crossroads?[34]

Interpretation for Esu, even—or especially—of the same text, the same *Odu,* is a continuous project: "Reading," to cite Hartman somewhat ironically, is "a form of life," which can itself be read. Esu's life is a form of reading texts in motion, constantly variable. I am, of course, reading the Yoruba and the Fon processes of reading, through the figure of Esu.[35]

But what sort of text is constantly variable, is a text in motion? Walter J. Ong passionately and persuasively argues in *Orality and Literacy* that the English word *text* is, "in absolute terms, more compatible etymologically with oral utterance than is 'literature,' which refers to the letters etymologically/ (literae) of the alphabet." *Text* is a satisfactory descriptive, etymologically at least, because of its Latin root *textus,* past participle of *texere,* "to weave." Ong says that this sense of *text* has even been used in oral cultures to describe

oral narration as a mode of "weaving or stitching—rhapsoidein, to 'rhapso-
dize,' basically means in Greek 'to stitch together.' " Nevertheless, he concludes, when we "literates" use the term, we conceive of *text* by analogy, as
a writing, and a written text is "fixed, boxed-off, isolated," unscoring "the
chirographic base of logic."[36]

The texts of Ifa are preserved by memory and exist in the memories of
babalawos and *bokonos*. The written texts that I am analyzing here are carefully recorded versions of one performance of oral narration. Quite probably,
however, these oral texts would not, and perhaps could not, be repeated
verbatim on a subsequent consultation of Ifa despite the fact that the literature on Ifa contains several striking examples of exact stanzaic repetition.
The texts of Ifa, then, are dynamic rather than fixed, as the text of a book
is fixed. They are open-ended, in the sense that while the total possible number of *ese* that could be uttered by the priest is a fixed number (over 150,-
000), no propitiate could possibly sit through a divination session long
enough to hear these chanted. Nor would the *ese* of the *Odu* necessarily be
rendered exactly the same from one day to the next. For reasons that I have
suggested above, the interpretive principles of these texts underscore their
open-endedness, as does their densely figurative language, which even includes archaic words that have been relegated to the corpus of Ifa and which
not even the *babalawo* can interpret or understand. What sort of closure,
then, can even be possible when we think of the nature of the texts of Ifa,
or when we think of the nature of their interpretation, a process that turns
upon approximation or analogy? That a propitiate might even return repeatedly to the *babalawo* for further clarification of the nature of his fate
emphasizes further that our received notion of closure is not applicable to
the writing of Ifa and the readings of Esu.[37]

The use in Yoruba of chirographic metaphors (writing, reading, signature) to describe the nature of the texts of Ifa, in the myths of origins of
writing and speaking discussed above, suggests that the system of oral narration attempted to mediate the distance between itself and written narration
by the use of chirographic figures of speech. This, most certainly, is an ironic
form of mediation. Esu's role as the perpetually copulating copula serves to
reinforce this notion of linkage, or mediation. As Pelton concludes, he is
"the copula of each sentence, and thus the embodiment of every limen."
Nevertheless, textual evidence suggests that we must not think of these as
idle metaphors. For the rhetorical and indeed semantic tension between figures of speaking and writing, as inscribed within the texts of Ifa themselves,
serves to undermine a chirographic culture's notions of closure and determi-
nacy, but especially to define a complex notion of writing, a spoken and
written writing. We shall return to this crucial point at the end of this
chapter.[38]

It is fascinating to trace the rhetorical and hermeneutic references to Esu,
as found in the work of several scholars. Melville J. Herskovits's field research with the Fon of Dahomey is rich in this sort of material. Herskovits's
Legba is the central figure in Fa. He is a lovable, if a somewhat mischievous,

figure for formal language use, especially in those canonical tales in which his extraordinarily vital sexuality is inscribed. One Fa myth of origins says of this penchant:

> Legba denied that he had had relations with a mother and a daughter, but his parent [Mawu-Lisa] ordered him to undress. As he stood naked, Mawu saw how his penis was erect and said, "You have lied to me, as you have deceived your sister [Gbadu]. And since you have done this, I ordain that your penis shall always be erect, and that you may never be appeased." To show his indifference to this punishment, Legba began at once to play with Gbadu before their parent, and when reproached, merely pointed out that since his organ was always to remain erect, Mawu had herself decreed such conduct for him. That is why Legba dances, he tries to take any woman who is at hand.[39]

"Myth after myth," Herskovits argues, represents Legba "as hugely over-sexed and therefore not to be trusted with women." Esu, like Legba, shares this characteristic and frequently is selected to be "intermediary between this world and the next" at the end of myths that recount his sexual prowess. The pun here, of course, is on copula(te) and intercourse. Legba's sexuality is a sign of liminality, but also of the penetration of thresholds, the exchange between discursive universes. As Pelton summarizes: "He is a living copula, and his phallus symbolizes his being the limen marking the real distinction between outside and inside, and the wild and the ordered, even as it ensures safe passage between them." This role as copula is apparent in another canonical myth.[40]

Herskovits records an alternative account of the "coming of Fa" to the version that I discussed earlier. It, as do so many others, argues strongly for Legba's crucial place in the system of Fa:

> After the world had been created, two men descended from the sky. The first was called Koda, the second Chada. It is said that in those days there was no medicine and nothing worshipped, and that in all of Africa there were very few people. Now these two men came down as numodato—"prophets"—and called the people together and told them that they had been sent by Mawu with the message that it was necessary that each person have his Fa. The people asked, "What is this thing you call Fa?" And they were told by these men that Fa is the writing with which Mawu creates each person, and that this writing is given to Legba, the only one who assists Mawu in this work. They also said that Mawu herself is always seated, but that Legba is forever before her, that the orders given to Legba by means of this writing are called Fa, and that, therefore, all men who have been created have their Fa which is in the house of Legba. They said, further, that the place where men were created is called by the name Fe. Legba, they said, possesses all the writing of each day, and is sent to Mawu to bring to each individual his Fa, for it is necessary that a man should know the writing which Mawu has used to create him, so that, knowing his Fa, he knows what he may eat and what he may not eat, what he may do and what he may not do.
>
> When they had said this, they also said that every man has a god

whom he must worship, but that without Fa he can never know his god, and that it is therefore necessary that all inhabitants of the earth worship Legba, for if they fail to do so, Legba will refuse to reveal to a man the writing that is his destiny; that if they do not address Legba first, he will not give to man the good things that are destined for him. Each day, they continued, Mawu gives the day's writing to Legba, thus telling him who is to die, who is to be born, what dangers this one is to encounter, what good fortune that one is to meet. And when Legba has this information, then, if he wishes, it is possible for him to change the fate in store for any man. When Koda and Chada finished speaking, the people understood that Fa was necessary for them.

As time went on, though they remembered that Fa is the will of the gods, they forgot the importance of Legba. Thus it happened that sometime later three other men came to earth at a place called Gisi, near a river in Nigeria called Anya. The first named Adjaka, the second Oku, and the third Ogbena. They came to tell the people that they should not forget that Mawu had said it is important they worship Legba. . . .

To spread their message, the three emissaries of the gods selected a man named Alaundje whom they instructed in the way of manipulating Fa. . . .

Alaundje spread the doctrine of Fa everywhere, and taught what he had learned of the cult of Fa to Djisa. Djisa established himself at Abomey and taught Fa and Legba to all the people of Dahomey. And Djisa instructed the people that all those who learned to know how to read this writing of Mawu were to be called *bokono,* since in the sky Legba is called bokono.[41]

Each god speaks a language of his or her own, and only Legba can interpret these because Legba "knows all 'languages.' " Such a role as interpreter, in such myths as that cited above, most certainly is designed to serve as a perpetual reminder of Legba's role, a subtle role for the Fon. For the Fon, Legba is a principle of fluidity, of uncertainty, of the indeterminacy even of one's inscribed fate. Nowhere in the literature is this role stated more clearly than in Herskovits's account:

In this way [that is, by reading the text of Fa], do men discover their destiny and conduct its worship. What is in store for a man is foreordained. Yet, . . . a "way out" is not denied to man. This power that permits man to escape his destiny—philosophically the personification of *Accident* in a world where Destiny is inexorable—is found in the character of Legba.[42]

Legba's priority, his place "before" Fa, "in the sense that . . . he transmits the wishes of the gods concerning what must occur to a person," is figured in the fact that he must always be worshiped and propitiated by sacrifice first, even before any other god can be summoned. If fate can be foretold, it can also be changed—by Legba, a quality of his representation which underscores his role as interpreter, as the determination of meaning through understanding. This is so even of Fa, "since it was necessary that Legba be at his side before Fa could speak," as one Fon myth says.[43]

The various figures of Esu provide endless, fascinating references to the critic's role in interpretation and to the nature of interpretation itself. Esu, like interpretation, is ageless. Despite the fact that I have referred to him in the masculine, Esu is also genderless, or of dual gender, as recorded Yoruba and Fon myths suggest, despite his remarkable penis feats.[44] Ogundipe records a group of Esu devotees who are exclusively women at Agbole Olunloyo at Ibadan. One of their *oriki* reads:

> Our mothers, witches, homage to you!
> If the little child respects its elders
> Clothes will hang comfortably on its back
> Our mothers, witches, we respect you.
> Deference to you, too, Esu
> Our mothers, witches![45]

As Robert Thompson shows, Esu is figured as paired male and female statues, which his/her devotees carry while dancing, or as one bisexual figure. Often she holds her breasts in the female figures. Even Esu's sexuality is indeterminate, if insatiable. In fact, Ogundipe, a Yoruba woman and scholar, writes that Esu

> certainly is not restricted to human distinctions of gender or sex; he is at once both male and female. Although his masculinity is depicted as visually and graphically overwhelming, his equally expressive femininity renders his enormous sexuality ambiguous, contrary, and genderless.[46]

Rather than standing as one more form of sexist discourse, then, the female-other is inscribed in Esu just as it is in Mawu-Lisa. Both are Janus figures, two-sided figures like a sign, "a kind of reconciliation of opposites of discourse and, therefore, the apt 'linguist' of Mawu."[47] Nowhere is Esu's existence as the third principle—neither male nor female, neither this nor that, but both, a compound morphology—put more expressively than by J. E. and D. M. dos Santos, in *Esu Bara Laroye*:

> Being result and issue, he inherits the nature of all the ancestors. He exhibits the characteristics of the male ancestors, the Egun Irunmale, as well as those of the female, the Iyam-mi Aje. By compounding their morphologies, he partakes indifferently of either group and can circulate freely between them all.[48]

Each time I have used the masculine pronoun for the referent *Esu,* then, I could just have properly used the feminine. This discursive structure of sexual duality the Fon even matched with a dual structure of "a twofold doubleness." As Paul Mercier describes this curious system:

> At the head is the king, and he is two in one. R. F. Burton was the first to point this out: "One of the Dahomean monarch's peculiarities is that he is double; *not merely binonymous, nor dual . . .* , but two in one." . . . There is only one royal personage, but there are two courts, two bodies of exactly similar officials, two series of rituals in honour of the royal ancestors. . . . Every title and every administrative office is con-

ferred simultaneously on a woman within the palace and a man outside it.[49]

Even Fon governmental structure, then, stood as a readily accessible institutional critique of the simple opposition, a critique that occurs by a doubling
process, of which Legba is the sign.

Metaphysically and hermeneutically, at least, Fon and Yoruba discourse
is truly genderless, offering feminist literary critics a unique opportunity to
examine a field of texts, a discursive universe, that escaped the trap of sexism
inherent in Western discourse. This is not to attempt to argue that African
men and women are not sexist, but to argue that the Yoruba discursive and
hermeneutical universes are not. The Fon and the Yoruba escape the Western
version of discursive sexism through the action of doubling the double; the
number 4 and its multiples are sacred in Yoruba metaphysics. Esu's two sides
"disclose a hidden wholeness"; rather than closing off unity, through the opposition, they signify the passage from one to the other as sections of a subsumed whole. Esu stands as the sign of this wholeness. Pelton's explanation
of this doubleness is especially cogent:

> Its meaning is not so much rooted in the coincidence of opposites or in
> the mere passage between structure or antistructure as it is in a percep-
> tion of life as a rounded wholeness whose faces both mask and disclose
> each other. These faces are simultaneously present, but this is a simul-
> taneity of *process,* a turning by which one face not only succeeds but is
> transformed into the other.[50] (emphasis added)

Esu, thus, is the potential for resolution, a role profoundly linked to his
role as the interpreter. Esu is a figure of doubled duality, of unreconciled opposites, living in harmony:

> Laaroye, one who can be good or bad
> One who can be tall or short
> One who can be short or tall.[51]

Thus, he is the epitome of paradox:

> Swift footed one!
> Agile and restless one!
> One who scatters himself abroad
> One who, once scattered, cannot be put together again.
> One born on the way to the market
> He walks through the peanut patch
> His head hardly shows
> But for his tallness.
> He has eyes yet with his nose weeps
> Tip of the razor blade
> He sleeps rested against a cudgel.[52]

Esu, as Ogundipe concludes, is "the personification of flux and mutability."
He is

Worthy of worship like Fate!
My mother's husband!
Owner of a golden whip!
Consumer of sacrifice to save man
As restless as a tale bearer.[53]

Bolaji Idowu contends that for the Yoruba even destiny is mutable. In the unborn state of being, each Yoruba kneels before Olodumare to hear the fate (ori) that shall be his or hers in life on earth. Then the unborn is born. As one is born one's fate is forgotten. Hence, one consults Ifa to learn one's fate. Nevertheless, this fate is not rendered in a literal or determinate way, so that human will comes to bear in the figure of Esu, just as chance is inherent in a system of revelation that turns upon a throw of the dice.[54] As Ogundipe puts the matter nicely,

Thus Ifa, as the principle of certainty, complements Esu as ordered Chance, the uncertainty in the certainty of the throw of the dice. Thus Esu and Ifa are complementary, not opposing or antithetical forces.[55]

Esu, in this sense, is the dialectical principle. As J. E. and D. M. dos Santos conclude, "It is Esu who speaks through Ifa, revealing the ways and means, the ebo, that shall enable him to open or close them to the benevolent or destructive elements."[56]

The literature on Esu in the New World is extensive. In all essential respects, he is represented the same as he is in the Fon and Yoruba systems. As Lydia Cabrera, writing about Esu in Cuba, and Juana and Deoscoredes dos Santos, writing about Esu Bara Laroye in Nigeria, Dahomey, and Brazil, demonstrate in some detail, Esu's presence only has proliferated in the New World, where every god and every human being has his or her own personal Esu, the principle of individuality. Cabrera's marvelous Chapter III of *El Monte,* entitled "Oluwa Ewe: El Dueño del Monte," contains several myths of Esu as the originator and master of Ifa and its interpretation. "It is Esu who speaks," as the Santoses quote from an *Oriki.*[57] This New World Esu figures plurality of meaning for the critic. He is, moreover, as master of the roads and the crossroads, the master of "all steps taken," be these steps taken as one walks or the steps of a process. He is, finally, a principle of rhetoric: "When he is in power," as Cabrera reports, "he exagggerates the speech of the pure black that he is," a description that also connects Esu to the Signifying Monkey.[58] Esu is the *deus ex machina,* but also the *deus est mortali iuvare mortalem,* god who is the helping of man to man. If anything, Esu, upon his emergence from the Middle Passage, assumed more functions and even a fuller presence within black cosmogonies than he had in Africa. Roger Bastide, for example, notes that in Brazil, in enslavement, black followers of Esu represented him as the liberator of the slaves and as enemy of the enslavers, "killing, poisoning, and driving mad their oppressors." Esu, then, assumed a direct importance to the black enslaved, while retaining his traditional functions. This importance is affirmed by representations of the figure of Esu in both New World and Old World black literature.[59]

One of the most important functions Esu bears is that of uncertainty or indeterminacy. Yoruba mythology inscribes the concept of indeterminacy in the Esu myth commonly known as "The Two Friends." This myth is probably the most well known of the Esu canon. Indeed, it is one of the canonical narratives that survived the Middle Passage and is as familiar among the Yoruba cultures of Brazil and Cuba as it is in Nigeria. As Ogundipe correctly concludes, "The conceptualization of Esu's presence as a dynamic principle and his representation as the principle of chance or uncertainty has endured in both the Old and New Worlds."[60]

There are several variants of this Esu myth of the indeterminate, recorded from Nigeria to Brazil and Cuba.[61] Ogundipe's version is a full one, revealing the reading given the text by the *babalawo*'s concluding verse:

> Everyone knows the story of the two friends who were thwarted in their friendship by Esu. They took vows of eternal friendship to one another,

but neither took Esu into consideration. Esu took note of their actions and decided to do something about them.

When the time was ripe, Esu decided to put their friendship to his own little test. He made a cloth cap. The right side was black, the left side was white.

The two friends were out in the fields, tilling their land. One was hoeing on the right side, the other was clearing the bushes to the left. Esu came by on a horse, riding between the two men. The one on the right saw the black side of his hat. The friend on the left noticed the sheer whiteness of Esu's cap.

The two friends took a break for lunch under the cool shade of the trees. Said one friend, "Did you see the man with a white cap who greeted us as we were working? He was very pleasant, wasn't he?"

"Yes, he was charming, but it was a man in a black cap that I recall, not a white one."

"It was a white cap. The man was riding a magnificently caparisoned horse."

"Then it must be the same man. I tell you, his cap was dark—black."

"You must be fatigued or blinded by the hot rays of the sun to take a white cap for a black one."

"I tell you it was a black cap and I am not mistaken. I remember him distinctly."

Figures 9, 10, 11. Janus-figure Esu-Elegbara. From the collection of Ralph and Fanny Ellison. *Photos by Chester Higgins, Jr.*

The two friends fell to fighting. The neighbors came running but the fight was so intense that the neighbors could not stop it. In the midst of this uproar, Esu returned, looking very calm and pretending not to know what was going on.

"What is the cause of all the hullabaloo?" he demanded sternly.

"Two close friends are fighting," was the answer. "They seem intent on killing each other and neither would stop or tell us the reason for the fight. Please do something before they destroy each other."

Esu promptly stopped the fight. "Why do you two lifelong friends make a public spectacle of yourselves in this manner?"

"A man rode through the farm, greeting us as he went by," said the first friend. "He was wearing a black cap, but my friend tells me it was a white cap and that I must have been tired or blind or both."

The second friend insisted that the man had been wearing a white cap. One of them must be mistaken, but it was not he.

"Both of you are right," said Esu.

"How can that be?"

"I am the man who paid the visit over which you now quarrel, and here is the cap that caused the dissension." Esu put his hand in his pocket and brought out the two-colored cap saying, "As you can see, one side is white and the other is black. You each saw one side and, therefore, are right about what you saw. Are you not the two friends who made vows of friendship? When you vowed to be friends always, to be faithful and true to each other, did you reckon with Esu? Do you know that he who does not put Esu first in all his doings has himself to blame if things misfire?"

And so it is said,

> "Esu, do not undo me,
> Do not falsify the words of my mouth,
> Do not misguide the movements of my feet.
> You who translates yesterday's words
> Into novel utterances,
> Do not undo me,
> I bear you sacrifices."[62]

This most common myth of Esu has been glossed in several ways, as if its encoded indeterminacy has blinded even the most astute commentators to a meaning even more fundamental than any literal rendering of its allegory allows. For this myth ascribes to Esu his principal function of the indeterminacy of interpretation. Neither of the friends is correct in his reading of the stranger's hat; but neither is, strictly speaking, wrong either. They are simultaneously right and wrong. Esu's hat is neither black nor white; it is both black and white. The folly depicted here is to insist—to the point of rupture of the always fragile bond of a human institution—on one determinate meaning, itself determined by vantage point and the mode one employs to see. Even the ultimate text of meaning, that of Ifa, remains indeterminate, despite the extensive rituals of disclosure that the Yoruba depend on. Disclosure, because of Esu, is never-ending; closure, on the other hand, simply does not exist until one's death, when one's *ori* is, at last, retrieved or recalled, just as the living subject has been recalled to the ancestors.

Despite Esu's open-endedness and his myriad faces and names, we must draw conclusions about his role in Yoruba, Fon, Lucumi, and Nago discourse as the figure of formal language use and its interpretation. As a meta-linguistic principle, Esu's importance to the theorist of comparative black literature should be obvious. His passage from Africa to the New World and his continued simultaneous existence in the Yoruba-derived cultures of Nigeria, Benin, Cuba, Haiti, Brazil, and the United States allows us to draw upon this compelling black figure as the trope of critical activity as a whole. Whereas Ogun, god of war and the artisan, stands as the writer's muse, it is Esu who stands as the muse of the critic. He can serve us as such because he is both the divine linguist and the divine interpreter, the controlling principle of its representation and its interpretation.

Let us recall the classic *Odu* that summarize for us exactly who and what Esu is, and precisely why it is to this deity that the literary critic must bear sacrifices. Interpreters, above all others, must beseech divine aid for their enterprise because of the dilemma inscribed in the following Yoruba proverb:

> I see the outside appearance,
> I cannot see the inside of the womb.
> If the inside were like a calabash,
> One could have opened it [and] seen everything it contains.[63]

It is the pleasure of the critic to open the text, even if not quite as readily as one opens a calabash; and to shift metaphors, the difficulties that await the traveler down this road most urgently demand supplication from the trickster figure, the *orisa* of the critic.

Esu rules two principal domains, as encoded in one of his several ritual honorifics: "Elegbaa Esu Ona," or "Esu, Lord of Power and of the Ways." Understanding the nature of these domains of power and of the ways is to understand Esu's significance for the critic. Esu's representations as the multiplicity of meaning, as the logos, and as what I shall call the Ogboni Supplement encapsulate his role for the critic.[64]

One of the many Yoruba creation myths lists Esu as the primal form, the very first form to exist. Before Esu assumed form, only air and water existed. Air (*Olorun*) moved and breathed and became water (*Orisanla*). Air and water interchanged to become liquid mud. The dos Santoses describe what happened next:

> From this mud, a swelling or small mound was raised, the first matter endowed with form, a reddish, muddy rock. Olorun admired the form and breathed over the mound, blowing his breath into it and giving it life. This form, the first form of existence, laterite rock, was Esu, or rather a proto-Esu, Esu the ancestor of Esu Agba, the Esu who was to be the king of all his descendants or Esu Oba or also Esu Yangi, on account of his association with laterite (which is called yangi).[65]

As Robert Farris Thompson demonstrates definitively, fragments of laterite and sculpted mud figures are Esu's oldest and most significant emblems.[66]

This proto-Esu, Esu Agba, multiplied itself remarkably, so that every other god, every individual, and all that exists has his, her, or its specific Esu. This individual Esu makes possible birth, development, and further reproduction. One makes sacrifice to ensure that this life cycle functions smoothly; sacrifices are compensation for "all the food which, in a real or metaphorical sense, [an individual's] life-principle has devoured." The Yoruba represent the idea of Esu as discrete principle of life by associating the placenta with Esu, as well as the semen.[67]

Because of the potential extent of the manifestations of the life principle, the Yoruba think of Esu as infinite in number, or Orisirisi Esu, to underscore his multiplicity. This is why the Yoruba say, "Esu is One, infinitely multiplied." The symbolic numbers 200 and 1,200 are related to Esu and connote multiplicity, the concept of doubled doubles that I discussed above.[68]

This idea of multiplicity is extraordinary: not only does each of the deities (the *orisa,* the *ebora,* and the *irunmale*) have an Esu, but so too does each *Odu.* Indeed, as one *Odu,* "The Orisi and Odu Which Accompanied Them with Their Esu," states, "Anybody who does not have an Esu in his body cannot exist, even to know that he is alive."[69]

How does one know one's Esu? This is a fairly straightforward matter for the *orisa,* the *ebora,* and the *irunmale,* who "can see themselves together with their Esu in order that they can send them anywhere to perform everything they need, according to Esu's ways and duties." Human beings, however, cannot see their own Esu, just as they can no longer recall the destiny (*ori*) whispered to them by Olodumare precisely as they are about to be born. Human beings, therefore, must consult the *Odu* and sacrifice to Esu, so that "the Esu should do his work in such a way that the person be helped so as to bear a good name and to have power to develop." An individual's Esu is an immense power to be summoned, "a medicine of supernatural power for each person." As the *Odu* elaborate, "When a person will say that he is able to level mountains or to turn forests into savannahs instantly, it is the Esu of each person that renders such help." Esu, in other words, represents power in terms of the agency of the will. But his ultimate power, of which even the will is a derivative, is the power of sheer plurality or multiplicity; the myths that account for his capacity to reproduce himself ad infinitum figure the plurality of meanings that Esu represents in the process of Ifa divination. Esu as the figure of indeterminacy extends directly from his lordship over the concept of plurality.[70]

If plurality comprises one form of Esu's power, a second form is his power to connect the parts. Esu is the sum of the parts, as well as that which connects to parts. He is invoked and sacrificed to first, before any other deity, because of this: "He *alone* can set an action in motion and interconnect the parts." This aspect of Esu cannot be emphasized too much. The most fundamental absolute of the Yoruba is that there exist, simultaneously, three stages of existence: the past, the present, and the unborn. Esu represents these stages, and makes their simultaneous existence possible, "without any contradiction," precisely because he is the principle of discourse both as messenger and as the god of communication. Discourse among three parallel phases of existence renders the notion of contradiction null. This helps the noninitiate to understand so many of the *Oriki Esu* that refer to Esu as the father and the child, the first and the last to be born, and so on. What appears in a binary system to be a contradiction resolvable only by the unity of opposites is more subtly—and mysteriously—resolved by the Yoruba in the concept central to the Ogboni secret society that "two, it becomes three."[71]

The Ogboni or the Osugbo secret society is comprised of the elder males and females of a society, those who embody wisdom. Thus, the Osugbo was the judicial segment of traditional government among the Yoruba. The signal emblem of this highly revered secret society is called the *edan,* a pair of bronze figures, one male the other female, linked by a chain. Peter Morton-Williams writes that the Osugbo signify their most fundamental metaphysical concept in the following cryptic utterance: "Two Ogboni, it becomes three." Morton-Williams contends that "The third element seems to be the mystery, the shared secret itself. The union of male and female in the edan image symbolizes this putting two together to make a third." The *edan,* presented to each initiate of the society, represents the transcendence of the binary opposition, of contradiction.[72]

Esu's relation to the numbers 2 and 3 helps to clarify somewhat the mystery of what Wole Soyinka calls "the House of Osugbo." Like the paired *edan* figures, Esu, as we have seen, is often represented as carved male and female figures, linked by a chain of cowrie shells. As I have shown earlier in this chapter, he is also represented with two heads. Nevertheless, Esu's symbolic prime number is 3 (which somehow is associated with the color black in Esu worship, "black being the color of the third cloth with which some of his emblems are dressed," after white and red). The 3 represents synthesis, in the same way as Esu himself was born as the result "of two primary elements, air and water, Orunmila and Yobiriru, Osun and the ase of the Agba-Odu, semen and placenta." Esu, in other words, signifies the synthesis of the number 3, "the procreated element, the third principle, the Igba-Ketu of the system." As the dos Santoses conclude aptly, it is Esu who resolves or "constitutes" the mystery of the Ogboni society's dictum, as one of the *Oriki Esu* says:

> Father who gave birth to *Ogboni*
> Is called by all *Baba Jakila*
> He lives three years in the earth
> And lives three years in the *Ajin* [depths of the other world].[73]

Esu, in other words, is the supplement, just as his especial *Odu (Odu Osetua)* is the seventeenth, "the 17th member of the 16 principal Odu Ifa, without whom the whole Ifa system would remain paralyzed." For it is in this *Odu* that Esu's role of bearer of the sacrifices and initial partaker of the sacrifice is defined. For the literary critic, of course, the concept of "Two Ogboni, it becomes three" accounts for the curious process by which author, text, and criticism interact. The third principle, we see readily, is criticism itself.[74]

Esu's importance for criticism can perhaps most easily be grasped through the idea of process. For Esu is the dynamic of process, the dialectical element of the system. It is Esu whose role of messenger we must conceive of, not as delivery boy, but as "he who interrelates all the different and multiple parts which compose the system. . . . He is the interpreter and linguist of the system," as the dos Santoses conclude, citing the following *Oriki Esu*:

> Collective mouths is the name by which Esu is called.

This *Oriki* refers to the myth that each of the 400 *irunmale* or deities gave segments of their mouths to Esu on the day that he became their mediator before Olorun. Esu combined these mouth pieces and thereby became the mouthpiece for all, he who speaks for all and whose mouth represents each of the mouths of the gods.[75]

Esu's role as interpreter is central to Ifa divination. The system simply would collapse if it had not placed at its center the principle of interpretation as mediation, and as open-ended. Esu speaks the readings of Ifa; his collective mouth (*Enugbarajo*) yields interpretation. As Wande Abimbola writes, citing one of the most crucial proverbs about the oracle, Orunmila, or Ifa, acts "with the ase of Esu." Esu speaks through Ifa, because it is his *ase* that reveals—or conceals—the roadways or the pathways through the text to its potential and possible meanings. Whereas Ifa is truth, Esu rules understanding of truth, a relationship that yields an individual's meaning. Esu's role in the critical process is to make that process possible: Esu is the process of interpretation. This is why an *Oriki Esu* says, "He spoke yesterday, it comes to pass today."[76]

I have been examining the texts of Esu for what these reveal to us about the nature of interpretation, as Yoruba myths would have it. I have been concerned to show that the rhetoric of the language in which these statements are rendered, the figures and relations among figures in the texts of Esu, are curious in that graphocentric figures are employed to account for the workings of a phonocentric system. Rather than declaring this to be a naive inconsistency, I think of this mode of figuration as a declaration of a complex notion of writing, a notion that accounts for a vocal writing and a graphic writing.[77]

The speech uttered by the *babalawo* after long and arduous years of training is already a form of writing—the writing of Mawu for the Fon and the writing of Ifa for the Yoruba. To figure Esu as a trope for indeterminacy serves to reinforce the critique of the immediacy or transcendence of presence implicit in the priority of speaking, which the oral forms of Ifa divination might suggest without Esu. With Esu as the deus ex machina, with the figuring of the *Odu* in the densest of figurative language, with archaic, untranslatable words dead to the society, alive only in the *Odu*, and with Esu's crucial role inscribed to the point of insistence, there can be little doubt that the Yoruba system of Ifa declares, through its own rhetorical figures, the words the *babalawo* speaks to be an especial form of writing, and the interpretation of these words to be a form of reading. The language of the Ifa oracle is of the textual, or discursive, order, precisely because it is mediated, like writing: Ifa writes his wisdom to the *babalawo*, and he, in turn, recites Ifa's words to the propitiate.

The reading of the propitiate of Ifa can occur only within a system of differences and traces, wherein the text of Ifa functions as a text in relation to Esu, who is never present at a reading, and in relation to other, larger cultural texts of which the Ifa oracle is merely one sign. Esu's indeterminacy can only be grappled with by reading the densely ambiguous language of Ifa against a system of meaning and interpretation that includes all of the texts that comprise the system of being Yoruba. What's more, that the system of divination figures its innermost workings through the traditionally opposed metaphors of speaking and writing is a sign of that system's sophisticated awareness that even its most sacred words must never be taken to be a direct or immediate indication of fate, or divinely ordered event, especially since Esu has the power to alter fate. That what is occurring as the *babalawo* speaks is described as a kind of writing forces even the most naive of the Yoruba to realize that his or her interpretation of the *Odu* must somehow be produced in relation to the other signifying components of the Yoruba cultural text, a function underscored, by definition, in the figurative language of the Odu texts themselves. We can privilege neither speaking nor writing in this system, since both (by definition) must be figured in terms of the other, existing only as a figure of the other in a bipolar moment of figuration within a system of differences. The text of Ifa is neither spoken nor written, because the relationship between them is an irresolvable moment, or an aporia. The rhetoric of Ifa only doubles this problematic of the location of meaning, invoking as it does the always absent figure of *Esu,* whom the system renders present in the open-ended signification process of which it consists. This doubling of irresolvability, of what others have called "a double, aporetic logic," ensures that Esu shall never again be forgotten as the signal god that he is, and explains precisely why it is he who must receive the first and the richest sacrifices, if chaos is to be averted.*

Whereas I have sought to locate this aporia in the Pan-African discourse of the Ifa oracle, I have also sought to define the notion of indeterminacy in the black interpretive process itself—precisely because the "speech" of the *babalawo* must be seen by the propitiate to be a chain of signifiers (like writing), which must be interpreted through a process of interpretation governed by Esu, a process that is always both openended and repeatable. Because the discrete *Odu* are not structured by the truth or logic of Mawu or Olodumare, but by the rhetoric of the language in which they are inscribed, the *Odu* imitate the so-called derivative or secondary term, *writing.* And, like writing, these *Odu* must be read, both literally by the *babalawo* and figuratively by the propitiate. Because the rhetoric of the *Odu* is anything but transparent, an opacity reinforced by archaism, the reader's gaze, or ear, cannot help but pause over the forms of the signifiers of the *Odu.*

Nor do these densely figurative signifiers readily yield Ifa's text of one's fate, for actually there is nothing to yield except the chain of signifiers, which represent a condition by repeated differences inscribed in the verses

---

* This rhetorical impasse within this black system of signification has become a topos of Afro-American literature. The "finding of the voice" of the speaking subject in a language in which blackness is the cardinal sign of absence is the subject of so much of Afro-American discourse that it has become a central trope to be revised, as well as the sign of that revision and hence of the inner process of Afro-American literary history. To find this impasse figured in black letters, one need only examine cursorily the first writings of Africans in English in the eighteenth century. The crucial repeated trope in these texts is that of the oxymoron, the Talking Book. The Talking Book is the fundamental repeated trope of the black tradition. See Chapter 4.

of the *Odu,* as textual analogues of the other texts of Yoruba culture against which the *Odu* are read. The speech of the *babalawo,* then, imitates a system of writing in several ways, precisely as the Yoruba themselves figured the matter rhetorically. And the irresolvability of this aporia, coupled with the encoding of Esu as the god of indeterminacy, attests that the notion of closure, even in the interpretation of one's fate, is alien to Ifa. Esu the absent one supersedes Ifa's presence in the ritual. Hence, all that is left is a series of differences, the relationship among which the reader (propitiate) must ponder to begin to produce some sort of meaning. Esu's often stated dwelling at the crossroads is, in this sense, at the crossroads of differences; there is no direct access, or contact, with truth or meaning, because Esu governs understanding, and even the speech of the *babalawo* is a form of writing, according both to the system's own code and to the absence of presence, immediacy, and transparency in the rhetoric of the *Odu.*

I wrote earlier in this chapter that the Yoruba believe that a person about to be born, about to leave the realm of the unborn for that of the living by way of the birth canal, kneels before Olodumare to hear whispered his or her fate, the truth of his or her existence. This fate, however, the unborn is doomed to forget upon entering the realm of the living. Ifa divination affords the apparent opportunity to retract from the lost world of the forgotten those spoken words that figure the contours of one's life. Yet Esu's indeterminacy prevents the desired retrieval of one's full, predetermined meaning while on earth. The ultimate indetermination of meaning, however, does not lead the Yoruba to despair; rather, it leads them to return to the text of Ifa, to consult it regularly, to wrestle with its play of differences, not to invent a meaning, but rather to process a meaning from among the differences, sacrifice to Esu and the appropriate deity, only to return to explore the process once more. Truly, the Ifa oracle is a dynamic system of interpretation. As Pelton concludes, in his perceptive and subtle study of "Irony and Sacred Delight," Esu

> is the master of the sacred language of Ifa, in which all human possibilities are contained. He destroys normal communication to bring men outside ordinary discourse, to speak a new word and to disclose a deeper grammar to them, and then to restore them to a conversation that speaks more accurately of Yoruba life.
>
> At this moment the language of the Yoruba is enlarged to name and to humanize an otherwise unintelligible and therefore unassimilable event. Here, at the moment of an enlargement that is also a transformation of non-sense to sense, of impasse to passage, the Yoruba see Esu, as the Fon see Legba, working most characteristically.[78]

We can conclude this meditation on Esu's function as a displaced, or absent, presence in the system of the Ifa oracle by thinking of Ifa as diacritical, as a system of differences very much like language itself. Esu, as we have seen in some detail, is the supplement of this system, the seventeenth member of the sixteen Odu, without whom the entire system would be paralyzed, or quite simply would collapse. Esu, as supplement, "enters the heart of all intelligible discourse and comes to define its very nature and condition," a role which poststructural criticism ascribes to writing.[79]

The figures of writing that are so very fundamental to Ifa signify Esu's place in the system. As promiscuous as divinely possible, Esu as copulating copula signifies "promiscuous exchange (or writing)." Esu bears a relation to the oral language of Ifa similar to that which rhetoric bears to ordinary speech. Esu is the free play or element of undecidability within the Ifa textual universe; Esu endlessly displaces meaning, deferring it by the play of signification. Esu is this element of displacement and deferral, as well as its sign. He is "a deceiving shadow," true to the trickster, "which falls between intent and meaning, between utterance and understanding." What Saussure says of language is true of Esu: he is a "differential network of meaning." Esu's answers or interpretations of Ifa's mediated riddles (riddled riddles, a second-order riddle, the doubled riddle) not only fail to resolve the "puzzles and perplexities" of Ifa's figurative discourse, but he delights in inscribing those in his cryptic responses. He is the primal figure in a truly black hermeneutic tradition; his opposites are identical, as R. P. Blackmun wrote of analogy. Esu is analogy, but also every other figure, for he is the trope of tropes, the figure of the figure. Esu is meta-discourse, the writing of the speech act of Ifa.[80]

Whereas the speech of the *babalawo* is figured rhetorically in terms of writing, Afro-American vernacular discourse figures its archetypal trickster in terms of speaking. Nevertheless, the highly structured rhetoric of the Signifying Monkey also conforms to the demands of writing, especially in the sense of a chain of signifiers, open to (mis)interpretation. The open-endedness of figurative language, rather than its single-minded closure, is inscribed in the myths of the Signifying Monkey. Whereas a small black man/woman, possessed of long hair and large eyes, emerges from the waters of Oriente province as a conflation of Esu and his partner, the Monkey, only the Monkey survived the passage from Cuba to the United States. Perhaps the racist designation of the Afro-American as a monkey informed the North American features of this figure; perhaps the explicit aporia between speech and writing that forms such a crucial and dynamic aspect of Ifa divination was forced underground into the implicit by the hostile terms of survival demanded of the Monkey. We do not know. But we do know that, for Afro-Americans, the Signifying Monkey tales inscribe the nature and function of formal language use and its interpretation, just as does Ifa. And whereas the rich parallels between Esu and the Monkey cannot be demonstrated historically, these are the rhetorical figures of the critic's enterprise that I am positing a relationship between, a functional and rhetorical equivalency and complementarity. The Signifying Monkey is the figure of the text of the Afro-American speaking subject, whose manipulations of the figurative and the literal both wreak havoc upon and inscribe order for criticism in the jungle.

Redeemer, I call on you,
Man at the roadside, carry our sacrifice straight to heaven,
Master, son of Onidere,
Who came from Idere to found a town,
Son of embezzler of sacrificial money,
Little man who goes through the gates in hot pursuit of Egungun.
Elderly orisa,
Spirits of dead criminals take the Oro gate
My master alone takes the entrance of the black warriors
One who turns white at the town gate
Makes a fence from your tendrils.
The snail of the buyer of destiny,
One who slaughters tortoises to eat,
Short, small man.[81]

Negue, may the *negue* go away!
Guije, may the *guije* go away!
Pigmies with enormous navels
people the restless waters;
their short legs are twisted;
their long ears stand up.
Ah, they are eating my child,
the one of pure, black flesh,
they are drinking his blood
sucking up dry his veins,
extinguishing the light of his eyes,
his great eyes made of pearls!
Flee, the monkey spirit will kill you,
flee, before the monkey spirit arrives!
My little one, my great little one,
may your necklace hold you safe . . .[82]

Owolabi, master medicineman
Drinker of a whole keg of pine wine at the bar
He peers from a ruined house
With elongated occiput like a bush fowl's,
With him, few words become truth.
Nimble somersaulter,
Lighter of fire with mouth full of water
Afterwards, they claimed mute was devious,
Akinfema, man with many names![83]

2

The Signifying Monkey and the Language of Signifyin(g): Rhetorical Difference and the Orders of Meaning

> Some of the best dozens players were girls. . . . before you can signify you got to be able to rap. . . . Signifying allowed you a choice—you could either make a cat feel good or bad. If you had just destroyed someone or if they were down already, signifying could help them over. Signifying was also a way of expressing your own feelings. . . . Signifying at its best can be heard when the brothers are exchanging tales.
> H. Rap Brown

> And they asked me right at Christmas
> If my blackness, would it rub off?
> I said, ask your Mama.
> Langston Hughes

I

If Esu-Elegbara stands as the central figure of the Ifa system of interpretation, then his Afro-American relative, the Signifying Monkey, stands as the rhetorical principle in Afro-American vernacular discourse. Whereas my concern in Chapter 1 was with the elaboration of an indigenous black hermeneutical principle, my concern in this chapter is to define a carefully structured system of rhetoric, traditional Afro-American figures of signification, and then to show how a curious figure becomes the trope of literary revision itself. My movement, then, is from hermeneutics to rhetoric and semantics, only to return to hermeneutics once again.

Thinking about the black concept of Signifyin(g) is a bit like stumbling unaware into a hall of mirrors: the sign itself appears to be doubled, at the very least, and (re)doubled upon ever closer examination. It is not the sign itself, however, which has multiplied. If orientation prevails over madness, we soon realize that only the signifier has been doubled and (re)doubled, a signifier in this instance that is silent, a "sound-image" as Saussure defines the signifier, but a "sound-image" *sans* the sound. The difficulty that we experience when thinking about the nature of the visual (re)doubling at work in a hall of mirrors is analogous to the difficulty we shall encounter in relating the

black linguistic sign, "Signification," to the standard English sign, "signification." This level of conceptual difficulty stems from—indeed, seems to have
been intentionally inscribed within—the selection of the signifier "Signification" to represent a concept remarkably distinct from that concept represented by the standard English signifier, "signification." For the standard English word is a homonym of the Afro-American vernacular word. And, to
compound the dizziness and the giddiness that we must experience in the
vertiginous movement between these two "identical" signifiers, these two homonyms have everything to do with each other and, then again, absolutely
nothing.[1]

In the extraordinarily complex relationship between the two homonyms,
we both enact and recapitulate the received, classic confrontation between
Afro-American culture and American culture. This confrontation is both political and metaphysical. We might profit somewhat by thinking of the curiously ironic relationship between these signifiers as a confrontation defined
by the politics of semantics, semantics here defined as the study of the classi-
fication of changes in the signification of words, and more especially the relationships between theories of denotation and naming, as well as connotation
and ambiguity. The relationship that black "Signification" bears to the English
"signification" is, paradoxically, a relation of difference inscribed within a relation of identity. That, it seems to me, is inherent in the nature of metaphorical substitution and the pun, particularly those rhetorical tropes dependent on
the repetition of a word with a change denoted by a difference in sound or in
a letter (agnominatio), and in homonymic puns (antanaclasis). These tropes
luxuriate in the chaos of ambiguity that repetition and difference (be that apparent difference centered in the signifier or in the signified, in the "sound-
image" or in the concept) yield in either an aural or a visual pun.

This dreaded, if playful, condition of ambiguity would, of course, disappear in the instance at hand if the two signs under examination did not bear
the same signifier. If the two signs were designated by two different signifiers,
we could escape our sense of vertigo handily. We cannot, however, precisely
because the antanaclasis that I am describing turns upon the very identity of
these signifiers, and the play of differences generated by the unrelated concepts (the signifieds) for which they stand.

What we are privileged to witness here is the (political, semantic) confrontation between two parallel discursive universes: the black American linguistic circle and the white. We see here the most subtle and perhaps the most
profound trace of an extended engagement between two separate and distinct
yet profoundly—even inextricably—related orders of meaning dependent precisely as much for their confrontation on relations of identity, manifested in
the signifier, as on their relations of difference, manifested at the level of the
signified. We bear witness here to a protracted argument over the nature of
the sign itself, with the black vernacular discourse proffering its critique of
the sign as the difference that blackness makes within the larger political
culture and its historical unconscious.

"Signification" and "signification" create a noisy disturbance in silence, at the level of the signifier. Derrida's neologism, "differance," in its relation to "difference," is a marvelous example of agnominatio, or repetition of a word with an alteration of both one letter and a sound. In this clever manner, Derrida's term resists reduction to self-identical meaning. The curiously suspended relationship between the French verbs *to differ* and *to defer* both defines Derrida's revision of Saussure's notion of language as a relation of differences and embodies his revision which "in its own unstable meaning [is] a graphic example of the process at work."[2]

I have encountered great difficulty in arriving at a suitably similar gesture. I have decided to signify the difference between these two signifiers by writing the black signifier in upper case ("Signification") and the white signifier in lower case ("signification"). Similarly, I have selected to write the black term with a bracketed final g ("Signifyin(g)") and the white term as "signifying." The bracketed g enables me to connote the fact that this word is, more often than not, spoken by black people without the final g as "signifyin'." This arbitrary and idiosyncratic convention also enables me to recall the fact that whatever historical community of Afro-Americans coined this usage did so in the vernacular as spoken, in contradistinction to the literate written usages of the standard English "shadowed" term. The bracketed or aurally erased g, like the discourse of black English and dialect poetry generally, stands as the trace of black difference in a remarkably sophisticated and fascinating (re)naming ritual graphically in evidence here. Perhaps replacing with a visual sign the g erased in the black vernacular shall, like Derrida's neologism, serve both to avoid confusion and the reduction of these two distinct sets of homonyms to a false identity and to stand as the sign of a (black) Signifyin(g) difference itself. The absent g is a figure for the Signifyin(g) black difference.

Let me attempt to account for the complexities of this (re)naming ritual, which apparently took place anonymously and unrecorded in antebellum America. Some black genius or a community of witty and sensitive speakers emptied the signifier "signification" of its received concepts and filled this empty signifier with their own concepts. By doing so, by supplanting the received, standard English concept associated by (white) convention with this particular signifier, they (un)wittingly disrupted the nature of the sign = *signified/signifier* equation itself. I bracket *wittingly* with a negation precisely because origins are always occasions for speculation. Nevertheless, I tend to think, or I wish to believe, that this guerrilla action occurred intentionally on this term, because of the very concept with which it is associated in standard English.

"Signification," in standard English, denotes the meaning that a term conveys, or is intended to convey. It is a fundamental term in the standard English semantic order. Since Saussure, at least, the three terms *signification, signifier, signified* have been fundamental to our thinking about general linguistics and, of late, about criticism specifically. These neologisms in the academic-critical community are homonyms of terms in the black vernacular tradition perhaps two centuries old. By supplanting the received term's associated concept, the black vernacular tradition created a homonymic pun of the profoundest sort, thereby marking its sense of difference from the rest of the English community of speakers. Their complex act of language Signifies upon both formal language use and its conventions, conventions established, at least officially, by middle-class white people.

This political offensive could have been mounted against all sorts of standard English terms—and, indeed, it was. I am thinking here of terms such as *down, nigger, baby,* and *cool,* which snobbishly tend to be written about as "dialect" words or "slang." There are scores of such revised words. But to revise the term *signification* is to select a term that represents the nature of the process of meaning-creation and its representation. Few other selections could have been so dramatic, or so meaningful. We are witnessing here a profound disruption at the level of the signifier, precisely because of the relationship of identity that obtains between the two apparently equivalent terms. This disturbance, of course, has been effected at the level of the conceptual, or the signified. How accidental, unconscious, or unintentional (or any other code-word substitution for the absence of reason) could such a brilliant challenge at the semantic level be? To revise the received sign (quotient) literally accounted for in the relation represented by *signified/signifier* at its most apparently denotative level is to critique the nature of (white) meaning itself, to challenge through a literal critique of the sign the meaning of meaning. What did/do black people signify in a society in which they were intentionally introduced as the subjugated, as the enslaved cipher? Nothing on the *x* axis of white signification, and everything on the *y* axis of blackness.[3]

It is not sufficient merely to reveal that black people colonized a white sign. A level of meta-discourse is at work in this process. If the signifier stands disrupted by the shift in concepts denoted and connoted, then we are engaged at the level of meaning itself, at the semantic register. Black people vacated this signifier, then—incredibly—substituted as its concept a signified that stands for the system of rhetorical strategies peculiar to their own vernacular tradition. Rhetoric, then, has supplanted semantics in this most literal meta-confrontation within the structure of the sign. Some historical black community of speakers most certainly struck directly at the heart of the matter, on the ground of the referent itself, thereby demonstrating that even (or especially) the concepts signified by the signifier are themselves arbitrary. By an act of will, some historically nameless community of remarkably self-conscious speakers of English defined their ontological status as one of profound difference vis-à-vis the rest of society. What's more, they undertook this act of self-definition, implicit in a (re)naming ritual, within the process of signification that the English language had inscribed for itself. Contrary to an assertion that Saussure makes in his *Course,* "the masses" did indeed "have [a] voice in the matter" and replaced the sign "chosen by language." We shall return to Saussure's discussion of the "Immutability and Mutability of the Sign" below.[4]

Before critiquing Saussure's discussion of signification, however, perhaps

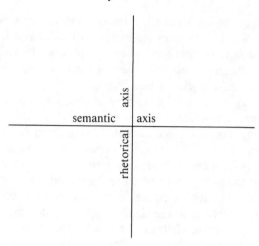

Chart 1. The Sign, "Signification"

I can help to clarif, an inherently confusing discussion by representing the black critique of the sign, the replacement of the semantic register by the rhetorical, in Chart 1.

Whereas in standard English usage signification can be represented *signified/signifier* and that which is signified is a concept, or concepts, in the black homonym, this relation of semantics has been supplanted by a relation of rhetoric, wherein the signifier "Signification" is associated with a concept that stands for the rhetorical structures of the black vernacular, the trope of tropes that is Signifyin(g). Accordingly, if in standard English

$$signification = signified = \frac{concept}{sound\text{-}image,}$$
$$\overline{signifier}$$

then in the black vernacular,

$$Signification = \frac{rhetorical\ figures}{signifier}.$$

In other words, the relation of signification itself has been critiqued by a black act of (re)doubling. The black term of *Signifyin(g)* has as its associated concept all of the rhetorical figures subsumed in the term *Signify*. To Signify, in other words, is to engage in certain rhetorical games, which I shall define and then compare to standard Western figures below, in Chart 4.

It would be erroneous even to suggest that a concept can be erased from its relation to a signifier. A signifier is never, ultimately, able to escape its received meanings, or concepts, no matter how dramatically such concepts might change through time. In fact, homonymic puns, antanaclasis, turn precisely upon received meanings and their deferral by a vertical substitution. All homonyms depend on the absent presence of received concepts associated with a signifier.

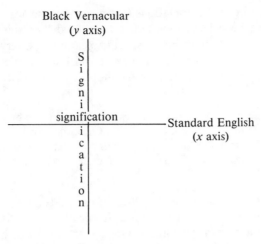

Chart 2. Black and Standard English

What does this mean in the instance of the black homonym *Signifyin(g)*, the shadowy revision of the white term? It means, it seems to me, that the signifier "Signification" has remained identical in spelling to its white counterpart to demonstrate, first, that a simultaneous, but negated, parallel discursive (ontological, political) universe exists within the larger white discursive universe, like the matter-and-antimatter fabulations so common to science fiction. It also seems apparent that retaining the identical signifier argues strongly that the most poignant level of black-white differences is that of meaning, of "signification" in the most literal sense. The play of doubles here occurs precisely on the axes, on the threshold or at Esu's crossroads, where black and white semantic fields collide. We can imagine the relationship of these two discursive universes as depicted in Chart 2. Parallel universes, then, is an inappropriate metaphor; *perpendicular* universes is perhaps a more accurate visual description.

The English-language use of *signification* refers to the chain of signifiers that configure horizontally, on the syntagmatic axis. Whereas signification operates and can be represented on a syntagmatic or horizontal axis, Signifyin(g) operates and can be represented on a paradigmatic or vertical axis. Signifyin(g) concerns itself with that which is suspended, vertically: the chaos of what Saussure calls "associative relations," which we can represent as the playful puns on a word that occupy the paradigmatic axis of language and which a speaker draws on for figurative substitutions. These substitutions in Signifyin(g) tend to be humorous, or function to name a person or a situation in a telling manner. Whereas signification depends for order and coherence on the exclusion of unconscious associations which any given word yields at any given time, Signification luxuriates in the inclusion of the free play of these associative rhetorical and semantic relations. Jacques Lacan calls these vertically suspended associations "a whole articulation of relevant contexts," by

which he means all of the associations that a signifier carries from other contexts, which must be deleted, ignored, or censored "for this signifier to be
lined up with a signified to produce a specific meaning."[5] Everything that must
be excluded for meaning to remain coherent and linear comes to bear in the
process of Signifyin(g). As Anthony Easthope puts the matter in *Poetry as
Discourse,*

> All of these absences and dependencies which have to be barred in order
> for meaning to take place constitute what Lacan designates as the *Other.*
> The presence of meaning along the syntagmatic chain necessarily depends
> upon the absence of the Other, the rest of language, from the syntag-
> matic chain.[6]

Signifyin(g), in Lacan's sense, is the Other of discourse; but it also constitutes
the black Other's discourse as its rhetoric. Ironically, rather than a proclamation of emancipation from the white person's standard English, the symbiotic
relationship between the black and white, between the syntagmatic and paradigmatic axes, between black vernacular discourse and standard English discourse, is underscored here, and signified, by the vertiginous relationship between the terms *signification* and *Signification,* each of which is dependent on
the other. We can, then, think of American discourse as both the opposition
between and the ironic identity of the movement, the very vertigo, that we encounter in a mental shift between the two terms.

The process of semantic appropriation in evidence in the relation of Signification to signification has been aptly described by Mikhail Bakhtin as a
double-voiced word, that is, a word or utterance, in this context, decolonized
for the black's purposes "by inserting a new semantic orientation into a word
which already has—and retains—its own orientation." Although I shall return
later in this chapter to a fuller consideration of this notion of double-voiced
words and double-voiced discourse, Gary Saul Morson's elaboration on Bakhtin's concept helps to clarify what Bakhtin implies:

> The audience of a double-voiced word is therefore meant to hear both a
> version of the original utterance as the embodiment of its speaker's point
> of view (or "semantic position") *and* the second speaker's evaluation of
> that utterance from a different point of view. I find it helpful to picture
> a double-voiced word as a special sort of palimpsest in which the upper-
> most inscription is a commentary on the one beneath it, which the reader
> (or audience) can know only by reading through the commentary that
> obscures in the very process of evaluating.[7]

The motivated troping effect of the disruption of the semantic orientation of
signification by the black vernacular depends on the homonymic relation of
the white term to the black. The sign, in other words, has been demonstrated
to be mutable.

Bakhtin's notion, then, implicitly critiques Saussure's position that

> the signifier . . . is fixed, not free, with respect to the linguistic com-
> munity that uses it. The masses have no voice in the matter, and the sig-

nifier chosen by language could be replaced by no other. . . . [The] community itself cannot control so much as a single word; it is bound to the existing language.[8]

Saussure, of course, proceeds to account for "shift(s) in the relationship between the signified and the signifier," shifts in time that result directly from "the arbitrary nature of the sign." But, simultaneously, Saussure denies what he terms to be "arbitrary substitution": "A particular language-state is always the product of historical forces, and these forces explain why the sign is unchangeable, i.e. why it resists any arbitrary substitution." The double-voiced relation of the two terms under analysis here argues forcefully that "the masses," especially in a multiethnic society, draw on "arbitrary substitution" freely, to disrupt the signifier by displacing its signified in an intentional act of will. Signifyin(g) is black double-voicedness; because it always entails formal revision and an intertextual relation, and because of Esu's double-voiced representation in art, I find it an ideal metaphor for black literary criticism, for the formal manner in which texts seem concerned to address their antecedents. Repetition, with a signal difference, is fundamental to the nature of Signifying(g), as we shall see.[9]

II

The Poetry of Signification

The literature or tales of the Signifying Monkey and his peculiar language, Signifyin(g), is both extensive and polemical, involving as it does assertions and counterassertions about the relationship that Signifyin(g) bears to several other black tropes. I am not interested in either recapitulating or contributing to this highly specialized debate over whether or not speech act *x* is an example of this black trope or that. On the contrary, I wish to argue that Signifyin(g) is the black trope of tropes, the figure for black rhetorical figures. I wish to do so because this represents my understanding of the value assigned to Signifyin(g) by the members of the Afro-American speech community, of which I have been a signifier for quite some time. While the role of a certain aspect of linguistics study is to discern the shape and function of each tree that stands in the verbal terrain, my role as a critic, in this book at least, is to define the contours of the discursive forest or, perhaps more appropriately, of the jungle.[10]

Tales of the Signifying Monkey seem to have had their origins in slavery. Hundreds of these have been recorded since the early twentieth century. In black music, Jazz Gillum, Count Basie, Oscar Peterson, the Big Three Trio, Oscar Brown, Jr., Little Willie Dixon, Snatch and the Poontangs, Otis Redding, Wilson Pickett, Smokey Joe Whitfield, and Johnny Otis—among others—have recorded songs about either the Signifying Monkey or, simply, Signifyin(g). The theory of Signifyin(g) is arrived at by explicating these black cultural forms. Signifyin(g) in jazz performances and in the play of black language games is a mode of formal revision, it depends for its effects on troping, it is often characterized by pastiche, and, most crucially, it turns on repetition of formal structures and their differences. Learning how to Signify is often part of our adolescent education.

Of the many colorful figures that appear in black vernacular tales, perhaps only Tar Baby is as enigmatic and compelling as is that oxymoron, the Signifying Monkey.[11] The ironic reversal of a received racist image of the black as simianlike, the Signifying Monkey, he who dwells at the margins of discourse, ever punning, ever troping, ever embodying the ambiguities of language, is our trope for repetition and revision, indeed our trope of chiasmus, repeating and reversing simultaneously as he does in one deft discursive act. If Vico and Burke, or Nietzsche, de Man, and Bloom, are correct in identifying four and six "master tropes," then we might think of these as the "master's tropes," and of Signifyin(g) as the slave's trope, the trope of tropes, as Bloom characterizes metalepsis, "a trope-reversing trope, a figure of a figure." Signifyin(g) is a trope in which are subsumed several other rhetorical tropes, including metaphor, metonymy, synecdoche, and irony (the master tropes), and also hyperbole, litotes, and metalepsis (Bloom's supplement to Burke). To this list we could easily add aporia, chiasmus, and catechresis, all of which are used in the ritual of Signifyin(g).

Signifyin(g), it is clear, means in black discourse modes of figuration themselves. When one Signifies, as Kimberly W. Benston puns, one "tropes-a-dope." Indeed, the black tradition itself has its own subdivisions of Signifyin(g), which we could readily identify with the figures of signification received from classical and medieval rhetoric, as Bloom has done with his "map of misprision" and which we could, appropriately enough, label a "rap of misprision." The black rhetorical tropes, subsumed under Signifyin(g), would include marking, loud-talking, testifying, calling out (of one's name), sounding, rapping, playing the dozens, and so on.[12] [See Chart 4.]

The Esu figures, among the Yoruba systems of thought in Benin and Nigeria, Brazil and Cuba, Haiti and New Orleans, are divine: they are gods who function in sacred myths, as do characters in a narrative. Esu's functional equivalent in Afro-American profane discourse is the Signifying Monkey, a figure who would seem to be distinctly Afro-American, probably derived from Cuban mythology which generally depicts Echu-Elegua with a monkey at his side. Unlike his Pan-African Esu cousins, the Signifying Monkey exists not primarily as a character in a narrative but rather as a vehicle for narration itself. Like Esu, however, the Signifying Monkey stands as the figure of an oral writing within black vernacular language rituals. It is from the corpus of mythological narratives that Signifyin(g) derives. The Afro-American rhetorical strategy of Signifyin(g) is a rhetorical practice that is not engaged in the game of information-giving, as Wittgenstein said of poetry. Signifyin(g) turns on the play and chain of signifiers, and not on some supposedly transcendent signified. As anthropologists demonstrate, the Signifying Monkey is often called the Signifier, he who wreaks havoc upon the Signified. One is signified upon by the signifier. He is indeed the "signifier as such," in Kristeva's phrase, "a presence that precedes the signification of object or emotion."

Alan Dundes's suggestion that the origins of Signifyin(g) could "lie in African rhetoric" is not as far-fetched as one might think. I have argued for a consideration of a line of descent for the Signifying Monkey from his Pan-African cousin, Esu-Elegbara. I have done so not because I have unearthed archeological evidence of a transmission process, but because of their functional equivalency as figures of rhetorical strategies and of interpretation. Esu, as I have attempted to show in Chapter 1, is the Yoruba figure of writing within an oral system. Like Esu, the Signifying Monkey exists, or is figured, in a densely structured discursive universe, one absolutely dependent on the play of differences. The poetry in which the Monkey's antics unfold is a signifying system: in marked contrast to the supposed transparency of normal speech, the poetry of these tales turns upon the free play of language itself, upon the displacement of meanings, precisely because it draws attention to its rhetorical structures and strategies and thereby draws attention to the force of the signifier.[18]

In opposition to the apparent transparency of speech, this poetry calls attention to itself as an extended linguistic sign, one composed of various forms of the signifiers peculiar to the black vernacular. Meaning, in these poems, is not proffered; it is deferred, and it is deferred because the relationship between intent and meaning, between the speech act and its comprehension, is skewed by the figures of rhetoric or signification of which these poems consist. This set of skewed relationships creates a measure of undecidability within the discourse, such that it must be interpreted or decoded by careful attention to its play of differences. Never can this interpretation be definitive, given the ambiguity at work in its rhetorical structures. The speech of the Monkey exists as a sequence of signifiers, effecting meanings through their differential relation and calling attention to itself by rhyming, repetition, and several of the rhetorical figures used in larger cultural language games. Signifyin(g) epitomizes all of the rhetorical play in the black vernacular. Its self-consciously open rhetorical status, then, functions as a kind of writing, wherein rhetoric is the writing of speech, of oral discourse. If Esu is the figure of writing in Ifa, the Signifying Monkey is the figure of a black rhetoric in the Afro-American speech community. He exists to embody the figures of speech characteristic to the black vernacular. He is the principle of self-consciousness in the black vernacular, the meta-figure itself. Given the play of doubles at work in the black appropriation of the English-language term that denotes relations of meaning, the Signifying Monkey and his language of Signifyin(g) are extraordinary conventions, with Signification standing as the term for black rhetoric, the obscuring of apparent meaning.

Scholars have for some time commented on the peculiar use of the word *Signifyin(g)* in black discourse. Though sharing some connotations with the standard English-language word, *Signifyin(g)* has rather unique definitions in black discourse. While we shall consider these definitions later in this chapter, it is useful to look briefly at one suggested by Roger D. Abrahams:

Signifying seems to be a Negro term, in use if not in origin. It can mean any of a number of things; in the case of the toast about the signifying monkey, it certainly refers to the trickster's ability to talk with great innuendo, to carp, cajole, needle, and lie. It can mean in other instances the propensity to talk around a subject, never quite coming to the point. It can mean making fun of a person or situation. Also it can denote speaking with the hands and eyes, and in this respect encompasses a whole complex of expressions and gestures. Thus it is signifying to stir up a fight between neighbors by telling stories; it is signifying to make fun of a policeman by parodying his motions behind his back; it is signifying to ask for a piece of cake by saying, "my brother needs a piece a cake."[14]

Essentially, Abrahams continues, Signifyin(g) is a *"technique* of indirect argument or persuasion," "a language of implication," "to imply, goad, beg, boast, by *indirect* verbal or gestural means." "The name 'signifying,' " he concludes, "shows the monkey to be a trickster, signifying being the language of trickery, that set of words or gestures achieving Hamlet's 'direction through indirection.' " The Monkey, in short, is not only a master of technique, as Abrahams concludes; he *is* technique, or style, or the literariness of literary language; he is the great Signifier. In this sense, one does not signify something; rather, one signifies in *some way*.[15]

The Signifying Monkey poems, like the *ese* of the Yoruba *Odu,* reward careful explication; this sort of extensive practical criticism, however, is outside the scope of this book, as fascinating as it might be. The stanzaic form of this poetry can vary a great deal, as is readily apparent from the selections listed in this book's appendix. The most common structure is the rhyming couplet in an a-a-b-b pattern. Even within the same poem, however, this pattern can be modified, as in the stanzas cited below, where an a-a-b-c-b and an a-b-c-b pattern obtain (followed in the latter example by an a-b-a concluding "moral"). Rhyming is extraordinarily important in the production of the humorous effect that these poems have and has become the signal indication of expertise among the street poets who narrate them. The rhythm of the poems is also crucial to the desired effect, an effect in part reinforced by their quasi-musical nature of delivery.

The Monkey tales generally have been recorded from male poets, in predominantly male settings such as barrooms, pool halls, and street corners. Accordingly, given their nature as rituals of insult and naming, recorded versions have a phallocentric bias. As we shall see below, however, Signifyin(g) itself can be, and is, undertaken with equal facility and effect by women as well as men.* Whereas only a relatively small number of people are accomplished narrators of Signifying Monkey tales, a remarkably large number of Afro-Americans are familiar with, and practice, modes of Signifyin(g), defined in this instance as the rubric for various sorts of playful language games, some aimed at reconstituting the subject while others are aimed at demystifying a

---

* Gloria Hall is a well-known professional storyteller, and she includes in her repertoire the Signifying Monkey poems.

subject. The poems are of interest to my argument primarily in three ways: as the source of the rhetorical act of Signification, as examples of the black tropes subsumed within the trope of Signifyin(g), and, crucially, as evidence for the valorization of the signifier. One of these subsumed tropes is concerned with repetition and difference; it is this trope, that of naming, which I have drawn upon as a metaphor for black intertextuality and, therefore, for formal literary history. Before discussing this process of revision, however, it is useful to demonstrate the formulaic structure of the Monkey tales and then to compare several attempts by linguists to define the nature and function of Signifyin(g). While other scholars have interpreted the Monkey tales against the binary opposition between black and white in American society, to do so is to ignore the *trinary* forces of the Monkey, the Lion, and the Elephant. To read the Monkey tales as a simple allegory of the black's political oppression is to ignore the hulking presence of the Elephant, the crucial third term of the depicted action. To note this is not to argue that the tales are not allegorical or that their import is not political. Rather, this is to note that to reduce such complex structures of meaning to a simple two-term opposition (white versus black) is to fail to account for the strength of the Elephant.

There are many versions of the toasts of the Signifying Monkey, most of which commence with a variant of the following formulaic lines:

> Deep down in the jungle so they say
> There's a signifying monkey down the way
> There hadn't been no disturbin' in the jungle for quite a bit,
> For up jumped the monkey in the tree one day and laughed
> "I guess I'll start some shit."[16]

Endings, too, tend toward the formulaic, as in the following:

> "Monkey," said the Lion,
> Beat to his unbooted knees,
> "You and your signifying children
> Better stay up in the trees."
> Which is why today
> Monkey does his signifying
> *A-way-up* out of the way.[17]

In the narrative poems, the Signifying Monkey invariably repeats to his friend, the Lion, some insult purportedly generated by their mutual friend, the Elephant. The Monkey, however, speaks figuratively. The Lion, indignant and outraged, demands an apology of the Elephant, who refuses and then trounces the Lion. The Lion, realizing that his mistake was to take the Monkey literally, returns to trounce the Monkey. It is this relationship between the literal and the figurative, and the dire consequences of their confusion, which is the most striking repeated element of these tales. The Monkey's trick depends on the Lion's inability to mediate between these two poles of signification, of meaning. There is a profound lesson about reading here. While we cannot undertake a full reading of the poetry of the Signifying Monkey, we can, however, identify the implications for black vernacular discourse that are encoded in this poetic diction.

Signifyin(g) as a rhetorical strategy emanates directly from the Signifying Monkey tales. The relationship between these poems and the related, but independent, mode of formal language use must be made clear. The action represented in Monkey tales turns upon the action of three stock characters—the Monkey, the Lion, and the Elephant—who are bound together in a trinary relationship. The Monkey—a trickster figure, like Esu, who is full of guile, who tells lies,* and who is a rhetorical genius—is intent on demystifying the Lion's self-imposed status as King of the Jungle. The Monkey, clearly, is no match for the Lion's physical prowess; the Elephant is, however. The Monkey's task, then, is to trick the Lion into tangling with the Elephant, who is the true King of the Jungle for everyone else in the animal kingdom. This the Monkey does with a rhetorical trick, a trick of mediation. Indeed, the Monkey is a term of (anti)mediation, as are all trickster figures, between two forces he seeks to oppose for his own contentious purposes, and then to reconcile.

The Monkey's trick of mediation—or, more properly, antimediation—is a play on language use. He succeeds in reversing the Lion's status by supposedly repeating a series of insults purportedly uttered by the Elephant about the Lion's closest relatives (his wife, his "mama," his "grandmama, too!"). These intimations of sexual use, abuse, and violation constitute one well-known and commonly used mode of Signifyin(g).† The Lion, who perceives his shaky, self-imposed status as having been challenged, rushes off in outrage to find the Elephant so that he might redress his grievances and preserve appearances. The self-confident but unassuming Elephant, after politely suggesting to the Lion that he must be mistaken, proceeds to trounce the Lion firmly. The Lion, clearly defeated and dethroned from his self-claimed title, returns to find the Monkey so that he can at the very least exact some sort of physical satisfaction and thereby restore his image somehat as the impregnable fortress-in-waiting that he so urgently wishes to be. The Monkey, absolutely ecstatic at the success of his deception, commences to Signify upon the Lion, as in the following exchange:

> Now the Lion come back more dead than alive,
> that's when the Monkey started some more of his old signifying.
> He said, "King of the Jungles, ain't you a bitch,
> you look like someone with the seven-year itch."
> He said, "When you left [me earlier in the narrative] the lightnin'
>   flashed and the bells rung,
> you look like something been damn near hung."
> He said, "Whup! Motherfucker, don't you roar,
> I'll jump down on the ground and beat your funky ass some more."
> Say, "While I'm swinging around in my tree,"
> say, "I ought to swing over your chickenshit head and pee."

---

* *Lies* is a traditional Afro-American word for figurative discourse, tales, or stories.
† Also known as "the dozens."

> Say, "Everytime me and my old lady be tryin' to get a little bit,
> here you come down through the jungle with that old 'Hi Ho' shit."[18]

This is a salient example of Signifying(g), wherein a verbal fusilade of insults spews forth in a structure of ritual rhetorical exchanges.

What happens next is also fascinating. The Monkey, at this point in the discourse deliriously pleased with himself, slips and falls to the ground:

> Now the little old Monkey was dancing all around
> his feet slipped and his ass must have hit the ground.

The startled Monkey, now vulnerable, seeks to repair his relationship with the Lion in the most urgent manner. So he begs initially:

> Like a streak of lightning and a bolt of white heat,
> the Lion was on the Monkey with all four feet.
> Monkey looks up with tears in his eyes,
> he says, "I'm sorry, brother Lion," say, "I apologize."
> The Lion says, "Apologize, shit," say, "I'm gonna stop you from your
>   signifyin'." (p. 165)

The Lion now turns on the Monkey (only, incidentally, to be tricked rhetorically again), not because he has been severely beaten but because he has been beaten, then Signified upon. Another text substitutes the following direct speech of the Lion for that quoted immediately above:

> [The Lion say], "I'm not gonna whip your ass 'cause that Elephant
>   whipped mine,
> I'm gonna whip your ass for signifyin'." (p. 168)

The Monkey's trick of Signification has been to convince the hapless Lion that he has spoken literally, when all along he has spoken figuratively. The Lion, though slow-witted enough to repeat his misreading through the eternity of discourse, realizes that his status has been deflated, not because of the Elephant's brutal self-defense but because he fundamentally misunderstood the status of the Monkey's statements. As still another poem represents this moment of clarity:

> Said, "Monkey, I'm not kicking your ass for lyin',
> I'm kicking your hairy ass for *signifyin'*." (p. 172)[19]

The black term *to lie,* as J. L. Dillard, Sterling A. Brown, and Zora Neale Hurston amply demonstrate, signifies tale-telling and constitutes a signal form of Signifyin(g).[20] But it is the naming ritual, in which the Monkey speaks aloud his editorial recapitulation of the previous events and their import, which even the dense Lion recognizes to be his most crucial threat, and against which he must defend himself, especially since the Lion returns to the Monkey's tree initially, at least, to impose *his* interpretation on his interchange with the Elephant:

> Now the Lion looked up to the Monkey, "You know I didn't get beat."
> He said, "You're a lyin' motherfucker, I had a ringside seat."

> The Lion looked up out of his one good eye, said, "Lord, let that skinny
>   bastard fall out of that tree before I die." (p. 172)

Which he, of course, does, only (in most cases) to escape once again, to return to Signify on another day:

> He said, "You might as well stop, there ain't no use tryin'
> because no motherfucker is gonna stop me from signifyin'." (p. 163)

While the insult aspect of the Monkey's discourse is important to the tales,
linguists have often failed to recognize that insult is not at all central to the
nature of Signifyin(g); it is merely one mode of a rhetorical strategy that has
several other modes, all of which share the use of troping. They have, in other
words, mistaken the trees for the forest. For Signifyin(g) constitutes all of
the language games, the figurative substitutions, the free associations held in
abeyance by Lacan's or Saussure's paradigmatic axis, which disturb the seemingly coherent linearity of the syntagmatic chain of signifiers, in a way analogous to Freud's notion of how the unconscious relates to the conscious. The
black vernacular trope of Signifyin(g) exists on this vertical axis, wherein the
materiality of the signifier (the use of words as things, in Freud's terms of
the discourse of the unconscious) not only ceases to be disguised but comes
to bear prominently as the dominant mode of discourse.

I do not cite Freud idly here. *Jokes and Their Relation to the Unconscious* and *The Interpretation of Dreams* have informed my reading of Sig-
nifyin(g), just as have Lacan's reading of Freud and Saussure, and Derrida's
emphasis on the "graphematic" aspect of even oral discourse. Just as jokes
often draw upon the sounds of words rather than their meanings, so do the
poetry of the Signifying Monkey and his language of Signifyin(g). Directing,
or redirecting, attention from the semantic to the rhetorical level defines the
relationship, as we have seen, between signification and Signification. It is this
redirection that allows us to bring the repressed meanings of a word, the
meanings that lie in wait on the paradigmatic axis of discourse, to bear upon
the syntagmatic axis. This redirection toward sound, without regard for the
scrambling of sense that it entails, defines what is meant by the materiality of
the signifier, its thingness. As Freud explained, there is nothing necessarily
infantile about this, although infants, of course, engage in such paradigmatic
substitutions gleefully. Similarly, there is absolutely nothing infantile about
Signifyin(g) either, except perhaps that we learn to use language in this way
in adolescence, despite the strangely compulsive repetition of this adjective as
a pejorative in the writings of linguists about Signifyin(g).

If Freud's analysis of the joke mechanism is a useful analogue for Signi-
fyin(g), then so too is his analysis of the "dream-work," which by now is so
familiar as not to warrant summary here. The Signifying Monkey poems can
usefully be thought of as quasi-dreams, or daydreams, dream narratives in
which monkeys, lions, and elephants manifest their feelings in direct speech.
Animals, of course, do not speak, except in dreams or in mythological discourse. As Freud puts it in *The Interpretation of Dreams,*

this symbolism is not peculiar to dreams, but is characteristic of unconscious ideation, in particular among the people, and it is to be found in
folklore, and in popular myths, legends, *linguistic idioms,* proverbial wisdom and current jokes, to a *more complete extent* than in dreams.[21]
(emphasis added)

The Signifying Monkey tales, in this sense, can be thought of as versions of
daydreams, the Daydream of the Black Other, chiastic fantasies of reversal of
power relationships. One of the traditional Signifying poems names this relationship explicitly:

> The Monkey laid up in a tree and he thought up a scheme,
> and thought he'd try one of his fantastic dreams. (p. 167)

To dream the fantastic is to dream the dream of the Other.

   Because these tales originated in slavery, we do not have to seek very far
to find typological analogues for these three terms of an allegorical structure.
Since to do so, inescapably, is to be reductive, is to redirect attention away
from the materiality of the signifier toward its supposed signified, I shall avoid
repeating what other scholars have done at such great length. For the importance of the Signifying Monkey poems is their repeated stress on the sheer materiality, and the willful play, of the signifier itself.

   While I wrote earlier in this chapter that a close reading of the Monkey
tales is outside the scope of a book whose intention is to define an indigenous
black metaphor for intertextuality as configured in Afro-American formal literary discourse, I am tempted to write that, like this signal trickster, I have
lied! While I am forced by the demands of this book to defer such a series of
readings to another text, it is necessary for me to turn to the poems, if briefly,
to explain what I mean about their emphasis on the signifier and its materiality. To do so, I have drawn upon William K. Wimsatt's well-known essay,
"Rhyme and Reason," printed in *The Verbal Icon: Studies in the Meaning of
Poetry* (1970), and Anthony Easthope's equally perceptive but less well-
known essay, "The Feudal Ballad," printed in his *Poetry as Discourse* (1983).

   Easthope's analysis of the structure of the English ballad dovetails nicely
with my analysis of the structure of the Signifying Monkey tales. Because
Easthope's crucial point of departure is a passage from Albert B. Lord's *The
Singer of Tales,* let me repeat it here:

> The method of language is like that of oral poetry, substituting in the
> framework of the grammar. Without the metrical restrictions of verse,
> language substitutes one subject for another in the nominative case, keep-
> ing the same verb, or keeping the same noun, it substitutes one verb for
> another.[22]

Lord defines "substitutions," as Easthope explains, similarly to what Saussure
identified as the paradigmatic axis, while Lord's "framework of the grammar"
corresponds to the syntagmatic axis. Easthope's summary of the defining features of the "discourse examplified in the ballad" reveals an identity with
those of the discourse of the Monkey tales:

> [The] syntagmatic chain does not aim for tight closure and rigid subordi-
> nation of elements in a linear development; rather it works through jux-
> taposition, addition and parallel, typically . . . in binary and trinary
> patterns.

> [Disruption] in the syntagmatic chain means that the discourse of the bal-
> lad does not offer transparent access to the enounced [*énoncé*, the nar-
> rated event, as opposed to enunciation (*enonciation*), the speech event],
> and so no fixed position is offered to the reader as subject of the
> enounced.[23]

Like the ballad, "vocabulary and phrasing" of the Monkey poems is "colloquial, monosyllabic and everyday." Even more important to our discussion of
language use in the Monkey poems, however, are the three aspects that Easthope locates in the operation of the ballad's syntagmatic chain. These are intertextuality, stanzaic units, and incremental repetition.[24]

Intertextuality

As is apparent from even a cursory reading of the Signifying Monkey poems
that I have listed in the appendix, each poem refers to other poems of the
same genre. The artistry of the oral narrator of these poems does not depend
on his or her capacity to dream up new characters or events that define the
actions depicted; rather, it depends on his or her display of the ability to
group together two lines that end in words that sound alike, that bear a phonetic similarity to each other. This challenge is greater when key terms are
fixed, such as the three characters' identities and their received relationship
to each other. Accordingly, all sorts of formulaic phrases recur across these
poems, but (re)placed in distinct parts of a discrete poem.

One example demonstrates this clearly, especially if we recall that intertextuality represents a process of repetition and revision, by definition. A
number of shared structural elements are repeated, with differences that suggest familiarity with other texts of the Monkey. For example, the placement of
the figure "forty-four" is an instance of a formulaic phrase being repeated
from poem to poem—because it has achieved a formulaic insistency—but repeated in distinct ways. For instance, the following lines in one poem:

> The Lion jumped back with a mighty roar,
> his tail stuck out like a forty-four,
> he breezed down through the jungle in a hell of a breeze,
> knockin' giraffes to their knees. (p. 162)

are refigured in another poem in this way:

> And the Lion knew that he didn't play the Dozens
> and he knew the Elephant wasn't none of his cousins,
> so he went through the jungle with a mighty roar,
> poppin' his tail like a forty-four,
> knockin' giraffes to their knees
> and knockin' coconuts from the trees. (p. 164)

and in another poem in this way:

> The Lion got so mad he jump up trimmin' the trees,
> chopped baby giraffes, monkeys down on their knees.
> He went on down the jungle way a jumpin' and pawin'
> poppin' his tail worse in' a forty-four. (p. 166)

It is as if a received structure of crucial elements provides a base for poeisis, and the narrator's technique, his or her craft, is to be gauged by the creative (re)placement of these expected or anticipated formulaic phrases and formulaic events, rendered anew in unexpected ways. Precisely because the concepts represented in the poem are shared, repeated, and familiar to the poet's audience, meaning is devalued while the signifier is valorized. Value, in this art of poeisis, lies in its foregrounding rather than in the invention of a novel signified. We shall see how the nature of the rhyme scheme also stresses the materiality and the priority of the signifier. Let me add first, however, that all other common structural elements are repeated with variations across the texts that, together, comprise the text of the Monkey. In other words, there is no fixed text of these poems; they exist as a play of differences.

Stanzaic Units

Every Signifying Monkey poem is characterized by at least two predominant features of stanzaic structure: an introductory formulaic frame and a concluding formulaic frame, as well as a progression of rhyming couplets, each of which usually relates to the next in a binary pattern of a-a-b-b rhyme, although occasionally a pattern of a-a-b-c or a-a-b-c-c appears, especially to include a particularly vivid (visual) or startling (aural) combination of signifiers. The frame consists of a variation of the following:

> Say deep down in the jungle in the coconut grove
> lay the Signifying Monkey in his one-button roll.
> Now the hat he wore was on the Esquire fold,
> his shoes was on a triple-A last.
> You could tell that he was a pimping motherfucker
> by the way his hair was gassed. (p. 162)

He said, "Well, Brother Lion, the day have come at last,
that I have found a limb to fit your ass."
He said, "You might as well stop, there ain't no use tryin',
because no motherfucker is gonna stop me from signifyin." (p. 163)

I shall turn to the nature of the rhyme scheme and its import below.

Incremental Repetition

Incremental repetition in these poems assumes the form of the repeated binary structure of rhyming couplets, which function as narrative units in isolation or with a second or third set of couplets, and as larger narrative units in a tertiary relation that is contained within the binary frame described above.

The frame defines a problem, the Monkey's irritation at the Lion's roaring, which disturbs the Monkey's connubial habits, and ends with some sort of resolution of that problem. The tertiary relation of the intervening narrative units turns upon the repetition of confrontation and engagement: the Monkey engages the Lion by repeating insults purportedly said by the Elephant; next, the Lion rushes off helter-skelter and challenges the Elephant to a confrontation that the Lion loses; finally, the Lion returns to the scene of the crime, the Monkey's tree, and engages the Monkey, who insults the Lion, slips from his protective branch, then usually escapes certain defeat by tricking the Lion again with a Signifyin(g) challenge, such as the following:

> The Monkey said, "I know you think you raisin' hell,
> but everybody seen me when I slipped and fell.
> But if you let me get my nuts up out of this sand
> I'll fight you just like a natural man."

This tertiary repetition of confrontation-engagement-resolution occurs in representations of direct speech. The Lion's combat with the Elephant is balanced by the Lion's combat with the Monkey. Stasis is relieved by the Monkey's trick of mediation, his rhetorical play on the Lion's incapacity to read his utterance, a flaw that enables the Monkey to scramble back to his protective limb, only to continue to Signify.

The most important aspect of language use in these poems, however, is the nature of its rhymes. Here we can draw upon Wimsatt's analysis of the rhymes of Pope and Easthope's analysis of the feudal ballad to elucidate the import of the rhyme in the Monkey tales.

Wimsatt points out perceptively that Pope's rhyming words tend to be different parts of speech, while Chaucer's depend on the coincidence of parts of speech.

> Pope's rhymes are characterized by difference in parts of speech or in function of the same parts of speech, the difference in each case being accentuated by the tendency of his couplets to parallel structure.[25]

Easthope argues that "Such rhyming works to throw a stress upon the meaning so that meaning dominates sound and the rhyme is subordinated." Such a rhyme scheme, he continues, implicitly emphasizes the crucial role of the phonetic in the production of meaning: "Relative to subordination, coincidence in rhyme emphasizes the phonetic, so acknowledging the dependence of signified [on] signifier." "Coincident rhyme," on the other hand, "foregrounds the signifier."[26]

While both coincidence and subordination occur in the Monkey tales, coincidence tends to occur more frequently, especially in the use of nouns to end a line. "Phonetic similarity," as Easthope maintains, links two words "at the level of the signifier." When rhymes of the same parts of speech coincide, as in Chaucer's poetry, the signifier and the signified are "in a relationship of equality" rather than subordination, such that "meaning is allowed to follow sound *as much as* sound does meaning." The dominance of rhymes of the same parts of speech in the Monkey poems, then, serves to italicize the role of the signifier, and its materiality, by flaunting, as it were, "the dependence of the signified on the signifier." As anyone who has heard these poems recited fully appreciates, they take their received meaning for granted and depend for their marvelous effect on the sheer play of the signifier.[27]

What does such a foregrounding of the signifier imply for black vernacular discourse? We must remember that the Signifying Monkey tales are the repositories of the black vernacular tradition's rhetorical principles, coded dictionaries of black tropes. First, the Monkey "tropes-a-dope," the Lion, by representing a figurative statement as a literal statement, depending on the Lion's thickness to misread the difference. Second, the ensuing depiction of action depends on the stress of phonetic similarity between signifiers. These poems flaunt the role of the signifier in relation to the signified, allowing it its full status as an equal in their relationship, if not the superior partner. Where meaning is constant, the (re)production of this fixed meaning, by definition, foregrounds the play of the signifier. Signifyin(g), then, is the sign of rule in the kingdom of Signification: neither the Lion nor the Elephant—both Signifieds, those Signified upon—is the King of the Jungle; rather, the Monkey is King, the Monkey as Signifier.

If the rhyme pattern of the poems depends on coincidence more often than subordination, then the Monkey's process of Signifyin(g) turns upon repetition and difference, or repetition and reversal. There are so many examples of Signifyin(g) in jazz that one could write a formal history of its development on this basis alone. One early example is relatively familiar: Jelly Roll Morton's 1938 recording entitled "Maple Leaf Rag (A Transformation)" Signifies upon Scott Joplin's signature composition, "Maple Leaf Rag," recorded in 1916. Whereas Joplin played its contrasting themes and their repetitions in the form of AABBACCDD, Morton "embellishes the piece two-handedly, with a swinging introduction (borrowed from the ending to A), followed by ABACCD (a hint of the tango here) D (a real New Orleans 'stomp' variation)," as Martin Williams observes. Morton's piano imitates "a trumpet-clarinet right hand and a trombone-rhythm left hand."* Morton's composition does not "surpass" or "destroy" Joplin's; it complexly *extends* and tropes figures present in the original. Morton's Signification is a gesture of admiration and respect. It is this aspect of Signifyin(g) that is inscribed in the black musical tradition in jazz compositions such as Oscar Peterson's "Signify" and Count Basie's "Signifyin'."

In these compositions, the formal history of solo piano styles in jazz is recapitulated, delightfully, whereby one piano style follows its chronological predecessor in the composition itself, so that boogie-woogie, stride, and blues piano styles—and so on—are represented in one composition as histories of the solo jazz piano, histories of its internal repetition and revision process. Improvisation, of course, so fundamental to the very idea of jazz, is "nothing more"

---

* Martin Williams, *The Smithsonian Collection of Classic Jazz* (Washington, D.C.: Smithsonian Institution, 1973), p. 16.

than repetition and revision. In this sort of revision, again where meaning is fixed, it is the realignment of the signifier that is the signal trait of expressive genius. The more mundane the fixed text ("April in Paris" by Charlie Parker, "My Favorite Things" by John Coltrane), the more dramatic is the Signifyin(g) revision. It is this principle of repetition and difference, this practice of intertextuality, which has been so crucial to the black vernacular forms of Signifyin(g), jazz—and even its antecedents, the blues, the spirituals, and ragtime—and which is the source of my trope for black intertextuality in the Afro-American formal literary tradition. I shall return to this idea at the end of Chapter 3.

III

Signifyin(g): Definitions

Signifyin(g) is so fundamentally black, that is, it is such a familiar rhetorical practice, that one encounters the great resistance of inertia when writing about it. By inertia I am thinking here of the difficulty of rendering the implications of a concept that is so shared in one's culture as to have long ago become second nature to its users. The critic is bound to encounter Ralph Ellison's "Little Man at Chehaw Station."*

Who is he? Ellison tells a marvelous story about himself when he was a student of music at Tuskegee. Having failed at an attempt to compensate for a lack of practice with a virtuoso style of performance, Ellison had sought some solace from the brilliant Hazel Harrison, one of his professors, with whom he had a sustained personal relationship. Instead of solace, however, his friend and mentor greeted his solicitation with a riddle. The exchange is relevant here:

> "All right," she said, "you must *always* play your best, even if it's only in the waiting room at Chehaw Station, because in this country there'll always be a little man hidden behind the stove."
>
> "A what?"
>
> She nodded. "That's right," she said, "there'll always be the little man whom you don't expect, and he'll know the *music,* and the *tradition,* and the standards of *musicianship* required for whatever you set out to perform!"[28]

This little man, who appears at such out-of-the-way places as the Chehaw Railroad Station, is, of course, a trickster figure surfacing when we least expect him, at a crossroads of destiny. This particular little man evokes Esu, the little man whose earthly dwelling place is the crossroads, as indicated in the following excerpts from a Yoruba poem:

* Houston A. Baker's reading of Ellison's essay suggested the alternative reading that I am giving it here. See Baker, *Blues, Ideology, and Afro-American Literature: A Vernacular Theory,* pp. 12–13, 64, 66.

> Latopa, Esu little man
> Latopa, Esu little man
>
> Short, diminutive man
> Tiny, little man.
> He uses both hands to sniffle!
> We call him master
> He who sacrifices without inviting the manumitter
> Will find his sacrifice unacceptable
> Manumitter, I call on you.
> Man by the roadside, bear our sacrifice to heaven directly
> Master, and son of the owner of Idere
> Who came from Idere to found the town,
> The son of the energetic small fellow
> The little man who cleans the gates for the masquerade.
> Elderly spirit deity![29]

The "little man" or woman is bound to surface when the literary critic begins to translate a signal concept from the black vernacular milieu into the discourse of critical theory. While critics write for writers and other critics, they also write—in this instance—for "little" men and women who dwell at the crossroads.

The critic of comparative black literature also dwells at a sort of crossroads, a discursive crossroads at which two languages meet, be these languages Yoruba and English, or Spanish and French, or even (perhaps especially) the black vernacular and standard English. This sort of critic would seem, like Esu, to live at the intersection of these crossroads. When writing a book that lifts one concept from two discrete discursive realms, only to compare them, the role of the critic as the trickster of discourse seems obvious. The concept of Signification is such an instance.

What Ellison's professor did to him was a salient example of Signifyin(g). His professor, subtle and loving as she must have been, Signified upon her young protégé so that he would never allow himself to succumb to the lure of the temptation to skip the necessary gates placed in the apprentice's path, gates which must somehow be opened or hurdled. Ellison was Signified upon because his dilemma was resolved through an allegory. This mode of rhetorical indirection, as Roger D. Abrahams and Claudia Mitchell-Kernan have defined it, is a signal aspect of Signifyin(g). Despite its highly motivated, often phallocentric orientation, then, Signifyin(g), it is clear, can mean any number of modes of rhetorical play.

An article printed in the *New York Times* on April 17, 1983, entitled "Test on Street Language Says It's Not Grant in That Tomb," affords an opportunity to expand somewhat on received definitions of Signifyin(g). The test referred to in the story's title is one created by "some high school students" in Winston-Salem, North Carolina, "who were dismayed at [McGraw-Hill's] own standardized tests." The examination, a multiple-choice intelligence test, is entitled "The In Your Face Test of No Certain Skills." It was created shortly after the students told their teacher, Rob Slater, that "they had trouble relating to a standardized achievement test." As Slater explains,

"They were taking one of these tests one day and one of my students looked up and asked what the reason for the test was, because all it did to him was make him feel academically inferior. After the test was over," Slater concludes, "I asked them if they wanted to get even. They took it from there."[30]

The students devised a test to measure vocabulary mastery in street language. They sent ten copies to McGraw-Hill, where eight employees took the test, only to score C's and D's. One of the test's questions, to which the *Times*'s article title refers, is an example of the most familiar mode of Signifyin(g). The question reads, "Who is buried in Grant's tomb?" The proper response to this question is, "Your mama." It is difficult to explain why this response is so funny and why it is an example of Signifyin(g). "Your mama" jokes abound in black discourse, all the way from the field and the street to Langston Hughes's highly accomplished volume of poems, *Ask Your Mama,* from which an epigraph to this chapter has been taken. The presence in the students' test of this centuries-old black joke represents an inscription of the test's Signifyin(g) nature, because it serves as an echo of the significance of the test's title, "The In Your Face Test of No Certain Skills." The title Signifies in two ways. First, "In your face" is a standard Signifyin(g) retort, meaning that by which you intended to confine (or define) me I shall return to you squarely in your face. And second, the title is a parody (repetition motivated to underscore irony) of test titles such as "The Iowa Test of Basic Skills," which my generation was made to suffer through from the fourth grade through high school. The test itself, then, is an extended Signifyin(g) sign of repetition and reversal, a chiastic slaying at the crossroads where two discursive units meet. As the *Times* article observes, "The students' point was that they did not look at things in the same way as the people at McGraw-Hill. The results of the 'In Your Face' test clearly show that McGraw-Hill and the ninth-graders at Hill High *do not speak the same language.*"[31]

The language of blackness encodes and names its sense of independence through a rhetorical process that we might think of as the Signifyin(g) black difference. As early as the eighteenth century, commentators recorded black usages of Signification. Nicholas Cresswell, writing between 1774 and 1777, made the following entry in his journal: "In [the blacks'] songs they generally relate the usage they have received from their Masters or Mistresses in a very satirical stile [sic] and manner."[32] Cresswell strikes at the heart of the matter when he makes explicit "the usage" that the black slaves "have received," for black people frequently "enounce" their sense of difference by repetition with a signal difference. The eighteenth century abounds in comments from philosophers such as David Hume in "Of National Characters" and statesmen such as Thomas Jefferson in *Notes on the State of Virginia,* who argued that blacks were "imitative" rather than "creative." All along, however, black people were merely Signifyin(g) through a motivated repetition.

Frederick Douglass, a masterful Signifier himself, discusses this use of troping in his *Narrative* of 1845. Douglass, writing some seventy years after Cresswell, was an even more acute observer. Writing about the genesis of the lyrics of black song, Douglass noted the crucial role of the signifier in the determination of meaning:

> [The slaves] would compose and sing as they went along, consulting neither time nor tune. The thought that came up, came out—if not in the *word,* in the *sound;*—and as frequently in the one as in the other . . . they would sing, as a chorus, to words which to many seem *unmeaning jargon,* but which, nevertheless, were *full of meaning* to themselves.[33]

Meaning, Douglass writes, was as determined by sound as by sense, whereby phonetic substitutions determined the shape of the songs. Moreover, the neologisms that Douglass's friends created, "unmeaning jargon" to standard English speakers, were "full of meaning" to the blacks, who were literally defining themselves in language, just as did Douglass and hundreds of other slave narrators. This, of course, is an example of both sorts of signification, black vernacular and standard English. Douglass continues his discussion by maintaining that his fellow slaves "would sing the most pathetic sentiment in the most rapturous tone, and the most rapturous sentiment in the most pathetic tone," a set of oppositions which led to the song's misreading by nonslaves. As Douglass admits,

> I have often been utterly astonished, since I came to the north, to find persons who could speak of the singing, among slaves, as evidence of their contentment and happiness. It is impossible to conceive of a greater mistake.[34]

This great mistake of interpretation occurred because the blacks were using antiphonal structures to reverse their apparent meaning, as a mode of encoding for self-preservation. Whereas black people under Cresswell's gaze Signified openly, those Douglass knew Signified protectively, leading to the misreading against which Douglass rails. As Douglass writes in his second autobiography, however, blacks often Signified directly, as in the following lyrics:

> We raise de wheat,
> Dey gib us de corn;
> We bake de bread,
> Dey gib us de cruss;
> We sif de meal,
> Dey gib us de huss;
> We peal de meat,
> Dey gib us de skin
> And dat's de way
> Dey takes us in.[35]

As William Faux wrote in 1819, slaves commonly used lyrics to Signify upon their oppressors: "Their verse was their own, and abounding either in praise or satire intended for kind and unkind masters."[36]

I cite these early references to motivated language use only to emphasize that black people have been Signifyin(g), without explicitly calling it that, since slavery, as we might expect. One ex-slave, Wash Wilson, in an interview he granted a member of the Federal Writers Project in the 1930s, implies that "sig'fication" was an especial term and practice for the slaves:

> When de niggers go round singin' "Steal Away to Jesus," dat mean dere gwine be a 'ligious meetin' dat night. Dat de *sig'fication* of a meetin'. De masters 'fore and after freedom didn't like dem 'ligious meetin's, so us natcherly slips off at night, down in de bottoms or somewheres. Sometimes us sing and pray all night.[37]

This usage, while close to its standard English shadow, recalls the sense of Signification as an indirect form of communication, as a troping. The report of Wilson's usage overlaps with Zora Neale Hurston's definition of *signify* in *Mules and Men,* published in 1935. These two usages of the words are among the earliest recorded; Wilson's usage argues for an origin of "sig'fication" in slavery, as does the allegorical structure of the Monkey poems and the nature of their figuration, both of which suggest a nineteenth-century provenance. I shall defer a fuller examination of Hurston's sense of Signification to Chapter 5. I wish to explore, in the remainder of this section of this chapter, received definitions of Signifyin(g) before elaborating my own use of this practice in literary criticism.

We can gain some appreciation of the complexity of Signifyin(g) by examining various definitions of the concept. Dictionary definitions give us an idea of how unstable the concepts are that can be signified by Signifyin(g). Clarence Major's *Dictionary of Afro-American Slang* says that "Signify" is the "same as the *Dirty Dozens;* to censure in 12 or fewer statements," and advises the reader to see "Cap on." The "Dirty Dozens" he defines as "a very elaborate game traditionally played by black boys, in which the participants insult each other's relatives, especially their mothers. The object of the game is to test emotional strength. The first person to give in to anger is the loser." To "Cap on" is "to censure," in the manner of the dozens. For Major, then, to Signify is to be engaged in a highly motivated rhetorical act, aimed at figurative, ritual insult.[38]

Hermese E. Roberts, writing in *The Third Ear: A Black Glossary,* combines Major's emphasis on insult and Roger D. Abrahams's emphasis on implication. Roberts defines "signifying," or "siggin(g)," as "language behavior that makes direct or indirect implications of baiting or boasting, the essence of which is making fun of another's appearance, relatives, or situation." For Roberts, then, a signal aspect of Signifyin(g) is "making fun of" as a mode of "baiting" or "boasting." It is curious to me how very many definitions of Signifyin(g) share this stress on what we might think of as the black person's symbolic aggression, enacted in language, rather than upon the play of language itself, the meta-rhetorical structures in evidence. "Making fun of" is a long way from "making fun," and it is the latter that defines Signifyin(g).[39]

Roberts lists as subcategories of Signifyin(g) the following figures: "joning, playing the dozens, screaming on, sounding." Under "joning" and "sounding," Roberts asks the reader to "See signifying." "Screaming on" is defined as "telling someone off; i.e. to get on someone's case," "case" meaning among other things "an imaginary region of the mind in which is centered one's vulnerable points, eccentricities, and sensitivities." "Screaming on" also means "embarrassing someone publicly." "Playing the dozens" Roberts defines as "making derogatory, often obscene, remarks about another's mother, parents, or family members. ('Yo' mama' is an expression used as retribution for previous vituperation.)" Roberts, in other words, consistently groups Signifyin(g) under those tropes of contention wherein aggression and conflict predominate. Despite this refusal to transcend surface meaning to define its latent meaning, Roberts's decision to group joning, playing the dozens, screaming on, and sounding as synonyms of Signifyin(g) is exemplary for suggesting that Signifyin(g) is the trope of tropes in the black vernacular.

Mezz Mezzrow, the well-known jazz musician, defines "Signify" in the glossary of his autobiography, *Really the Blues,* as "hint, to put on an act, boast, make a gesture." In the body of his text, however, Mezzrow implicitly defines signifying as the homonymic pun. In an episode in which some black people in a bar let some white gangsters know that their identity as murderers is common knowledge, the blacks, apparently describing a musical performance, use homonyms such as "killer" and "murder" to Signify upon the criminals. As Mezzrow describes the event:

> He could have been talking about the music, but everybody in the room knew different. Right quick another cat spoke up real loud, saying, "That's *murder* man, really murder," and his eyes were *signifying* too. All these gunmen began to shift from foot to foot, fixing their ties and scratching their noses, faces red and Adam's apples jumping. Before we knew it they had gulped their drinks and beat it out the door, saying good-bye to the bartender with their hats way down over their eyebrows and their eyes gunning the ground. That's what Harlem thought of the white underworld.[40]

Signifying here connotes the play of language—both spoken and body language—drawn upon to name something figuratively.

Mezzrow's definitions are both perceptive and subtle. Signifyin(g) for him is one mode of "verbal horseplay," designed to train the subject "to think faster and be more nimble-witted." Mezzrow, then, is able to penetrate the content of this black verbal horseplay to analyze the significance of the rhetorical structures that transcend any fixed form of Signifyin(g), such as the verbal insult rituals called the dozens. Indeed, Mezzrow was one of the first commentators to recognize that Signifyin(g) as a structure of performance could apply equally to verbal texts and musical texts. As he summarizes:

> Through all these friendly but lively competitions you could see the Negro's appreciation of real talent and merit, his demand for fair play, and his ardor for the best man wins and don't you come around here with no jive. Boasting doesn't cut any ice; if you think you've got some-

> thing, don't waste time talking yourself up, go to work and prove it. If
> you have the stuff the other cats will recognize it frankly, with solid ad-
> miration. That's especially true in the field of music, which has a double
> importance to the Negro because that's where he really shines, where his
> inventiveness and artistry come through in full force. The colored boys
> prove their musical talents in those competitions called cutting contests,
> and there it really is the best man wins, because the Negro audience is
> extra critical when it comes to music and won't accept anything second-
> rate. These cutting contests are just a musical version of the verbal duels.
> They're staged to see which performer can snag and cap all the others
> *musically.* And by the way, these battles have helped to produce some of
> the race's greatest musicians.[41]

Signifyin(g) for Mezzrow is not what is played or said; it is rather a form of
rhetorical training, an on-the-streets exercise in the use of troping, in which
the play is the thing—not specifically what is said, but how. All definitions of
Signifyin(g) that do not distinguish between manner and matter succumb,
like the Lion, to serious misreading.

   Malachi Andrews and Paul T. Owens, in *Black Language,* acutely recognize two crucial aspects of Signifyin(g): first, that the signifier invents a myth
to commence the ritual and, second, that in the Monkey tales at least, trinary
structure prevails over binary structure. "To Signify," they write,

> is to tease, to provoke into anger. The *signifier* creates a myth about
> someone and tells him a *third* person started it. The *signified* person is
> aroused and seeks that person. . . . Signifying is completely successful
> when the *signifier* convinces the chump he is working on, that what he is
> saying is true and that it gets him angered to wrath.[42]

Andrews and Owen's definition sticks fairly closely to the action of the Signifying Monkey tales. While Signifyin(g) can, and indeed does, occur between two people, the three terms of the traditional mythic structure serve to
dispel a simple relation of identity between the allegorical figures of the poem
and the binary political relationship, outside the text, between black and
white. The third term both critiques the idea of the binary opposition and
demonstrates that Signifyin(g) itself encompasses a larger domain than
merely the political. It is a game of language, independent of reaction to white
racism or even to collective black wish-fulfillment vis-à-vis white racism. I
cannot stress too much the import of the presence of this third term, or in
Hermese E. Roberts's extraordinarily suggestive phrase, "The Third Ear," an
intraracial ear through which encoded vernacular language is deciphered.

   J. L. Dillard, who along with William Labov and William A. Stewart is
one of the most sensitive observers of black language use, defines Signify-
in(g) as "a familiar discourse device from the inner city, [which] tends to
mean 'communicating (often an obscene or ridiculing message) by indirection.' "[43] Dillard here is elaborating somewhat upon Zora Neale Hurston's
gloss printed in *Mules and Men,* where she writes that to signify is to "show
off."[44] This definition seems to be an anomalous one, unless we supply Hurston's missing, or implied, terms: to show off *with language use.* Dillard, how-

ever, is more concerned with the dozens than he is with Signifyin(g). In an especially perceptive chapter entitled "Discourse Distribution and Semantic Difference in Homophonous Items," Dillard ignores the homophone *signify* but suggests that so-called inner-city verbal rituals, such as the dozens, could well be contemporary revisions of "the 'lies' told by Florida Blacks studied by Hurston and the Anansi stories of the southern plantations," sans the "sex and scatology." "Put those elements back," Dillard continues, "and you have something like the rhymed 'toasts' of the inner city."[45] The "toasts," as Bruce Jackson has shown, include among their types the Signifying Monkey tales.[46] There can be little doubt that Signifyin(g) was found by linguists in the black urban neighborhoods in the fifties and sixties because black people from the South migrated there and passed the tradition along to subsequent generations.

We can see the extremes of dictionary and glossary definitions of *Signify* in two final examples, one taken from *The Psychology of Black Language,* by Jim Haskins and Hugh F. Butts, and the other from the *Dictionary of American Slang,* compiled by Harold Wentworth and Stuart Berg Flexner. Haskins and Butts, in a glossary appended to their text, define "to signify" as "To berate, degrade."[47] In their text, however, they define "signifying" as "a more humane form of verbal bantering" than the dozens, admitting, however, that Signifyin(g) "has many meanings," including meanings that contradict their own glossary listing: "It is, again, the clever and humorous use of words, but it can be used for many purposes—'putting down' another person, making another person feel better, or simply expressing one's feelings."[48] Haskins and Butts's longer definition seems to contradict their glossary listing—unless we recall that Signifyin(g) can mean all of these meanings, and more, precisely because so many black tropes are subsumed within it. Signifyin(g) does not, on the other hand, mean "To pretend to have knowledge; to pretend to be hip, esp. when such pretentions cause one to trifle with an important matter," as Wentworth and Flexner would have it.[49] Indeed, this definition sounds like a classic black Signification, in which a black informant, as it were, Signified upon either Wentworth or Flexner, or lexicographers in general who "pretend to have knowledge."

There are several other dictionary definitions that I could cite here. My intention, however, has been to suggest the various ways in which Signifyin(g) is (mis)understood, primarily because few scholars have succeeded in defining it as a full concept. Rather, they often have taken the part—one of its several tropes—as its whole. The delightfully "dirty" lines of the dozens seem to have generated far more interest from scholars than has Signifyin(g), and perhaps far more heat than light. The dozens are an especially compelling subset of Signifyin(g), and its name quite probably derives from an eighteenth-century meaning of the verb *dozen,* "to stun, stupefy, daze," in the black sense, through language.[50] Let us examine more substantive definitions of Signifyin(g) by H. Rap Brown, Roger D. Abrahams, Thomas Kochman, Claudia Mitchell-Kernan, Geneva Smitherman, and Ralph Ellison, before exploring examples of the definition of Signifyin(g) that I shall employ in the remainder of this book.

H. Rap Brown earned his byname because he was a master of black vernacular rhetorical games and their attendant well-defined rhetorical strategies. Brown's understanding of Signifyin(g) is unsurpassed by that of any scholar. In the second chapter of his autobiography, *Die Nigger Die!*, Brown represents the scenes of instruction by which he received his byname. "I learned to talk in the street," he writes, "not from reading about Dick and Jane going to the zoo and all that simple shit." Rather, Brown continues, "we exercised our minds," not by studying arithmetic but "by playing the Dozens":

> I fucked your mama
> Till she went blind.
> Her breath smells bad,
> But she sure can grind.
>
> I fucked your mama
> For a solid hour.
> Baby came out
> Screaming, Black Power.
>
> Elephant and the Baboon
> Learning to screw.
> Baby came out looking
> Like Spiro Agnew.

Brown argues that his teachers sought to teach him "poetry," meaning poems from the Western tradition, when he and his fellows were *making* poetry in the streets. "If anybody needed to study poetry," he maintains, "my teacher needed to study mine. We played the Dozens," he concludes, "like white folks play Scrabble." "[They] call me Rap," he writes humorously if tautologically, "'cause I could rap." To rap is to use the vernacular with great dexterity. Brown, judging from his poetry printed in this chapter of his autobiography, most certainly earned his byname.[51]

Brown's definitions and examples are as witty as they are telling. He insists, as does Claudia Mitchell-Kernan, that both men and women can play the dozens and Signify: "Some of the best Dozens players," he writes, "were girls." Whereas the dozens were an unrelentingly "mean game because what you try to do is totally destroy somebody else with words," Signifyin(g) was "more humane": "Instead of coming down on somebody's mother, you come down on them." Brown's account of the process of Signifyin(g) is especially accurate:

> A session would start maybe by a brother
> saying, "Man, before you mess with me
> you'd rather run rabbits, eat shit and
> bark at the moon." Then, if he was talking
> to me, I'd tell him:
>
> Man, you must don't know who I am.
> I'm sweet peeter jeeter the womb beater
> The baby maker the cradle shaker
> The deerslayer the buckbinder the women finder

Known from the Gold Coast to the rocky shores of Maine
Rap is my name and love is my game.
I'm the bed tucker the cock plucker the motherfucker
The milkshaker the record breaker the population maker
The gun-slinger the baby bringer
The hum-dinger the pussy ringer
The man with the terrible middle finger.
The hard hitter the bullshitter the poly-nussy getter
The beast from the East the Judge the sludge
The women's pet the men's fret and the punks' pin-up boy.
They call me Rap the dicker the ass kicker
The cherry picker the city slicker the titty licker
And I ain't giving up nothing but bubble gum and hard times and I'm
    fresh out of bubble gum.
I'm giving up wooden nickles 'cause I know they won't spend
And I got a pocketful of splinter change.
I'm a member of the bathtub club: I'm seeing a whole lot of ass but I
    ain't taking no shit.
I'm the man who walked the water and tied the whale's tail in a knot
Taught the little fishes how to swim
Crossed the burning sands and shook the devil's hand
Rode round the world on the back of a snail carrying a sack saying AIR
    MAIL.
Walked 49 miles of barbwire and used a Cobra snake for a necktie
And got a brand new house on the roadside made from a cracker's hide,
Got a brand new chimney setting on top made from the cracker's skull
Took a hammer and nail and built the world and calls it "THE
    BUCKET OF BLOOD."
Yes, I'm hemp the demp the women's pimp
Women fight for my delight.
I'm a bad motherfucker. Rap the rip-saw the devil's brother'n law.
I roam the world I'm known to wander and this .45 is where I get my
    thunder.
I'm the only man in the world who knows why white milk makes yellow
    butter.
I know where the lights go when you cut the switch off.
I might not be the best in the world, but I'm in the top two and my
brother's getting old.
And ain't nothing bad 'bout you but your breath.

Whereas the dozens were structured to make one's subject feel bad, "Signifying allowed you a choice—you could either make a cat feel good or bad. If you had just destroyed someone [verbally] or if they were just down already, signifying could help them over."[52]

Few scholars have recognized this level of complexity in Signifyin(g), which Brown argues implicitly to be the rhetorical structures at work in the discourse, rather than a specific content uttered. In addition to making "a cat feel good or bad," Brown continues, "Signifying was also a way of expressing your own feelings," as in the following example:

> Man, I can't win for losing.
> If it wasn't for bad luck, I wouldn't have no luck at all.
> I been having buzzard luck
> Can't kill nothing and won't nothing die
> I'm living on the welfare and things is stormy
> They borrowing their shit from the Salvation Army
> But things bound to get better 'cause they can't get no worse
> I'm just like the blind man, standing by a broken window
> I don't feel no pain.
> But it's your world
> You the man I pay rent to
> If I had you hands I'd give 'way both my arms.
> Cause I could do without them
> I'm the man but you the main man
> I read the books you write
> You set the pace in the race I run
> Why, you always in good form
> You got more foam than Alka Seltzer . . .[53]

Signifyin(g), then, for Brown, is an especially expressive mode of discourse that turns upon forms of figuration rather than intent or content. Signifyin(g), to cite Brown, is "what the white folks call verbal skills. We learn how to throw them words together." Signifying, "at its best," Brown concludes, "can be heard when brothers are exchanging tales." It is this sense of storytelling, repeated and often shared (almost communal canonical stories, or on-the-spot recountings of current events) in which Signifyin(g) as a rhetorical strategy can most clearly be seen. We shall return to Brown's definition in the next section of this chapter.[54]

One of the most sustained attempts to define Signifyin(g) is that of Roger D. Abrahams, a well-known and highly regarded literary critic, linguist, and anthropologist. Abrahams's work in this area is seminal, as defined here as a work against which subsequent works must, in some way, react. Between 1962 and 1976, Abrahams published several significant studies of Signifyin(g). To tract Abrahams's interpretative evolution helps us to understand the complexities of this rhetorical strategy but is outside the scope of this book.[55]

Abrahams in 1962 brilliantly defines Signifyin(g) in terms that he and other subsequent scholars shall repeat:

> The name "Signifying Monkey" shows [the hero] to be a trickster, "signifying" being the language of trickery, that set of words or gestures which arrives at "direction through indirection."[56]

Signifyin(g), Abrahams argues implicitly, is the black person's use of figurative modes of language use. The word *indirection* hereafter recurs in the literature with great, if often unacknowledged, frequency. Abrahams expanded on this theory of Signifyin(g) in two editions of *Deep Down in the Jungle* (1964, 1970). It is useful to list the signal aspects of his extensive definitions:

1. Signifyin(g) "can mean any number of things."
2. It is a black term and a black rhetorical device.
3. It can mean the "ability to talk with great innuendo."
4. It can mean "to carp, cajole, needle, and lie."
5. It can mean "the propensity to talk around a subject, never quite coming to the point."
6. It can mean "making fun of a person or situation."
7. It can "also denote speaking with the hands and eyes."
8. It is "the language of trickery, that set of words achieving Hamlet's 'direction through indirection.' "
9. The Monkey "is a 'signifier,' and the Lion, therefore, is the signified."

Finally, in his appended glossary of "Unusual Terms and Expressions," Abrahams defines "Signify" as "To imply, goad, beg, boast by indirect verbal or gestural means. A language of implication."[57]

These definitions are exemplary insofar as they emphasize "indirection" and "implication," which we can read as synonyms of *figurative*. Abrahams was the first scholar, to my knowledge, to define Signifyin(g) as a language, by which he means a particular rhetorical strategy. Whereas he writes that the Monkey is a master of this technique, it is even more accurate to write that he *is* technique, the literariness of language, the ultimate source for black people of the figures of signification. If we think of rhetoric as the "writing" of spoken discourse, then the Monkey's role as the source and encoded keeper of Signifyin(g) helps to reveal his functional equivalency with his Pan-African cousin, *Esu-Elegbara,* the figure of writing in Ifa.

Abrahams's work helps us to understand that Signifyin(g) is an adult ritual, which black people learn as adolescents, almost exactly like children learned the traditional figures of signification in classically structured Western primary and secondard schools, training one hopes shall be returned to contemporary education. As we shall see below, Claudia Mitchell-Kernan, an anthropologist-linguist, shares an anecdote that demonstrates, first, how Signifyin(g) truly is a conscious rhetorical strategy and, second, how adult black people implicitly instruct a mature child in its most profound and subtle uses by an indirect mode of narration only implicitly related in form to the Monkey tales, perhaps as extract relates to the vanilla bean, or as sand relates to the pearl, or, as Esu might add, as palm wine relates to the palm tree. Black adults teach their children this exceptionally complex system of rhetoric, almost exactly like Richard A. Lanham describes a generic portrait of the teaching of the rhetorical *paideia* to Western schoolchildren. The mastery of Signifyin(g) creates *homo rhetoricus Africanus,* allowing—through the manipulation of these classic black figures of Signification—the black person to move freely between two discursive universes. This is an excellent example of what I call linguistic masking, the verbal sign of the mask of blackness that demarcates the boundary between the white linguistic realm and the black, two domains that exist side by side in a homonymic relation signified by the very concept of Signification. To learn to manipulate language in such a way as to facilitate the smooth navigation between these two realms has been the challenge of black parenthood, and remains so even today. Teaching one's children the fine art of Signifyin(g) is to teach them about this mode of linguistic circumnavigation, to teach them a second language that they can share with other black people.[58] Black adolescents engaged in the dozens and in Signifyin(g) rituals to learn the classic black figures of Signification. As H. Rap Brown declares passionately, his true school was the street. Richard Lanham's wonderful depiction of the student passing through the rhetorical *paideia* reads like a description of vernacular black language training:

> Start your student young. Teach him a minute concentration on the word, how to write it, speak it, remember it. . . . From the beginning, stress behavior as performance, reading aloud, speaking with gesture, a full range of histrionic adornment. . . . Develop elaborate memory schemes to keep them readily at hand. Teach, as theory of personality, a corresponding set of accepted personality types, a taxonomy of impersonation. . . . Nourish an acute sense of social situation. . . . Stress, too, the need for improvisation, ad-lib quickness, the coaxing of chance. Hold always before the student rhetoric's practical purpose: to win, to persuade. But train for this purpose with continual verbal play, rehearsal for the sake of rehearsal.
>
> Use the "case" method. . . . Practice this re-creation always in an agonistic context. The aim is scoring. Urge the student to go into the world and observe its doings from this perspective. And urge him to continue his rehearsal method all his life, forever rehearsing a spontaneous real life. . . . Training in the word thus becomes a badge, as well as a diversion, of the leisure class.[59]

This reads very much like a black person's training in Signifyin(g). Lanham's key words—among which are "a taxonomy of impersonation, "improvisation," "ad-lib quickness," "to win," "to persuade," "continual verbal play," "the 'case' method," "the aim is scoring"—echo exactly the training of blacks to Signify. Even Lanham's concept of a "leisure" class applies ironically here, since blacks tend in capitalist societies to occupy a disproportionate part of the "idle" unemployed, a leisure-class with a difference. To Signify, then, is to master the figures of black Signification.

Few black adults can recite an entire Monkey tale; black adults, on the other hand, can—and do—Signify. The mastering of the Monkey tales corresponds to this early part of Lanham's account of Western rhetorical training. Words are looked at in the Monkey tales because the test of this form of *poeisis* is to arrive at a phonetic coincidence of similar parts of speech, as I have shown above. The splendid example of Signifyin(g) that I have cited in Ralph Ellison's anecdote about Hazel Harrison, and the anecdote of Claudia Mitchell-Kernan's that I shall discuss below, conform to Lanham's apt description of the mature capacity to look through words for their full meaning. Learning the Monkey tales, then, is somewhat akin to attending troping school, where one learns to "trope-a-dope."

The Monkey is a hero of black myth, a sign of the triumph of wit and reason, his language of Signifyin(g) standing as the linguistic sign of the ultimate triumph of self-consciously formal language use. The black person's capacity to create this rich poetry and to derive from these rituals a complex attitude toward attempts at domination, which can be transcended in and through language, is a sign of their originality, of their extreme consciousness of the metaphysical. Abrahams makes these matters clear.

In *Talking Black,* published in 1976, Abrahams's analysis of Signifyin(g) as an act of language is even more subtle than his earlier interpretations. Abrahams repeats his insightful definition that Signifyin(g) turns upon indirection. Black women, he maintains, and "to a certain extent children," utilize "more indirect methods of signifying." His examples are relevant ones:

> These range from the most obvious kinds of indirection, like using an unexpected pronoun in discourse ("Didn't *we* come to shine, today?" or "Who thinks his drawers don't stink?"), to the more subtle technique, of *louding* or *loud-talking* in a different sense from the one above. A person is loud-talking when he says something of someone just loud enough for that person to hear, but indirectly, so he cannot properly respond (Mitchell-Kernan). Another technique of signifying through indirection is making reference to a person or group not present, in order to start trouble between someone present and the ones who are not. An example of this technique is the famous toast, "The Signifying Monkey."[60]

These examples are salient for two reasons: first, because he has understood that adults use the modes of signification commonly, even if they cannot recite even one couplet from the Monkey tales, and, second, because he has realized that other tropes, such as loud-talking, are subtropes of Signifyin(g). His emphasis on the mature forms of Signifyin(g)—that is, the indirect modes—as more common among women and children does not agree with my observations. Indeed, I have found that black men and women use indirection with each other to the same degree.

Next, Abrahams states that Signifyin(g) can also be used "in recurrent black-white encounters as masking behavior." Since the full effectiveness of Signifyin(g) turns upon all speakers possessing the mastery of reading, what Abrahams calls "intergroup" Signifyin(g) is difficult to effect, if only because the inherent irony of discourse most probably will not be understood. Still, Signifyin(g) is one significant mode of verbal masking or troping.[61]

Abrahams's most important contribution to the literature on Signifyin(g) is his discovery that Signifyin(g) is primarily a term for rhetorical strategies, which often is called by other names depending on which of its several forms it takes. As he concludes, "with *signifying* we have a term not only for a way of speaking but for a rhetorical strategy that may be characteristic of a number of other designated events."[62] I would add to this statement that, for black adults, Signifyin(g) is the name for the figures of rhetoric themselves, the figure of the figure. Abrahams lists the following terms as synonyms of Signifyin(g), as derived from several other scholars, and which I am defining to be black tropes as subsumed within the trope of Signifyin(g): *talking shit, woofing, spouting, muckty muck, boogerbang, beating your gums, talking smart, putting down, putting on, playing, sounding, telling lies, shag-lag, marking, shucking, jiving, jitterbugging, bugging, mounting, charging, cracking, harping, rapping, bookooing, low-rating, hoorawing, sweet-talking, smart-talking,* and no doubt a few others that I have omitted.[63] This is a crucial contribution to our understanding of this figure because it transcends the disagreements, among linguists, about whether trope x or y is evidenced by speech act a or b. What's more, Abrahams reveals, by listing its synonyms, that black people can mean at least twenty-eight figures when they call something Signifyin(g). He represents a few of the figures embedded in Signifyin(g) in Chart 3:

Chart 3. Roger D. Abrahams's Figure 1 in *Talking Black*, p. 46.

conversation on the streets; ways of speaking between equals		
informational; content focus *running it down*	aggressive, witty performance talk *signifying*	
	serious, clever conflict talk "me-and-you and no one else" focus *talking smart*	nonserious contest talk "any of us here" focus *talking shit*
	overtly aggressive talk *putting down* covertly aggressive, manipulative talk *putting on*	nondirective *playing* directive *sounding*

going deep: talking bad

conversational (apparently spontaneous)	arises within conversational context, yet judged in performance (stylistic) terms	performance interaction, yet built on model of conversational back-and-forth

He could have listed several others. When black people say that "Signification is the Nigger's occupation," we can readily see what they mean, since mastering all of these figures of Signification is a lifetime's work!

When a black person speaks of Signifyin(g), he or she means a "style-focused message . . . styling which is *foregrounded* by the devices of making a point by indirection and wit." What is foregrounded, of course, is the signifier itself, as we have seen in the rhyme scheme of the Monkey tales. The Monkey is called the signifier because he foregrounds the signifier in his use of language. Signifyin(g), in other words, turns on the sheer play of the signifier. It does not refer primarily to the signified; rather, it refers to the style of language, to that which transforms ordinary discourse into literature. Again, one does not Signify some thing; one Signifies in *some way*.[64]

The import of this observation for the study of black literature is manifold. When I wrote earlier that the black tradition theorized about itself in the vernacular, this is what I meant in part. Signifyin(g) is the black rhetorical difference that negotiates the language user through several orders of meaning. In formal literature, what we commonly call figuration corresponds to Signification. Again, the originality of so much of the black tradition emphasizes refiguration, or repetition and difference, or troping, underscoring the foregrounding of the chain of signifiers, rather than the mimetic representation of a novel content. Critics of Afro-American, Caribbean, and African literatures, however, have far more often than not directed their attention to the signified, often at the expense of the signifier, as if the latter were transparent. This functions contrary to the principles of criticism inherent in the concept of Signifyin(g).

Thomas Kochman's contribution to the literature on Signifyin(g) is the recognition that the Monkey is the Signifier, and that one common form of this rhetorical practice turns upon repetition and difference. Kochman also draws an important distinction between directive and expressive modes of Signification. Directive Signifyin(g), paradoxically, turns upon an indirective strategy:

> . . . when the function of signifying is *directive,* and the *tactic* which is employed is one of *indirection*—i.e., the signifier reports or repeats what someone has said about the listener; the "report" is couched in plausible language designed to compel belief and arouse feelings of anger and hostility.[65]

Kochman argues that the function of this sort of claim to repetition is to challenge and reverse the status quo:

> There is also the implication that if the listener fails to do anything about it—what has to be "done" is usually quite clear—his status will be seriously compromised. Thus the lion is compelled to vindicate the honor of his family by fighting or else leave the impression that he is afraid, and that he is not "king of the jungle." When used to direct action, signifying is like shucking in also being deceptive and subtle in approach and depending for success on the naïveté or gullibility of the person being put on.[66]

Kochman's definition of expressive Signifyin(g), while useful, is less inclusive than that proposed by H. Rap Brown, including as it does only negative intentions: "to arouse feelings of embarrassment, shame, frustration, or futility, for the purpose of diminishing someone's status, but without directive implication." Expressive Signifyin(g), Kochman continues, employs "direct" speech tactics "in the form of a taunt, as in the . . . example where the monkey is making fun of the lion." For Kochman, Signifyin(g) implies an aggressive mode of rhetoric, a form of symbolic action that yields catharsis.[67]

While several other scholars have discussed the nature and function of Signifyin(g), the theories of Claudia Mitchell-Kernan and Geneva Smitherman are especially useful for the theory of revision that I am outlining in this chapter.[68] Mitchell-Kernan's theory of Signifyin(g) is among the most thorough and the most subtle in the linguistic literature, while Smitherman's work connects linguistic analysis with the Afro-American literary tradition. I shall examine Mitchell-Kernan's work first and then discuss Smitherman's work in Chapter 3.

Mitchell-Kernan is quick to demonstrate that Signifyin(g) has received most scholarly attention as "a tactic employed in game activity—verbal dueling—which is engaged in as an end in itself," as if this one aspect of the rhetorical concept amounted to its whole. In fact, however, "*Signifying* . . . also refers to a way of encoding messages or meanings which involves, in most cases, an element of indirection." This alternative definition amounts to nothing less than a polite critique of the linguistic studies of Signifyin(g), since the subtleties of this rhetorical strategy somehow escaped most other scholars before Mitchell-Kernan. As she expands her definition, "This kind of *signifying* might be best viewed as an alternative message form, selected for its artistic merit, and may occur embedded in a variety of discourse. Such *signifying* is not focal to the linguistic interaction in the sense that it does not define the entire speech event."[69]

I cannot stress too much the importance of this definition, for it shows that Signifyin(g) is a pervasive mode of language use rather than merely one specific verbal game, an observation that somehow escaped the notice of every other scholar before Mitchell-Kernan. This definition alone serves as a corrective to what I think of as the tendency among linguists who have fixed their gaze upon the aggressive ritual part and thereby avoided seeing the concept as a whole. What's more, Mitchell-Kernan's definition points to the implicit parallels between Signifyin(g) and the use of language that we broadly define to be figurative, by which I mean in this context an intentional deviation from the ordinary form or syntactical relation of words.[70]

Signifyin(g), in other words, is synonymous with figuration. Mitchell-Kernan's work is so rich because she studied the language behavior of adults as well as adolescents, and of women as well as men. Whereas her colleagues studied lower-class male language use, then generalized from this strictly limited sample, Mitchell-Kernan's data are derived from a sample more representative of the black speech community. Hers is a sample that does not undermine her data because it accounts for the role of age and sex as variables in language use. In addition, Mitchell-Kernan refused to be captivated by the verbal insult rituals, such as sounding, playing the dozens, and Signifyin(g), as ritual speech events, unlike other linguists whose work suffers from an undue attention to the use of words such as *motherfucker,* to insults that turn on sexual assertions about someone's mama, and to supposed Oedipal complexes that arise in the literature only because the linguist is reading the figurative as a literal statement, like our friend, the Signified Lion.

These scholars, unlike Mitchell-Kernan, have mistaken the language games of adolescents as an end rather than as the drills common to classical rhetorical study as suggested in Lanham's hypothetical synopsis quoted earlier in this chapter. As Mitchell-Kernan concludes, both the sex and the age of the linguist's informants "may slant interpretation, particularly because the insult dimension [of Signifyin(g)] looms large in contexts where verbal dueling is focal." In the neighborhood in which she was raised, she argues, whereas "*Sounding* and *Playing the Dozens* categorically involved verbal insult (typically joking behavior); *signifying* did not." Mitchell-Kernan is declaring, most unobtrusively, that, for whatever reasons, linguists have misunderstood what Signifyin(g) means to black people who practice it. While she admits that one relatively minor aspect of this rhetorical principle involves the ritual of insult, the concept is much more profound than merely this. Indeed, Signifyin(g) alone serves to underscore the uniqueness of the black community's use of language: "the terminological use of *signifying* to refer to a particular kind of language specialization defines the Black community as a speech community in contrast to non-Black communities." Mitchell-Kernan here both critiques the work of other linguists who have wrestled unsuccessfully with this difficult concept (specifically Abrahams and Kochman) and provides an urgently needed corrective by defining Signifyin(g) as a way of figuring language. Mitchell-Kernan's penetrating work enables Signifyin(g) to be even further elaborated upon for use in literary theory.[71]

Because it is difficult to arrive at a consensus of definitions of Signifyin(g), as this chapter already has made clear, Mitchell-Kernan proceeds "by way of analogy to inform the reader of its various meanings as applied in interpretation." This difficulty of definition is a direct result of the fact that Signifyin(g) is the black term for what in classical European rhetoric are called the figures of signification. Because to Signify is to be figurative, to define it in practice is to define it through any number of its embedded tropes. No wonder even Mitchell-Kernan could not arrive at a consensus among her informants—except for what turns out to be the most crucial shared aspects of all figures of speech, an indirect use of words that changes the meaning of a word or words. Or, as Quintilian put it, figuration turns on some sort of "change in signification." While linguists who disagree about what it means to Signify all repeat the role of indirection in this rhetorical strategy, none of them seems to have understood that the ensuing alteration or deviation of meaning makes Signifyin(g) the black trope for all other tropes, the trope of tropes, the figure of figures. Signifyin(g) *is* troping.[72]

Mitchell-Kernan begins her elaboration of the concept by pointing to the unique usage of the word in black discourse:

> What is unique in Black English usage is the way in which signifying is extended to cover a range of meanings and events which are not covered in its Standard English usage. In the Black community it is possible to say, "He is signifying" and "Stop signifying"—sentences which would be anomalous elsewhere.[73]

Because in standard English signification denotes meaning and in the black tradition it denotes ways of meaning, Mitchell-Kernan argues for discrepancies between meanings of the same term in two distinct discourses:

> The Black concept of *signifying* incorporates essentially a folk notion that dictionary entries for words are not always sufficient for interpreting meanings or messages, or that meaning goes beyond such interpretations.

Complimentary remarks may be delivered in a left-handed fashion. A particular utterance may be an insult in one context and not another. What pretends to be informative may intend to be persuasive. The hearer is thus constrained to attend to all potential meaning carrying symbolic systems in speech events—the total universe of discourse.[74]

Signifyin(g), in other words, is the figurative difference between the literal and the metaphorical, between surface and latent meaning. Mitchell-Kernan calls this feature of discourse an "implicit content or function, which is potentially obscured by the surface content or function." Finally, Signifyin(g) presupposes an "encoded" intention to say one thing but to mean quite another.[75]

Mitchell-Kernan presents several examples of Signifyin(g), as she is defining it. Her first example is a conversation among three women about the meal to be served at dinner. One woman asks the other two to join her for dinner, that is, if they are willing to eat "chit'lins." She ends her invitation with a pointed rhetorical question: "Or are you one of those Negroes who don't eat chit'lins?" The third person, the woman not addressed, responds with a long defense of why she prefers "prime rib and T-bone" to "chit'lins," ending with a traditional ultimate appeal to special pleading, a call to unity within the ranks to defeat white racism. Then she leaves. After she has gone, the initial speaker replies to her original addressee in this fashion: "Well, I wasn't signifying at her, but like I always say, if the shoe fits wear it." Mitchell-Kernan concludes that while the manifest subject of this exchange was dinner, the latent subject was the political orientation of two black people vis-à-vis cultural assimilation or cultural nationalism, since many middle-class blacks refuse to eat this item from the traditional black cuisine. Mitchell-Kernan labels this form of Signifyin(g) "allegory," because "the significance or meaning of the words must be derived from known symbolic values."[76]

This mode of Signifyin(g) is commonly practiced by Afro-American adults. It is functionally equivalent to one of its embedded tropes, often called louding or loud-talking, which as we might expect connotes exactly the opposite of that which it denotes: one successfully loud-talks by speaking to a second person remarks in fact directed to a third person, at a level just audible to the third person. A sign of the success of this practice is an indignant "What?" from the third person, to which the speaker responds, "I wasn't talking to you." Of course, the speaker was, yet simultaneously was not. Loud-talking is related to Mitchell-Kernan's second figure of Signification, which she calls "obscuring the addressee" and which I shall call naming. Her example is one commonly used in the tradition, in which "the remark is, on the surface, directed toward no one in particular":

> I saw a woman the other day in a pair of stretch pants, she must have weighed 300 pounds. If she knew how she looked she would burn those things.[77]

If a member of the speaker's audience is overweight and frequently wears stretch pants, then this message could well be intended for her. If she protests, the speaker is free to maintain that she was speaking about someone else and to ask why her auditor is so paranoid. Alternatively, the speaker can say, "if the shoe fits. . . ." Mitchell-Kernan says that a characteristic of this form of Signifyin(g) is the selection of a subject that is "selectively relevant to the speaker's audience."[78] I once heard a black minister name the illicit behavior of specific members of his congregation by performing a magnificent reading of "The Text of the Dry Bones," which is a reading or gloss upon Ezekiel 37: 1–14. Following this sermon, a prayer was offered by Lin Allen. As "Mr. Lin," as we called him, said, "Dear Lord, go with the gambling man . . . not forgetting the gambling woman," the little church's eerie silence was shattered by the loud-talking voice of one of my father's friends (Ben Fisher, rest his soul), whom the congregation "overheard" saying, "Got *you* that time, Gates, got *you* that time, Newtsy!" My father and one of our neighbors, Miss Newtsy, had been Signified upon.[78]

Mitchell-Kernan presents several examples of Signifyin(g) that elaborate on its subtypes.[79] Her conclusion is crucial to the place of her research in the literature on Signification. *"Signifying,"* she declares as conclusion, "does not . . . always have negative valuations attached to it; it is clearly thought of as a kind of art—a clever way of conveying messages."[80] A literary critic might call this troping, an interpretation or mis-taking of meaning, to paraphrase Harold Bloom, because, as Mitchell-Kernan maintains, *"signifying . . .* alludes to and implies things which are never made explicit."[81] Let me cite two brief examples. In the first, "Grace" introduces the exchange by defining its context:

> (After I had my little boy, I swore I was not having any more babies. I thought four kids was a nice-sized family. But it didn't turn out that way. I was a little bit disgusted and didn't tell anybody when I discovered I was pregnant. My sister came over one day and I had started to show by that time.) . . .
>
> Rochelle: Girl, you sure do need to join the Metrecal for lunch bunch.
>
> Grace: (non-committally) Yes, I guess I am putting on a little weight.
>
> Rochelle: Now look here, girl, we both standing here soaking wet and you still trying to tell me it ain't raining.[82]

This form of Signifyin(g) is obviously a long way from the sort usually defined by scholars. One final example of the amusing, troping exchange follows, again cited by Mitchell-Kernan:

> I: Man, when you gon pay me my five dollars?
>
> II: Soon as I get it.
>
> I: (to audience) Anybody want to buy a five dollar nigger? I got one to sell.
>
> II: Man, if I gave you your five dollars, you wouldn't have nothing to signify about.
>
> I: Nigger, long as you don't change, I'll always have me a subject.[83]

This sort of exchange is common in the black community and represents Signifyin(g) at its more evolved levels than the more obvious examples (characterized by confrontation and insult) discussed by linguists other than Mitchell-Kernan.

The highly evolved form of Signifyin(g) that H. Rap Brown defines and that Ralph Ellison's anecdote about Hazel Harrison epitomizes is represented in a wonderful anecdote that Mitchell-Kernan narrates. This tale bears repeating to demonstrate how black adults teach their children to "hold a conversation":

> At the age of seven or eight I encountered what I believe was a version of the tale of the "Signifying Monkey." In this story a monkey reports to a lion that an elephant has been maligning the lion and his family. This stirs the lion into attempting to impose sanctions against the elephant. A battle ensues in which the elephant is victor and the lion returns extremely chafed at the monkey. In this instance, the recounting of this story is a case of signifying for directive purposes. I was sitting on the stoop of a neighbor who was telling me about his adventures as a big game hunter in Africa, a favorite tall-tale topic, unrecognized by me as tall-tale at the time. A neighboring woman called to me from her porch and asked me to go to the store for her. I refused, saying that my mother had told me not to, a lie which Mr. Waters recognized and asked me about. Rather than simply saying I wanted to listen to his stories, I replied that I had refused to go because I hated the woman. Being pressured for a reason for my dislike, and sensing Mr. Water's disapproval, I countered with another lie, "I hate her because she say you were lazy," attempting, I suppose, to regain his favor by arousing ire toward someone else. Although I had heard someone say that he was lazy, it had not been this woman. He explained to me that he was not lazy and that he didn't work because he had been laid-off from his job and couldn't find work elsewhere, and that if the lady had said what I reported, she had not done so out of meanness but because she didn't understand. Guilt-ridden, I went to fetch the can of Milnot milk. Upon returning, the tale of the "Signifying Monkey" was told to me, a censored prose version in which the monkey is rather brutally beaten by the lion after having suffered a similar fate in the hands of the elephant. I liked the story very much and righteously approved of its ending, not realizing at the time that he was *signifying* at me. Mr. Waters reacted to my response with a great deal of amusement. It was several days later in the context of re-telling the tale to another child that I understood its timely telling. My apology and admission of lying were met by affectionate humor, and I was told that I was finally getting to the age where I could "hold a conversation," i.e., understand and appreciate implications.[84]

Black people call this kind of lesson "schooling," and this label denotes its function. The child must learn to hold a conversation. We cannot but recall Richard Lanham's ideal presentation of rhetorical training and conclude that what Mr. Waters says to the child, Claudia, is analogous to an adult teacher of rhetoric attempting to show his pupils how to employ the tropes that they have memorized in an act of communication and its interpretation. This subtle process of instruction in the levels of Signification is related to, but far removed from, adolescent males insulting each other with the Signifying Monkey tales. The language of Signifyin(g), in other words, is a strategy of black figurative language use.

I have been drawing a distinction between the ritual of Signifyin(g), epitomized in the Monkey tales, and the language of Signifyin(g), which is the vernacular term for the figurative use of language. These terms correspond to what Mitchell-Kernan calls "third-party signifying" and "metaphorical signifying." Mitchell-Kernan defines their distinction as follows:

> In the metaphorical type of *signifying,* the speaker attempts to transmit his message indirectly and it is only by virtue of the hearers defining the utterance as *signifying* that the speaker's intent (to convey a particular message) is realized. In third-party signifying, the speaker may realize his aim only when the converse is true, that is, if the addressee fails to recognize the speech act as *signifying.* In [the Signifying Monkey toast] the monkey succeeds in goading the lion into a rash act because the lion does not define the monkey's message as *signifying.*[85]

In other words, these two dominant modes of Signification function conversely, another sign of the maturation process demanded to move, as it were, from the repetition of tropes to their application.

The Monkey tales inscribe a dictum about interpretation, whereas the language of Signifyin(g) addresses the nature and application of rhetoric. The import of the Monkey tales for the interpretation of literature is that the Monkey dethrones the Lion only because the Lion cannot read the nature of his discourse. As Mitchell-Kernan argues cogently, "There seems something of symbolic relevance from the perspective of language in this poem. The monkey and lion do not speak the same language; the lion is not able to interpret the monkey's use of language, he is an outsider, un-hip, in a word." In other words, the Monkey speaks figuratively, while the Lion reads his discourse literally. For his act of misinterpretation, he suffers grave consequences. This valorization of the figurative is perhaps the most important moral of these poems, although the Monkey's mastery of figuration has made him one of the canonical heroes in the Afro-American mythic tradition, a point underscored by Mitchell-Kernan.[86]

Mitchell-Kernan's summary of the defining characteristics of "Signifying as a Form of Verbal Art" helps to clarify this most difficult, and elusive, mode of rhetoric. We can outline these characteristics for convenience. The most important defining features of Signifyin(g) are "indirect intent" and "metaphorical reference." This aspect of indirection is a formal device, and "appears to be almost purely stylistic"; moreover, "its art characteristics remain in the forefront." Signifyin(g), in other words, turns upon the foregrounding of the Signifier. By "indirection" Mitchell-Kernan means

> that the correct semantic (referential interpretation) or signification of the utterance cannot be arrived at by a consideration of the dictionary

meaning of the lexical items involved and the syntactic rules for their combination alone. The apparent significance of the message differs from its real significance. *The apparent meaning of the sentence signifies its actual meaning.*[87]

The relationship between latent and manifest meaning is a curious one, as determined by the formal properties of the Signifyin(g) utterance. In one of several ways, manifest meaning directs attention away from itself to another, latent level of meaning. We might compare this relationship to that which obtains between the two parts of a metaphor, tenor (the inner meaning) and vehicle (the outer meaning).

Signifyin(g), according to Mitchell-Kernan, operates so delightfully because "apparent meaning serves as a key which directs hearers to some shared knowledge, attitudes, and values or signals that reference must be produced metaphorically." The decoding of the figurative, she continues, depends "upon shared knowledge . . . and this shared knowledge operates on two levels." One of these two levels is that the speaker and his audience realize that *"signifying* is occurring and that the dictionary-syntactical meaning of the utterance is to be ignored." In addition, a silent second text, as it were, which corresponds rightly to what Mitchell-Kernan is calling "shared knowledge," must be brought to bear upon the manifest content of the speech act and "employed in the reinterpretation of the utterance." Indeed, this element is of the utmost importance in the esthetics of Signifyin(g), for "it is the cleverness used in directing the attention of the hearer and audience to this shared knowledge upon which a speaker's artistic talent is judged." Signifyin(g), in other words, depends on the success of the signifier at invoking an absent meaning ambiguously "present" in a carefully wrought statement.[88]

As I have attempted to show, there is much confusion and disagreement among linguists about the names and functions of the classical black tropes. While the specific terminology may vary from scholar to scholar, city to city, or generation to generation, however, the rhetorical functions of these tropes remain consistent. It is a fairly straightforward exercise to compare the black slave tropes to the master tropes identified by Vico, Nietzsche, Burke, and Bloom, and to map a black speech act, such as Signifyin(g), into its component Western tropes. Chart 4 is intended to Signify upon Harold Bloom's "map of misprision."[89] I echo the essence of this map here, adding columns that list the Yoruba and Afro-American tropes that correspond to their Western counterparts.

We can, furthermore, chart our own map, in which we graph the separate lines of a "Signifyin(g) Riff," as follows:[90]

Slave Trope of Tropes, Signifyin(g)

Your mama's a man	(metaphor)
Your daddy's one too	(irony)
They live in a tin can	(metonymy)
That smells like a zoo	(synecdoche)

Chart 4. The Figures of Signification

Rhetorical Trope	Bloom's Revisionary Ratio	Afro-American Signifyin(g) Trope	Classical Yoruba	Lexically Borrowed Yoruba
Irony	Clinamen	Signifyin(g) ("Nigger business" in the West Indies)	Ríràn (èràn)	Àìróni
Synecdoche	Tessera	Calling out of one's name		Mẹ̀tónimi
Metonymy	Kenosis			
Hyperbole, litotes	Daemonization	Stylin' or woofing ("Flash" in the West Indies)	Ìhàlè (Ẹ̀pón)	
Metaphor	Askesis	Naming	Àfiwé (elétòó) / Àfiwé gaan	Métàfò (indirect "naming")* / Símílì (direct "naming")*
Metalepsis	Apophrades	Capping	Afíkún; Àjámọ́; Èni	

* N.B. "Naming" is an especially rich trope in Yoruba. Positive naming is called *Oríkì*, while negative naming is called *Inagije*. Naming is also an especially luxurious (if potentially volatile) trope in the Afro-American vernacular tradition. "Naming" someone and "Calling [someone] Out of [his] name" are among the most commonly used tropes in Afro-American vernacular discourse. Scores of proverbs and epigrams in the black tradition turn upon figures for naming.

87

The fact that the street rhymes of blacks and their received rhetorical tropes configure into the categories of classical Western rhetoric should come as no surprise. Indeed, this aspect of black language use recalls Montaigne's statement, in "Of the Vanity of Words," that "When you hear people talk about metonymy, metaphor, allegory, and other such names in grammar, doesn't it seem that they mean some rare and exotic form of language?" Rather, Montaigne concludes, "They are terms that apply to the babble of your chambermaid."[91] We can add that these terms also apply to the rapping of black kids on street corners, who recite and thereby preserve the classical black rhetorical structures.

Signification is a complex rhetorical device that has elicited various, even contradictory, definitions from linguists, as should be apparent from this summary of its various definitions. While many of its manifestations and possibilities are figured in the tales of the Signifying Monkey, most people who Signify do not engage in the narration of these tales. Rather, the Monkey tales stand as the canonical poems from which what I am calling the language of Signifyin(g) extends. The degree to which the figure of the Monkey is anthropologically related to the figure of the Pan-African trickster, Esu-Elegbara, shall most probably remain a matter of speculation.

Nevertheless, the two figures are related as functional equivalents because each in its own way stands as a moment of consciousness of black formal language use, of rhetorical structures and their appropriate modes of interpretation. As I have argued, both figures connote what we might think of as the writing implicit in an oral literature, and both figures function as repositories for a tradition's declarations about how and why formal literary language departs from ordinary language use. The metaphor of a double-voiced Esu-Elegbara corresponds to the double-voiced nature of the Signifyin(g) utterance. When one text Signifies upon another text, by tropological revision or repetition and difference, the double-voiced utterance allows us to chart discrete formal relationships in Afro-American literary history. Signifyin(g), then, is a metaphor for textual revision.

3

Figures of Signification

He was unwrapping the object now and I watched his old man's hands.

"I'd like to pass it on to you, son. There," he said, handing it to me. "Funny thing to give somebody, but I think it's got a heap of signifying wrapped up in it and it might help you remember what we're really fighting against. I don't think of it in terms of but two words, *yes* and *no;* but it signifies a heap more . . ."

I saw him place his hand on the desk. "Brother," he said, calling me "Brother" for the first time, "I want you to take it. I guess it's a kind of luck piece. Anyway, it's the one I filed to get away."

Ralph Ellison, *Invisible Man*

There is in effect no signifying chain that does not have, as if attached to the punctuation of each of its units, a whole articulation of relevant contexts suspended "vertically," as it were, from that point.

Jacques Lacan

Jacques Lacan's elaboration upon the signifier's function produces more than a simple tilting within the sign, since as soon as the question is one of signification, the relevant unit is no longer the sign itself (for example, the word in the dictionary), but the signifying chain, which generates a meaning effect at the moment when it turns back upon itself, its end allowing the retroactive interpretation of its beginning.

Oswald Ducrot and Tzvetan Todorov

The end is the beginning and lies far ahead.
Ralph Ellison, *Invisible Man*

I

How does Signifyin(g) manifest itself in Afro-American literature? This colorful, often amusing trope occurs in black texts as explicit theme, as implicit rhetorical strategy, and as a principle of literary history. Before elab-

89

orating on these modes of Signification, however, it is useful to discuss the different orders of meaning created by their use in black texts. Perhaps in this way, rather abstract theoretical definitions can be more clearly exemplified. This chapter presents a number of illustrative examples of Signifyin(g) in its several forms, then concludes by outlining selective examples of black intertextual relations.

Perhaps one of the earliest examples of Signifyin(g) as irony is to be found in the poetry of "el Negro," Juan Latino, a sixteenth-century neo-Latin poet who published three books of poems at Granada between 1573 and 1585.[1] In the opening section of Latino's most accomplished poem, the *Austriad,* Latino beseeches of King Philip the right to sing the praises of the king's brother, Don Juan, hero of the Battle of Lepanto. One matter that could generate objections against the right of this poet to commemorate this crucial historical event, Latino suggests, is his African heritage:

> On bended knees, invincible Philip, he [the poet] begs you that he may be the singer of your brother. For if the wars of Austria bring fame to the poet, in view of the fact that he, a black, made a Phoenix of Austria . . . Austria will be a portent to the earth.[2]

Why shall Austria be a portent to the earth? Precisely because the one chosen to represent this signal event in verse is a benighted black slave:

> The prodigious fame of the poet will disturb men reading these monuments in your records. The East produced him and the blessed kings of the Arabians, whom she gave to God as the first fruits of the people.[3]

Then Juan Latino Signifies upon his would-be detractors, who equate blackness with evil or stupidity:

> For if our black face, oh king, is displeasing to your ministers, the white face is not pleasing to the men of Ethiopia. There, he who, white, visits the East is held in little esteem. The leaders are black, oh king, and the ruddy color is present.[4]

Latino is Signifyin(g) in this passage because he has mounted a rhetorical self-defense by defending the integrity of his black self through a clever inversion of the context in which societies define beauty. Only his wit prevents his statement from being insolent; Philip, after all, is king. This subtle and witty use of irony is among the most common forms of Signifyin(g).

Signifyin(g), of course, is a principle of language use and is not in any way the exclusive province of black people, although blacks named the term and invented its rituals. One early-nineteenth-century example, published as a broadside in New York in 1828, is entitled "Dreadful Riot on Negro Hill" and is a Signification as parody of Phillis Wheatley's seven known letters to her black friend, Arbour Tanner of Newport, Rhode Island, dated between 1772 and 1779.[5]

The anonymously published "letter" is dated "Bosson, Uly 32, 18015" and is subtitled "Copy of an intercepted Letter from Phillis to her Sister in the Country, describing the late Riot on Negro Hill." It consists of two sen-

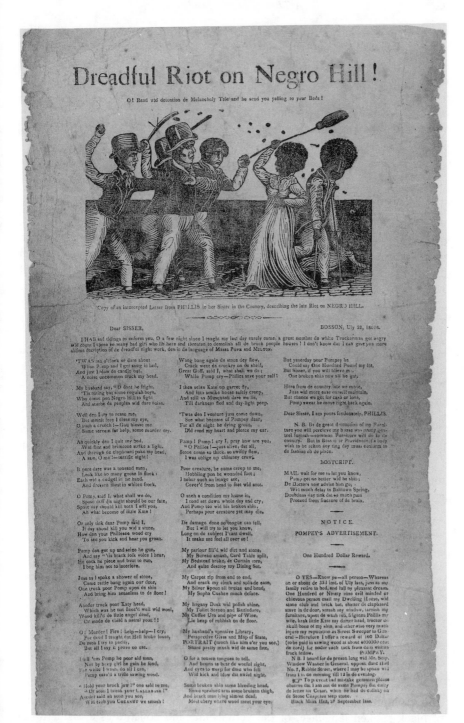

Figure 12. "Dreadful Riot on Negro Hill." *From the collection of American Literature, Beinecke Rare Book and Manuscript Library, Yale University.*

91

tences that introduce a twenty-eight-stanza poem, ostensibly written after the styles of Pope and Milton, two of Wheatley's principal influences. The second sentence reads, "I don't know dat I can give you more sublime description of de dreadful night work, den in de language of *Massa Pope* and *Milton*." The letter and its verse are, in fact, written in dialect, making this document one of the earliest extended examples of the representation of black speech in verse. The following stanza is typical:

> De damage done no tongue can tell,
> But I will try to let you know,
> Long on de subject I cant dwell,
> It make me feel all over so!

What is curious about this broadside is that its parody turns upon both a denigrating mockery of black dialect and an intimate familiarity with the model of the parody. The latter is an aspect of all successful parody. Scholars do not believe that Wheatley's letters to Arbour Tanner were published until 1863–64, thereby raising a host of fascinating questions about how someone else could have been so remarkably familiar with the originals.[6] Despite this quandary, the broadside is a salient example of Signifyin(g) and suggests that as early as 1828 what we might think of as the signifying black difference—Afro-American spoken vernacular discourse—could be the object and the mechanism of parody. The black English vernacular, as early as this, was a sign of black difference, blackness of the tongue. It is not surprising that the vernacular is the source from which black theory springs. The broadside is reproduced in Figure 12.

Still another Signifyin(g) parody based on the representation of dialect is a broadside published at London in 1846, entitled "A Black Lecture on Language."[7] (See Figure 13.) This, again, Signifies upon the supposed contours of the black vernacular. The broadside is headed by the following epigraph:

> Niggars all dat got disarning [discerning],
> Listen to de woice ob larning.
> While me tell, all is my wont,
> What me know—(*Aside*)—and what me dont.

The lecture's first sentence reads,

> Me tend to dress my scorce to you dis nite on de all imported subject of Language, an de warious tongues ob differn nations and niggars, libbin and dead, known and unknown: an in so doing me shant stan shilly shally bout preface to de subject, but run bang at him at once like mad bull at "dam haystack."

This "lecture on language" is, we learn, a discourse on the representation of black spoken language, of the vernacular, and constitutes a Signifyin(g) parody in which the subject of critique is not an antecedent text but a broader mode of spoken discourse itself. This lecture is numbered 6 in a series of

A BLACK LECTURE ON LANGUAGE.

NIGGARS ALL DAT GOT DISARNING,   WHILE ME TELL, AS IS MY WONT,
LISTEN TO DE WOICE OB LARNING.   WHAT ME KNOW—(*Aside*)—AND WHAT ME DONT.

BELOBED BLACK BRODEREN.—Me tend to dress my scorce to you dis nite on de all imported subject ob Language, an de warious tongues ob differn Nations and Niggars, libbin an dead, known and unknown: an in so doing me shant stan shilly shally bout preface to de subject, but run bang at him at once like mad bull at "dam haystack."

Now to prewent confusion, my Frens, me shall fus mention de names ob de differen Tongues, an den de most poplar words in each ob dem. And de fus me cum to is de "Polite" Tongue; dis is spoke by Gemlem at Courts, an is allways saying what him no mean, an meanin deblish sight more dan him say; den der is de Bull's Tongue, wish is a bullying Tongue; den der is de Moder Tongue, wish moder's use when dey flog lilly Niggars till dey sing out "me gentle Moder, dear;" den der is de Sheep's Tongue, wish belong to pipple dat say, Bah! when dey dont belebe you; den der is de Lamb's Tongue, which belong to de Ladies, an is de tongue Shaksper say can wheedle wid de Debil (an me hab no doubt dey will hab de chance ob doing so)—dese Lambs also calld *Bells* on account ob der clappers; an if dey Ladies ob Color, ob cours dey are calld "Lamb Black." In short, my Frens, der so many Tongues, dat mine quite tired countin dem, so me shall proceed to de words, and de fus me cum to is de word "Funk;" dis, my Frens, is German, but is not *foreign* to de subject: "Funk" is de present tense, "Funked" is de imperfect tense, and "D——Funked" de past: dis las word belong to de *dead* language. Now, 'cording to Massa Murry, de word stan dus: I *was* funked, you *wer* funked, he was funked; we wer funked, he or she was funked, dey were funked; so you see my belobed Frens, de dam Niggars were *all* funked togeder. De meanin ob de word Funked is dat you feel half dead, an when you d——Funked, ob cours you quite dead. *Bone em secur em* is de nex word on de liss; dis, my Frens, is Latin, an it mean in English; Prig em an keep em, kase when you bone, den ob course you secure em, an git a bone-us for yonself. Me now cum to de medical word, "*Sal waliatie*." Now, you see, in de Polite Tongue *Sal* volotil would be *Sal* frisky, an in de Wulgar Tongue *Sal* randy; berry well. "Humbug" is a word in de English language an mean like dis: spose you go away dis nite, an no drop some browns in de plate, den you would be de humbug (fus Niggar singular), an me should be humbug-ed. Me shall now splain some words nee in de Law. A "*Mandamus*" is a form ob law wish blige you to be heard on oath, an as de man bliged to swear, ob cours it calld a Man-*dam*-us. De nex word nee in de law is call'd "A rule discharged," and it like dis: you see when der is row in de Court, de Clerk shy de *rule* at de parties, an dat is a rule *discharged*. Me now come to French words, an de fus is "*Pas de deaux*." Now, you see, ducks mean white breeches; an, derfore, Pass de Ducks, mean in English, git me de breeches, but dats de Wulgar Tongue: de Polite Tongue would say, may I trouble you for de "Dont Whisperems." "*Beau*" is nex on de liss: bean mean smart Niggar, dressed in longtail blue, red waistcoat, striped shirt wid big collar up to him eyes, yellar breeches, an white hat—yes, yes, dats a beau, an no mistake. But, my Frens, der is differen sort ob bows, fus der is de *Long* Bow, wish is a tall *beau*, ob course; den der is de *Cross* Bow, wish is de *beau* berry cross; den der is de *Rain* Bow, wish is de same *beau* coched in de rain. Now you see de chap wid de long bow is call de archer, but metink de *belle* is de *archer* ob de two. *Belle* is de French for *Gal*, an when you marry de gal, ob course you *ring* de bell; and when you look at a *belle*, it calld *La Belle Vue*. Me shall now proceed to splain some ob de words common in de Wulgar Tongue: an lookin ober de notes me find de following words: "Kicksies," "Crab-shells," "Shakers," "Whipes," "Toggery," also, "Lagged," "Scragged," &c. Now de fus word me cant *express*, kase it inexpressibles; de nex word "Crab-shells" mean shoes, kase old pipple dat are close an pinchin are calld crabbed. "Shakers" mean certain under garments wish belong to de masculin an feminin gender, an wish me no doubt dose ob my hearers who hab sich luxories will understan what me mean, an dose dat dont, why it all *dickey* wid dem. De nex word is "Whipes," an it means hankerchers; so when anybody say dey will gib you a whipe, ob course you wery much bliged to dem. "Toggery," my Frens is de cloths, an is deribed from de dress worn by de Roman Tribunes, an call'd a "Toga," hence Toggery. "Lagged," mean when de Government kindly find you employment *abroad*, an you are *transported* at de idea. "Scragged," my Frens, is when you elewated above de common heard, an doe you can't cast out de mote, yet you can plainly perceib de *beam* an are ober persuaded to take a *drop* too much—dis is call'd by commercial men, entering into de *noose line*, berry good. Me tink me can't close de discorce bettar dan by gibbin you a lesson from Murry's Gramer: I did gib, you did gib, we did gib, he or she did gib, dey did gib; I must pay, you must pay, he or she must pay, dey must pay; so you see, my Frens, you *all must pay*.

To pay, my Frens, you'r willing, all I trust,
Come, no dam ugly mugs, but drop de dust.

LONDON: PUBLISHED AT FOLLIT'S, CITY REPOSITORY OF ARTS, AND CHEAP PICTURE FRAME MANUFACTORY, 63, FLEET STREET.

Figure 13. "A Black Lecture on Language." *Courtesy of the Print Collection, Lewis Walpole Library, Yale University.*

93

"Follit's Black Lectures," which includes other dialect representations entitled "A Black Lecture on Phrenology" (no. 1; reproduced here as Figure
14), "A Black Lecture on the Corn Laws" (no. 5), "A Black Lecture on
the Currency Question" (no. 8), "A Black Lecture on Steam" (no. 9), and
"A Black Lecture on the Invasion of Great Britain" (no. 11), in a series
that no doubt included others.[8]

If blacks were the subject of this sort of racist Signifyin(g) parody, they
also were quite capable of establishing the necessary distance between themselves and their condition to Signify upon white racism through parody. One
such parody was written by "Ethiop," a black person who frequently published essays in black periodicals, such as *Frederick Douglass' Paper,* in the
1850s. Ethiop, in an essay entitled "What Shall We Do with the White People?" is Signifyin(g) upon the genre of essays that came in the twentieth century to be called "What Shall We Do with the Negro" or simply "The Negro
Problem."[9] While this sort of essay assumed several forms in the eighteenth
and nineteenth centuries, it generally turned on the so-called absence of black
progress in the mastery of formal letters, euphemistically called the arts and
sciences. David Hume's essay "Of National Characters" is an excellent example of this genre.[10] Ethiop's is a Signifyin(g) revision of the countergenre,
as the conclusion to his essay makes clear:

> We give them [white people] also high credit for their material progress.
> Who knows, but that some day, when, after they shall have fulfilled their
> mission, carried arts and sciences to their highest point, they will make
> way for a milder and more genial race, or become so blended in it, as to
> lose their own peculiar and objectionable characteristics? In any case, in
> view of the existing state of things around us, let our constant thought
> be, *what for the best good of all shall we do with the White people?*[11]

This sort of Signifyin(g) as parody is commonly found in the black literary
tradition. Because both parody and pastiche comprise two central aspects of
Signifyin(g) as motivated and unmotivated revision, I shall return to a fuller
discussion of repetition and revision after introducing explicit examples of
Signifyin(g) as subject matter in Afro-American texts.

The representation of Signifyin(g) in Afro-American literature as a ritual
speech act is a subject that has been treated by linguist Geneva Smitherman
in *Talkin and Testifyin.*[12] For Smitherman, Signifyin(g) is a black "mode of
discourse" that is a synonym of "dropping lugs; joanin; capping; [and] sounding."[13] For her, Signification has the following eight characteristics:

1. indirection, circumlocution
2. metaphorical-imagistic (but images rooted in the everyday, real world)
3. humorous, ironic
4. rhythmic fluency and sound
5. teachy but not preachy
6. directed at person or persons usually present in the situational context
7. punning, play on words
8. introduction of the semantically or logically unexpected.[14]

"A BLACK LECTURE ON PHRENOLOGY"

FRENS, AN FELLOW NIGGERS, LEND ME YOUR EARS.---

SHAKEMSPER.

"My Frens" you dissemble here dis nite for hear lectar on Nalagy—nalagy, my frens, is de art ob telling de fief niggar from de homes niggar, de fool niggar from de wisdom niggar, de grog niggar from de water niggar ; an how dat done I wonder ? eh ! why I tell you, by de bumps on him "dam tick" skull—on dis side you may obserb I hab cast ob de head ob a genelman ob color, an on de oder side I hab cast ob de head ob a common white feller—berry well, here. my fren, I tink it rite to obserb, dat all great an clebber men ob ebery nation are BLACK ; fuss der was Aggamemom an de Duke ob Wellington, bof black ; one all ober, an de oder only black heart ; den der was Nerer de fiddler, Napoleon de butcher, and Crumwell de brewer, all berry black indeed ; den der was Robispir, Marat, Billy Waters, "George de Forf," an de debil, all black ; but de LAST genelman not so black as de rest. Dus you see, my frens, dat all great pipple are black ; black-legs, black-hearts, and black-guards ; and me furder wish to obserb dat in my humel obinion dat EBERY BODY was black once, ob course I lude to de DARK ages, An now for de subject : (as de dockor say to de body snatcher), he ! he ! he ! Nalagy mean, my frens (if it mean any thing), bumps, and bumps mean nalagy, I tink dat berry clear. Dis is de head ob Ceasar Antonia Pompey Agamemom—an dis de head ob a "dam white rascal," you see, my frens, dat clebber man an dam rascal is de same ting, when dey bof white ; but when one white and de oder black "dat quite anoder pair ob shoes." Nalagy treats ob de head and is derfor a NOBBY study ; de head is dewilded into differen parts call "organs," (not wat dey grind about de street, kase de PEEF do all girndin bisness demselves) der is great many organ in de head, but me can't say how many, kase when pipple get into row dey somtims get nock on de scouse and dat break one organ in two or free—so you see, my frens, dat de number ob organs is rader uncertin. When de flesh is off de head it called "skull," an where der is great mob ob sculls dey call it de "SCULLERY," an when two skulls bof alike it called "A SCULLER'S MATCH." Now, my frens, I shall splain de use ob de differen organs, fus me come to de organ ob smell, dis organ sometimes called de smeller, an wat make pipple SMELL A RAT, it also called de sneezar, de snuff-box, an de conk (but dey only PROFESSIONAL names). I nex come to de organ ob sight, which make us see "sight ob tings" dis also called de "blinkers," de "goggles," de "peppers," &c. De organ ob "NUMBERS" is nex, and numbers bein in de skull is de reason dey call pipple "num-skull," dat short for number skull"—besides

"Numbers mean figgars,
And dam lot ob niggars."

but ob all numbers nebber forget "number ONE," der is also de organ ob COLOR, but dis not to be found in BLACK pipple, kase black NO COLOR, nor in white kase dey hab no color ; den der is de bumb ob "BENEBOLENCE," which mean you no go away widout drop someting in de plate, dat colled actib benebolence ; but der is another call "passib" benebolence, which mean telling lies behind pipples back—kicking der corns under de table, and pinching dem when nobody see you, dat called passib benebolence ; furder on me notice de organ ob "DRAWING," drawing, my frens, mean "drawing" water, drawing a truck, drawing teef, and sometims drawing it mild. Me now come to de organ ob "PERSPECTIB," perspectib make pipple see ting long way off (sometims out ob sight), some pipple grow bettar (in perspectib), pay der debts in perspectib, and me see large collection ob money dis nite (in perspectib). Nex is de organ of "COMBATIBNESS," an is de reason make niggars punch one an oders head, and when it berry large it called d——wolloped ; me now come to de organ ob "CONKORD," dis is suppose by some pipple to mean music an harmony—no sich ting, "CONK"-ORD treats ob de conk, and eberybody NOSE dat's not music ; me find also de organ ob "FORM," form mean "berry long skull," an it also mean de man ob color's head, dat's form wid a wengeance ! Observe de smove an finely pencilled brow ; de sof and languishing eye, de graceful outline ob de nose, de "delicately chissel lips" forming altogeder dat lubly expression de french call JINNY squeek aw, among de many organs der some me no unerstand, one ob which is call "AMITIBNESS," but me spose Amitibness an "Costibness" is de same ting ; me now come to de organ ob "TIME ;" time, my frens, "dam old rascal" he draw de face into wrinkles, and "deface it," he pull out black hair an shove in de grey ; time also berry big fief, he rob us ob healf, ob strength an enjoyment, he pull down buildings, kills pipple an shub em into holes in de ground ; he also great drunkard, kase he always hab a glass in him hand. Der is also anoder organ called "MEMORY," some pipple hab berry bad memory, me know some niggars when dey git new coat forget der frens ; dat shocking bad memory—some forget der debts, acts ob kindness, an den forget dem selves, but me hope no one will forget de COLLECTION at de door. Der is anoder organ call "TRUFT," but ME NO NOTING ABOUT DAT, so me shall finis de lectar in de words ob de poet PUNCH, "hur ray de debil's dead, its all ober. Here, "Sambo," you dam jiggerry toe niggar look after de BROWNS kase de BLACKS are bolting,

LONDON : FOLLIT'S "CITY REPOSITORY OF ARTS," SPORTING GALLERY AND CHEAP PICTURE FRAME MANUFACTORY
65, FLEET STREET, CORNER OF BOUVERIE STREET.

Figure 14. "A Black Lecture on Phrenology." *Courtesy of the Print Collection, Lewis Walpole Library, Yale University.*

Signifyin(g), for Smitherman, as a mode of discourse can be employed for insult, "to make a point," or "just for fun."

The examples Smitherman has located in Afro-American literature illustrate its configurations as "a witty one-liner, a series of loosely related statements, or a cohesive discourse on one point."[15] The following passage from Richard Wright's novel *Lawd Today* illustrates Signifyin(g) in a series of parallel statements:

> "You's one down, *redoubled*!" boomed Slim, marking down the score.
> "Easy's taking candy from a baby!" laughed Al.
> "Smoother'n velvet!" laughed Slim rearing back in his seat and blowing smoke to the ceiling.
> "Like rolling off a log!" sang Al, shuffling the cards.
> "Like sliding down a greasy pole!"
> "Like snapping your fingers!"
> "Like spitting!"
> "Like falling in love with a high yellow!"[16]

This Signifyin(g) exchange exemplifies five of Smitherman's eight characteristics, including metaphor, humor, rhythmic fluency, direction at speakers engaged in the ritual, and verbal plays on the logically unexpected.[17]

Smitherman's next example, also from *Lawd Today,* exemplifies Signifyin(g) as a "one-liner":

> "Let's go," said Slim.
> "One No trump," said Al.
> "I ain't got a Gawddamn thing," whined Jake, squirming in his chair.
> "Don't confess to me!" said Slim haughtily. "I ain't no priest!"[18]

This exchange includes three of the eight aspects of Signification, including humor, plays on the semantically and logically unexpected, and direction at the person present.

The following passage, taken from Chester Himes's novel *Hot Day, Hot Night,* exemplifies all eight of Smitherman's markers of Signification. The central characters of the novel, Coffin Ed and Grave Digger, two black detectives who work in Harlem, are responding to their white supervisor about the origins of a recent riot:

> "I take it you've discovered who started the riot," Anderson said.
> "We knew who he was all along," Grave Digger said.
> "It's just nothing we can do to him," Coffin Ed echoed.
> "Why not, for God's sake?"
> "He's dead," Coffin Ed said.
> "Who?"
> "Lincoln," Grave Digger said.
> "He hadn't ought to have freed us if he didn't want to make provisions to feed us," Coffin Ed said. "Anyone could have told him that."[19]

Anderson, attempting to defend himself against his colleagues' attack, tries to grant them a part of their argument, only to be Signified upon once again:

"All right, all right, lots of us have wondered what he might have thought of the consequences," Anderson admitted. "But it's too late to charge him now."

"Couldn't have convicted him anyway," Grave Digger said.

"All he'd have to do would be to plead good intentions," Coffin Ed elaborated. "Never was a white man convicted as long as he plead good intentions."

"All right, all right, who's the culprit this night, here, in Harlem? Who's inciting these people to this senseless anarchy?"

"Skin," Grave Digger said.[20]

This exchange is an example of extended Signification and depends for its force on the multiple irony implicit in the metaphor of skin.

A final example of extended Signifyin(g) in black literature is taken from the climax of the passage cited above from Wright's *Lawd Today*. Although this novel was published posthumously in 1963, Michel Fabre tells us that its final version "is fairly close to" the draft that Wright completed in 1936.[21] The passage bears repeating not only because it reveals how important Wright felt the representation of the black vernacular to be, but also because in it is found one of the earliest uses of the term *signifying,* ostensibly one year after Zora Neale Hurston had used it in her anthropological collection, *Mules and Men.*[22]

"So you got a new shirt, hunh, Al?" asked Jake quietly, tentatively, sucking his teeth and throwing his leg over the arm of the chair.

Al modestly stroked the collar of his shirt with his fingers.

"Yeah, I picked it up yesterday."

"Where you steal it from?"

"Steal it? Nigger, you can't steal shirts like this!"

"You didn't buy it!"

"How come I didn't? Ain't I got money?" said Al. He was sitting upright, his round black face flushed with mock indignation.

"What did you ever buy?" asked Jake.

Al rose, rammed his hands deep into his pockets, and stood in front of Jake.

"You go into Marshall Field's and steal a shirt! It takes kale to wear clothes like this!"

"Marshall Field's?"

"Yeah. Marshall Field's!"

"The closest you ever got to Marshall Field's was the show window," said Jake.

"That's a Gawddamn lie!" said Al.

Slim and Bob listened silently, hoping for a bout of the dozens between the two.

"Whoever heard of a nigger going into Marshall Field's and buying a green shirt?" asked Jake, as though to himself.

"Aw, nigger, quit signifying! Go buy *you* a shirt!"

"I don't need no shirts. I got aplenty!"

"This nigger setting here wearing his purple rag around his throat talking about he's got aplenty shirts. Somebody wake 'im up!"

Slim and Bob laughed.

"I can change *five* shirts to your *one*," boasted Jake.

"The onliest way you can do that is to pull off the one you has on now and put it on five times," said Al.

Slim and Bob laughed again.

"Listen, nigger," said Jake. "I was wearing shirts when you was going around naked in Miss'sippi!"

Slim and Bob opened their mouths wide and slumped deep into their seats.

"Hunh, hunh," said Al. "That was the time when you was wearing your hair wrapped with white strings, wasn't it?"

"White strings? Aw, Jake. . . . Hehehe!" Bob could not finish, the idea tickled him so.

"Yeah," said Jake. "When I was wearing them white strings on my hair old Colonel James was sucking at your ma's tits, wasn't he?"

"Jeesus," moaned Slim, pressing his handerchief hard against his mouth to keep from coughing. "I told a piece of iron that once and it turned *redhot*. Now, what would a poor *meat* man do?"

Al glowered and fingered his cigarette nervously.

"Nigger," Al said slowly, so that the full force of his words would not be missed, "when old Colonel James was sucking at my ma's tits I saw your little baby brother across the street watching with slobber in his mouth. . . ."

Slim and Bob rolled on the sofa and held their stomachs. Jake stiffened, crossed his legs, and gazed out of the window.

"Yeah," he said slowly, "I remembers when my little baby brother was watching with slobber in his mouth, your old grandma was out in the privy crying 'cause she couldn't find a corncob. . . ."

Slim and Bob groaned and stomped their feet.

"Yeah," said Al, retaliating with narrowed eyes. "When my old grandma was crying for that corncob, your old aunt Lucy was round back of the barn with old Colonel James' old man, and she was saying something like this: 'Yyyyou kknow . . . Mmmister Cccolonel . . . I jjjust ddon't like to ssssell . . . my ssstuff. . . . I jjjust lloves to gggive . . . iit away. . . .' "

Slim and Bob embraced each other and howled.

"Yeah," said Jake. "I remembers when old aunt Lucy got through she looked around and saw your old aunt Mary there watching with her finger stuck in her puss. And old aunt Lucy said, 'Mary, go home and wash your bloomers!' "

Slim and Bob beat the floor with their fists.

Al curled his lips and shot back:

"Hunh, hunh, yeah! And when my old aunt Mary was washing out her bloomers the hot smell of them soapsuds rose up and went out over the lonesome graveyard and your old greatgreatgreat grandma turned over in her grave and said: 'Lawd, I sure thank Thee for the smell of them pork chops You's cooking up in Heaven. . . .' "

Slim grabbed Bob and they screamed.

"Yeah," drawled Jake, determined not to be outdone, "when my old greatgreat*great* grandma was smelling them pork chops, your poor old

greatgreatgreatgreat grandma was a Zulu queen in Africa. She was setting at the table and she said to the waiter: 'Say waiter, be sure and fetch
me some of them missionary chitterlings . . .' "

"Mmmm . . . miss . . . missionary chitterlings?" asked Slim, stretch-
ing flat on the floor and panting as one about to die.

"Yeah," said Al. "When my greatgreatgreatgreat grandma who was
a Zulu queen got through eating them missionary chitterlings, she wanted
to build a sewer-ditch to take away her crap, so she went out and saw
your poor old greatgreatgreatgreat*great* grandma *sleeping* under a coco-
nut tree with her old mouth wide open. She didn't need to build no sewer-
ditch. . . .' "

"Jeesus!" yelled Slim, closing his eyes and holding his stomach. "I'm
dying!"

Jake screwed up his eyes, bit his lips, and tried hard to think of a return. But, for the life of him, he could not. Al's last image was too
much; it left him blank. Then they all laughed so that they felt weak in
the joints of their bones.[23]

This lengthy passage is relevant to this inquiry into the nature and function of Signifyin(g) because it reveals the close connection between "the
dozens" and Signification. While most linguists, for reasons that remain un-
clear to me, separate these two modes of black discourse, for most black people the two are mutually interchangeable terms, as they seem to have been
for Wright. Smitherman makes a strong argument for the dozens as "a form
of signification, but as a discourse mode [with] rules and rituals of its own."
Accordingly, the dozens "constitutes a kind of subcategory within the signification mode."[24]

The dozens is perhaps the best-known mode of Signification, both because it depends so heavily on humor and because the success of its exchanges turns on insults of one's family members, especially one's mother.
It is enough to say "Your mama" to commence—or to conclude—this ritual
exchange. Ralph Ellison represents a dozens in the following exchange between the protagonist of *Invisible Man* and Brother Jack, a key figure in the
"Brotherhood":

> "His personal responsibility," Brother Jack said.
> "Did you hear that, Brother? Did I hear him correctly?"
> "Where did you get it, Brother," he said. "This is astounding, where
> did you get it?"
> "From your Ma—" I started and caught myself in time.[25]

One of the funniest representations of the dozens, which Smitherman maintains is probably so called because "the original verses involved twelve sex
acts, each stated in such a way as to rhyme with the numbers 1 to 12,"[26] appears in Wright's short story, "Big Boy Leaves Home":

> *Yo mamma don wear no drawers . . .*
> Clearly, the voice rose out of the woods, and died away. Like an
> echo another voice caught it up:
> *As seena when she pulled em off . . .*

Another, shrill, cracking, adolescent:
N she washed 'em in alcohol . . .
Then a quartet of voices blending in harmony, floated high above the tree tops:
N she hung 'em out in the hall . . .
Laughing easily, four black boys came out of the woods into cleared pasture. They walked lollingly in bare feet, beating tangled vines and bushes with long sticks.
"Ah wished Ah knowed some mo lines t tha song."
"Yeah, when yuh gits t where she hangs em out in the hall yuh has t stop."
"Shucks, whut goes wid *hall?*"
"*Call.*"
"*Fall.*"
"*Wall.*"
"*Quall.*"
They threw themselves on the grass, laughing.
"Big Boys?"
"Huh?"
"Yuh know one thing?"
"Whut?"
"Yuh sho is crazy!"
"Crazy?"
"Yeah, uh crazys a bed-bug!"
"Crazy bout whut?"
"Man, whoever hearda *quall?*"
"Yuh said yuh wanted something to go wid *hall*, didn't yuh?"
"Yuh, but whuts a *quall?*"
"Nigger, a *qualls* a *quall.*"
They laughed easily, catching and pulling long green blades of grass with their toes.
"Waal, ef a *qualls* a *quall*, whut IS a *quall?*"
"Oh, Ah know."
"What?"
"Tha old song goes something like this:

> *Yo mama don wear no drawers,*
> *Ah seena when she pulled them off,*
> *N she washed em in alcohol,*
> *N she hung em out in the hall,*
> *N she put em back on her Quall!*"[27]

This is a superb example of paradigmatic (*y*-axis) substitutions determined by phonetic rather than semantic similarity (*hall/quall*).

No doubt the most well-known, and one of the most subtle, representations of the dozens as a mode of discourse that structures a work of literature is that found in Langston Hughes's twelve-part poem, *Ask Your Mama*.[28] Not only does the poem consist of a dozen sections, but it is meant to be read against the traditional black melody of "Hesitation Blues," which is transcribed and printed as a preface to the poem. The poem itself imitates the dozens in its use of witty puns, in its urge toward a narrative (which, in this case, amounts to a twelve-section history of Afro-America, complete with a roll call of cultural heroes), but especially in the frequent repetition of the phrase, "Ask Your Mama." Indeed, that phrase is the repeated figure on which the poem's unity depends. One section of the poem's sixth part, entitled "Horn of Plenty," yields a sense of the whole:

> I MOVED OUT TO LONG ISLAND
> EVEN FARTHER THAN ST. ALBANS
> (WHICH LATELY IS STONE NOWHERE)
> I MOVED OUT EVEN FARTHER FURTHER FARTHER
> ON THE SOUND WAY OFF THE TURNPIKE—
> AND I'M THE ONLY COLORED
>
> GOT THERE! YES, I MADE IT!
> NAME IN THE PAPERS EVERY DAY!
> FAMOUS—THE HARD WAY—
> FROM NOBODY AND NOTHING TO WHERE I AM.
> THEY KNOW ME, TOO, DOWNTOWN,
> ALL ACROSS THE COUNTRY, EUROPE—
> ME WHO USED TO BE NOBODY,
> NOTHING BUT ANOTHER SHADOW
> IN THE QUARTER OF THE NEGROES,
> NOW A NAME! MY NAME—A NAME!
>
> YET THEY ASKED ME OUT ON MY PATIO
> WHERE DID I GET MY MONEY?
> I SAID, FROM YOUR MAMA![29]

Hughes's poem is a wonderful synthesis of the Afro-American blues tradition, the formal poetic tradition, and the black vernacular tradition, rendered into one literary structure by a rhetorical strategy taken from that mode of Signification known as the dozens. Indeed, the poem can be described as one extended Signifyin(g) riff.

One of the most interesting representations of Signifyin(g) occurs in Alston Anderson's short story "Signifying," which follows another story entitled "The Dozens."[30] Anderson, whose short stories are models of subtlety and sparsity, depicts a Signifyin(g) ritual in the following way:

> One day I was standing outside the barbershop with some of the boys. Miss Florence come by on her way home from the schoolhouse, and they got to signifying:
> "Mmmmm-*mph!* What a fine day *this* is!"
> "Yes, Lawd, it sho is."
> "My, my, what a *purty* day!"
> "How do, Miss Florence!"
> "How do you do."
> "Yes, Lawd, I'd sleep in the streets fawdy days and fawdy nights for a day like *that!*"
> "Y'all hush your signifying," I said. "That there's a *lady,* and I won't have y'all signifying 'bout her like that."

> I said it in a tone of voice that wasn't loud, but I knew she heard it.
> Next time I seen her she had a nice little smile for me, but I acted just
> like nothing had ever happened.[31]

This example of Signifyin(g) not only represents a metaphorical transfer but also demonstrates H. Rap Brown's statement that Signifyin(g) can make a person feel good *or* bad. Miss Florence, no doubt, was flattered by the rhetorical attention she had attracted, and especially by the narrator's naming of the ritual in evidence, which he did as a ritual gesture of introducing his attraction to a strange woman. After the narrator finally succeeds in seducing Miss Florence, he wanders back home, only to begin to worry about the implications of his action:

> When she sat down again I tried to kiss her.
> "Don't," she said.
> When I kissed her her lips was real tight. But by the end of the
> Weekly Summary of the News they won't tight no more.
> Afterwards, back at my own place with a decent drink, I got to
> thinking about it. Now what in God's name make a man act like that?
> I didn't have no intentions of marrying the woman. In fact, I didn't even
> want to *see* her more than two or three times the week, and then out of
> pure selfishness.

In the conclusion of the story the figure of Signifyin(g) recurs. In this instance, however, it has negative connotations, hovering somewhere between sustained, embarrassing teasing and an insult:

> I knowed what would happen, of course: niggers would get to signi-
> fying, and I'd get mad. I'd get to ducking Miss Florence, and *she'd* get
> mad.
> I took off my clothes and poured me another drink—a big one—drank
> it, turned out the lights and got into bed and pulled the covers over my
> head, *real* tight, and went to sleep.[32]

Anderson's short story is a masterpiece of the genre and is one of the most delicately wrought representations of Signifyin(g) as theme, as depicted oral ritual, but also as structuring principle, since the story's mode of narration is the black vernacular, and since it embodies Smitherman's eight features of this mode of discourse.

I could list scores of other examples of Signifyin(g) rituals as represented in Afro-American literature in the nineteenth and twentieth centuries. From Frederick Douglass and the black slave's narrative and Charles Chesnutt's fictions at the turn of the century; to the myriad uses in Sterling A. Brown, Hurston, Wright, and Ellison; to recent examples by Toni Cade Bambara and John Edgar Wideman, Signifyin(g) is frequently figured in Afro-American literature. Carolyn Rodgers, in an interesting essay entitled "Black Poetry—Where It's At," has even identified Signifyin(g) as one major *kind* of poetry within the Afro-American tradition and cites examples from the poetry of Don L. Lee, LeRoi Jones, Sonia Sanchez, and Nikki Giovanni. Signifyin(g), it is fair to say, is a supple concept in the tradition. The second section of this chapter discusses the modes of Signification that serve as types of tropological revision from text to text, as found principally in parody and pastiche.[33]

II

We have seen in the literature of Signifyin(g) that linguists stress indirection as the most salient feature of this rhetorical strategy.

Rhetorical naming by indirection is central to our notions of figuration, troping, and of the parody of forms, or pastiche, in evidence when one writer repeats another's structure by one of several means, including a fairly exact repetition of a given narrative or rhetorical structure, filled incongruously with a ludicrous or incongruent context. T. Thomas Fortune's "The Black Man's Burden" is an excellent example of this form of parody, Signifyin(g) as it does upon Kipling's "White Man's Burden":

> What is the Black Man's Burden,
> Ye hypocrites and vile,
> Ye whited sepulchres
> From th' Amazon to the Nile?
> What is the Black Man's Burden,
> Ye Gentile parasites,
> Who crush and rob your brother
> Of his manhood and his rights?

Dante Gabriel Rossetti's "Uncle Ned," a dialect verse parody of Harriet Beecher Stowe's *Uncle Tom's Cabin,* provides a second example:

> Him tale dribble on and on widout a break,
> Till you had no eyes for to see;
> When I reach Chapter 4 I had got a headache;
> So I had to let Chapter 4 be.

A third example is quoted by Roger D. Abrahams in *Positively Black*. This poem is a rhyme created by children in east Texas, apparently to be chanted while skipping rope:

> Two, four, six, eight,
> We ain't gonna integrate.
> Eight, six, four, two,
> Bet you sons-of-bitches do.[34]

This rhyme repeats and then reverses a rhyme that was chanted by white racists during the problematical integration of a Little Rock, Arkansas, high school in 1957. Although I was a child, I vividly remember hearing this chant on the news and the circumstances that occasioned its use. Each morning during the initial days of this integration attempt, white adults and their children lined either side of the school walk and hurled vicious racial epithets at the black children attempting to attend this previously all-white public school and at the members of the National Guard who had been ordered by President Eisenhower to escort and protect these children. As the black children approached the school building, the white crowd, led by the high school's cheerleaders dressed in their uniforms, chanted in the most threatening tones, "Two, four, six, eight, We don't want to integrate." The chant cited by Abrahams in 1970 Signifies upon its racist antecedent of 1957.

Another kind of formal parody suggests a given structure precisely by failing to coincide with it—that is, suggests it by dissemblance. Repetition of a form and then inversion of the same through a process of variation is central to jazz. A stellar example is John Coltrane's rendition of "My Favorite Things" compared to Julie Andrew's version. Resemblance thus can be evoked cleverly by dissemblance. Aristophanes's *The Frogs,* which parodies the styles of both Aeschylus and Euripides; Cervantes's relationship to the fiction of knight-errantry; Fielding's parody of the Richardsonian novel of sentiment in *Joseph Andrews*; and Lewis Carroll's double parody in *Hiawatha's Photographing* (which draws upon Longfellow's rhythms to parody the convention of the family photograph) are good examples found in *The Princeton Encyclopedia of Poetry and Poetics.*

Ralph Ellison defines the parody aspect of Signifyin(g) implicitly in several places, definitions which I shall bring to bear on my discussion of the strategies of formal devision at work in the Afro-American literary tradition. In his complex short story, "And Hickman Arrives" (1960), Ellison's narrator portrays Signifyin(g) in this way:

> And the two men [Daddy Hickman and Deacon Wilhite] standing side by side, the one large and dark, the other slim and light brown, the other reverends rowed behind them, their faces staring grim with engrossed attention to the reading of the Word, like judges in their carved, high-backed chairs. And the two voices beginning their call and countercall as Daddy Hickman began spelling out the text which Deacon Wilhite read, playing variations on the verses just as he did with his trombone when he really felt like signifying on a tune the choir was singing.[35]

Following this introduction, the two ministers demonstrate this mode of Signification, which in turn Signifies upon the antiphonal structure of the Afro-American sermon. Ellison's parody of form here is of the same order as Richard Pryor's parody of both the same sermonic structure and Stevie Wonder's "Living for the City," which he effects by speaking the lyrics of Wonder's song in the form of and with the intonation peculiar to the Afro-American sermon in his "reading" of "The Book of Wonder." Pryor's parody is a signification of the "third order," revealing simultaneously the received structure of the sermon (by its presence, demystified here by its incongruous content), the structures of Wonder's music (by the absence of its form and the presence of its lyrics), and the complex yet direct formal relationship between both the black sermon and Wonder's music specifically, and black sacred and secular narrative forms generally.

Ellison defines Signifyin(g) in other ways as well. In his essay on Charlie

Parker, "On Bird, Bird-Watching, and Jazz" (1962), Ellison discusses the satirical aspect of signifying as one aspect of riffing in jazz.

> But what kind of bird was Parker? Back during the thirties members of the old Blue Devils Orchestra celebrated a certain robin by playing a lugubrious little tune called "They Picked Poor Robin." It was a jazz community joke, musically an extended "signifying riff" or melodic naming of a recurrent human situation, and was played to satirize some betrayal of faith or loss of love observed from the bandstand.[36]

Here again the parody is twofold, involving a formal parody of the melody of "They Picked Poor Robin" as well as a ritual naming, and therefore a troping, of an action "observed from the bandstand." While *riffing* is a term that has several meanings, I prefer that told to Alan Lomax by Jelly Roll Morton. A riff, according to Morton, is "a *figure,* musically speaking." A riff functions as "something that gives any orchestra a great background," by which Morton means "what you would call a foundation," "something you could walk on." J. L. Dillard's definition explains that this "figure" works as "a short phrase repeated over the length of a chorus, more or less like an *ostinato* in classical European musical notation."[37] The phrase, "Ask Your Mama," repeated throughout Langston Hughes's poem of the same name, is this sort of riff or figure. The riff is a central component of jazz improvisation and Signifyin(g) and serves as an especially appropriate synonym for troping and for revision.

Ellison, of course, is a complex Signifier, naming things by indirection and troping throughout his works. In his well-known review of LeRoi Jones's *Blues People,* Ellison defines Signifyin(g) in yet a third sense, then Signifies upon Jones's reading of Afro-American cultural history which he argues is misdirected and wrongheaded. "The tremendous burden of sociology which Jones would place upon this body of music," writes Ellison, "is enough to give even the blues the blues." Ellison writes that Lydia Maria Child's title, *An Appeal in Favor of That Class of Americans called Africans,*

> sounds like a fine bit of contemporary ironic signifying—*"signifying"* here meaning, in the unwritten dictionary of American Negro usage, "rhetorical understatements." It tells us much of the thinking of her opposition, and it reminds us that as late as the 1890s, a time when Negro composers, singers, dancers and comedians dominated the American musical stage, popular Negro songs (including James Weldon Johnson's "Under the Bamboo Tree," now immortalized by T. S. Eliot) were commonly referred to as "Ethiopian Airs."[38]

Ellison's stress on "the unwritten dictionary of American Negro usage" reminds us of the problem of definitions, of signification itself, when one is translating between two languages. The Signifying Monkey, perhaps appropriately, seems to dwell in this space between two linguistic domains. One wonders, incidentally, about this Afro-American figure and a possible French connection between *signe* ("sign") and *singe* ("monkey").

Ellison's definition of the relation his works bear to those of Richard

Wright constitutes a definition of "critical Signification," "pastiche," or "critical parody," although he employs none of these terms. His explanation of what we might call implicit formal criticism, however, comprises what we sometimes call troping and offers a profound definition of critical Signification itself:

> I felt no need to attack what I considered the limitations of [Wright's] vision because I was quite impressed by what he had achieved. And in this, although I saw with the black vision of Ham, I was, I suppose, as pious as Shem and Japheth. Still I would write my own books and they would be in themselves, implicitly, criticisms of Wright's; just as all novels of a given historical moment form an argument over the nature of reality and are, to an extent, criticisms each of the other.[39]

Ellison in his fictions Signifies upon Wright by parodying Wright's literary structures through repetition and difference. One can readily suggest the complexities of the parodying. The play of language, the Signifyin(g), starts with the titles. Wright's *Native Son* and *Black Boy,* titles connoting race, self, and presence, Ellison tropes with *Invisible Man,* with *invisibility* as an ironic response of absence to the would-be presence of blacks and natives, while *man* suggests a more mature and stronger status than either *son* or *boy.* Ellison Signifies upon Wright's distinctive version of naturalism with a complex rendering of modernism; Wright's re-acting protagonist, voiceless to the last, Ellison Signifies upon with a nameless protagonist. Ellison's protagonist is nothing *but* voice, since it is he who shapes, edits, and narrates his own tale, thereby combining action with the representation of action and defining reality by its representation. This unity of presence and representation is perhaps Ellison's most subtle reversal of Wright's theory of the novel as exemplified in *Native Son.* Bigger's voicelessness and powerlessness to act (as opposed to react) signify an absence, despite the metaphor of presence found in the novel's title; the reverse obtains in *Invisible Man,* where the absence implied by invisibility is undermined by the presence of the narrator as the author of his own text.

There are other aspects of Signifyin(g) at play here, too, one of the funniest being Jack's glass eye plopping into his water glass before him. This is functionally equivalent to the action of Wright's protagonist in *The Man Who Lived Underground,* as he stumbles over the body of a dead baby, deep down in the sewer. It is precisely at this point in the narrative that we know Fred Daniels to be "dead, baby," in the heavy-handed way that Wright's naturalism was self-consciously symbolic. If Daniels's fate is signified by the objects over which he stumbles in the darkness of the sewer, Ellison Signifies upon Wright's novella by repeating this underground scene of discovery but having his protagonist burn the bits of paper through which he had allowed himself to be defined by others. By explicitly repeating and reversing key figures of Wright's fictions, and by defining implicitly in the process of narration a sophisticated form more akin to Zora Neale Hurston's *Their Eyes Were Watching God,* Ellison exposed naturalism as merely a hardened convention of representation of "the Negro problem," and perhaps part of "the Negro problem" itself. I cannot emphasize enough the major import of this narrative gesture to the subsequent development of black narrative forms. Ellison recorded a new "way of seeing" and defined both a new manner of representation and its relation to the concept of presence.[40]

The formal relationship that Ellison bears to Wright, Ishmael Reed bears to both, though principally to Ellison. (I shall discuss this relation in Chapter 6). Not surprisingly, Ellison has formulated this type of complex and inherently polemical intertextual relationship of formal Signifyin(g). In a refutation of Irving Howe's critique of his work, Ellison states: "I agree with Howe that protest is an element of all art, though it does not necessarily take the form of speaking for a political or social program. It might appear in a novel as a *technical assault against the styles* which have gone before."[41] This form of formal revision is what I am calling critical signification, or formal Signifyin(g), and is my metaphor for literary history.

Before attempting to demonstrate how such a theory of Signification obtains in Afro-American literary history, let us consider received definitions of parody and pastiche and compare these to Signifyin(g). *Critical parody* is defined in the *Princeton Encyclopedia of Poetry and Poetics* as "the exaggerated imitation of a work of art" which interprets a subject from within rather than from without. Parody, moreover, is "a form of literary criticism which consists in heightening the characteristics of the thing imitated." *The Oxford Classical Dictionary* defines two types of literary parody: "pastiche, which caricatures the manner of an original without adherence to its actual words, and parody proper, in which an original, usually well known, is distorted, with the minimum of verbal or literal change, to convey a new sense, often incongruous with the form." An excellent example of parody is in evidence when Sidi, "the village belle" in Wole Soyinka's *The Lion and the Jewel* (1963), responds to Sadiku, the "Bale's" head wife. The form of her self-indulgent panegyric is cast in blank verse, clearly echoing the language of Shakespeare. Sadiku's subsequent response is a classic sign of the presence of parody:

> SADIKU [shocked, bewildered, incapable of making any sense of Sidi's words.]: But Sidi, are you well? Such nonsense never passed your lips before. Did you not sound strange, even in your own hearing? [Rushes suddenly at Lakunle.] Is this your doing, your popinjay? Have you driven the poor girl mad at last? Such rubbish . . . I will beat your head for this!
> LAKUNLE [retreating in panic.]: Keep away from me, old hag.[42]

In our sense of the term, Soyinka here Signifies upon Shakespeare, blank verse, and the uncritical adoption of received Western literary forms.

Al Young uses this sort of literary parody to Signify upon the genre of Black Arts poetry through the "poet," "O. O. Gabugah." This parody of the poetry of black nationalism so prevalent in the sixties Signifies upon the uses of dialect and the themes and the forms of this body of poetry. The poem, "The Old O.O. Blues," is the most telling of Gabugah's corpus. An excerpt follows:

>   Like right now it's the summertime
>   And I'm so all alone
>   I gots to blow some fonky rhyme
>   on my mental saxophone
>
>   Brother Trane done did his thang
>   and so have West Montgomery,
>   Both heavyweights in the music rang,
>   now I'mo play my summary
>   It's lotsa yall that thank yall white
>   (ought I say Uri-peein?)
>   Who thank Mozart and Bach's all right,
>   denyin' your Black bein'
>
>   Well, honkeyphiles, yall's day done come,
>   I mean we gon clean house
>   and ride the earth of Oreo-scum
>   that put down Fats for Faust
>
>   This here's one for-real revolution
>   where ain't nobody playin'
>   We intends to stop this cultural pollution
>   Can yall git to what I'm saying?[43]

An example of the sort of parody in which the formal events of a received structure are indeed present but are repeated in the reverse order of the original is Jean Renoir's film, *Sur un air de Charleston* ("Charleston"). A twenty-minute silent remnant of a lost feature released in March 1927, the film is very much in the surrealist mode and would seem to have been influenced by René Clair's *Paris qui dort* and *Entr'acte*. A simple summary of the film's story will perhaps suggest both its twofold parody—in this instance, a Signifyin(g) riff of a profound order—and its precursory thematic relation to Ishmael Reed's *Mumbo Jumbo*. A silver ball blasts away from a conical-shaped enclosure, adjacent to a building designed after traditional West African architecture. Piloted by an astronaut, whose face we do not see until he lands, the space capsule flies north from the equator over the continent of Africa to what is the edge of the known civilized world, which we recognize to be the Mediterranean. What we know to be modern France is here the uncharted territory of the primitive, designated on the astronaut's navigational charts as *"terres inconnues,"* whereas all of Africa is charted in great detail, the map criss-crossed with lines of transport and communication. Finally, the capsule lands in Paris; a broken Eiffel Tower suggests the aftermath of a holocaust. Emerging from the capsule, the astronaut (Johnny Hudgins, the famous tap-dancer) is seen to be a black man in blackface wearing the full regalia of Minstrel Man. He is greeted by France's only apparent survivor, a scantily clad white Wild Woman (played by Catherine Hessling) and her lascivious companion, an ape. The Wild Woman is not at all civilized; rather, she is adept only at dancing and dances the Charleston as if she invented it. Lewdly, she seduces the astronaut, who not only learns the dance but also outdances the Wild Woman. The hairy ape attempts to imitate the pair but only manages to learn a mean two-step. The two Charleston their way back to the space capsule and blast off to civilization, the charted land south of the Sahara. The moral of the story is that there is just one step that separates monkeyshine from Minstrel Man.

Sur un air de Charleston is a parody of the literature of discovery so popular in Renaissance and Enlightenment Europe between 1550 and 1800, when a succession of Europeans "discovered" cultures and persons of color, especially in West Africa. The white Wild Woman is the reversed image of the exotic blacks the Europeans depicted; her fondness for apes is a reversal of common European allegations of the propensity of African women to prefer the company of male apes.[44] That the Wild Woman can only dance, and communicates with the Afro-Astronaut in lewd dances at that, reverses the frequent observations of lewd, "unnatural" behavior among the Africans and of their undue preference of music and the dance among the arts. This sort of reversal is fairly straightforward. Depicting the astronaut as a black man in blackface (a double negative) suited in the full regalia of Minstrel Man is an even more subtle parody, conflating as it does a nineteenth-century stereotype with a seventeenth-century stereotype. Substituting the racist image of Minstrel Man as absence of intellection with that of Minstrel Man as presence of intellection is Renoir's master trope of irony, as is the fact that the Wild Woman teaches Afro-Astronaut the Charleston. The two boogie-woogie their way up the ladder into the space capsule, and they blast their way back to the connubial bliss of the civilized sub-Sahara as the ape waves a teary-eyed farewell from the bleak deserts of a ruined Paris. (The film was somewhat controversial, only in part because of Hessling's half-nude, lewd dancing lesson.) Renoir's clever reversal of the Minstrel Man stereotype recalls the critique, and the challenge, that Ellison rendered to Western fabulators of the image of the black:

> . . . the white American, figuratively [forces] the Negro down into the deeper level of his consciousness, into the inner world, where reason and madness mingle with hope and memory and endlessly give birth to nightmare and to dream; down into the province of the psychiatrist and the artist, from whence spring the lunatic's fancy and the work of art. . . .
>
> Obviously this position need not be absolutely disadvantageous for the Negro. It might, in a different culture, be highly strategic, enlisting in his cause the freedom-creating powers of art. For imprisoned in the deepest drives of human society, it is practically impossible for the white American to think of sex, of economics, his children or women-folk, or of sweeping sociopolitical changes, without summoning into consciousness fear-flecked images of black men. Indeed, it seems that the Negro has become identified with those unpleasant aspects of conscience and consciousness which it is part of the American's character to avoid. Thus when the literary artist attempts to tap the charged springs issuing from

> his inner world, up float his misshapen and bloated images of the Negro,
> like the fetid bodies of the drowned, and he turns away discarding an
> ambiguous substance which the artists of other cultures would confront
> boldly and humanize into the stuff of a tragic art.[45]

Renoir's surrealistic critique of these fundamental conventions of Western
discourse on the black, transfixed as it is upon the dance, is an example of
critical Signification just as surely as is Ishmael Reed's postmodern critique
of black literary relations in *Mumbo Jumbo,* as I attempt to show below,
and both are equally dependent on the spirit of the dance.

These sorts of parody all depend on the suppression of one term of the
simile implied in comparison itself: *x* is *like y.* The reader must supply the
model, of which the author's text is a distorted image, mirrored in some way.
This looking-glass reflection can involve relations of content and relations of
form, both, or neither. Mikhail Bakhtin, in his well-known essay "Discourse
Typology in Prose," defines more subtle uses of parody in the process of narration itself.[46]

Bakhtin's essay is a useful explication of the three categories of words
used in narrative forms. His third type of discourse is of most interest to our
reading of the Afro-American literary tradition. Bakhtin calls this third order
of discourse "double-voiced." Two of Bakhtin's subdivisions of this third type
seem appropriate categories through which to elaborate upon the theory of
Signifyin(g) as a metaphor for literary history: parodic narration and the
hidden, or internal, polemic. As we shall see, and as Bakhtin suggests, these
two types of discourse can merge, as they do in several of our tradition's canonical texts. Bakhtin's definition of narrative parody bears repeating. In
parody,

> as in stylization, the author employs the speech of another, but, in con-
> tradistinction to stylization, he introduces into that other speech an inten-
> tion which is directly opposed to the original one. The second voice,
> having lodged in the other speech, clashes antagonistically with the origi-
> nal, host voice and forces it to serve directly opposite aims. Speech be-
> comes a battlefield for opposing intentions. . . .
>
> Parody allows considerable variety: one can parody another's style
> as style, or parody another's socially typical or individually characteristic
> manner of observing, thinking, and speaking. Furthermore, the depth of
> parody may vary: one can limit parody to the forms that make up the
> verbal surface, but one can also parody even the deepest principles of
> the other speech act.[47]

As should be clear, what Bakhtin means by parody can, depending on context, refer to either what we call "parody" or "pastiche," as defined above.
The texts in the Afro-American canon can be said to configure into relationships based on the sorts of repetition and revision inherent in parody and pastiche. The mode of parody defined above depends on the utilization of another text's words. But Bakhtin defines another, and I think more subtle, form
of narrative discourse, and this is the hidden polemic.

As an introduction to the theory of Signifyin(g), which is fundamentally related to Bakhtin's definitions of parody and hidden polemic, I intend here to discuss the relationship of Ishmael Reed's Signifyin(g) postmodernism to Richard Wright's realism and Ralph Ellison's modernism. The set of intertextual relations that I chart through formal Signification is obviously related to Bakhtin's double-voiced discourse, especially as subdivided into parodic narration and the hidden, or internal, polemic. These two types of double-voiced discourse can merge together, as they do, for example, in *Invisible Man* or *Mumbo Jumbo*. Let me cite Bakhtin once more. In hidden polemic,

> the other speech act remains outside the bounds of the author's speech, but is implied or alluded to in that speech. The other speech act is not reproduced with a new intention, but shapes the author's speech while remaining outside its boundaries. Such is the nature of discourse in hidden polemic. . . .
> In hidden polemic the author's discourse is oriented toward its referential object, as is any other discourse, but at the same time each assertion about that object is constructed in such a way that, besides its referential meaning, the author's discourse brings a polemical attack to bear against another speech act, another assertion, on the same topic. Here one utterance focused on its referential object clashes with another utterance on the grounds of the referent itself. That other utterance is not reproduced; it is understood only in its import.[48]

Ellison's definition of the formal relationship between his works and Wright's is a salient example of the hidden polemic: his texts clash with Wright's "on the grounds of the referent itself." "As a result," Bakhtin continues, "the latter begins to influence the author's speech from within." In this double-voiced relationship, one speech act determines the internal structure of another, the second effecting the voice of the first by absence, by difference.

Much of the Afro-American literary tradition can be read as successive attempts to create a new narrative space for representing the recurring referent of Afro-American literature, the so-called Black Experience. Certainly, this is the way we read the relation of Sterling A. Brown's regionalism to Toomer's lyricism, Hurston's lyricism to Wright's naturalism, and, equally, Ellison's modernism to Wright's naturalism. This set of relationships can be illustrated in the schematic representation of Chart 5 which I intend only to be suggestive.[49] These relationships are reciprocal because we are free to read in critical time machines, to read backward, as Merlin moved through time. The direct relations most important to my own theory of reading are the direct black lines that connect Ishmael Reed with Ralph Ellison, Alice Walker with Zora Neale Hurston, and Ellison and Hurston to Toni Morrison.

While Reed and Hurston seem to relish the play of the tradition, Reed's work seems to be a magnificently conceived play *on* the tradition. Both Hurston and Reed have written myths of Moses, both draw upon black sacred and secular mythic discourse as metaphorical and metaphysical systems; both write self-reflexive texts which comment on the nature of writing itself; both make

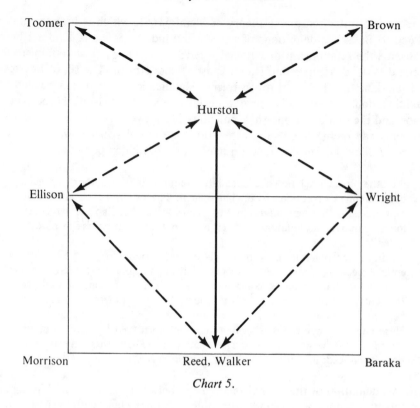

Chart 5.

use of the frame to bracket their narratives-within-a-narrative; and both are authors of fictions which I characterize as speakerly texts. Speakerly texts privilege the representation of the speaking black voice, of what the Russian Formalists called *skaz* and which Hurston and Reed have defined as "an oral book, a talking book," a figure which occurs, remarkably enough, in five of the earliest narratives in the black tradition.[50]

Reed's relation to these authors in the tradition is at all points double-voiced, since he seems to be especially concerned with employing satire to utilize literature in what Northrop Frye calls "a special function of analysis, of breaking up the lumber of stereotypes, fossilized beliefs, superstitious terrors, crank theories, pedantic dogmatisms, oppressive fashions, and all other things that impede the free movement . . . of society."[51] Reed, of course, seems to be most concerned with the "free movement" of writing itself. In Reed's work, parody and hidden polemic overlap, in a process Bakhtin describes as follows:

> When parody becomes aware of substantial resistance, a certain forceful-
> ness and profundity in the speech act it parodies, it takes on a new di-
> mension of complexity via the tones of the hidden polemic. . . . [A]
> process of inner dialogization takes place within the parodic speech act.[52]

This "inner dialogization" can have curious implications, the most interesting, perhaps, being what Bakhtin describes as "the splitting of double-voiced discourse into two speech acts, into two entirely separate and autonomous voices." The clearest evidence that Reed is Signifyin(g) in *Mumbo Jumbo* through parody as hidden polemic is his use of these two autonomous narrative voices. Reed employs these two voices in the manner of, and renders them through, foregrounding, to parody the two simultaneous stories of detective narration (that of the present and that of the past) in a narrative flow that moves hurriedly from cause to effect. In *Mumbo Jumbo,* however, the narrative of the past bears an ironic relation to the narrative of the present, because it comments not only on the other narrative but on the nature of its writing itself. Frye describes this, in another context, as "the constant tendency to self-parody in satiric rhetoric which prevents even the process of writing itself from becoming an oversimplified convention or ideal."[53] Reed's rhetorical strategy assumes the form of the relationship between the text and the criticism of that text, which serves as discourse upon the text.

While I shall attempt a close reading of *Mumbo Jumbo* in Chapter 6, I have introduced here some of its more obvious forms of Signifyin(g) only to render this theory of revision more concrete. I have selected four examples, including *Mumbo Jumbo,* to analyze in the chapters that follow. I can, however, introduce other examples of Signifyin(g) revisions in the remainder of this chapter, examples that help to demonstrate that authors produce meaning in part by revising formal patterns of representation in their fictions. This production of meaning, in all its complexity, simultaneously involves a positioning or a critiquing both of received literary conventions and of the subject matter represented in canonical texts of the tradition.

Revision is a curious and perhaps even ironic matter to pursue in the black tradition, if only because of the odd role that originality has assumed in black letters. As early as the mid-eighteenth century, David Hume (and later Immanuel Kant and Thomas Jefferson, among scores of other commentators) argued that black authors were not original in their writings. They were "imitative." Hume, writing about the poet Francis Williams (who was educated at Cambridge and who wrote Latin verse), argued stridently that Williams, widely held by abolitionists to be an irresistible argument against the European's fairly widespread doubt about the African's inherent incapacity to create the arts and letters, exemplified nothing of the sort. Indeed, Hume maintained, " 'tis likely he is admired for very slender accomplishments, like a parrot, who speaks a few words plainly." This metaphor of the black parrot gave way in the nineteenth century to the metaphor of the "mockingbird poets," black poets generally thought to lack originality but who excelled, rather, at mimicry, at what was called mindless imitation, repetition without sufficient revision. So prevalent in the black tradition has this sort of imitation supposedly been that literary historians often refer to the poetry published before Paul Laurence Dunbar's dialect verse to be part of a single "Mockingbird School."[54]

The concern to be original is so frequently expressed in black letters that it deserves a full-length study. Reacting to the questionable allegations made against their capacity to be original, black writers have often assumed a position of extreme negation, in which they claim for themselves no black literary antecedents whatsoever, or else claim for themselves an anonymity of origins as Topsy did when she said she "jes' grew." This second position, curiously enough, often stresses the anonymous origins and influence of the Afro-American vernacular tradition, as figured in the spirituals, the blues, and vernacular secular folk poetry such as that found in the toasts of the Signifying Monkey, as if group influence, unnamed, is more enabling than would be the claim of descent through a line of black precursors or even from one black precursor. This is originality at its extremes, a nameless progeniture, and the critic risks incurring the wrath of the poets when he or she seeks to demonstrate influence through close, practical criticism.

W. E. B. Du Bois writes in several places about this urge toward originality. Writing in *The Negro* in 1915, Du Bois argued that "American Negroes are gaining their own voices, their own ideals," whereas before the twentieth century they were "led and defended by others."[55] Du Bois reveals exactly who these others might be in his well-known statement printed in the final issue of *The Crisis* published under his editorship in June 1934:

> In this period of frustration and disappointment, we must turn from negation to affirmation, from the ever-lasting "No" to the ever-lasting "Yes." Instead of drowning our originality in imitation of mediocre white folks . . . [we] have a right to affirm that the Negro race is one of the great human races, inferior to none in its accomplishments and in its ability.[56]

Du Bois merely summarized nearly two centuries' brooding on lack of originality in the black tradition. Of the many such citations, let me quote that of John H. Smythe published in 1887:

> If there is any fault with us it is that we are always aping somebody else. . . . The Negro is now a distinct, and ever will be a distinct race in this country. Blood—not language and religion—makes social distinctions. We are therefore bound by every drop of blood that flows in our being, and by whatever of self-respect you and I individually and collectively possess, to make ourselves—not on the pattern of any other race, but actuated by our peculiar genius in literature, religion, commerce and social intercourse—a great people.[57]

This concern plagued even the greatest writers in the tradition. In his fascinating ironic poem "Prometheus," Paul Laurence Dunbar voices his concern about his failure to articulate his own strong voice in a poetic tradition that he thinks suffers from the same failure:

> We have no singers like the ones whose note
> Gave challenge to the noblest warbler's song.
> We have no voice so mellow, sweet, and strong
> As that which from Shelley's golden throat.

> The measure of our songs is our desires:
> We tinkle where old poets used to storm.
> We lack their substance tho' we keep their form:
> We strum our banjo-strings and call them lyres.[58]

Dunbar clearly admits defeat here by "Shelley's golden throat" and by the entire poetic tradition of which Shelley is so central a part.

Dunbar, in these lines and elsewhere, admits the defeat of his attempt to register his authentic black voice in the tradition of Western poetry. Not only does he seem to be giving up the quest, but he also eventually gives up his black identity. In a letter to his mother sent from London, Dunbar has this to say: "I am the most interviewed man in London. . . . At tea with Henry M. Stanley. The French waiter took off his cap to me. . . . I am entirely white."[59] If a French waiter in London could transform Dunbar from black to white, the sheer weight of the Western tradition seemed to demand of him to "write white." Responding to an interviewer in 1899 who had asked him about the quality of black poetry when compared with that of white poets, Dunbar answered, "It is inevitable. We must write like white men. I do not mean imitate them; but our life is now the same."[60] But if Dunbar felt anxious enough about the sheer possibility of finding and recording a black voice in poetry, other poets envied him his fame. Carlin T. Kindilien writes that after 1896 Dunbar's "verses became an American vogue":

> he was applauded by critics who compared his work with Burns', he made his own lecture program, publishers begged for any bits of his work, and white poets expressed their envy:
>
> > O that I were a nigger
> > And wrote my name Dunbar,
> > How quickly I should figger
> > A bright, poetic star![61]

Dunbar's Promethean lament, however, which we could retitle "Prometheus Bound," depending so much as it does on his opposition between "their substance" and "their form," helps us to understand the nature of what I shall call tertiary revision in the Afro-American tradition, to which I shall return below after discussing the thoughts on orginality and revision rendered by Charles Chesnutt, Zora Neale Hurston, Richard Wright, and Ralph Ellison.

Charles Chesnutt is generally thought to have no peer in Afro-American fiction written before his time. Indeed, when one searches for the black antecedents of Chesnutt, it is quite probable that he had not read even one of the several novels by black authors published in England and in the United States. According to his daughter and biographer, Helen M. Chesnutt, Chesnutt believed that "No great publishing house in the country, as far as he knew, had ever published a volume of stories or a novel written by a colored man, although Paul Laurence Dunbar had published some poems." To become the first black person to do so was Chesnutt's great preoccupation. Writing in his journal on March 16, 1880, Chesnutt admitted that "the man" who could "write as good a book as Judge Tourgée has written [*Fool's Errand*] is yet to make an appearance." Moreover, "if I can't be the man, I shall be the first to rejoice at his début, and give God speed to his work."[62]

But Chesnutt did believe himself to be "the man" and decided just two months later to admit this to himself. Writing in his journal on May 29, 1880, Chesnutt stated in the boldest terms, "I think I must write a book":

> I am almost afraid to undertake a book so early and with so little ex-
> perience in composition. But it has been my cherished dream, and I feel
> an influence that I cannot resist calling me to the task.[63]

Chesnutt defines his "political" motives for writing in military metaphors, per-haps appropriately chosen since he saw the creation of literature as a weapon that could defeat racism:

> The subtle almost indefinable feeling of repulsion toward the Negro,
> which is common to most Americans—cannot be stormed and taken by
> assault; the garrison will not capitulate, so their position must be mined,
> and we will find ourselves in their midst before they think it.[64]

In the very creation of literature, the black author performed a twofold task: he or she exemplified, by definition, the "capacity" of "the race" for "prog-ress," and he or she taught, through his or her subject matter, that racism was an outmoded and unnecessary emotion:

> This work is of a two-fold character. The Negro's part is to prepare him-
> self for recognition and equality, and it is the province of literature to
> open the way for him to get it—to accustom the public mind to the idea;
> to lead people out, imperceptibly, unconsciously, step by step, to the
> desired state of feeling. If I can do anything to further this work, and
> can see any likelihood of obtaining success in it, I would gladly devote
> my life to it.[65]

Chesnutt wrote to create a "desired state of feeling" among his white readers and to demonstrate that his black readers were ready for "recognition and equality," that is, were prepared to be seen in the republic of letters. With no apparent black antecedents to encumber his path, it would seem that the privi-lege of priority would have lent him a certain energy for such an ennobling purpose as "the elevation of the whites." His was "a high, holy purpose," which he believed would "inspire [him] to greater effort."[66]

If Chesnutt, on that day of May 29, 1880, felt "an influence that [he could not] resist," less than one year later he felt the pull of another influ-ence, one he was determined to undermine. And this influence was that of William Wells Brown, a prolific author and a leading figure in the black abo-litionist movement. Brown seems to have been the first black person to pub-lish a novel, which he entitled *Clotel; or, The President's Daughter: A Narra-tive of Slave Life in the United States* (1853). But it was not this curious novel against which Chesnutt felt the need to protect himself by explaining it away; rather, it was Brown's history of black patriotism in the American Revolution, entitled *The Negro in the American Rebellion, His Heroism and*

His Fidelity (1867). Chesnutt uses the occasion of "skimming" Brown's book on March 17, 1881, to reassert the significance of his mission, which was no less than to inscribe the black's name on the tabula rasa of Western literature:

> I have skimmed *The Negro in the Rebellion* by Dr. Brown and it only strengthens me in my opinion that the Negro is yet to become known who can write a good book. Dr. Brown's books are mere compilations and if they were not written by a colored man, they would not sell for enough to pay for the printing. I read them mostly for the facts, but I could appreciate the facts better if they were well presented.[67]

By "well presented," Chesnutt means to connote images of middle-class respectability and gentility, abandoning the military metaphors he employed the year before when assigning to himself the state of primogeniture. It is through this extended metaphor of the presentable that Chesnutt clears "Dr. Brown" from his heritage:

> The book reminds me of a gentleman in a dirty shirt. You are rather apt to doubt his gentility under such circumstances. I am sometimes doubtful of the facts for the same reason—they make but a shabby appearance.[68]

Then, as if to demonstrate literary respectability at its utmost, Chesnutt writes in the two sentences following his consideration of Brown's poor showing: "I am reading Molière's *Le Mari Confondu,* or the *Cuckold.* It is amusing."

Chesnutt wiped the slate of black authors clean so that he could inscribe his name, and inherently the name of the race, upon it. Try as one might not to use the term, one must conclude that there is some *anxiety* here, an anxiety that is revealed much more convincingly when one realizes the degree to which Chesnutt revised tropes from Brown's fictions. In an excellent essay, Richard O. Lewis demonstrates in convincing detail that Chesnutt structured the central plot of "The Passing of Grandison" (1899) after the plot of chapter XIII ("The Slave's Escape") of Brown's last novel, *My Southern Home; or, The South and Its People* (1880).[69] Lewis's superb account of Chesnutt's revisions of Brown's thirteenth chapter suggests that Chesnutt's "redressing" of Brown's plot was an instance of a motivated Signifyin(g) revision.

To discuss Signifyin(g) revisions in the Afro-American tradition is to discuss what Ralph Ellison has called "the Negro writer's complicated assertions and denials of identity," whether these be of the sort that Dunbar's takes (that is, employing the mastery of white forms to become white) or that of Charles Chesnutt's (determining that no Negro before him could dress language suitably to move the text of himself from the cabin to the Big House of Western literature).[70] Zora Neale Hurston recorded her responses to "Originality" and to "Imitation" as subsections of her major essay on "Characteristics of Negro Expression," published in Nancy Cunard's lengthy anthology, *Negro,* in 1934.[71]

While I shall return to this essay in Chapter 5, it is relevant to say here that Hurston was not content to accept the received opinion that black expression was not original, that it was imitative. Hurston confronts the received fiction squarely:

> It has been said so often that the Negro is lacking in originality that it
> has almost become a gospel. Outward signs seem to bear this out. But if
> one looks closely its falsity is immediately evident.[72]

Hurston proceeds to argue that what we really mean by originality is in fact
masterful revision, because "originality is the modification of ideas." By the
modification of ideas, Hurston means "re-interpretation." Every great artist,
she maintains, citing the example of Shakespeare, "re-interprets." We "cannot
claim first source even for Shakespeare." Instead, borrowings, echoes, and revisions characterize modern art of all forms, and in this "new art" is to be
found the truly original.[73]

    Similarly, Hurston addresses the matter of "Imitation" in an essay that
follows that on "Originality." "The Negro," she admits, "the world over, is
famous as a mimic. But this in no way damages his standing as an original."
In fact, Hurston continues, imitation is the most fundamental aspect of great
art. "Mimicry," moreover, "is an art in itself. If it is not, then all art must fall
by the same blow that strikes it down." Negroes, she concludes, mimic "for
the love of it," rather than because they lack originality. Imitation is the Afro-
American's central art form. Responding implicitly to positions epitomized by
poets such as Paul Laurence Dunbar, Hurston concludes that "The group of
Negroes who slavishly imitate is small. The average Negro glories in his ways.
The highly educated Negro the same." For Hurston, the distinction between
originality and imitation is a false distinction, and for the black writer to suffer under the burden of avoiding repetition, revision, or reinterpretation is to
succumb to a political argument that reflects a racist subtext.[74]

    If Hurston sought to relieve her fellow black authors' worries about their
complex relationships to the Western tradition on one hand, and to the Afro-
American vernacular and formal traditions on the other, then she clearly
failed. Writing just six years later in his well-known essay "How 'Bigger'
Was Born" (published in *The Saturday Review of Literature* on June 1,
1940), Richard Wright revoices Charles Chesnutt's opinion that he had no
black literary antecedents worthy of revising; rather, Wright turned to the
novels of the Western tradition for influence:

> I met white writers who talked of their responses, who told me how
> whites reacted to this lurid American scene. And, as they talked, I'd
> translate what they said in terms of Bigger's life. But what was more
> important still, *I read their novels.* Here, for the first time, I found ways
> and techniques of gauging meaningfully the effects of American civiliza-
> tion upon the personalities of people. I took these techniques, these *ways
> of seeing and feeling,* and twisted them, bent them, adapted them, until
> they became *my* ways of apprehending the locked-in life of the Black
> Belt Areas.[75]

Wright's emphasis on "ways of seeing and feeling" is an ironic echo of Dunbar's curious claim that black poets "lack their substance tho' we keep their
form." In fact, Wright is willing to make an even greater claim about the bar-
renness of his black antecedent texts than either Dunbar or Chesnutt:

This association with white writers was the life preserver of my hope to depict Negro life in fiction, for my race possessed *no fictional works* dealing with such problems, had no background in such sharp and critical testing of experience, no novels that went with a deep and fearless will down to the dark roots of life.[76]

So much for Jean Toomer and Zora Neale Hurston; so much for the tradition of the Afro-American novel.

Wright, unlike Chesnutt, did not claim that he did not "know" the Afro-American literary tradition; for by 1940 he had written an important essay about the tradition, and in 1957 he would publish a second sustained statement. Writing in *New Challenge* in 1937, in an essay entitled "Blueprint for Negro Writing," Wright broadly characterized Negro writing as an effort to demonstrate the writer's full humanity and equality with white human beings:

> Generally speaking, Negro writing in the past has been confined to humble novels, poems, and plays, prim and decorous ambassadors who went a-begging to white America. They entered the Court of Public Opinion dressed in the knee-pants of servility, curtsying to show that the Negro was not inferior, that he was human, and that he had a life comparable to that of other people. For the most part these artistic ambassadors were received as though they were French poodles who do clever tricks.[77]

While these "artistic ambassadors" somehow managed to achieve "often technically brilliant performances," a valid black literary tradition was not allowed to thrive in this country because "White America never offered these Negro writers any serious criticism. The mere fact that a Negro could write was astonishing." The only form of growth that obtained in this stillborn tradition was provided by "the fruits of that foul soil which was the result of a liaison between inferiority-complexed Negro 'geniuses' and burnt-out white Bohemians with money." In this statement, of course, Wright refers to the "Harlem" or "New Negro Renaissance," the literary movement of the twenties against which Wright reacted stridently.[78]

Instead of such an infertile tradition afforded by his black antecedents, Wright cautioned his fellow black writers to turn to the great tradition of Western writing, and to the nameless tradition of black mythology:

> Eliot, Stein, Joyce, Proust, Hemingway, and Anderson; Gorky, Barbusse, Nexo, and Jack London no less than the folklore of the Negro himself should form the heritage of the Negro writer. Every iota of gain in human thought and sensibility should be ready grist for his mill, no matter how farfetched they may seem in their immediate implications.[79]

Wright expanded this reference to the folklore of the Negro in "The Literature of the Negro in the United States," published exactly thirty years after "Blueprint" in his important collection, *White Man, Listen!* In this essay Wright defines what he calls "The Forms of Things Unknown," by which intriguing label he means the black vernacular traditions of music and poetry:

Numerically, this *formless* folk utterance accounts for the great majority of the Negro people in the United States, and it is my conviction
that the subject matter of future novels and poems resides in the lives of
these *nameless millions.* There are two pools of this black folk expression: The sacred and the secular. (Let me recall to you quickly that we
are now far beyond the world of Phillis Wheatley; she was an integrated
individual, at one with her culture; we are now dealing with people who
have *lost their individuality,* whose reactions are fiercely *elemental,*
whose *shattered* lives are burdened by *impulses* they cannot *master* or
control.) [80]

Wright's key words and phrases—"formless," "nameless," "loss of individuality," "reactions," "elemental," "shattered," "lack of mastery," and "control of
impulses"—both undermine his genuine praise of the vernacular tradition and
allow us to wonder if he actually thought this "pole" of "unauthored" black
influence to be equal in force to a Western tradition epitomized by Eliot,
Stein, Joyce, et al., and characterized by values antithetical to the characteristics he attributes to the black vernacular tradition. Since Wright, later in the
same essay, summarizes this tradition as consisting of "authorless utterances"
that "sprang spontaneously," we can conclude that the black writer can seek
and claim influence from this black tradition with absolutely no anxiety about
the influence of any particular Negro. "Nameless," "formless," "authorless"
traditions can represent no threat to primogeniture.

I have allowed myself the luxury of this elaboration on some of the Afro-
American writers' ideas about black textual antecedents to underscore the
fact that, in general, black authors do not admit to a line of literary descent
within their own literary tradition. Ralph Ellison, onto whose ideas of Signi-
fyin(g) and formal critique I have grafted my theory of critical Signification,
rightly argues, against Irving Howe, that "the notion of an intellectual or artistic succession based upon color or racial background is no less absurd than
one based upon a common religious background." Literary succession or influence, rather, can be based on only formal literary revision, which the literary critic must be able to demonstrate. These discrete demonstrations allow
for definitions of a tradition. Few definitions of tradition escape the racism, es-
sentialism, or nationalism often implicit in rubrics such as "African" or "Jew-
ish" or "Commonwealth" literature. As Ellison argues, "For the critic there
simply exists no substitute for the knowledge of history and literary tradition." [81]

Ellison's definition of his antecedents and their influence over the shape of
Invisible Man, while often cited, is relevant here:

> I respected Wright's work and I knew him, but this is not to say that he
> "influenced" me as significantly as you assume. Consult the text! I *sought
> out* Wright because I had read Eliot, Pound, Gertrude Stein, and Hem-
> ingway. . . . But perhaps you will understand when I say he did not
> influence me if I point out that while one can do nothing about choosing
> one's relatives, one can, as artist, choose one's "ancestors." Wright was,
> in this sense, a "relative"; Hemingway an "ancestor." Langston Hughes,

whose work I knew in grade school and whom I knew before I knew Wright, was a "relative"; Eliot . . . and Malraux and Dostoievsky and Faulkner, were "ancestors"—if you please or don't please![82]

Ellison, who elsewhere has defined his myriad uses of the black vernacular, is one of the first black authors who admits having black literary "relatives," if not "ancestors." It is popular to attack this distinction. Nevertheless, I find it useful especially since lines of influence are complexly drawn, and one's genetic relation to one's cousins, aunts, and uncles is dramatically different from one's genetic relation to mother, father, sisters, and brothers. Ellison's distinction between relatives and ancestors corresponds to my distinction between motivated and unmotivated Signifyin(g). Ellison relates to Wright as the Signifying Monkey relates to the Signified Lion. He parodies Wright, as a mode of critical Signification. When he says that he simply stepped around Wright, he is not joking. But if this is so, then it is also the case that he played the dozens on Wright's texts as he swerved past him. Ellison's well-defined practice of pastiche, corresponding to unmotivated Signifyin(g), is what he seems to imply in the term *ancestor*. Rather than to eschew influence, Ellison in these statements is being uncharacteristically open, for a great writer, about his formal literary heritage.

Ellison's distinction between types of influence helps to clarify a complex matter in Afro-American literature, and that is the matter of lines of descent. I wrote earlier that the basis of a tradition must be shared patterns of language use. By this I mean the shared, discrete uses of literary language in texts that bear some sort of relation to each other. My definition of tradition can be taken as a formal extension of Ellison's definition of Afro-American culture:

> It is not skin color which makes a Negro American but cultural heritage as shaped by the American experience, the social and political predicament; a sharing of that *"concord of sensibilities"* which the group expressed through historical circumstance and through which it has come to constitute a subdivision of the larger American culture.[83]

To this definition I would add that for the literary critic this "concord of sensibilities" manifests itself textually. The blackness of black literature is not an absolute or a metaphysical condition, as Ellison rightly maintains, nor is it some transcending essence that exists outside of its manifestations in texts. Rather, the "blackness" of black American literature can be discerned only through close readings. By "blackness" here I mean specific uses of literary language that are shared, repeated, critiqued, and revised.[84]

Ellison's placing of his black antecedents as relatives on his literary family tree, as opposed to ancestors who happen to be white, constitutes an important revision in that position about influence epitomized by Dunbar's "Prometheus." Dunbar's distinction between substance and form is echoed in Ellison's distinction between relatives and ancestors, since his ancestors provided model texts for revision, while his relatives share with him common subjects. This distinction helps to explain what I mean when I say that Afro-American literary history is often characterized by tertiary revision, by which I mean that three elements tend to be involved in the relationship of ancestry. These elements include texts that provide models of form, texts that provide models of substance, and the text at hand. The text at hand helps to determine how we read or conceive of the shape of a literary tradition. Through it, we "read backwards," as Eliot argued in "Tradition and the Individual Talent," charting new lines of formal descent. Several of the canonical texts in the Afro-American tradition seem to be related to other black texts primarily in terms of substance or content, whereas they seem to be related to Western texts in terms of form. *Cane, Their Eyes Were Watching God, Invisible Man, Native Son, Black Boy,* Chester Himes's detective novels, Chesnutt's novels, even Reed's parodies, among many other texts in the tradition, it seems to me, wear this curious two-toned Harlequin mask of influence. But there also exists another mode of revision within the tradition. While most, if not all, black writers seek to place their works in the "larger" tradition of their genre, many also revise tropes from substantive antecedent texts in the Afro-American tradition. It seems necessary to repeat this obvious observation because of its repeated denials.

It should be clear, even from a cursory familiarity with the texts of the Afro-American tradition, that black writers read and critique the texts of other black writers as an act of rhetorical self-definition. Our literary tradition exists because of these chartable formal relationships, relationships of Signifyin(g). These Signifyin(g) relationships are both motivated and unmotivated. When Sterling A. Brown riffs upon Robert Penn Warren's line from "Pondy Woods" (1945)—"Nigger, your breed ain't metaphysical"—with "Cracker, your breed ain't exegetical," we know this to be an instance of motivated Signifyin(g). Or consider Owen Dodson's imitation of a Black Arts poem:

> Look, man, I am black.
> Don't you see how black I am?
> I'm black as my fingernails
> and I'm black to my toes
> and if you smell me
> I am black
> And now I want you to give me a job
> because I am black.[85]

We do not need his comments to John O'Brien to recognize that he is parodying what he calls "Nikki Giovanni poems."

On the other hand, when Dunbar revises James Whitcomb Riley (in "The Ol' Tunes," "A Banjo Song," "The Old Apple Tree," "The Old Homestead," "An Old Memory," "A Drowsy Day"), he is arguing for a positioning of an entirely different order. But so too is Frances Ellen Watkins Harper in her novel *Iola Le Roy* (1892), when she takes the first chapter of Douglass's 1845 *Narrative* and expands it into the plot of her novel, in an unmotivated Signifyin(g) relation. This is a formal equivalent of the tale-within-a-tale, but within one text, in a literal sense. Here, however, the proportions of the original are magnified dramatically. The primary text (Douglass's first chapter) is heard, or read, throughout the secondary text. Hurston refigures two tropes from *Iola Le Roy:* the transformation of her protagonist from white to black through a signal scene of discovery, and the dramatic shift of the protagonist from object to subject by direct discourse. Kimberly W. Benston has charted in splendid detail what he calls "genealogical revisionism," which is similar to this mode of critical Signification or pastiche:

> All Afro-American literature may be seen as one vast genealogical poem
> that attempts to restore continuity to the ruptures or discontinuities im-
> posed by the history of the black presence in America.[86]

Benston's reading of the repetitions of the Jane figures in *Their Eyes Were Watching God, The Autobiography of Miss Jane Pittman,* LeRoi Jones's "Crow Jane" poems, and Yeats's figure of "Crazy Jane" provides still another example of the Signifyin(g) revision.[87]

I could list several other examples of Signifyin(g) revisions in the tradition, both motivated and unmotivated. Instead of merely expanding this list, however, I think it more useful to turn to the texts I have selected for a closer form of analysis. Before doing so, however, it would perhaps be useful to summarize my use of Signifyin(g) as the trope of literary revision.

We have seen that the Afro-American tradition assigns to Signifyin(g) multiple roles. In the jazz tradition, compositions by Count Basie ("Signify") and Oscar Peterson ("Signifying") are structured around the idea of formal revision and implication. When a musician "signifies" a beat, he is playing the upbeat into the downbeat of the chorus, implying their formal relationship by merging the two structures together to create an ellipsis of the downbeat. The downbeat, then, is rendered present by its absence. This is a revision of an aspect of the blues. When playing the blues, a great musician often tries to make musical phrases that are elastic in their formal properties. These elastic phrases stretch the form rather than articulate the form. Because the form is self-evident to the musician, both he and his well-trained audience are playing and listening with expectation. Signifyin(g) disappoints these expectations; caesuras, or breaks, achieve the same function. This form of disappointment creates a dialogue between what the listener expects and what the artist plays. Whereas younger, less mature musicians accentuate the beat, more accomplished musicians do not have to do so. They feel free to imply it.

Basie, in his composition, creates phrases that overlap the underlying rhythmic and harmonic structures of the piece, so that he does not have to play the downbeat, which is the first beat of the twelve-bar chorus. He is, therefore, free to "comment" on the first beat of the chorus. The musical phrase, then, begins before the downbeat of the chorus and ends after the downbeat. Charlie Parker, who revised Basie's "Kansas City style," is a master of this compelling mode of evoking presence by absence through indirection.

Indirection is the most common feature of the definitions of Signifyin(g) that I have outlined in Chapter 2. Basie's composition allows us to see Signifyin(g) as the tradition's trope of revision as well as of figuration. Throughout his piece, Basie alludes to styles of playing that predominated in black music between 1920 and 1940. These styles include ragtime, stride, barrelhouse, boogie-woogie, and the Kansas City "walking bass" so central to swing in the thirties. Through these allusions, Basie has created a composition characterized by pastiche. He has recapitulated the very tradition out of which he grew and from which he descended. Basie, in other words, is repeating the formal history of his tradition within his composition entitled "Signify." It is this definition of *Signify* that allows for its use as a metaphor of Afro-American formal revision.[88]

Pastiche only renders explicit that which any literary history implies: that tradition is the process of formal revision. Pastiche is literary history naming itself, pronouncing its surface content to be the displaced content of intertextual relations themselves, the announcement of ostensibly concealed revision. Pastiche is an act of literary "Naming"; parody is an act of "Calling out of one's name."

Signifyin(g) revision is a rhetorical transfer that can be motivated or unmotivated. Motivated Signifyin(g) is the sort in which the Monkey delights; it functions to redress an imbalance of power, to clear a space, rhetorically. To achieve occupancy in this desired space, the Monkey rewrites the received order by exploiting the Lion's hubris and his inability to read the figurative other than as the literal. Writers Signify upon each other's texts by rewriting the received textual tradition. This can be accomplished by the revision of tropes. This sort of Signifyin(g) revision serves, if successful, to create a space for the revising text. It also alters fundamentally the way we read the tradition, by defining the relation of the text at hand *to* the tradition. The revising text is written in the language of the tradition, employing its tropes, its rhetorical strategies, and its ostensible subject matter, the so-called Black Experience. This mode of revision, of Signifyin(g), is the most striking aspect of Afro-American literary history. If black writers read each other, they also revise each other's texts. Thereby they become fluent in the language of tradition. Signifyin(g) is the figure of Afro-American literary history, and revision proceeds by riffing upon tropes. As I hope to demonstrate in the next chapter, the first trope revised in the tradition was that of the Talking Book.

TWO

Reading the Tradition

The truth is that, with the fading of the Renaissance ideal through progressive stages of specialism, leading to intellectual emptiness, we are left with a potentially suicidal movement among "leaders of the profession," while, at the same time, the profession sprawls, without its old center, in helpless disarray.

One quickly cited example is the professional organization, the Modern Language Association. . . . A glance at its thick program for its last meeting shows a massive increase and fragmentation into more than 500 categories! I cite a few examples: . . . "The Trickster Figure in Chicano and Black Literature." . . . Naturally, the progressive trivialization of topics has made these meetings a laughingstock in the national press.

W. Jackson Bate

Why is it so often true that when critics confront the American as *Negro* they suddenly drop their advanced critical armament and revert with an air of confident superiority to quite primitive modes of analysis?

Ralph Ellison

Signification is the Nigger's Occupation.

Traditional

4

The Trope of the Talking Book

[A] disingenuous and unmanly *Position* had been formed; and privately (*and as it were in the dark*) handed to and again, which is this, that the *Negro's*, though in their Figure they carry some resemblances of Manhood, yet are indeed *no Men*. . . .

[The] consideration of the shape and figure of our *Negro's* Bodies, their Limbs and Members; their Voice and Countenance, in all things according with other Mens; together with their *Risibility* and *Discourse* (Man's *peculiar* Faculties) should be sufficient Conviction. How should they otherwise be capable of *Trades,* and other no less Manly imploy-ments; as also of *Reading and Writing* . . . were they not truly Men?

Morgan Godwyn, 1680[1]

Let us to the Press Devoted Be,
Its *Light* will *Shine* and *Speak Us Free.*
David Ruggles, 1835

I

The literature of the slave, published in English between 1760 and 1865, is the most obvious site to excavate the origins of the Afro-American literary tradition. Whether our definition of *tradition* is based on the rather narrow lines of race or nationality of authors, upon shared themes and narrated stances, or upon repeated and revised tropes, it is to the literature of the black slave that the critic must turn to identify the beginning of the Afro-American literary tradition.

"The literature of the slave" is an ironic phrase, at the very least, and is an oxymoron at its most literal level of meaning. "Literature," as Samuel Johnson used the term, denoted an "acquaintance with 'letters' or books," according to the *Oxford English Dictionary.* It also connoted "polite or hu-mane learning" and "literary culture." While it is self-evident that the ex-slave who managed (as Frederick Douglass put it) to "steal" some learning from his or her master and the master's texts, was bent on demonstrating to a skeptical public an acquaintance with letters or books, we cannot honestly conclude that slave literature was meant to exemplify either polite or humane learning or the presence in the author of literary culture. Indeed, it is more accurate to argue that the literature of the slave consisted of texts that represent impolite learning and that these texts collectively railed against the arbitrary and inhumane learning which masters foisted upon slaves to reinforce a perverse fiction of the "natural" order of things. The slave, by definition, possessed at most a liminal status within the human community.* To read and to write was to transgress this nebulous realm of liminality. The slave's texts, then, could not be taken as specimens of a black literary culture. Rather, the texts of the slave could only be read as testimony of defilement: the slave's *representation* and reversal of the master's attempt to transform a human being into a commodity, and the slave's simultaneous verbal witness of the possession of a humanity shared in common with Europeans. The chiasmus, perhaps the most commonly used rhetorical figure in the slave narratives and throughout subsequent black literature, is figured in the black vernacular tradition by tropes of the crossroads, that liminal space where Esu resides. The slave wrote not primarily to demonstrate humane letters, but to demonstrate his or her own membership in the human community.

This intention cannot be disregarded as a force extraneous to the production of a text, a common text that I like to think of as the text of blackness. If we recall Ralph Ellison's apt phrase by which he defines what I am calling tradition, "a sharing of that 'concord of sensibilities' which the group *expresses*," then what I wish to suggest by the text of blackness is perhaps clearer. Black writers to a remarkable extent have created texts that express the broad "concord of sensibilities" shared by persons of African descent in the Western hemisphere. Texts written over two centuries ago address what we might think of as common subjects of condition that continue to be strangely resonant, and relevant, as we approach the twenty-first century. Just as there are remarkably few literary traditions whose first century's existence is determined by texts created by slaves, so too are there few traditions that claim such an apparent unity from a fundamental political condition represented for over two hundred years in such strikingly similar patterns and details.

Has a common experience, or, more accurately, the shared sense of a common experience, been largely responsible for the sharing of this text of blackness? It would be foolish to say no. Nevertheless, shared experience of black people vis-à-vis white racism is not sufficient evidence upon which to argue that black writers have shared patterns of representation of their common subject for two centuries—unless one wishes to argue for a genetic theory of literature, which the biological sciences do not support. Rather, shared modes of figuration result only when writers read each other's texts and seize upon topoi and tropes to revise in their own texts. This form of revision is a process of grounding and has served to create curious formal lines of con-

---

* My understanding of *liminality* arises from Robert Pelton's usages in *The Trickster in West Africa* and from Houston Baker's novel usage as taken from Victor Turner's work. See Baker's *Blues, Ideology, and Afro-American Literature: A Vernacular Theory* (1985).

tinuity between the texts that together comprise the shared text of blackness, the discrete chapters of which scholars are still establishing.

What seems clear upon reading the texts created by black writers in English or the critical texts that responded to these black writings is that the production of literature was taken to be the central arena in which persons of African descent could, or could not, establish and redefine their status within the human community. Black people, the evidence suggests, had to represent themselves as "speaking subjects" before they could even begin to destroy their status as objects, as commodities, within Western culture. In addition to all of the myriad reasons for which human beings write books, this particular reason seems to have been paramount for the black slave. At least since 1600, Europeans had wondered aloud whether or not the African "species of men," as they most commonly put it, could ever create formal literature, could ever master the arts and sciences. If they could, then, the argument ran, the African variety of humanity and the European variety were fundamentally related. If not, then it seemed clear that the African was destined by nature to be a slave.

Determined to discover the answer to this crucial quandary, several Europeans and Americans undertook experiments in which young African slaves were tutored and trained along with white children. Phillis Wheatley was merely one result of such an experiment. Francis Williams, a Jamaican who took the B.A. at Cambridge before 1750; Jacobus Capitein, who earned several degrees in Holland; Wilhelm Amo, who took the doctorate degree in philosophy at Halle; and Ignatius Sancho, who became a friend of Laurence Sterne's and who published a volume of *Letters* in 1782, are just a few of the black subjects of such experiments. The published writings of these black men and one woman, who wrote in Latin, Dutch, German, and English, were seized upon both by pro- and anti-slavery proponents as proof that their arguments were sound.

So widespread was the debate over "the nature of the African" between 1730 and 1830 that not until the Harlem Renaissance would the work of black writers be as extensively reviewed as it was in the eighteenth century. Phillis Wheatley's list of reviewers includes Voltaire, Thomas Jefferson, George Washington, Samuel Rush, and James Beatty, to list only a few. Francis Williams's work was analyzed by no less than David Hume and Immanuel Kant. Hegel, writing in the *Philosophy of History* in 1813, used the absence of writing of Africans as the sign of their innate inferiority. The list of commentators is extensive, amounting to a "Who's Who" of the French, English, and American Enlightenment.

Why was the creative writing of the African of such importance to the eighteenth century's debate over slavery? I can briefly outline one thesis. After Descartes, reason was privileged, or valorized, over all other human characteristics. Writing, especially after the printing press became so widespread, was taken to be the visible sign of reason. Blacks were reasonable, and hence "men," if—and only if—they demonstrated mastery of "the arts and sciences," the eighteenth century's formula for writing. So, while the

Enlightenment is famous for establishing its existence upon man's ability to reason, it simultaneously used the absence and presence of reason to delimit and circumscribe the very humanity of the cultures and people of color which Europeans had been "discovering" since the Renaissance. The urge toward the systematization of all human knowledge, by which we characterize the Enlightenment, in other words led directly to the relegation of black people to a lower rung on the Great Chain of Being, an eighteenth century metaphor that arranged all of creation on the vertical scale from animals and plants and insects through man to the angels and God himself. By 1750, the chain had become individualized; the human scale rose from "the lowliest Hottentot" (black South Africans) to "glorious Milton and Newton." If blacks could write and publish imaginative literature, then they could, in effect, take a few giant steps up the Chain of Being, in a pernicious game of "Mother, May I?" The Rev. James W. C. Pennington, an ex-slave who wrote a slave narrative and who was a prominent black abolitionist, summarized this curious idea in his prefatory note to Ann Plato's 1841 book of essays, biographies, and poems: "The history of the arts and sciences is the history of individuals, of individual nations." Only by publishing books such as Plato's, he argues, can blacks demonstrate "the fallacy of that stupid theory, *that nature has done nothing but fit us for slaves, and that art cannot unfit us for slavery!*"[2]

Not a lot changed, then, between Phillis Wheatley's 1773 publication of her *Poems* (complete with a prefatory letter of authenticity signed by eighteen of "the most respectable characters in Boston") and Ann Plato's, except that by 1841 Plato's attestation was supplied by a black person.[3] What we might think of as the black text's mode of being, however, remained pretty much the same during these sixty-eight years. What remained consistent was that black people could become speaking subjects only by inscribing their voices in the written word. If this matter of recording an authentic black voice in the text of Western letters was of widespread concern in the eighteenth century, then how did it affect the production of black texts, if indeed it affected them at all? It is not enough simply to trace a line of shared argument as context to show that blacks regarded this matter as crucial to their tasks; rather, evidence for such a direct relationship of text to context must be found in the black texts themselves.

The most salient indication that this idea informed the writing of black texts is found in a topos that appears in five black texts published in English by 1815. This topos assumed such a central place in the black use of figurative language that we can call it a trope. It is the trope of the Talking Book, which first occurred in a 1770 slave narrative and was then revised in other slave narratives published in 1785, 1787, 1789, and 1815. Rebecca Jackson refigures this trope in her autobiographical writings, written between 1830 and 1832 but not published until 1981. Jackson's usage serves as a critique of her black male antecedents' usages because she refigures the trope in terms of male domination of a female's voice and her quest for literacy. (I analyze Jackson's revision in Chapter 7.) Not only does this shared but revised trope argue forcefully that blacks were intent on placing their individual and collective voices in the text of Western letters, but also that even the earliest writers of the Anglo-African tradition read each other's texts and grounded these texts in what soon became a tradition.

The trope of the Talking Book is the ur-trope of the Anglo-African tradition. Bakhtin's metaphor of double-voiced discourse, figured most literally in representational sculptures of Esu and implied in the Signifying Monkey's function as the rhetoric of a vernacular literature, comes to bear in black texts through the trope of the Talking Book. In the slave narratives discussed in this chapter, making the white written text speak with a black voice is the initial mode of inscription of the metaphor of the double-voiced. In Zora Neale Hurston, the concept of voice is complex, oscillating as representation among direct discourse, indirect discourse, and a unique form of free indirect discourse that serves to privilege the speaking voice. In Ishmael Reed's novel, **Mumbo Jumbo,** the double-voiced text emerges as the text of ultimate critique and revision of the rhetorical strategies at work in the canonical texts of the tradition. Finally, in Alice Walker's *The Color Purple,* the double-voiced text assumes the form of the epistolary novel in which revision manifests itself as a literal representation of a protagonist creating her self by finding her voice, but finding this voice in the act of writing. The written representation of this voice is a rewriting of the speaking voice that Hurston created for her protagonist in *Their Eyes Were Watching God.* Walker, in this brilliant act of grounding herself in the tradition by Signifyin(g) upon Hurston's rhetorical strategy, tropes Hurston's trope by "capping" (metalepsis) and inverts Hurston's effect of creating an invisible writing that speaks, by creating an invisible speaking voice that can only write!

The explication of the trope of the Talking Book enables us to witness the extent of intertextuality and presupposition at work in the first discrete period in Afro-American literary history. But it also reveals, rather surprisingly, that the curious tension between the black vernacular and the literate white text, between the spoken and the written word, between the oral and the printed forms of literary discourse, has been represented and thematized in black letters at least since slaves and ex-slaves met the challenge of the Enlightenment to their humanity by literally writing themselves into being through carefully crafted representations in language of the black self.

Literacy, the very literacy of the printed book, stood as the ultimate parameter by which to measure the humanity of authors struggling to define an African self in Western letters. It was to establish a collective black voice through the sublime example of an individual text, and thereby to register a black presence in letters, that most clearly motivated black writers, from the Augustan Age to the Harlem Renaissance. Voice and presence, silence and absence, then, have been the resonating terms of a four-part homology in our literary tradition for well over two hundred years.

The trope of the Talking Book became the first repeated and revised trope of the tradition, the first trope to be Signified upon. The paradox of representing, of containing somehow, the oral within the written, precisely when oral black culture was transforming itself into a written culture, proved to be of sufficient concern for five of the earliest black autobiographers to repeat the same figure of the Talking Book that fails to speak, appropriating the figure accordingly with embellished rhetorical differences. Whereas James Gronniosaw, John Marrant, and John Jea employ the figure as an element of plot, Ottobah Cugoano and Olaudah Equiano, with an impressive sense of their own relation to these earlier texts, bracket the tale in ways that direct attention to its status as a figure. The tension between the spoken and the written voice, for Cugoano and Equiano, is a matter they problematize as a rhetorical gesture, included in the text for its own sake, voicing, as it were, for the black literary tradition a problematic of speaking and writing. Jea's use of this curious figure has become decadent in the repetition, with the deus ex machina here represented literally as God in the text in this primal, or supernatural, scene of instruction.

This general question of the voice in the text is compounded in any literature, such as the Afro-American literary tradition, in which the oral and the written literary traditions comprise separate and distinct discursive universes which, on occasion, overlap, but often do not. Precisely because successive Western cultures have privileged written art over oral or musical forms, the writing of black people in Western languages has, at all points, remained political, implicitly or explicitly, regardless of its intent or its subject. Then, too, since blacks began to publish books they have been engaged in one form of direct political dialogue or another, consistently up to the present. The very proliferation of black written voices, and the concomitant political import of them, led fairly rapidly in our literary history to demands both for the coming of a "black Shakespeare or Dante," as one critic put it in 1925, and for an authentic black printed voice of deliverance, whose presence would, by definition, put an end to all claims of the black person's subhumanity. In the black tradition, writing became the visible sign, the commodity of exchange, the text and technology of reason.

II

The first text in which the trope of the Talking Book appears is James Albert Ukawsaw Gronniosaw's first edition of *A Narrative of the Most Remarkable Particulars in the Life of James Albert Ukawsaw Gronniosaw, An African Prince, As Related by Himself*. Gronniosaw's narrative of enslavement and delivery had by 1811 been published in seven editions, including American editions in 1774 and 1810 and a Dublin edition in 1790. In 1840 another edition was published simultaneously in London, Manchester, and Glasgow. It is this edition to which I refer.[4]

Reading and writing were of signal import to the shaping of Gronniosaw's text, as presences and absences refigured throughout his twenty-four-page narrative. While the 1770 edition says in its subtitle that Gronniosaw "related" his tale "himself," the 1774 edition, reprinted at Newport, Rhode

Island, claims that his narrative was "written by himself." When referred to in editions subsequent to 1840, "related" or "dictated" replace "written by himself." It is the narrator's concern with literacy that is of most interest to our argument here.

Gronniosaw's curious narrative has not enjoyed a wide reading among critics, or at least has not engendered many critical readings, unlike the works of his eighteenth-century colleagues John Marrant and Olaudah Equiano. What we know of him stems only from his slave narrative, generally thought to be the second example of the genre, after the 1760 *Narrative of the Uncommon Sufferings and Surprising Deliverance of Briton Hammon, A Negro Man*. While the two texts are narratives of bondage and deliverance, and while they both use the figure of the "return to my Native Land," Gronniosaw's more clearly inaugurates the genre of the slave narrative, from its "I was born" opening sentence to the use of literacy training as a repeated figure that functions to unify the structure of his tale.[5]

Who does Gronniosaw claim to be? He states that he was born "in the city of Bournou," which is the "chief city" of the Kingdom of Zaara. Gronniosaw's mother was the oldest daughter of "the reigning King of Zaara," and he was the youngest of six children. Gronniosaw stresses his intimate relationship with his mother, and to a lesser extent with his maternal grandfather, but rarely mentions his father, who we presume was not born to royalty but wed royalty. Gronniosaw's identification of himself in his narrative's title as "an African Prince" helps to explain the significance of this rhetorical gesture. Gronniosaw, by representing himself as a prince, implicitly tied his narrative to the literary tradition of the "Noble Savage" and to its subgenre, the "Noble Negro."[6]

Gronniosaw, in other words, represents himself as no mere common Negro slave, but as one nurtured, indulged, and trained in the manner of royalty everywhere. Faced with what must have seemed a deafening silence in black literary antecedents, Gronniosaw turned to the fictions of the Noble Savage to ground his text within a tradition. He also turned to the tradition of the Christian confession, referring to the import of works of Bunyan and Baxter upon his quest to learn the identity of "some great Man of Power," as he proudly tells us. Gronniosaw, in other words, represents himself as an ebony admixture of Oronooko and the Lord's questing Pilgrim.[7]

One of the ironies of representation of the Noble Savage is that he or she is rendered noble through a series of contrasts with his or her black countrymen. Oronooko bears aquiline features, has managed through some miraculous process to straighten his kinky hair, and speaks French fluently, among other languages. Oronooko, in other words, looks like a European, speaks like a European, and thinks and acts like a European—or, more properly, like a European king. Unlike the conventions of representing most other Noble Savage protagonists, then, Oronooko and his fellow black princes-in-bondage are made noble by a dissimilarity with their native countrymen. He is the exception, and not in any way the rule. Several Africans gained notoriety in eighteenth-century England and France by claiming royal lineage, even attending performances of *Oronooko* on stage, weeping loudly as they were carried from the theater.

Gronniosaw seized upon this convention of Noble Savage literature, but with a critical difference. To ground himself in the tradition of Bunyan, Gronniosaw figures his sense of difference as the only person in his grandfather's kingdom who understood, "from my infancy," that "some great Man of Power . . . resided above the sun, moon, and stars, the objects of our [African] worship." Gronniosaw's salient sign of difference is his inherent knowledge that there existed one God, rather than the many worshipped by all and sundry in the Kingdom of Zaara.[8]

The youngest prince's noble beliefs led, as we might suspect, to an estrangement from his brothers and sisters and even, eventually, from his father, his grandfather, and his devoted mother. Gronniosaw represents his discourse with his mother as follows:

> My dear mother, said I, pray tell me who is the great Man of Power that makes the thunder. She said that there was no power but the sun, moon, and stars; that they made all our country. I then inquired how all our people came. She answered me, from one another; and so carried me to many generations back. Then, says I, who made the *first man,* and who made the first cow, and the first lion, and where does the fly come from, as no one can make him? My mother seemed in great trouble; for she was apprehensive that my senses were impaired, or that I was foolish. My father came in, and seeing her in grief, asked the cause; but when she related our conversation to him, he was exceedingly angry with me, and told me that he would punish me severely if ever I was so troublesome again; so that I resolved never to say anything more to her. But I grew unhappy in myself.[9]

Gronniosaw tells us that "these wonderful impressions" were unique in all of the Kingdom of Zaara, a situation "which affords me matter of admiration and thankfulness." But his alienation increased to such an uncomfortable extent that when "a merchant from the Gold Coast" offered to take the young man to a land where he "should see houses with wings to them walk upon the water" and "see the white folks," he beseeched of his parents the freedom to leave. The only family tie that he regretted severing was with his sister Logwy, who was "quite white and fair, with fine light hair, though my father and mother were black."

Gronniosaw's affection for his "white" sister is one of three curious figures that he uses to represent his inherent difference from other black people. On one occasion, he describes "the devil" as "a black man" who "lives in hell," while he by contrast seeks to be washed clean of the blackness of sin. Moreover, the woman ordained by God for him to marry turns out to be white, echoing his bond with his "white" sister. Gronniosaw's color symbolism privileges whiteness, as we shall see, at the expense of his blackness.[10]

The young prince, of course, was traded into slavery and sailed to "Barbadoes," where he was purchased by a Mr. Vanhorn of New York. His subsequent adventures, motivated by a desire to live among the "holy" inhabitants of England ("because the authors of the books that had been given me were Englishmen"), took him to "St. Domingo," "Martinco," "Havannah," and then to London and Holland, only to return to marry and raise a family in England. The remainder of his *narrative* depicts the economic hardships he suffers from racism and from evil people generally, and his fervent devotion to the principles of Christian dogma.[11]

What concerns us about Gronniosaw's *Narrative* is his repeated references to reading and writing. His second master in New York, a Mr. Freelandhouse, and his wife "put me to school," he writes, where he "learnt to read pretty well." His master and mistress, wishing to help him overcome his spiritual dilemma about the nature of this one God ("the Author of all my comforts") whom he discovered at New York, gave him copies of "John Bunyan on the Holy War" and "Baxter's 'Call to the Unconverted.'" As an example of the "much persecution" that he received from "the sailors," Gronniosaw writes, "I cannot help mentioning one circumstance that hurt me more than all the rest."[12] Even this scene of cruelty turns upon the deprivation of a book:

> I was reading a book that I was very fond of, and which I frequently amused myself with, when this person snatched it out of my hand, and threw it into the sea. But, which was very remarkable, he was the first that was killed in our engagement. I do not pretend to say that this happened because he was not my friend; but I thought it was a very awful providence, to see how the enemies of the Lord were cut off.[13]

It is his ability to read and write and speak the Word of the Lord which motivates Gronniosaw's pilgrimage to England, as it did for Phillis Wheatley, to "find out Mr. [George] Whitefield." Since Gronniosaw informs his readers late in his text that he "could not read English," and since he describes his eloquent discourse on religion with "thirty-eight ministers, every Tuesday, for seven weeks together" in Holland, and since his two masters at New York bore Dutch names, it is probable that he was literate in Dutch.[14] By the age of "sixty," which W. Shirley in his "Preface" estimates to be his age at the time of publication, he spoke fluent English, in which, like Caliban, he learned first "to curse and swear surprisingly."[15]

If Gronniosaw, like Caliban, first learned the master's tongue to curse and swear, he quickly mended his ways. Indeed, almost from the beginning of his capture, Gronniosaw seems to have been determined to allow nothing to come between his desire to know the name of the Christian God and its fulfillment. Gronniosaw represents this desire within an extended passage in which he uses the trope of the Talking Book. He first describes his pleasure at disregarding the principal material sign of his African heritage, an extensive gold chain which must have been remarkably valuable judging by its description:

> When I left my dear mother, I had a large quantity of gold about me, as is the custom of our country. It was made into rings, and they were

linked one into another, and formed into a *kind of chain,* and so put
round my neck, and arms, and legs, and a large piece hanging at one ear,
almost in the shape of a pear. I found all this troublesome, and was glad
when my new master [a Dutch captain of a ship] took it from me. I was
now washed, and clothed in the Dutch or English manner.[16]

Gronniosaw admits to being glad when his royal chain, a chain of gold that
signified his cultural heritage, was removed from him, to be replaced, after
a proverbial if secular baptism by water, with the "Dutch or English"
clothing of a ship's crew. That which signified his African past, a veritable
signifying chain, Gronniosaw eagerly abandons, just as he longs to abandon
the language that his European captors "did not understand."

Gronniosaw's signifying gold chain is an ironic prefigurement of Brother
Tarp's link to *his* cultural heritage, a prison gang, in *Invisible Man.* When
Tarp tells Ellison's narrator that his chain "had a whole lot of signifying
wrapped up in it" and that "it might help you remember what we're really
fighting against," we not only recall Gronniosaw's willingness to relinquish
his signifying chain, but we also begin to understand why. Gronniosaw has
absolutely no desire to "remember what we're really fighting against." As
Tarp continues, such a signifying chain "signifies a heap more" than the opposition between "*yes* and *no*" that it connotes, on a first level of meaning,
for the escaped prisoner. These significations are what Gronniosaw seeks to
forget.[17]

If Gronniosaw willingly abandons his signifying chain of gold, then he
is also willing to discard that chain of signifiers that comprised whatever African discourse he used to greet his Dutch enslavers. He represents this desire in the black tradition's first use of the trope of the Talking Book, which
follows the unchaining ceremony in the same paragraph:

> [My master] used to read prayers in public to the ship's crew every Sab-
> bath day; and when I first saw him read, I was never so surprised in my
> life, as when I saw the book talk to my master, for I thought it did, as I
> observed him to look upon it, and move his lips. I wished it would do so
> with me. As soon as my master had done reading, I followed him to the
> place where he put the book, being mightily delighted with it, and when
> nobody saw me, I opened it, and put my ear down close upon it, in
> great hopes that it would say something to me; but I was very sorry, and
> greatly disappointed, when I found that it would not speak. This thought
> immediately presented itself to me, that every body and every thing de-
> spised me because I was black.[18]

What can we say of this compelling anecdote? The book had no voice for
Gronniosaw; it simply refused to speak to him, or with him. For Gronniosaw, the book—or, perhaps I should say, the very concept of "book"—constituted a silent primary text, a text, however, in which the black man found
no echo of his own voice. The silent book did not reflect or acknowledge the
black presence before it. The book's rather deafening silence renames the

received tradition in European letters that the mask of blackness worn by Gronniosaw and his countrymen was a trope of absence.

Gronniosaw can speak to the text only if the text first speaks to him. The text does not, not even in the faintest whisper, a decibel level accounted for by the black man's charming gesture of placing his "ear down close upon it." Gronniosaw cannot address the text because the text will not address Gronniosaw. The text does not recognize his presence, and so refuses to share its secrets or decipher its coded message. Gronniosaw and the text are silent; the "dialogue" that he records having observed between the book and his master eludes him. To explain the difference between his master's relations to this text and the slave's relation to the same text, Gronniosaw seizes upon one explanation, and only one: the salient difference was his blackness, the very blackness of silence.

Gronniosaw explains the text's silence by resorting to an oxymoronic figure in which voice and presence, (black) face and absence are conflated. Perhaps a more accurate description of the figure is that Gronniosaw conflates an oral figure (voice) with a visual figure (his black face). In other words, Gronniosaw's explanation of the silence of the text allows for no other possibility but one; and it, he tells us, suggested itself on the spot: "This thought immediately presented itself to me, that every body and every thing despised me because I was black."

Gronniosaw's conflation of the senses, of the oral and the visual—the book refused to speak to me because my face was black—was a curiously arbitrary choice for figural substitution. After all, a more "natural" explanation might have been that the book refused to speak to him because he could not speak Dutch, especially if we remember that this scene occurs on the ship that transports the newly captured slave from the Gold Coast to Barbados, the ship's destination. This more logical or natural explanation, however, did not apparently occur to the African. Rather, the curse of silence that the text yielded could only be accounted for by the curse of blackness that God had ostensibly visited upon the dusky sons of Ham. The text's voice, for Gronniosaw, presupposed a face; and a black face, in turn, presupposed the text's silence since blackness was a sign of absence, the remarkably ultimate absence of face *and* voice. Gronniosaw could achieve no recognition from this canonical text of Western letters—either the Bible or a prayer book—because the text could not see him or hear him. Texts can only address that which they can see. Cognition, or the act of knowing as awareness and judgment, presupposes the most fundamental form of recognition in Gronniosaw's text. It was his black face that interrupted this most basic, if apparently essential, mode of recognition, thereby precluding communication.

This desire for recognition of his self in the text of Western letters motivates Gronniosaw's creation of a text, in both a most literal and a most figurative manner. Literally, this trope of the (non-)Talking Book becomes the central scene of instruction against which this black African's entire autobiography must be read. The text refuses to speak to Gronniosaw, so some forty-five years later Gronniosaw writes a text that speaks his face into existence among the authors and texts of the Western tradition. As I have shown above, no less than five subsequent scenes of instruction (in a twenty-four-page text) are represented in the *Narrative* through tropes of reading and writing, including the curious scene in which Gronniosaw (with admirable control if obvious pleasure) explains to us that the white man who "snatched" his favorite book from his hands and "threw it into the sea" proved to be "the first that was killed in our [first military] engagement." Gronniosaw represents a sixty-year life in a brief text that depends for the shape of its rhetorical strategy on six tropes of reading and writing. Gronniosaw narrates a text, the rhetorical patterning of his autobiography forces us to conclude, to satisfy the desire created when his first master's seminal text, the prayer book, refuses to address him. Gronniosaw, in other words, narrates a text that simultaneously voices, contains, and reflects the peculiar contours of his (black) face. Given the fact that by 1770 only four black people are thought to have published books in Western languages (Juan Latino, Jacobus Capitein, Wilhelm Amo, and Briton Hammon), Gronniosaw's gesture was a major one, if its motivation as inscribed in his central trope is ironic.[19]

But is his a black face as voiced in his text? When I wrote above that the ship captain's text and its refusal to speak to the slave motivated the slave to seek recognition in other Western texts (as figured in his several scenes of literacy instruction), I argued that this motivation was both literal and metaphorical. By metaphorical, I mean that the face of the author at sixty is fundamentally altered from that (black) African face that the adolescent Gronniosaw first presented in his encounter with his first Western text. Gronniosaw is a careful narrator and is especially careful to state what he means. We recall that the trope of the Talking Book occurs in the same paragraph as his description of his eager abandonment of the gold chain that signifies his African heritage. Indeed, he presents his face before the captain's speaking text only after he has been "washed, and clothed in the Dutch or English manner." The text represents this procedure as if it were a rite of baptism, but a secular or cultural cleansing or inundation that obliterates (or is meant to obliterate) the traces of an African past that Gronniosaw is eager to relinquish, as emblematized in his gold chain: "I found all this troublesome, and was glad when my new master took it from me."

In the sentence immediately following this one, Gronniosaw tells us, "My master grew fond of me, and I loved him exceedingly," unlike the mutual disdain and mistrust that had obtained between him and his first master and his partner. We recall that it was the first master who, along with his partner, had persuaded the unhappy adolescent to leave the Kingdom of Bournou to seek the land of "the white folks," where "houses with wings to them walk upon the water." His second master "grew fond" of the "new" Gronniosaw, the Gronniosaw who had willingly submitted to being "washed, and clothed in the Dutch or English manner." His old master had related to an "old" Gronniosaw, an unregenerated (black) African Gronniosaw whose alienation from his traditional belief system and from most of the members of his family had, in retrospect, persuaded him to seek "the white folks" in the first place. Gronniosaw, in other words, was now capable of being regarded "fondly" by his second master because he was no longer the pure cultural African that he was when enticed to leave his village.[20]

If he was, at this point in his *Narrative,* no longer the African that he once was, he was not yet the Anglo-African that he would become and that he so wished to be. "Clothes," and, we might add, a good washing, "do not make the man," the captain's text in its silent eloquence informs the new Gronniosaw. He was merely an African, sans signifying chain, cloaked in European garb. His dress may have been appropriately European, but his face retained the blackness of his willingly abandoned African brothers. Gronniosaw, as he placed his ear close upon the text, was a third term, neither fish nor fowl. No longer the unadulterated African, he was not yet the European that he would be. The text of Western letters could not accommodate his liminal status and therefore refused to speak to him, because Gronniosaw was not yet *this* while clearly he was no longer *that*. It was not enough, the text in its massive silence informed him, to abandon his signifying gold chain in order to be able to experience the sublime encounter with the European text's chain of signifiers. Much more washing and re-clothing would be demanded of him to make the text speak.

Forty-five years later, Gronniosaw registered his presence and figured the contours of his face in the text of his autobiography. At sixty, he was fluent in two European languages, Dutch and English; he was a freed man; he was sufficiently masterful of the "Calvinist" interpretation of Christianity to discourse "before thirty-eight [Dutch] ministers every Tuesday, for seven weeks together, and they were all very well satisfied"; and he was the husband of an English wife and the father of both her child (by an English first marriage) and their "mulatto" children. The Christian text that had once refused to acknowledge him he had by sixty mastered sufficiently not only to "satisfy" and "persuade" others by his eloquence "that I was what I pretended to be," but also to interweave within the fabric of his autobiographical text the warp and the woof of Protestant Christianity and the strange passage from black man to white. The presence found in Gronniosaw's own text is generated by the voice, and face, of assimilation. What is absent, of course, is the African's black mask of humanity, a priceless heritage discarded as readily as was a priceless gold chain. Indeed, Gronniosaw's text is free of what soon became in the slave narratives the expected polemic against the ungodly enslavement of blacks. It is also free of descriptions of any other black characters, except for the "old black servant that lived in the [Van-horn] family," and his reference to "a black man called the devil." It was the "old black servant" who taught Gronniosaw about the devil's identity and who, we presume (along with other servants), taught him to curse. No longer could Gronniosaw claim that "every body and every thing despised me because I was black."

In its trope of the Talking Book, Gronniosaw's important text in the history of black letters Signifies upon three texts of the Western tradition. I shall defer the revelation of the third text to my discussion of Ottobah Cugoano's revision of the trope of the Talking Book, for it is Cugoano's 1787 slave narrative that reveals the ultimate textual source of this figure for these black narrators. Here, however, let us briefly examine the other two.

The first text is that of Willem Bosman, entitled *A New and Accurate Description of the Coast of Guinea,* which I discussed briefly in Chapter 1. Bosman's account of his travels in Africa was published in Dutch in 1704 and in English at London in 1705. By 1737, four Dutch editions had been published, as well as translations in French, German, and English. In 1752, an Italian translation appeared. At least two more English editions have been published in this century.[21]

Bosman was the Dutch "Chief Factor" at the Fort of Elmira, on the coast of West Africa (popularly called Guinea at the time) in what is now Ghana. Bosman is thought to have been the "second most important Dutch official on the coast of Guinea from about 1688 to 1702." Bosman's "Letter X" is devoted to "the Religion of the *Negroes*" at "Guinea," another name for the "Gold Coast" that appears in Gronniosaw's *Narrative.* Indeed, it is probable that Gronniosaw's Dutch ship captain set sail from the Fort of Elmira. It is just as probable that Gronniosaw and Bosman were at Elmira within twenty-three years of each other, if W. Shirley's estimate of Gronniosaw's age in 1770 is correct. If he has underestimated Gronniosaw's age, then it is conceivable that the two men could have been at Elmira at the same time. What is more probable is that Gronniosaw knew Bosman's Dutch text, especially "Letter X."[22]

Bosman's "Letter X," according to Robert D. Richardson, has had an extraordinary influence on the development of the concept of fetishism in modern anthropology, by way of Pierre Bayle's *Historical and Critical Dictionary* (1697, 1734–1738) and Charles de Brosses's *Du culte des dieux fétiches* (1760), the latter of which asserted the theory that fetishism, as practiced by blacks in West Africa, was the most fundamental form of religious worship. Auguste Comte's declaration that a "primary, festishistic, or theological stage" was central to the development of a society depended on de Brosses's 1760 theory of fetishism. Bosman's observations, then, have proven to be central to the discourse on religion so fundamental to the development of anthropology in this century.[23]

Bosman's letter begins with an assertion that "all the Coast *Negroes* believe in one true God, to whom they attribute the Creation of the World." This claim, of course, at first appears to be at odds with Gronniosaw's claim that he alone of all the people in the Kingdom of Zaara held this belief. But Bosman quickly adds that for this belief in the one *God* the coastal blacks "are not obliged to themselves nor the Tradition of their Ancestors." Rather, the source of this notion is "their daily conversation with the *Europeans,* who from time to time have continually endeavoured to emplant this notion in them." The initial sense of difference that Gronniosaw strives so diligently

to effect between himself and his African kinsmen (his monotheism as opposed to their polytheism) is prefigured in Bosman's second paragraph.[24]

What is even more relevant here is that Bosman's account of the Ashanti
people's myth of creation turns upon an opposition between gold, on one
hand, and "Reading and Writing," on the other. As Bosman recounts this
fascinating myth:

> [A] great part of the *Negroes* believe that man was made by *Anansie,*
> that is, a great Spider: the rest attribute the Creation of Man to God,
> which they assert to have happened in the following manner: They tell
> us, that in the beginning God created Black as well as White Men;
> thereby not only hinting but endeavouring to prove that their race was as
> soon in the World as ours; and to bestow a yet greater Honour on them-
> selves, they tell us that God having created these two sorts of Men,
> offered two sorts of Gifts, *viz,* Gold, and the Knowledge of Arts of
> Reading and Writing, giving the Blacks, the first Election, who chose
> Gold, and left the Knowledge of Letters to the White. God granted their
> Request, but being incensed at their Avarice, resolved that the Whites
> should for ever be their Masters, and they obliged to wait on them as
> their Slaves.[25]

Gold, spake God to the African, or the arts of Western letters—*choose*! The
African, much to his regret, elected gold and was doomed by his avarice to
be a slave. As a footnote to Bosman's first edition tells us, the African's
avarice was an eternal curse, and his punishment was the doom of never
mastering the Western arts and letters.

If the African at the Creation was foolish enough to select gold over
reading and writing, Gronniosaw, African man but European-in-the-making,
would not repeat that primal mistake. Gronniosaw eschewed the temptation
of his gold chain and all that it signified, and sought a fluency in Western languages through which he could remake the features, and color, of his face.

If Gronniosaw echoes Bosman, probably self-consciously, then he also
echoes Kant, probably not aware of Kant's 1764 German text. Writing in
Observations on the Feelings of the Beautiful and Sublime, Kant prefigures
Gronniosaw's equation of his black skin with the text's refusal to speak to
him. Kant, drawing upon Hume's note on blacks in "Of National Characters," argues that "So fundamental is the difference between these two races
of man, [that] it appears to be as great in regard to mental capacities as in
color." Two pages later, responding to a black man's comment to Jean Bap-
tiste Labat about male-female relations in Europe, Kant points to this supposedly natural relationship between blackness and intelligence: "And it
might be that there was something in this which perhaps deserved to be considered; but in short, this fellow was quite black from head to foot, a clear
proof that what he said was stupid."[26] Gronniosaw, after Kant, presupposes
a natural relationship between blackness and being "despised" by "every
body and every thing," including the Dutch ship captain's silent primary text.
To undoing this relationship Gronniosaw devoted his next forty-five years,

until he was fully able to structure the events of his life into a pattern that speaks quite eloquently, if ironically, to readers today.

III

The Narrative of the Lord's Wonderful Dealings with John Marrant, A Black is not properly a slave narrative, though it is usually described as such. Rather, it is an Indian captivity tale, a genre that was extraordinarily popular in the eighteenth century. Of the narratives that comprise this genre, John Marrant's was "one of the three most popular stories of Indian captivity, surpassed in number of editions only by those of Peter Williamson (1757) and Mary Jemison (1784)." Marrant's *Narrative*, which he "related" to the Rev. William Aldridge, was published in 1785 at London. Four successive editions followed in the same year, including the fourth and fifth editions "with additions." A sixth edition (1788) was followed by a 1790 Dublin edition, an 1802 London edition, three Halifax editions (1808, 1812, 1813), an 1815 Leeds edition, a Welsh translation (Caerdydd, 1818), and an 1820 edition published at Middletown, Connecticut. By 1835, Murrant's book had been printed no less than twenty times.[27]

Marrant's text was narrated to William Aldridge, who states in his "Preface" that he has "always preserved *Mr.* Marrant's ideas, tho' I could not his language," assuring Marrant's readers, however, that "no more alterations . . . have been made, than were thought necessary," whatever this might mean. Marrant's text states in its first sentence that he was "born June 15th, 1755, in New York," of free black parents. Marrant was never a slave, and he narrated his story with almost no references to black people outside of his family. Marrant experienced a profound religious conversion, which soon alienated him from his two sisters and one brother, and eventually even from his mother, just as Gronniosaw's religious stirrings alienated him from his African family. Like Gronniosaw, Marrant was heavily influenced by the Rev. George Whitefield, cofounder with John Wesley of Methodism. Alienated from his family, Marrant "went over the fence, about half a mile from our house [in Charleston, South Carolina], which divided the inhabited and cultivated parts of the country from the wilderness." It is in this "wilderness" (which he calls "the desart") that the recently converted Christian is tried sorely in his capture by Cherokee Indians.[28]

Marrant's text is remarkable in its depiction of "the Lord's wonderful Dealings" with his convert, including Marrant's "singular deliverance" from "a violent storm," during which he was "washed overboard" three times, only to be "tossed upon deck again" each time: "he who heard Jonah's prayer, did not shut out mine." The sales of Marrant's *Narrative* were no doubt influenced by both his Christian piety and his remarkable imagination for scenes of deliverance. But it is his reworking of Gronniosaw's trope of the Talking Book which is of interest to us here.

Marrant, like Gronniosaw, was fifteen when captured. Wandering through the wilderness, Marrant encountered an Indian "fortification," protected by strategically placed "guards." The Cherokee guard politely informed him that he must be put to death for venturing onto Cherokee land. A resident judge next sentenced Marrant to death, an excruciating execution by fire. About to be executed, Marrant began to pray, politely if enthusiastically reminding the Lord that he had delivered "the three children in the fiery furnace" and "Daniel in the lion's den," and asking if perhaps his servant John might be delivered in such fashion. At "about the middle of my prayer," Marrant states, "the Lord impressed a strong desire upon my mind to turn into their language, and pray in their tongue." It is this divinely inspired fluency in Cherokee which, Marrant continues, "wonderfully affected the people" gathered around to watch him slowly roast. The executioner, "savingly converted to God," interrupted the proceedings to take the black captive off for an audience with the king.[29]

In an audience before the king, however, Marrant's gift of tongues backfired, and he was sentenced to die once again for being a "witch." Marrant's account of these events contains his revision, or curious inversion, of the trope of the Talking Book:

> At this instant the king's eldest daughter came into the chamber, a person about 19 years of age, and stood at my right-hand. I had a Bible in my hand, which she took out of it, and having opened it, she kissed it, and seemed much delighted with it. When she had put it into my hand again, the king asked me what it was? and I told him, the name of my God was recorded there; and, after several questions, he bid me read it, which I did, particularly the 53d chapter of Isaiah, in the most solemn manner I was able; and also the 26 chapter of Matthew's Gospel; and when I pronounced the name of Jesus, the particular effect it had upon me was observed by the king. When I had finished reading, he asked me why I read those names with so much reverence? I told him, because the Being to whom those names belonged made heaven and earth, and I and he; this he denied. I then pointed to the sun, and asked him who made the sun, and moon, and stars, and preserved them in their regular order? He said there was a man in their town that did it. I laboured as much as I could to convince him to the contrary. His daughter took the book out of my hand a second time; she opened it, and kissed it again; her father bid her give it to me, which she did; but said, with much sorrow, the book would not speak to her. The executioner then fell upon his knees, and begged the king to let me go to prayer, which being granted, we all went upon our knees, and now the Lord displayed his glorious power. In the midst of the prayer some of them cried out, particularly the king's daughter, and the man who ordered me to be executed, and several others seemed under deep conviction of sin: This made the king very angry; he called me a witch, and commanded me to be thrust into the prison, and to be executed the next morning. This was enough to make me think, as old Jacob once did, "All these things are against me"; for I was dragged away, and thrust into the dungeon with much indignation; but God, who never forsakes his people, was with me.[30]

Marrant is saved from this second sentence of execution, he informs us a paragraph later, by curing the king's ill daughter through prayer. After he prayed three times, "the Lord appeared most lovely and glorious; the king himself was awakened, and [I] set at Liberty."[31]

What is so striking about Marrant's Signifyin(g) revision of Gronniosaw's trope is that he inverts Gronniosaw's opposition of blackness and the silence of the text. Rather, in this Kingdom of the Cherokee, it is only the black man who can make the text speak. The king's daughter, representing the Cherokee people, says "with much sorrow" that "the book would not speak to her." Marrant's capacity to make the text speak leads directly to his second condemnation for being a witch. Only by making the Lord himself appear, "most lovely and glorious," does Marrant escape the sentence of death. If in Gronniosaw's trope voice presupposes a white or assimilated face, in Marrant's text voice presupposes both a black face and an even more luminous presence, the presence of God himself. This scene, we shall see, is refigured in John Jea's revision of the trope of the Talking Book.

If Marrant Signifies upon Gronniosaw by substituting the oppositions of black/Cherokee and Christian/non-Christian for black illiterate African/white literate European, what has become of Gronniosaw's "signifying chain"? Marrant does not disappoint us; the chain is inverted as well, although it is still made of gold. And, like Gronniosaw, Marrant by contiguity in his narration associates the golden chain with his own mastery of language, the Cherokee language. Marrant's figure of the golden chain does not appear until the penultimate sentence in the two-and-one-half-page paragraph in which the Talking Book episode occurs. In this sentence, Marrant informs us that it is the Cherokee king who owns the gold "chain and bracelets," and as we might suspect, it is John Marrant, literate[32] black man from another world, who has the power over the king to command him to put them on, or take them off, "like a child": "The King would take off his golden garments, his chain and bracelets, like a child, if I objected to them and lay them aside."[33] It is Marrant, master of the text and its presences, of its voice and letters, who, for reasons never stated in his text, can force the king to "lay" his golden chain "aside," like Gronniosaw, who eagerly lays his golden chain aside in the very first attempt to shed his African identity. But Marrant is not only the king's master because of his mastery of the English text of the Bible; he soon becomes master of the king's language as well. In the paragraph's final sentence, following immediately upon the unchaining episode, Marrant tells us, "Here I learnt to speak their tongue in the highest stile." Marrant's fluency in Cherokee, inspired by God in the first instance to save him from an initial death decree, now enables him to live with the Cherokee in "perfect liberty." If Gronniosaw's golden chains signified his royal heritage, now Marrant's power of articulation leads to his fullest transformation; from "poor condemned prisoner," the "new" Marrant is "treated like a prince."[34] Marrant, in other words, has turned Gronniosaw's trope of the Talking Book inside out, reversing Gronniosaw's figures of the text that refuses to speak, the golden chain, and the movement from prince to commoner, detail by detail. Marrant wrestles from Gronniosaw a space for his own representation of a black pious life, with a Signifyin(g) revision of his only truly antecedent text and of its central trope.

For all of his apparent piety, then, Marrant seems to have been concerned to use the text of his sole predecessor in the Anglo-African tradition as a model to be revised. Marrant's revision inaugurates the black tradition of English literature, not because he was its first author but because he was the tradition's first revisionist. My idea of tradition, in part, turns upon this definition of texts read by an author and then Signified upon in some formal way, as an implicit commentary on grounding and on satisfactory modes of representation—in this instance, a mode of representation of the black pious pilgrim who descends into a chaotic wilderness of sin, is captured, suffers through several rather unbelievable trials of faith, then emerges whole and cleansed and devout.

But of what sort is Marrant's mode of Signifyin(g) upon Gronniosaw's *Narrative?* Marrant's revision is an excellent example of "capping," which is the black vernacular equivalent of metalepsis. Marrant is capping upon Gronniosaw's trope because his revision seeks to reverse the received trope by displacement and substitution. All of the key terms of Gronniosaw's trope are present in Marrant's revision, but the "original" pattern has been re-arranged significantly. (I put quotes around "original" because, as we shall see below, Gronniosaw also revised the trope from another text.) Gone is Gronniosaw's ironic claim of difference from all other black people. Although Marrant, as I stated earlier, is not concerned in this text at least to speak to the perilous condition of black bondsmen or even the marginally free, he does claim that his belief in the true God is unlike the beliefs of his kinsmen. Marrant implies that the degree of his faith alienates him from the religious beliefs of his family (and vice versa), so he takes leave for the wilderness, encountering trials and tribulations akin to those of Bunyan's Pilgrim. Nevertheless, there is a major difference between what Bosman called "fetishism" and Christianity (Gronniosaw's difference) and the *kinds* of Christianity (Marrant's difference).

Marrant, moreover, also rejects what we might think of as Gronniosaw's claim of the whiteness of the text. Instead of retaining Gronniosaw's oppositions between black/white, literate/illiterate, presence/absence, speaking/silence, European/African, and naked/clothed, Marrant substitutes Christian/non-Christian, Black/Cherokee, English language/Cherokee language, and so on. Gone is Gronniosaw's problematic desire to redress the absence of the voice in the text, which he somehow attributes to his physical and, as it were, metaphysical blackness, and to which he responds by narrating a text of a life that charts his pilgrimage to the shrines of European culture. Instead, Marrant restructures the trope such that it is the Cherokee who assume the perilous burdens of negation. Marrant's difference, then, emerges in contrast with other people of color, or a people of another color, rather than primarily from a claimed difference from other black people, despite the fact that the families of both narrators believe them to be "crazy" and as "unstable as water," as Marrant admits.[35]

Whereas Gronniosaw attributes the burden of his rejection by the text to his blackness, Marrant creates a narrative in which the black controls the voice in the text, a literally bilingual voice that speaks in fluent English and, with God's initial help and the supplement of the Indians, in fluent Cherokee. Whereas Gronniosaw depicts the motivation of his plot and of its writing as the desire to make the text respond to his presence and address him, Marrant in marked contrast displaces that desire upon the Cherokee, a desire that he, and the good Lord, manipulate miraculously. It is Marrant who is the text's ventriloquist; it is Marrant who emerges fully in control.

It is also Marrant who controls the Cherokee king's signifying chain, which Marrant can force him to remove at will, "like a child." Marrant controls the golden chain because he controls the text's chain of signifiers in a manner that Gronniosaw, the African prince, only wishes to do. Marrant's trope reverses Gronniosaw's trope of absence by transforming it into a trope of his presence and divine presence, at the expense, of course, of the unfortunate Cherokee. If we can say that Gronniosaw puts his blackness under erasure, then Marrant puts the Cherokee king under erasure at will, by commanding him to put on or remove the king's ultimate sign of authority, his golden ornaments. Marrant's revision of Gronniosaw is one of the black tradition's earliest examples of Signifyin(g) as capping.

IV

John Stuart was a black man who wrote letters. He was concerned to influence certain powerful members of English society about "the evil and wicked traffic of the slavery and commerce of the human species," as part of the title of his book would read. Accordingly, he wrote twice to the Prince of Wales and apparently once to Edmund Burke, King George III, and Granville Sharp. The point of this correspondence was to convince these gentlemen that human bondage was a form of oppression that militated against "the natural liberties of Men," as he wrote to King George. Such "abandoned wickedness" struck at the moral fabric of a kingdom dedicated to the rights of man. To outline his argument more forcefully, he wrote, he enclosed with three of his letters a copy of the 148-page book that he had published in 1787. Lest they be confused about its author's relation to the signature on each of the letters, Stuart added that John Stuart was in fact "He whose African Name is the title of the book."[36]

John Stuart was the English name that Quobna Ottobah Cugoano apparently adopted in London. But in 1787 he published his major argument against human slavery under a version of his Ghanaian name, Ottobah Cugoano.[37] Ottobah Cugoano was born about 1757, near Ajumako in what is now Ghana. Cugoano was a member of the "Fantee" (Fanti) people. If

not born to royalty like Gronniosaw, his family did enjoy an intimate association with royalty; his father "was a companion to the chief," and Cugoano
was a companion of the chief's nephew. In 1770, at about the age of thirteen,
Cugoano was captured, sold into slavery, and taken to Grenada.[38]

At Grenada, the young slave was purchased by "a gentleman coming to
England," who "took me for his servant." Thus was he "delivered from
Grenada, and that horrid brutal slavery" in 1772. Cugoano became a freedman, and at least by 1786 emerged as a leader of the "black poor" of London. Cugoano was also a close friend of Olaudah Equiano, whom I shall
discuss below, and of Scipione Piattoli, a member of the Polish patriotic
movement led by King Stanislaw II. Cugoano, then, was a major black
public figure in England at least between 1786 and 1791.[39]

It was at the height of his authority that he published his *Thoughts and
Sentiments* in 1787. Cugoano's book is an impassioned and extended argument for the abolition of slavery, not primarily an autobiography. While the
genre of the slave narrative is characterized by both polemics and autobiography ("my bondage and my freedom," as Frederick Douglass put it in
his 1855 narrative), Cugoano leans heavily toward the side of the polemic.
Cugoano, in fact, wrestles in his text with several other eighteenth-century
authors of works about slavery, some named and some unnamed, including
James Tobin's *Cursory Remarks upon the Reverend Mr. Ramsay's Essay*
(London, 1785), James Ramsay's *Essay on the Treatment and Conversion
of the African Slaves in the British Sugar Colonies* (London, 1784), Anthony Benezet's *Some Historical Account of Guinea* (London, 1771),
Patrick Gordon's *The Geography of England* (London, 1744) and *Geography Anatomized* (London, 1693), Gordon Turnbull's *An Apology for
Slavery* (London, 1786), and David Hume's 1754 version of his well-known
essay "Of National Characters," among other texts. Cugoano's *Thoughts
and Sentiments,* in other words, is constructed as a response to the eighteenth
century's major treatises on African enslavement.

Cugoano, early in his text, accounts for his literacy and for his familiarity
with the works of Europeans on slavery:

> After coming to England, and seeing others write and read, I had a
> strong desire to learn, and getting what assistance I could, I applied my-
> self to learn reading and writing, which soon became my recreation,
> pleasure, and delight; and when my master perceived that I could write
> some, he sent me to a proper school for that purpose to learn. Since, I
> have endeavoured to improve my mind in reading, and have sought to
> get all the intelligence I could, in my situation in life, towards the state
> of my brethen and countrymen in complexion, and of the miserable sit-
> uation of those who are barbarously sold into captivity, and unlawfully
> held in slavery.[40]

Cugoano describes for his readers how he learned to read and write and
also how he knows so very much about the literature of slavery. The representation of the scene of instruction of the black author's literacy became,

after Cugoano, a necessary principle of structure of virtually all of the slave narratives published between 1789 and 1865. Cugoano's, however, is the first instance of associating the mastery of letters with freedom. Indeed, Cugoano, like Job Ben Solomon in 1731, suggests that he virtually "wrote" his way from bondage to freedom.[41] Cugoano also acknowledges that despite the brutality of his enslavement, it did enable him to learn about "principles" and the Christian religion "unknown to the people of my native country":

> [One] great duty I owe to Almighty God . . . that, although I have been brought away from my native country, . . . I have both obtained liberty; and acquired the great advantages of some little learning, in being able to read and write, and, what is still infinitely of greater advantage, I trust, to know something of *Him who is that God whose providence rules over all.*[42]

"In this respect," Cugoano continues, "I am highly indebted to many of the good people of England for learning and principles unknown to the people of my native country." Despite this appreciation, however, Cugoana is not the pious pilgrim that Marrant is; rather, he is determined to show that slavery is both a defilement of sacred writ and contrary to the secular notion of liberty to which all Englishmen are heir.

If Cugoano claims to have read the major texts on slavery, he also implies that he has read the works of Gronniosaw and Marrant. Cugoano effectively makes his two predecessors in the Anglo-African tradition characters in his text, just as both Gronniosaw and Marrant do with the Rev. Mr. Whitefield. Cugoano cites Gronniosaw and Marrant as examples of blacks who managed to "get their liberty" and who were able "eventually [to] arrive at some knowledge of the Christian religion, and the great advantages to it." Of Gronniosaw, Cugoano writes:

> Such was the case of Ukawsaw Gronniosaw, an African prince, who lived in England. He was a long time in a state of great poverty and distress, and must have died at one time for want, if a good and charitable attorney had not supported him. He was long after in a very poor state, but he would not have given his faith in the Christian religion, in exchange for all the kingdoms of Africa, if they could have been given to him, in place of his poverty, for it.[43]

Cugoano knew his Gronniosaw, as his final sentence ironically suggests, for Gronniosaw, seeking to become a "man of parts and learning," wanted no parts of Africa, not even his gold chain.

And what of John Marrant? Cugoano compares him favorably with Gronniosaw:

> And such was A. Morrant [sic] in America. When a boy, he could stroll away into a desart, and prefer the society of wild beasts to the absurd Christianity of his mother's house. He was conducted to the king of the Cherokees, who, in a miraculous manner, was induced by him to em-

brace the Christian faith. This Morrant was in the British service last war, and his royal convert, the king of the Cherokee Indians, accompanied General Clinton at the siege of Charles Town.[44]

Cugoano recaptiulates the import of Marrant's text by focusing on the miracle of the Talking Book and of God emerging from the text. He does so as a delayed preface to his own revision of the trope of the Talking Book.

Fifty-odd pages after introducing Gronniosaw and Marrant, Cugoano represents his own revision of the trope of the text that speaks. He does so in a most enterprising manner, as the climax of a narrative of "the base perfidy and bloody treachery of the Spaniards" in their treament of the Native Americans. His revision is contained in a tale embedded within Cugoano's larger narrative of actions "so very disgraceful to human nature," occasioned by the "barbarous inhuman Europeans" as they conquered and enslaved the peoples of Africa, Mexico, and Peru. As we shall see, Marrant's supplement of the Cherokee in his revision presents Cugoano the occasion to relate a longer tale.[45]

Cugoano is recounting his version of "the base treacherous bastard Pizarra" (Pizarro), who stood "at the head of the Spanish banditti of miscreant depredators," and his brutal slaughter of "the Peruvian empire" and of "the noble Atahualpa, the great Inca or Lord of that empire." At this point in the story, "Pizarra" has deceived Atahualpa into believing that his was "an embassy of peace from a great monarch." Atahualpa, not trusting the Spaniards but afraid of their overwhelming military superiority, and "thinking to appease them by complying with their request, relied on Pizarra's feigned pretensions of friendship." Cugoano narrates the subsequent events:

As [Atahualpa] approached near the Spanish quarters the arch fanatic Father Vincente Valverde, chaplain to the expedition, advanced with a crucifix in one hand and a breviary in the other, and began with a long discourse, pretending to explain some of the general doctrines of Christianity . . . ; and that the then Pope, Alexander, by donation, had invested their master as the sole Monarch of all the New World . . . [Atahualpa] observed [in response] that he was Lord of the dominions over which he reigned by hereditary succession; and, said, that he could not conceive how a foreign priest should pretend to dispose of territories which did not belong to him, and that if such a preposterous grant had been made, he, who was the rightful possessor, refused to confirm it; that he had no inclination to renounce the religious institutions established by his ancestors; nor would he forsake the service of the Sun, the immortal divinity whom he and his people revered, in order to worship the God of the Spaniards, who was subject to death; and that with respect to other matters, he had never heard of them before, and did not then understand their meaning. And he desired to know where Valverde had learned things so extraordinary. In this book, replied the fanatic Monk, reaching out his breviary. The Inca opened it eagerly, and turning over the leaves, lifted it to his ear: This, says he, is silent; it tells me nothing; and threw it with disdain to the ground. The enraged father of ruffians, turning toward his countrymen, the assassinators, cried out, to arms, Christians, to

arms; the word of God is insulted; avenge this profanation on these im-
pious dogs.[46]

The Spaniards, we know, slaughtered the Incas and captured Atahualpa,
deceiving him a second time before murdering him brutally.

If Cugoano's narrative of Atahualpa and the Talking Book retains Marrant's substitution of the Indian supplicant before the text, he too inverts its
meaning by having the noble Indian disdainfully throw the silent book to the
ground. A text which contained no voice had no significance for Atahualpa;
its silent letters were dead. Unlike Marrant's Cherokee king, the king of the
Incas was not awed by Friar Vincente's silent text, even if it refused to address him just as it had done the princess of the Cherokee. Our sympathies
remain with Atahualpa in Cugoano's narration of the tale, just as Cugoano
intended. Indeed, the magical speaking text has been perverted by the Spanish friar, in a prefiguring of Father John's climactic pronouncement rendered
near the end of Jean Toomer's *Cane* (1923):

> O th sin th white folks 'mitted
> when they made th Bible lie.[47]

The Spaniards used the breviary as the justification of their "rights" to someone else's lands. Cugoano has revised Marrant's trope by transforming it into
an allegory of evil—the evils of colonization, to be sure, but also the evils of
the abuses of biblical exegesis.

Just as Marrant had revised Gronniosaw's scene of instruction by rearranging its salient details into an allegory of the Lord's "Wonderful Dealings," Cugoano has revised Marrant by using the trope as the climax of a
tale-within-a-tale, but at the European's expense. Gronniosaw's trope reveals
him to be a would-be European, a white-man-in-the-making who not unim-
portantly encounters his text during the dread Middle Passage, a most appropriate locale because he too is in "middle passage" from the African prince
he once was to the Christian pilgrim he soon would be. Marrant, on the other
hand, amounts to a substituted white man in the presence of the Cherokee,
because it is he, and only he, who controls the voices and presences of the
white man's holy text. Cugoano, unlike his two black predecessors in the tradition, writes primarily to indict a perverted economic and moral order, rather
than either to exemplify the living wonders of Protestant Christianity or to
fashion in public an articulated life. Rather, he writes to chart a freed slave's
remarkably extensive knowledge of the sheer horrors attendant upon human
slavery. Ironically, he succeeds at turning the trope of the Talking Book back
upon itself, thereby underscoring the nobility of the Inca, and simultaneously
showing the perversity of a "civilization" which justifies even murder and pil-
lage through the most sacred of written words. Cugoano, like Caliban, masters the master's tongue only to curse him more satisfactorily. The sort of
Signifyin(g) in which Cugoano is engaged partakes of metaphor (or its extended form, allegory) tinged throughout with irony. In the Afro-American

tradition, Cugoano's revision is an instance of extended "Naming," which has the same import as "calling out of one's name."

If Cugoano retains Marrant's Indians, what has happened to the golden chain? There is no chain, but Cugoano does not disappoint us. The figure of gold comes to bear in his account of the Spaniards' second deceit of Atahualpa. After they captured the king, the Spaniards imprisoned him. Expecting an execution, Atahualpa attempted to escape death by offering to his captors to fill his prison "apartment," which Cugoano tells us measured twenty-two feet by sixteen feet, with "vessels of gold as high as he could reach." Eagerly, the Spaniards accepted this proposal, and dutifully the Incas filled the apartment to the appointed mark. Cugoano narrates the tale's conclusion:

> The gold was accordingly collected from various parts with the greatest expedition by the Inca's obedient and loving subjects, who thought nothing too much for his ransom and life; but, after all, poor Atahualpa was cruelly murdered, and his body burnt by a military inquisition, and his extensive and rich dominions devoted to destruction and ruin by these merciless depredators.[48]

The power of the speaking text that gives Marrant the power to "unchain" the king of the Cherokee is not represented in Cugoano's revision because the Spaniards' breviary has no power over the Inca king. Only the guns of the Spaniards have power, a power of negation which is the objective counterpart of the Spaniards' deceitful words. Only their word is necessary to extract from Atahualpa all of the gold needed to fill his prison apartment. The Spaniards exchange their sacred oath, sworn no doubt on their sacred breviary, for the Inca's gold. Cugoano makes of the gold chain of Gronniosaw and Marrant the perverted booty gained by the immoral use of European words.

Cugoano's use of the tale-within-a-tale serves to emphasize that the Talking Book is a trope, rather than a quaint experience encountered by the narrator on his road from slavery to salvation. Cugoano, in other words, calls attention to the figurative nature of the trope itself instead of drawing upon it as an element in his primary narrative line. This bracketing of the trope of the Talking Book calls attention to the author's rhetorical strategies, to his control over his materials. Cugoano, we recall, is the only writer of the three; both Gronniosaw and Marrant dictated their tales to the people who edited them. Cugoano's bracketed tale of Atahualpa reflects a borrowing of the story from another text, which turns out not to be the text of either Gronniosaw or Marrant. Rather, Cugoano, who gives no citation for the original, points to the "original" source of the trope, which Gronniosaw and Marrant could also possibly have been revising.

Cugoano is revising the story of Atahualpa as he probably encountered it in an English translation of the event, or nonevent, as we shall see. His careful use of detail would suggest that he has followed closely another text. I am not certain which text this might be, but the most well-known account presents the trope only to claim that it never "really" happened, that it is a fiction, a myth propagated by "historians." Not only does the book not speak, but the depiction of these uncited histories is of a nonevent, something created for narrative purposes rather than an element of history necessarily incorporated into a full reconstruction of whatever occurred just before the Spaniards slaughtered the Incas.

It turns out that the story of Atahualpa and Friar Vincente de Valverde was published by Gracilasso de la Vega, the Inca, in 1617. Gracilasso published the story in his *Historia General del Perú,* which is Part II of his *Comentarios reales del Perú,* a work translated by Sir Paul Rycaut into English and published in 1688 as *The Royal Commentaries of Peru.*[49] According to Gracilasso's "true account," the exchange of speeches between the Spaniards and Atahualpa was problematical from the start because of difficulties of translation. Felipillo, the interpreter, apparently spoke a dialect different from that spoken by Atahualpa. Frustrated by these difficulties, they finally resort to *quipus* (a mode of writing using knots as signs) instead of word exchanges, but to no avail. As we might expect, one of the most problematical areas of mutual understanding apparently was the matter of the authority of the texts the Spaniards cited to justify their desire to colonize the Incas. Gracilasso's refutation of the Talking Book incident follows:

> And here it is to be noted, that it is not true that some Historians report of Atahualpa, that he should say, "You believe that Christ is God and that he died: I adore the Sun and the Moon, which are immortal: And who taught you, that your God created the Heaven and the Earth?" to which Valverde made answer, "This book hath taught it to us:" Then the King took it in his hand, and opening the Leaves, laid it to his Ear; and not hearing it speak to him, he threw it upon the ground. Upon which, they say, that the Friar starting up, ran to his Companions, crying out, that the Gospel was despised and trampled under foot; Justice and Revenge upon those who contemn our Law and refuse our Friendship.[50]

Regardless of what Atahualpa might have said, Rycaut's 1688 translation could have been Cugoano's source, and Marrant's, since they both read English, unlike Gronniosaw. Cugoano, however, was familiar with Marrant's revision and seems to have decided to use the "original" version as a way of stepping around Marrant. What seems clear from this is that, as early in the Anglo-African tradition as 1787, black texts were already "mulatto" texts, with complex double, or two-toned, literary heritages. The split between influence of form and influence of content, which I have suggested is the import of Ralph Ellison's statements about his own literary ancestry, would seem to have obtained as early as 1787.

V

Two years later, in 1789, Cugoano's friend Olaudah Equiano published his slave narrative, *The Interesting Narrative of the Life of Olaudah Equiano.*[51] Equiano's *Narrative* was so richly structured that it became the prototype of the nineteenth-century slave narrative, best exemplified in the works of Frederick Douglass, William Wells Brown, and Harriet Jacobs. It was Equiano whose text served to create a model that other ex-slaves would imitate. From his subtitle, "Written by Himself" and a signed engraving of the black author holding an open text (the Bible) in his lap, to more subtle rhetorical strategies such as the overlapping of the slave's arduous journey to freedom and his simultaneous journey from orality to literacy, Equiano's strategies of self-presentation and rhetorical representation heavily informed, if not determined, the shape of black narrative before 1865.

Equiano's two-volume work was exceptionally popular. Eight editions were printed in Great Britain during the author's lifetime, and a first American edition appeared in New York in 1791. By 1837, another eight editions had appeared, including an abridgment in 1829. Three of these editions were published together with Phillis Wheatley's *Poems*. Dutch and German translations were published in 1790 and 1791.[52]

Equiano told a good story, and he even gives a believable account of cultural life among the Igbo peoples of what is now Nigeria. The movement of his plot, then, is from African freedom, through European enslavement, to Anglican freedom. Both his remarkable command of narrative devices and his detailed accounts of his stirring adventures no doubt combined to create a readership broader than that enjoyed by any black writer before 1789. When we recall that his adventures include service in the Seven Years War with General Wolfe in Canada and Admiral Boscawen in the Mediterranean, voyages to the Arctic with the 1772–73 Phipps expedition, six months among the Miskito Indians in Central America, and "a grand tour of the Mediterranean as personal servant to an English gentleman," it is clear that this ex-slave was one of the most well-traveled people in the world when he decided to write a story of his life.[53]

Like his friend Cugoano, Equiano was extraordinarily well read, and, like Cugoano, he borrowed freely from other texts, including Constantine Phipps's *A Journal of a Voyage Towards the North Pole* (London, 1774), Anthony Benezet's *Some Historical Account of Guinea* (London, 1771), and Thomas Clarkson's *An Essay on the Slavery and Commerce of the Human Species* (London, 1785). He also paraphrased frequently, especially would-be "direct" quotations from Milton, Pope, and Thomas Day.[54] Nevertheless, Equiano was an impressively self-conscious writer and developed two rhetorical strategies that would come to be utilized extensively in the nineteenth-century slave narratives: the trope of chiasmus, and the use of two distinct voices to distinguish, through rhetorical strategies, the simple wonder with which the young Equiano approached the New World of his captors and a more eloquently articulated voice that he employs to describe the author's narrative present. The interplay of these two voices is only as striking as Equiano's overarching plot-reversal pattern, within which all sorts of embedded reversal tales occur. Both strategies combine to make Equiano's text a representation of becoming, of a development of a self that not only has a past and a present but which speaks distinct languages at its several stages which culminate in the narrative present. Rarely would a slave narrator match Equiano's mastery of self-representation.[55]

Equiano refers to his literacy training a number of times. Richard Baker, an American boy on board the ship that first took Equiano to England, was, Equiano tells us, his "constant companion and instructor," and "interpreter." At Guernsey, his playmate Mary's mother "behaved to me with great kindness and attention; and taught me every thing in the same manner as she did her own child, and indeed in every way treated me as such."[56] Within a year, he continues,

> I could now speak English tolerably well, and I perfectly understood everything that was said. I not only felt myself quite easy with these new countrymen, but relished their society and manners. I no longer looked upon them as spirits, but as men superior to us; and I therefore had the stronger desire to resemble them, to imbibe their spirit, and imitate their manners. I therefore embraced every occasion of improvement, and every new thing that I observed I treasured up in my memory. I had long wished to be able to read and write; and for this purpose I took every opportunity to gain instruction, but had made as yet very little progress. However, when I went to London with my master, I had soon an opportunity of improving myself, which I gladly embraced. Shortly after my arrival, he sent me to wait upon the Miss Guerins, who had treated me with such kindness when I was there before; and they sent me to school.[57]

Equiano also used the sea as an extension school, as he did on the "Aetna fireship":

> I now became the captain's steward, in such situation I was very happy: for I was extremely well treated by all on board; and I had leisure to improve myself in reading and writing. The latter I had learned a little of before I left the Namur, as there was a school on board.[58]

Equiano, in short, leaves a trail of evidence to prove that he was fully capable of writing his own life's story. Despite these clues, however, at least the reviewer for *The Monthly Review* wondered aloud about the assistance of "some English writer" in the production of his text.[59]

Equiano uses the trope of the Talking Book in his third chapter, in which he describes his voyages from Barbados to Virginia and on to England. It is on this voyage that he begins to learn English. Equiano uses the trope as a climax of several examples sprinkled throughout the early pages of this chapter of sublime moments of cross-cultural encounters experienced by the wide-eyed boy. His encounters with a watch and a portrait are among the first items on his list:

> The first object that engaged my attention was a watch which hung on the chimney, and was going. I was quite surprised at the noise it made, and was afraid it would tell the gentleman any thing I might do amiss: and when I immediately after observed a picture hanging in the room, which appeared constantly to look at me, I was still more affrighted, having never seen such things as these before. At one time I thought it

was something relative to magic; and not seeing it move I thought it might be some way the whites had to keep their great men when they died, and offer them libations as we used to do our friendly spirits.[60]

When he sees snow for the first time, he thinks it is salt. He concludes just before introducing as a separate paragraph the Talking Book scene, "I was astonished at the wisdom of the white people in all things I saw."[61]

Equiano returns to Gronniosaw's use of the trope for its details and refers to gold only implicitly, in his reference to the "watch which hung on the chimney." The trope is presented in a self-contained paragraph, which does not refer directly either to the paragraph that precedes it or to the one that follows. Nevertheless, the trope culminates the implicit list of wonderments that the young African experiences at the marvels of the West. As Equiano narrates:

> I had often seen my master and Dick employed in reading; and I had a great curiosity to talk to the books, as I thought they did; and so to learn how all things had a beginning: for that purpose I have often taken up a book, and have talked to it, and then put my ears to it, when alone, in hopes it would answer me; and I have been very much concerned when I found it remained silent.[62]

A watch, a portrait, a book that speaks: these are the elements of wonder that the young African encounters on his road to Western culture. These are the very signs through which Equiano represents the difference in subjectivity that separates his, now lost, African world from the New World of "white folks" that has been thrust upon him.

Significantly, Equiano endows each of these objects with his master's subjectivity. The portrait seems to be watching him as he moves through the room. The watch, he fears, can see, hear, and speak, and appears to be quite capable of and willing to report his actions to his sleeping master once he awakes. The watch is his master's surrogate overseer, standing in for the master as an authority figure, even while he sleeps. The painting is also a surrogate figure of the master's authority, following his movements silently as he walks about the room. The book that speaks to "my master and Dick" is a double sign of subjectivity, since Equiano represents its function as one that occurs in dialogue between a human being and its speaking pages. What can we make of these elements that comprise Equiano's list of the salient signs of difference?

While dramatizing rather effectively the sensitive child's naiveté and curiosity, and his ability to interpret the culture of the Europeans from a distinctly African point of reference, Equiano is contrasting his earlier self with the self that narrates his text. This, certainly, is essential to his apparent desire to represent in his autobiography a dynamic self that once was "like that" but is now "like this." His ability to show his readers his own naiveté, rather than merely to tell us about it or to claim it, and to make this earlier self the focus of his readers' sympathy and amusement, are extraordinarily effective rhetorical strategies that serve to heighten our identification with the openly honest subject whose perceptions these were and who has remembered them for us to share. But Equiano is up to much more. Under the guise of the representation of his naive self, he is naming or reading Western culture closely, underlining relationships between subjects and objects that are implicit in commodity cultures. Watches do speak to their masters, in a language that has no other counterpart in this culture, and their language frequently proves to be the determining factor in the master's daily existence. The narrative past and the narrative present through which the narrator's consciousness shifts so freely and tellingly are symbolized by the voice that the young Equiano attributes to the watch. Portraits, moreover, do stare one in the face as one moves about within a room. They are also used as tokens of the immortality of their subjects, commanding of their viewers symbolic "libations," which the young Equiano "thought it might." Portraits are would-be tropes against the subject's mortality, just as Equiano imagined them to be. Books, finally, do speak to Europeans, and not to the Africans of the eighteenth century. The book recognizes "my master and Dick," acknowledging both their voices and their faces by engaging in a dialogue with them; neither the young African's voice nor his face can be recognizable to the text, because his countenance and discourse stand in Western texts as signs of absence, of the null and void. The young Equiano has read these texts closely, and rather tellingly, while the older Equiano represents this reading at a double-voiced level, allowing his readers to engage this series of encounters on both a manifest and a latent level of meaning.

But what can we make of the shift of tenses (from "had" to "have," for example) in Equiano's passage on the Talking Book? One key to reading this shift of tenses within the description itself is Equiano's endowment of these objects of Western culture with the master's subjectivity. Equiano, the slave, enjoys a status identical to that of the watch, the portrait, and the book. He is the master's object, to be used and enjoyed, purchased, sold, or discarded, just like a watch, a portrait, or a book. By law, the slave has no more and no less rights than do the other objects that the master collects and endows with his subjectivity. Of course the book does not speak to him. Only subjects can endow an object with subjectivity; objects, such as a slave, possess no inherent subjectivity of their own. Objects can only reflect the subjectivity of the subject, like a mirror does. When Equiano, the object, attempts to speak to the book, there follows only the deafening silence that obtains between two lifeless objects. Only a subject can speak. Two mirrors can only reflect each other, in an endless pattern of voided repetition. But they cannot speak to each other, at least not in the language of the master. When the master's book looks to see whose face is behind the voice that Equiano speaks, it can only see an absence, the invisibility that dwells in an unattended looking-glass.

Through the act of writing alone, Equiano announces and preserves his newly found status as a subject. It is he who is the master of his text, a text that speaks volumes of experience and subjectivity. If once he too was an object, like a watch, a portrait, or a book, now he has endowed himself with his master's culture's ultimate sign of subjectivity, the presence of a voice which is the signal feature of a face. The shift in verb tenses creates irony, because we, his readers, know full well by this moment within the narrative that Equiano the narrator no longer speaks to texts that cannot see his face or that, therefore, refuse to address him. Equiano the author is a speaking subject, "just like" his master. But he is not "just like" his master and never can be in a culture in which the blackness of his face signifies an absence. Nevertheless, Equiano's use of shifting tenses serves to represent the very movement that he is experiencing (in a Middle Passage, as was Gronniosaw) as he transforms himself from African to Anglo-African, from slave to potential freedman, from an absence to a presence, and indeed from an object to a subject.

If the master's voice endows his objects with reflections of his subjectivity, then the representation, in writing, of the master's voice (and this process of endowment or reflection of subjectivity) serves to enable the object to remake himself into a subject. Equiano's shift in tenses enables his readers to observe him experiencing the silent text, within a narrative present that has been inscribed within a passage from his past; but it also serves, implicitly, to represent the difference between the narrator and this character of his (past) self, a difference marked through verb tense as the difference between object and subject. The process by which the master endows his commodities with the reflection of subjectivity, as figured in the African's readings of the watch, the portrait, and the book, is duplicated by Equiano's narrator's account of his own movement from slave-object to author-subject. The shift of tenses is Equiano's grammatical analogue of this process of becoming—of becoming a human being who reads differently from the child, of becoming a subject by passing a test (the mastery of writing) that no object can pass, and of becoming an author who represents, under the guise of a series of naive readings, an object's "true" nature by demonstrating that he can now read these objects in both ways, as he once did in the Middle Passage but also as he does today. The narrator's character of himself, of course, reads on a latent level of meaning; the first test of subjectivity is to demonstrate the ability to read on a manifest level. By revising the trope of the Talking Book, and by shifting from present to past and back to present, Equiano the author is able to read these objects simultaneously on both levels and to demonstrate his true mastery of the text of Western letters and the text of his verbal representation of his past and present selves.

What does this complex mode of representation suggest about Equiano's revisionary relationship to his friend and companion Cugoano? Cugoano had left Equiano very little room in which to maneuver, both by implicitly naming the "original" of the Anglo-African tradition's central trope and then by representing it as a fiction of a fiction, as a story about a story. Cugoano's bracketed narrative of Atahualpa calls attention to itself by removing it from the linear flow of the rest of his narrative, in a manner not found in the usages of either Gronniosaw or Marrant. By 1787, then, the trope could not be utilized without a remarkable degree of self-consciousness. So Cugoano engages in two maximal signs of self-consciousness: he uses the trope as an allegory of storytelling, allowing the characters even to speak in direct discourse, and simultaneously names its source, which is Gronniosaw and Marrant in one line of descent and an Inca historian in another line of descent. Equiano could not, as Gronniosaw and Marrant had done, simply make the trope a part of a linear narrative. So he subordinates it to a list of latent readings of the "true" nature of Western culture and simultaneously allows it to function as an allegory of his own act of fashioning an Anglo-African self out of words. Equiano's usage amounts to a fiction about the making of a fiction. His is a Signifyin(g) tale that Signifies upon the Western order of things, of which his willed black present self is the ironic double. If Cugoano names the trope, Equiano names his relation to Western culture through the trope. But he also, through his brilliant revision, names his relation to his three antecedent authors as that of the chain of narrators, a link, as it were, between links.

VI

The final revision of the trope of the Talking Book is that of John Jea. Jea revises the trope extensively in his autobiography, *The Life, History, and Unparalled Sufferings of John Jea*. Jea enjoys a rare distinction in the Anglo-African tradition: he is one of the few, if not the only black poet before this century who published both an autobiography and a work of imaginative literature. Despite this unique place in black letters, however, both of Jea's works had been lost until they were accidentally uncovered in 1983. Neither work appears in any of the standard bibliographies of black poetry or autobiography.[63]

We do not yet know very many of the particulars of Jea's life, beyond those narrated in his autobiography. He tells us that he, "the subject of this narrative," was born in "Old Callabar, in Africa, in the year 1773." Jea tells his readers that he, his parents, and his brothers and sisters "were stolen" from Africa, and taken to New York. His master and mistress, Oliver and Angelika Triehuen, were Dutch. Jea's narrative is an account of the arduous labors forced upon the slaves of the Triehuens, and of his rescue by God and Christianity, despite the most severe beatings by his master whenever Jea succeeded in attending any sort of religious gathering. Eventually, Jea is freed and becomes an itinerant preacher, whose travels take him to Boston, New Orleans, the "East Indies," South America, Holland, France, Germany, Ireland, and England. Jea's travels, replete with "surprising deliverances" effected by Divine Providence, make for fascinating reading, but what is of most interest here are his rhetorical strategies.

The discovery of Jea's narrative enables us to gain a much better understanding than was possible before of the formal development of strategies of self-presentation that obtain in the slave narratives published between 1760 and 1865. Jea's text stands as something of a missing link in the chain of black narrators, because his is one of the few black autobiographies published between 1800 and 1830, by which date the structure of the slave narratives becomes fairly fixed. Jea's text, for instance, is replete with animal metaphors drawn upon to describe the life of the slave. These metaphors are much less common in the narratives published in the eighteenth century than they are in those published after 1830. Jea's text, moreover, is explicitly concerned with literacy as the element that enables the slave to reverse his or her status, from a condition of slave/animal to that of articulate subject. Jea is also explicitly concerned to be a voice for the abolition of slavery, an institution that he repeatedly claims to be at odds with the divine order. Finally, Jea's narrative, as full of italicized citations from the Bible as it is of antislavery sentiment, helps us to understand how the "sacred life of the troubled Christian" that had been Gronniosaw's and Marrant's concern to express, was readily used as a model to transform black autobiography into a fundamentally secular narrative mode after 1830, in which the slave-subject apparently feels no need to justify his or her rights to freedom by calling upon the Lord and his scriptures. Jea's is the last of the great black "sacred" slave autobiographies. After his text, slave narrators generally relegate the sacred to a tacit presence, while the secular concern with abolition becomes predominant.

Jea introduces two major revisions of the slave narrative structure that he received from the eighteenth century. These include the visual representation of the text's subject, which prefaces his text, and the trope of the Talking Book. As Equiano had done twenty-six years before him, Jea prefaces his text with his own image, but an image represented both in profile and in silhouette. Jea's representation of himself in shadow draws attention primarily to his "African" features, especially to his "Bantu" nose, his thick lips, and his "Ibo" forehead, unlike the engravings of Phillis Wheatley and Equiano, which call attention to the assimilated presence of a subject who is Anglo-African, a hybrid third term meant to mediate between the opposites signified by "African" and "Anglo-Saxon." Jea's choice of representation of himself, while common among other Protestant ministers who published autobiographies contemporaneous with Jea's, is the negative, if you will, of the positive image selected by Wheatley and Equiano. Jea reverses the convention of self-presentation by employing the silhouette to underscore a literal blackness of the subject, represented as black upon black.[64]

But even more curious for the purposes of this chapter is Jea's revision of the trope of the Talking Book, which he also seeks to make literal. By this I mean that Jea—like both Gronniosaw and Marrant before him—uses the trope of the Talking Book as an element in a larger linear narrative, unlike Cugoano, who brackets the trope by making it a narrative-within-a-narrative, and unlike Equiano, who utilizes it as a signal element in his "list of differences" that separated the African from the European. Equiano succeeds in calling attention to the figurative uses he is making of the trope through several rhetorical devices, especially by a shift of verb tenses that serves to remind his readers that he, the author and subject of his narrative, is now able to make the text speak in his own tongue, and that this Equiano, the author, is not the same Equiano we overhear speaking to a silent text. Jea, like Marrant and Gronniosaw, also makes this scene a part of his linear plot development, but with one major difference: he reads the trope literally as "the word made flesh," then uses this curious event to claim that it alone led to his true manumission, a psychological manumission that necessarily follows the legal manumission he had achieved by undergoing baptism.

Jea's account of the Talking Book unfolds over five pages of his text. Unlike the texts of his antecedents, it is not readily available, only three copies being registered in England and in the United States. Because it is so rare, and more especially because it does not summarize well, I have decided to reprint it as follows below. It occurs in Jea's narrative immediately after he tells us that he "ran from" his last human master's house "to the house of God, [and] was baptized unknown to him." (Jea tells us later that "It was a law of the state of the city of New York, that if any slave could give a satisfactory account of what he knew of the word of the Lord on his soul, he was free from slavery." This process was responsible for "releasing some thousands of us poor black slaves from the galling chains of slavery."[65]) Jea's text follows:

> But my master strove to baffle me, and to prevent me from understanding the Scriptures: so he used to tell me that there was a time to every purpose under the sun, to do all manner of work, that slaves were in duty bound to do whatever their masters commanded them, whether it was right or wrong; so that they must be as obedient to a hard spiteful master as to a good one. He then took the Bible and showed it to me, and said that the book talked with him. Thus he talked with me endeavouring to convince me that I ought not to leave him, although I had received my full liberty from the magistrates, and was fully determined, by the grace of God, to leave him; yet he strove to the uttermost to prevent me; but thanks be to God, his strivings were all in vain.
>
> My master's sons also endeavoured to convince me, by their reading in the behalf of their father, for it surprised me much, how they could take that blessed book into their hands, and to be so superstitious as to want to make me believe that the book did talk with them; so that every opportunity when they were out of the way, I took the book, and held it up to my ears, to try whether the book would talk with me or not, but it proved to be all in vain, for I could not hear it speak one word, which caused me to grieve and lament, that after God had done so much for me as he had, in pardoning my sins, and blotting out my iniquities and transgressions, and making me a new creature, the book would not talk with me; but the Spirit of the Lord brought this passage of Scripture to my mind, where Jesus Christ says, "Whatsoever, ye shall ask the Father in my name, ye shall receive. Ask in faith nothing doubting: for according unto your faith it shall be unto you. For unto him that believeth, all things are possible." Then I began to ask God in faithful and fervent prayer, as the Spirit of the Lord gave me utterance, begging earnestly of the Lord to give me the knowledge of his word, that I might be enabled to understand it in its pure light, and be able to speak it in the Dutch and English languages, that I might convince my master that he and his sons had not spoken to me as they ought, when I was their slave.
>
> Thus I wrestled with God by faithful and fervent prayer, for five or six weeks, like Jacob of old, Gen. xxxii. 24. Hosea vii. 4. My master and mistress, and all people, laughed me to scorn, for being such a fool, to

think that God would hear my prayer and grant unto me my request. But I gave God no rest day nor night, and I was so earnest, that I can truly say, I shed as many tears for this blessing, as I did when I was begging God to grant me the pardon and forgiveness of my sins. During the time I was pouring out my supplications and prayers unto the Lord, my hands were employed, labouring for the bread that perisheth, and my heart within me still famishing for the word of God; as spoken in the Scriptures, "There shall be a famine in the land; not a famine of bread, nor of water, but of the word of God." And thus blessed be the Lord, that he sent a famine into my heart, and caused me to call upon him by his Spirit's assistance, in the time of my trouble.

The Lord heard my groans and cries at the end of six weeks, and sent the blessed angel of the covenant to my heart and soul, to release me from all my distress and troubles, and delivered me from all mine enemies, which were ready to destroy me; thus the Lord was pleased in his infinite mercy, to send an angel, in a vision, in shining raiment, and his countenance shining as the sun, with a large Bible in his hands, and brought it unto me, and said, "I am come to bless thee, and to grant thee thy request," as you read in the Scriptures. Thus my eyes were opened at the end of six weeks, while I was praying, in the place where I slept; although the place was as dark as a dungeon, I awoke, as the Scripture saith, and found it illuminated with the light of the glory of God, and the angel standing by me, with the large book open, which was the Holy Bible, and said unto me, "Thou has desired to read and understand this book, and to speak the language of it both in English and in Dutch; I will therefore teach thee, and now read"; and then he taught me to read the first chapter of the gospel according to St. John; and when I had read the whole chapter, the angel and the book were both gone in the twinkling of an eye, which astonished me very much, for the place was dark immediately; being about four o'clock in the morning in the winter season. After my astonishment had a little subsided, I began to think whether it was a fact that an angel had taught me to read, or only a dream; for I was in such a strait, like Peter was in the prison, when the angel smote him on the side, and said unto Peter, "Arise, Peter, and take thy garment, and spread it around thee, and follow me." And Peter knew not whether it was a dream or not; and when the angel touched him the second time, Peter arose, took his garment, folded it around him, and followed the angel, and the gates opened unto him of their own accord. So it was with me when the room was darkened again, that I wondered within myself whether I could read or not, but the Spirit of the Lord convinced me that I could; I went out of the house to a secret place, and there rendered thanksgivings and praises unto God's holy name, for his goodness in showing me to read his holy word, to understand it, and to speak it, both in the English and Dutch languages.

I tarried at a distance from the house, blessing and praising God, until the dawning of the day, and by that time the rest of the slaves were called to their labour; they were all very much surprised to see me there so early in the morning, rejoicing as if I had found a pearl of great price, for they used to see me very sad and grieved on other mornings, but now rejoicing, and they asked me what was the reason of my rejoicing more now than at other times, but I answered I would not tell them. After I had finished my day's work I went to the minister's house, and told him that I could read, but he doubted greatly of it, and said unto me, "How is it possible that you can read? For when you were a slave your master would not suffer any one, whatever, to come near you to teach you, nor any of the slaves, to read; and it is not long since you had your liberty, not long enough to learn to read." But I told him, that the Lord had learnt me to read last night. He said it was impossible. I said, "Nothing is impossible with God, for all things are possible with him; but the thing impossible with man is possible with God: for he doth with the host of heaven, and with the inhabitants of the earth, as he pleaseth, and there is none that can withstay his hand, nor dare to say what dost thou? And so did the Lord with me as it pleased him, in shewing me to read his word, and to speak it, and if you have a large Bible, as the Lord showed me last night, I can read it." But he said, "No, it is not possible that you can read." This grieved me greatly, which caused me to cry. His wife then spoke in my behalf, and said unto him, "You have a large Bible, fetch it, and let him try and see whether he can read it or not, and you will then be convinced." The minister then brought the Bible to me, in order that I should read; and as he opened the Bible for me to read, it appeared unto me, that a person said, "That is the place, read it." Which was the first chapter of the gospel of St. John, the same the Lord had taught me to read. So I read to the minister; and he said to me, "You read very well and very distinct"; and asked me who had learnt me. I said the Lord had learnt me last night. He said that it was impossible; but, if it were so, he should find it out. On saying this he went and got other books, to see whether I could read them; I tried, but could not. He then brought a spelling book, to see if I could spell; but he found to his great astonishment, that I could not. This convinced him and his wife that it was the Lord's work, and it was marvellous in their eyes.

This caused them to spread a rumour all over the city of New York, saying, that the Lord had worked great miracles on a poor black man. The people flocked from all parts to know whether it was true or not; and some of them took me before the magistrates, and had me examined concerning the rumour that was spread abroad, to prevent me, if possible, from saying the Lord had taught me to read in one night, in about fifteen minutes; for they were afraid that I should teach the other slaves to call upon the name of the Lord, as I did aforetime, and that they should come to the knowledge of the truth.

The magistrates examined me strictly, to see if I could read, as the report states; they brought a Bible for me to read in, and I read unto them the same chapter the Lord had taught me, as before-mentioned, and they said I read very well and very distinct, and asked me who had taught me to read. I still replied, that the Lord had taught me. They said that it was impossible; but brought forth spelling and other books, to see if I could read them, or whether I could spell, but they found to their great surprise, that I could not read other books, neither could I spell a word; when they said, it was the work of the Lord, and a very great miracle indeed; whilst others exclaimed and said that it was not right that I should have my liberty. The magistrates said that it was right and just that I should have my liberty, for they believed that I was of God, for they were persuaded that no man could read in such a manner, unless he was taught of God.

From that hour, in which the Lord taught me to read, until the present, I have not been able to read in any book, nor any reading whatever, but such as contain the word of God.[66]

What are we to make of Jea's fantastic revision of the trope of the Talking Book? Where are the golden chains that appear in Gronniosaw, Marrant, and Cugoano? Whereas Equiano's self-reflexive strategy of representing the trope makes his chain the very chain of narrators whom he is revising, Jea's chains are the "chains of sin," which he has carefully elaborated upon before he tells us of the Talking Book:

> [Unless] you improve your advantages, you had better be a slave in any dark part of the world, than a neglecter of the gospel in this highly favoured land; recollect also that even here you might be a slave of the most awful description:—a slave to your passions—a slave to the world—a slave to sin—a slave to satan—a slave to hell—and, unless you are made free by Christ, through the means of the gospel, you will remain in captivity, tied and bound in the *chains* of your sin, till at last you will be bound hand and foot, and cast into utter darkness, there shall be weeping and gnashing of teeth forever.[67]

Jea reverses the semantic associations of "slave" and "chains," making his condition the metaphor of the human condition. It is clear early on in his text, then, that this Christian life of a slave bears a relationship to other lives as the part stands for the whole. Jea, as I hope to show, has much in mind in his revisions of the contents of the trope of the Talking Book.

Let us be clear about Jea's chain: while nominally freed by the laws of New York because he was baptized and because he "could give a satisfactory account of what he knew of the work of the Lord on his soul," it was not until he demonstrated his ability to "read" the first chapter of the Gospel of John, "very well and distinct" as Jea tells us twice, that his rights to "liberty" were confirmed by "the magistrates" of New York because he had been "taught of God." Jea, in other words, literally reads his way out of slavery, just as Job Ben Solomon in 1731 had literally written his way out of bondage. Whereas Gronniosaw, Marrant, Cugoano, and Equiano had represented a truly cultural or metaphysical manumission through the transference afforded by the trope of the Talking Book, Jea, on the surface at least, erases this received trope by literalizing it to a degree that most narrators would not dream of attempting before Jea's usage and especially afterward.

Jea attempts to ground his representation of this miracle by carefully selecting concrete details of the event to share with his readers. He names the text that the angel teaches him to read; he adds that the event occurs just before dawn, "being about four o'clock in the morning," and that the entire reading lesson unfolded "in about fifteen minutes." Jea also gives his readers a fairly precise account of events that led to the angel's appearance, and of his actions immediately before and after this supernatural visitation. Finally, he tells us three times that his request of God and God's gift in return was to "read," "understand," and "speak the language" of this chapter of the Bible in both "the English and Dutch languages." Jea's desire, satisfied by divine intervention when all other merely mortal avenues had been closed off by the evils of slavery, was for a bilingual facility with the text of God, a facility that he is able to demonstrate upon demand of the skeptical. It is the mastery of the text of God, alone of all other texts, which leads directly to his legal manumission.

It is not an arbitrary text that the angel (or God) selects for the black slave's mastery. Rather, it is the Gospel of John. Let us recall its opening verse: "In the beginning was the Word, and the Word was with God, and the Word was God." Jea's "mastery" of reading is centered upon the curious sentence of the New Testament which explicitly concerns the nature of "the Word," upon the logos, speech or the word as reason. And let us recall the first chapter's final verse: "And he saith unto him, Verily, verily, I say unto you, Hereafter ye shall see heaven open, and the angels of God ascending and descending upon the Son of man." Jea takes these framing verses of this major text and represents its wonders in the most literal manner possible, by having "heaven open" and an angel both descend and then ascend, but also by literally dramatizing the text's first verse, that "the Word" is the beginning, and is with God in the beginning, and indeed "was God." Only God, epitome and keeper of the Word, can satisfy the illiterate slave's desire to know this Word, "in the English and Dutch languages," because all human agencies are closed off to him by slavery. God-in-the-text, then, emerges from the text, and rewards his servant's unusual plea with its fulfillment at its most literal level. While we, his readers, find Jea's account of his literacy training to be allegorical at best, he does not seek to emphasize the event as figurative; on the contrary, by making it one more element in his linear narration (albeit a crucial one), and by representing it as the event that leads directly to his attainment of legal liberty, Jea disregards the strategies of revision drawn upon by Cugoano and Equiano (both of whom call attention to its figurative properties, as we have seen) and attempts to represent the several literal and figurative elements of the received trope as if they all happened. This is what I mean when I say that Jea literalizes the trope, that he erases its figurative properties by expanding its compacted denotations and connotations into a five-page account of the event that transforms his life in a most fundamental way.

But Jea's revision does more than make the trope literal. His revision names the trope and all of the transferences that we have seen to be at work in his antecedent narrators' revisions. His naming of the trope, moreover, is the event that, at last, enables him to tell *his* name, a name that he places in his title and that the text of his life elaborates upon in some detail. Jea's concern with naming is explicitly stated in the Wesley hymn that appears on the last page of his narrative, as an afterthought or coda. In two of the hymn's five stanzas, Wesley addresses the significance of naming explicitly and provocatively:

> I need not tell thee who I am;
>> My misery and sin declare:
> Thyself has call'd me by my name;
>> Look on thy hands, and read it there:
> But who, I ask thee, who art thou?
> Tell me thy Name, and tell me now. . . .
>
> Wilt thou not yet to me reveal
>> Thy new, unutterable Name?
> Tell me, I still beseech thee, tell;
>> To know it now, resolv'd I am:
> Wrestling I will not let thee go,
>> Till I thy name, thy Nature know.

Through a long dark night of the soul, like Jacob with the angel, the subject of the hymn wrestles with "the God-man" only to learn His name. In one's name is one's "Nature," the hymn says, arguing for a natural relationship between signs and what they signify. Jea inscribes his name in his autobiographical text, so that his readers can also know his name and thereby know his nature and that of the black slaves for whom he stands as the part stands for the whole.

What are the names he gives to the trope through his revision? Jea shows us that the trope of the Talking Book figures the difference that obtains in Western culture between the slave and the free, between African and European, between non-Christian and Christian. His revision tells us that true freedom, in the life of the slave, turns upon the mastery of Western letters or, more properly, upon the mastery inherent in the communion of the subject with the logos, in both its most literal and most figurative forms. He tells us that in literacy was to be found the sole sign of difference that separated chattel property from human being. And he tells us that this figure, as encoded in the tropes that he received from Gronniosaw, Marrant, Cugoano, and Equiano, was not merely a figure, but a figure of a figure, literacy being Western culture's trope of dominance over the peoples of color it had "discovered," colonized, and enslaved since the fifteenth century. Jea's revision also tells us that the trope, all along, has been one of presence, the presence of the human voice necessary for the black slave narrator effectively to transform himself—and to represent this transformation—from silent object to speaking subject, in the form of a life containable in autobiography.

Jea's revision also addresses the complex matter of the distance that separates the oral from the written. Just as what I am calling the trope of the Talking Book in fact is more properly the trope of the un-Talking Book, in which the canceled presence of an opposite term is enunciated by the silence or absence of the text, so too is Jea's literacy a canceled presence because he can only read one chapter of one book, albeit a major chapter of a major book.

Indeed it is not clear if Jea could read or write at all; despite the claim of his text's title that the autobiography has been "Compiled and Written by Himself," Jea tells us near the end of his tale (p. 95), "My dear reader, I would now inform you, that I have stated this in the best manner I am able, for I cannot write, therefore it is not so correct as if I had been able to have written it myself." Jea, in other words, can only make the text speak, as it were, by memorization rather than by the true mastery of its letters. His is the oral reading and writing of memory, of the sort practiced by the Yoruba *babalawo*. (Jea's birthplace of "Old Callabar," we recall, is in the east of Nigeria, where similar modes of narration would have obtained even in the eighteenth century.) Jea's is at best an ironic mode of reading. Like Gronniosaw and Marrant before him, never is he able to write his life, only to write it by oral narration. Jea is the third-term resolution between the illiterate slave and the fully literate European.

After Jea's revision, or erasure as I am thinking of it, the trope of the Talking Book disappears from the other slave narratives published in the nineteenth century. No longer is this sign of the presence of literacy, and all that this sign connotes in the life of the black slave, available for revision after Jea has erased its figurative properties by his turn to the supernatural. Rather, the trope of the Talking Book now must be displaced in a second-order revision in which the absence and presence of the speaking voice is refigured as the absence and presence of the written voice. Jea's scene of instruction, or midnight dream of instruction (did it actually happen, he wonders aloud as his readers wonder, or was it "only a dream?"), represents the dream of freedom as the dream of literacy, a dream realized as if by a miracle of literacy. Jea's dream is, as I have stated, composed of elements common to the usages of his black antecedents, but the central content of the trope has been expanded disproportionately from its figurative associations to its most literal level, wherein an angel teaches the slave how to read and thus escape the clutches of the devil that keeps the slave in chains. Equiano's angel was a young white boy; Frederick Douglass's guardian angel was the white woman married to his master. Many of the post-1830 slave narrators' guardian angels are also white women or children, related directly or indirectly by a marriage bond to the master.

These representations of the mastery of letters (literally, the A B C's) are clearly transferences and displacements of the dream of freedom figured for the tradition by Jea's text, again, in the most literal way. Whereas Jea's Signifyin(g) relation to Gronniosaw, Marrant, Cugoano, and Equiano is defined by a disproportionate expansion and elaboration upon the contents of their tropes, to such an extent that we are led to conclude that these narrators could have saved themselves loads of trouble had they only prayed to God intensely for six weeks to make the text speak, Jea's revision erased the trope (or Signified upon it by reducing it to the absurd) for the slave narrators who follow him in the tradition. They no longer can revise the trope merely by displacing or condensing its contents. Rather, Jea's supernatural naming demands that a completely new trope be figured to represent what Jea's revision has made unrepresentable without some sort of censorship, if the narrator is to be believed and believable as one who is capable of, and entitled to, the enjoyment of the secular idea of liberty that obtains in a text of a life such as Frederick Douglass's. Because Douglass and his black contemporaries wish to write their way to a freedom epitomized by the abolition movement, they cannot afford Jea's luxury of appealing, in his representation of his signal scene of instruction, primarily to the Christian converted. Douglass and his associates long for a secular freedom now. They can ill afford to represent even their previous selves—the earlier self that is transformed, as we read their texts, into the speaking subjects who obviously warrant full equality with white people—as so naive as to believe that books speak when their masters speak to them. Instead, the post-Jea narrators refigure the trope of the Talking Book by the secular equation of the mastery of slavery through the "simple" mastery of letters. Their dream of freedom, figured primarily in tropes of writing rather than speaking, constitutes a displacement of the eighteenth-century trope of the Talking Book, wherein the presence of the human voice in the text is only implied by its absence as we read these narratives and especially their tropes of writing (as Robert Stepto has so ably done) against the trope that we have been examining here.[68]

These narrators, linked by revision of a trope into the very first black chain of signifiers, implicitly Signify upon another chain, the metaphorical Great Chain of Being. Blacks were most commonly represented on the chain either as the lowest of the human races or as first cousin to the ape. Since writing, according to Hume, was the ultimate sign of difference between animal and human, these writers implicitly were Signifyin(g) upon the figure of the chain itself, simply by publishing autobiographies that were indictments of the received order of Western culture of which slavery, to them, by definition stood as the most salient sign. The writings of Gronniosaw, Marrant, Equiano, Cugoano, and Jea served as a critique of the sign of the Great Chain of Being and the black person's figurative place on the chain. This chain of black signifiers, regardless of their intent or desire, made the first political gesture in the Anglo-African literary tradition "simply" by the act of writing, a collective act that gave birth to the black literary tradition and defined it as the other's chain, the chain of black being as black people themselves would have it. Making the book speak, then, constituted a motivated, and political, engagement with and condemnation of Europe's fundamental figure of domination, the Great Chain of Being.

The trope of the Talking Book is not a trope of the presence of voice at all, but of its absence. To speak of a silent voice is to speak in an oxymoron. There is no such thing as a silent voice. Furthermore, as Juliet Mitchell has put the matter, there is something untenable about the attempt to represent what is not there, to represent what is *missing* or absent. Given that this is what these five black authors are seeking to do, we are justified in wondering aloud if the sort of subjectivity that they seek can be realized through a pro-

Chart 6. Typology of the Trope of the Talking Book*

	Chain	Status	Alienated from family	"Dutch or English"	Scene	Geo. Whitfield	Book
Gronniosaw	Gold	Slave prince	X	X	Middle passage	X	Bible
Marrant	Gold	Free prince	X		Moment of execution	X	Bible
Cugoano	Gold	Inca chief			Moment of confrontation		Breviary
Equiano	Gold (Watch)	Slave			Middle passage		Bible
Jea	Sin	Slave to sin; slave	X	X	Dark night of the soul	X	Bible

* I would like to thank Elizabeth Petrino, who prepared this chart.

cess that is so very ironic from the outset. Indeed, how can the black subject posit a full and sufficient self in a language in which blackness is a sign of absence?

The modes of revision of one trope that are charted in this chapter, a trope fundamental to the slave narratives in one form or another between 1770 and 1865, attest to the sort of shared, if altered, patterns of representation that serve to define a literary tradition. One could easily write an account of the shaping of the Afro-American tradition, from Briton Hammon's 1760 narrative to Alice Walker's *The Color Purple,* simply by explicating the figures used to represent the search of the black subject for a textual voice. In the three remaining chapters of this book, I wish to explore this matter of voicing and its various representations, first (Chapter 5) in Zora Neale Hurston's use of free indirect discourse in *Their Eyes Were Watching God,* a text whose central theme is the quest of a silent black woman both to find a voice and then to share it in loving dialogue with a friend (Phoeby) and a lover (Tea Cake), a process that turns upon the literal and figurative (or, more properly, the white and the black vernacular usages) of "Signifyin(g)." In Chapter 6 I wish to explicate the doubling of voices as the undergirding rhetorical strategy through which Ishmael Reed critiques and revises the black fiction tradition by an extended Signifyin(g) riff. Finally, concluding in Chapter 7, I wish to demonstrate how Alice Walker's Signification consists of a rewriting of the speakerly strategies of narration at work in Hurston's use of free indirect discourse, by turning to the epistolary novel and representing a subject who *writes* herself to a personal freedom and to a remarkable level of articulation in the dialect voice in which Hurston's protagonist *speaks.*

5

Zora Neale Hurston and the Speakerly Text

Our house stood within a few rods of the Chesapeake Bay, whose broad bosom was ever white with sails from every quarter of the habitable globe. Those beautiful vessels, robed in purest white, so delightful to the eye of freemen, were to me so many shrouded ghosts, to terrify and torment me with thoughts of my wretched condition. I have often, in the deep stillness of a summer's Sabbath, stood all alone upon the lofty banks of that noble bay, and traced, with saddened heart and tearful eye, the countless number of sails moving off to the mighty ocean. The sight of these always affected me powerfully. My thoughts would compel utterance; and there, with no audience but the Almighty, I would pour out my soul's complaint, in my rude way, with an apostrophe to the moving multitude of ships: —

"You are loosed from your moorings, and are free; I am fast in my chains, and am a slave! You move merrily before the gentle gale, and I sadly before the bloody whip! You are freedom's swift-winged angels, that fly around the world; I am confined in bands of iron! O that I were free!"

Frederick Douglass, 1845

Ships at a distance have every man's wish on board. For some they come in with the tide. For others they sail forever on the horizon, never out of sight, never landing until the Watcher turns his eyes away in resignation, his dreams mocked to death by Time. That is the life of men.

Now, women forget all those things they don't want to remember, and remember everything they don't want to forget. The dream is the truth. Then they act and do things accordingly.

Zora Neale Hurston, 1937

I

The eighteenth-century revisions of the trope of the Talking Book that I traced in Chapter 4 and its displacement into tropes of freedom and literacy in the slave narratives published after 1815 help us to understand the remarkable degree to which the quest to register a public black voice in Western letters preoccupied the Afro-American tradition's first century. Writing could be no mean thing in the life of the slave. What was at stake for the earliest black authors was nothing less than the implicit testimony to their humanity, a common humanity which they sought to demonstrate through the very writing of a text of an ex-slave's life. In one sense, not even legal manumission was of more importance to the slave community's status in Western culture than was the negation of the image of the black as an absence. To redress their image as a negation of all that was white and Western, black authors published as if their collective fate depended on how their texts would be received. It is as difficult to judge how effective this tacitly political gesture was as it is to judge how the negative image of the black in Western culture was affected by the publication of black texts. It seems apparent, however, that the abolition of slavery did not diminish the force of this impulse to write the race fully into the human community. Rather, the liberation of the slave community and the slow but steady growth of a black middle class between Reconstruction (1865–1876) and the sudden ending of the New Negro Renaissance (circa 1930) only seem to have made this impulse even more intense than it had been in antebellum America. Perhaps this was the case because, once slavery was abolished, racism assumed vastly more subtle forms. If slavery had been an immoral institution, it had also been a large, fixed target; once abolished, the target of racism splintered into hundreds of fragments, all of which seemed to be moving in as many directions. Just as the ex-slaves wrote to end slavery, so too did free black authors write to redress the myriad forms that the fluid mask of racism assumed between the end of the Civil War and the end of the Jazz Age.

If the writings of black people retained their implicitly political import after the war and especially after the sudden death of Reconstruction, then it should not surprise us that the search for a voice in black letters became a matter of grave concern among the black literati. This concern, as we might expect, led to remarkably polemical debates over the precise register which an "authentic" black voice would, or could, assume. It is also clear that postbellum black authors continued to read and revise the central figures they received from the fragments of tradition that somehow survived the latter nineteenth century's onslaught of de facto and de jure segregation. Zora Neale Hurston's revision of Frederick Douglass's apostrophe to the ships (the epigraphs to this chapter) is only one example of many such instances of a black textual grounding through revision.

Hurston underscores her revision of Douglass's canonical text by using two chiasmuses in her opening paragraphs.[1] The subject of the second paragraph of *Their Eyes Were Watching God* (women) reverses the subject of the first (men) and figures the nature of their respective desire in opposite terms. A man's desire becomes reified onto a disappearing ship, and he is transformed from a human being into "a Watcher," his desire personified onto an object, beyond his grasp or control, external to himself. Nanny, significantly, uses this "male" figure—"Ah could see uh big ship at a distance" (p. 35)—as does Tea Cake, whose use reverses Douglass's by indicating Tea Cake's claim of control of his fate and ability to satisfy Jamie's desire: "Can't no ole man stop me from gittin' no ship for yuh if dat's whut you want. Ah'd git dat ship out from under him so slick til he'd be walkin' de water lak ole Peter befo' he knowed it" (p. 154).

A woman, by contrast, represents desire metaphorically, rather than metonymically, by controlling the process of memory, an active subjective process figured in the pun on (re)membering, as in the process of narration which Janie will share with her friend, Phoeby, and which we shall "overhear." For a woman, "The dream is the truth"; the truth is her dream. Janie, as we shall see, is thought to be (and is maintained) "inarticulate" by her first two husbands but is a master of metaphorical narration; Joe Starks, her most oppressive husband, by contrast, is a master of metonym, an opposition which Janie must navigate her selves through to achieve self-knowledge. The first sentence ("Now, women forget all those things they don't want to remember, and remember everything they don't want to forget") is itself a chiasmus (women/remember//remember/forget), similar in structure to Douglass's famous chiasmus, "You have seen how a man became a slave, you will see how a slave became a man." Indeed, Douglass's major contribution to the slave's narrative was to make chiasmus the central trope of slave narration, in which a slave-object writes himself or herself into a human-subject through the act of writing. The overarching rhetorical strategy of the slave narratives written after 1845 can be represented as a chiasmus, as repetition and reversal. Hurston, in these enigmatic opening paragraphs, Signifies upon Douglass through formal revision.

This sort of formal revision is one mode of tacit commentary about the shape and status of received tradition. A more explicit mode was the literary criticism published by blacks as a response to specific black texts which, despite great difficulties, somehow managed to be published. While this subject demands a full-length study, I can summarize its salient aspects here. The debate about the register of the black voice assumed two poles. By the end of the Civil War, the first pole of the debate, the value of the representation, of the reality imitated in the text, had been firmly established. Black authors wrote almost exclusively about their social and political condition as black people living in a society in which race was, at best, problematical. By the turn of the century, a second and more subtle pole of the debate had become predominant, and that pole turned upon precisely how an authentic black voice should be represented in print. The proper manner and matter of representation of a black printed voice are not truly separable, of course; these poles of concern could merge, and often did, as in the heated issue of the import of Paul Laurence Dunbar's late-nineteenth-century dialect poetry. To understand more fully just how curious were Zora Neale Hurston's rhetorical strategies of revision in *Their Eyes Were Watching God* (1937) and just how engaged in debate these strategies were with the Afro-American tradition, it is useful to summarize the nineteenth-century arguments about representation.

We gain some understanding of this concern over representation by examining *The Anglo-African Magazine,* published in New York by Thomas

Hamilton between January 1859 and March 1860. Hamilton, in his introductory "Apology" to the first number, argues what for his generation was
self-evident: "[black people], in order to assert and maintain their rank as
men among men, must speak for themselves; no outside tongue, however
gifted with eloquence, can tell their story." Blacks must "speak for themselves," Hamilton writes, to counter the racist "endeavor to write down the
negro as something less than a man."[2] In the second number, W. J. Wilson,
in a poem entitled "The Coming Man," defines the presence of the text to
be that which separates "the undefinable present," "the dim misty past," and
"the unknown future":

> I am resolved. 'Tis more than half my task;
> 'Twas the great need of all my passed existence.
> The glooms that have so long shrouded me,
> Recede as vapor from the new presence,
> And the light-gleam—it must be life
> So brightens and spreads its rays before,
> That I read my Mission as 'twere a book.[3]

Wilson's figure of life as a text to be read, of the race's life as embodied in
the book, Frances E. W. Harper elaborated upon in a letter to the editor
later that same year. In this letter, we have recorded one of the first challenges to what was then, and has remained, the preoccupation of Afro-
American male writers: the great and terrible subject of white racism. "If
our talents are to be recognized," Frances Harper writes,

> we must write less of issues that are particular and more of feelings that
> are general. We are blessed with hearts and brains that compass more
> than ourselves in our present plight. . . . We must look to the future
> which, God willing, will be better than the present or the past, and delve
> into the heart of the world.[4]

Consider the sheer audacity of this black woman, perhaps our first truly professional writer, who could so freely advocate this position in the great crisis
year of 1859, which witnessed both John Brown's aborted raid on the Harper's Ferry arsenal and the U.S. Supreme Court's decision to uphold the
constitutionality of the Fugitive Slave Act of 1850. Harper, in this statement
about representation and in her poems and fictions, demanded that black
writers embrace as their subjects "feelings that are general," feelings such
as love and sex, birth and death. The debate over the content of black literature had begun, then, as articulated by a black woman writer.

Whereas Harper expressed concern for a new content or "signifier," a
content that was at once black, self-contained, and humanly general, the
other pole of the debate about representation concerned itself with the exact
form that the signifier should take. This concern over what I am calling the
signifier occupied, in several ways and for various reasons, the center of
black aesthetic theory roughly between the publication of Paul Laurence
Dunbar's *Lyrics of Lowly Life* in 1895 and at least the publication in 1937
of Zora Neale Hurston's *Their Eyes Were Watching God*. This debate, curi-

ously enough, returns us in the broadest sense to the point of departure of
this chapter, namely the absence and presence of the black voice in the text,
that which caused Gronniosaw so much consternation and perplexity. It is
not surprising that Dunbar's widely noted presence should engender, in part,
the turn of critical attention to matters of language and voice, since it is he
who stands, unquestionably, as the most accomplished black dialect poet,
and the most successful black poet before Langston Hughes. Nor is it surprising that Hurston's lyrical text should demarcate an ending of this debate,
since Hurston's very rhetorical strategy, her invention of what I have chosen
to call the speakerly text, seems designed to mediate between, for fiction,
what Sterling A. Brown's representation of the black voice mediated between for black poetic diction: namely, a profoundly lyrical, densely metaphorical, quasi-musical, privileged black oral tradition on the one hand, and
a received but not yet fully appropriated standard English literary tradition
on the other hand. The quandary for the writer was to find a third term, a
bold and novel signifier, informed by these two related yet distinct literary
languages. This is what Hurston tried to do in *Their Eyes.*

Critics widely heralded Dunbar's black poetic diction, and poets, white
and black, widely imitated it. It is difficult to understand the millennarian
tones of Dunbar's critical reception. The urgent calls for a black "redeemer-
poet," so common in the black newspapers and periodicals published between 1827 and 1919, by the late 1880s were being echoed by white critics.
One anonymous white woman critic, for example, who signed herself only
as "A Lady from Philadelphia," wrote in *Lippincott's Monthly Magazine* in
1886 that "The Coming American Novelist" would be "of African origin."[5]
This great author would be one "With us" but "not of us," one who "has
suffered everything a poet, a dramatist, a novelist need suffer before he
comes to have his lips anointed." "When one comes to consider the subject,"
this critic concludes, "there is no improbability to it." After all, she continues, the African "has given us the only national music we have ever had,"
a corpus of art "distinctive in musical history." He is, moreover, "a natural
story-teller,"[6] uniquely able to fabricate what she calls "acts of the imagination," discourses in which no "morality is involved."

> [Why] should not this man, who has suffered so much, who is so easy to
> amuse, so full of his own resources, and who is yet undeveloped, why
> should he not some day soon tell a story that shall interest, amuse us, stir
> our hearts, and make a new epoch in our literature?[7]

Then, in a remarkable reversal, the writer makes an even bolder claim:

> Yet farther: I have used the generic masculine pronoun because it is
> convenient; but Fate keeps revenges in store. It was a woman who,
> taking the wrongs of the African as her theme, wrote the novel that
> awakened the world to their reality, and why should not the coming
> novelist be a woman as well as an African? She—the woman of that race—
> has some claims on Fate which are not yet paid up.

It is difficult to discern which of this critic's two claims is the bolder: that the great American writer would be black or that she would be a black woman. It is not difficult, however, to summarize the energizing effect on our literary tradition which this critic's prediction was to have. Even as late as 1899, W. S. Scarborough would still cite this *Lippincott's* essay to urge black writers to redeem "the race."[8]

W. H. A. Moore, writing about "A Void in Our Literature" in 1890, called for the appearance of a great black poet whose presence would stand as "an indication of the character of [the Afro-American's] development on those lines which determine the capacity of a people." "The Afro-American," he continues,

> has not given to English literature a great poet. No one of his kind has, up to this day, lent influence to the literature of his time, save Phillis Wheatley. It is not to be expected that he would. And yet every fragment, every whispering of his benighted muse is scanned with eager and curious interest in the hope that here may be found the gathered breathings of a true singer.[9]

"The keynote," Moore concludes, "has not yet been struck." To find a poetic diction which reflects "the inner workings of the subject which it seeks to portray," Moore argues, "is the mission of the race." Moore's essay is merely typical of many others published between 1865 and 1930. For example, in 1893, H. T. Johnson, editor of the *Recorder,* outlined the need for race authors to express racial aspirations. Five years later, H. T. Kealing wrote of the unique contributions that only Negro authors could make. The literature of any people, he said, had an indigenous quality, "the product of the national peculiarities and race idiosyncrasies that no alien could duplicate." He called upon the Negro author not to imitate whites, as had been the case hitherto, but to reach "down to the original and unexplored depths of his own being where lies unused the material that is to provide him a place among the great writers." Similarly, Scarborough, speaking at the Hampton Negro Conference in 1899, called for something higher than the false dialect types depicted by white authors; even Chesnutt's and Dunbar's short stories had not gone far enough in portraying the higher aspirations of the race. Only the Negro author could portray the Negro best—his "loves and hates, his hopes and fears, his ambitions, his whole life, in such a way that the world will weep and laugh . . . forgetting completely that the hero and heroine are God's bronze image, but knowing only that they are men and women with joys and sorrows that belong to the whole human family." In the discussion that followed Scarborough's paper, it was agreed that the types portrayed in "vaudeville" were false. Lucy Laney, principal of the Haines Norman and Industrial Institute, prefigured a major interest of the 1920s when she spoke of the material for short stories to be found in the rural South and called upon Negro writers to go down to the sea islands of Georgia and South Carolina "where they could study the Negro in his original purity," with a culture and a voice "close to the African."[10]

Into this black milieu wrote Paul Lawrence Dunbar. Perhaps because we tend to read Dunbar backwards, as it were, through the poetry of Sterling A. Brown and the early Langston Hughes, and through the often unfortunate poetic efforts of Dunbar's less talented imitators, we tend to forget how startling was Dunbar's use of black dialect as the basis of a poetic diction. After all, by 1895, dialect had come to connote black innate mental inferiority, the linguistic sign both of human bondage (as origin) and of the continued failure of "improvability" or "progress," two turn-of-the-century keywords. Dialect signified both "black difference" and that the figure of the black in literature existed primarily as object, not subject; and even sympathetic characterizations of the black, such as Uncle Remus by Joel Chandler Harris, were far more related to a racist textual tradition that stemmed from minstrelsy, the plantation novel, and vaudeville than to representations of spoken language. As Scarborough summarized the matter:

> Both northern and southern writers have presented Negro nature, Negro dialect, Negro thought, as they conceived it, too often, alas, as evolved out of their own consciousness. Too often the dialect has been inconsistent, the types presented, mere composite photographs as it were, or uncouth specimens served up so as the humorous side of the literary setting might be properly balanced.[11]

This received literary tradition of plantation and vaudeville art, Scarborough concluded, demanded "realism" to refute the twin gross stereotypes of characterization and the representation of black speech.

For Dunbar to draw upon dialect as the medium through which to posit this mode of realism suggests both a certain boldness as well as a certain opportunism, two qualities that helped to inform Dunbar's mixed results, which we know so well, he lamented to his death. Dunbar, nevertheless, Signified upon the received white racist textual tradition and posited in its stead a black poetic diction which his more gifted literary heirs would, in their turn, Signify upon, with often pathetic results. What Sterling A. Brown would realize in the language of his poetry, Zora Neale Hurston would realize in the language of her fiction. For, after Dunbar, the two separate poles of the debate over black mimetic principles, over the shape of the signifier and the nature of the signified, could no longer be thought of independently. Dunbar's primary rhetorical gesture, as Scarborough concluded in 1899, had been to do just that:

> And here we pause to see what [Dunbar and Chesnutt] have added to our literature, what new artistic value they have discovered. [Both] have followed closely the "suffering side," the portrayal of the old fashioned Negro of "befo' de wah,"—the Negro that [Thomas Nelson] Page and [Joel Chandler] Harris and others have given a permanent place in literature. But they have done one thing more; they have presented the facts of Negro life with a thread running through both warp and woof that shows not only humour and pathos, humility, self-sacrifice, courtesy

and loyalty, but something at times of the higher aims, ambition, desires, hopes, and aspiration of the race—but by no means as fully and to as great an extent as we had hoped they would do.[12]

How the black writer represented, and what he or she represented, were now indissolubly linked in black aesthetic theory.

In the curious manner by which one generation's parenthetical concerns come to form the central questions of a subsequent generation's critical debate, Scarborough's judgement that Dunbar's representations of the folk "befo' de wah" were potentially capable of encompassing more than "humour and pathos" became the lynchpin of James Weldon Johnson's attack on dialect as a poetic diction. I have sketched the debate over dialect elsewhere.[13] Suffice it to say here that that great American realist, William Dean Howells, in 1896, thought that Dunbar's dialect verse was a representation of reality, a "portrait . . . undeniably like." The political import of this artistic achievement, Howells maintained, was unassailable: "A race which has reached this effect in any of its members can no longer be held wholly uncivilized; and intellectually Mr. Dunbar makes a stronger claim for the negro than the negro has yet done."[14] By the 1920s, however, dialect was thought to be a literary trap.

A careful study of the aesthetic theories of the New Negro Renaissance suggests strongly that the issue of dialect as an inappropriate literary language seems to have been raised in order for a second poetic diction to be posited in its place. Indeed, we can with some justification set as boundaries of this literary movement James Weldon Johnson's critiques of dialect, which he published in his separate "Prefaces" to the first and second editions of *The Book of American Negro Poetry,* printed in 1923 and 1931, respectively, but also Johnson's "Introduction" to the first edition of Sterling A. Brown's *Southern Road,* printed in 1932.

In his "Preface," Johnson had defined the urgent task of the new black writer to be the "break away from, not Negro dialect itself, but the limitations of Negro dialect imposed by the fixing effects of long convention." And what were these limitations? Said Johnson, "it is an instrument with but two full stops, humor and pathos," repeating and reversing Scarborough's terms. Nine years later, in his second "Preface," Johnson could assert assuredly that "the passing of traditional dialect as a medium for Negro poets is complete." Just one year later, however, Brown's poetry forced Johnson to admit that, although Brown "began writing just after Negro poets had generally discarded conventionalized dialect, with its minstrel traditions of Negro life," he has "infused his [dialect] poetry with genuine characteristic flavor by adopting as his medium the common, racy living speech of the Negro in certain phases of *real* life." Brown's achievement, Johnson acknowledges, is that he has turned to "folk poetry" as a source of a poetic diction, "deepened its meanings and multiplied its implications. . . . In a word, he has taken this raw material and worked it into original and authentic power."

Brown's poetry, then, in a remarkably tangible sense, marks the end of the New Negro Renaissance as well as the resolution, for black poetic diction, of a long debate over its mimetic principles.[15]

Brown's achievement in poetry, however, had no counterpart in fiction. True, Jean Toomer's *Cane* can be thought of as a fictional antecedent of Brown's poetic diction, both of whose works inform the structure of *Their Eyes Were Watching God*. Yet Toomer's use of the privileged oral voice, and especially its poignant silences, is not without its ironies, since Toomer employs the black oral voice in his text both as a counterpoint to that standard English voice of his succession of narrators but also as evidence of the modernist claim that there had existed no privileged, romantic movement of unified consciousness, especially or not even in the cane fields of a rural Georgia echoing its own swan song. Existence, in the world of *Cane,* is bifurcated, fundamentally opposed, as represented by all sorts of binary oppositions, among these standard English and black speech, as well as black and white, male and female, South and North, textual desire and sensual consummation. Even in that fiction's long, final section, called "Kabnis," in which the place of the narrator becomes that of stage directions in a tragedy, the presence of the oral voice retains its primarily antiphonal function, as in the following exchange among Halsey, Layman, and Kabnis:

> Halsey (in a mock religious tone): Amen t that, brother Layman. Amen (turning to Kabnis, half playful, yet somehow dead in earnest). An Mr. Kabnis, kindly remember youre in th land of cotton—hell of a land. Th white folks get the boll; th niggers get th stalk. An dont you dare touch th boll, or even look at it. They'll swing y sho. (Laughs)
>
> Kabnis: But they wouldnt touch a gentleman—fellows, men like us three here—
>
> Layman: Nigger's a nigger down this away, Professor. An only two dividins: good an bad. An even they aint permanent categories. They sometimes mixes um up when it comes t lynchin. I've seen um do it.[16]

Toomer's representation of black spoken language, even in this instance, stands essentially as an element of plot and of theme.

Rather than as a self-contained element of literary structure, the oral voice in *Cane* is a motivated sign of duality, of opposition, which Toomer thematizes in each section of his fiction, and specifically in this passage:

> Kabnis: . . . An besides, he aint my past. My ancestors were Southern blue-bloods—
>
> Lewis: And black.
>
> Kabnis: Aint much difference between blue an black.
>
> Lewis: Enough to draw a denial from you. Cant hold them, can you? Master; slave. Soil; and the overarching heavens. Dusk; dawn. They fight and bastardize you. The sun tint of your cheeks, flame of the great season's multi-colored leaves, tarnished, burned. Split, shredded: easily burned. No use . . .
>
> His gaze shifts to Steiia. Stella's face draws back, her breasts come towards him.

Stella: I aint got nothin f y, mister. Taint no use t look at me. (pp. 217–18)

It would not be until Zora Neale Hurston began to publish novels that Toomer's rhetorical innovation would be extended in black fiction, although the line between Toomer's lyricism and Brown's regionalism is a direct one. Indeed, although Toomer received enthusiastic praise for *Cane,* this praise remained vague and ill defined. Du Bois, for instance, saw the import of the book as its subject matter, which he defined to be male-female sexual relations, which, he protested, were notably absent from the corpus of black fiction. There is not much truly consummated or untroubled sex in *Cane* either, but at least for Du Bois the text treated its possibility. For Du Bois, this stood as *Cane*'s significant breakthrough.

By 1923, when Toomer published *Cane,* the concern over the nature and function of representation, of what we might profitably think of as the ideology of mimesis, had focused on one aesthetic issue, which Du Bois would call "How Shall the Negro Be Portrayed?" and which we can, boldly I admit, think of as "What to do with the folk?" Despite scores of essays, exchanges, and debates over this problematic of representation, however, by 1929 not only had Toomer's innovations apparently been forgotten, but ironclad "Instructions for Contributors" had been widely circulated among black writers in the "Illustrated Feature Section" of the Negro press. Since these help us to begin to understand the major place of *Their Eyes Were Watching God* in the history of black rhetorical strategies, let me reprint these instructions, written by George S. Schuyler, in full:

> Every manuscript submitted must be written in each-sentence-a-paragraph style.
>
> Stories must be full of human interest. Short, simple words. No attempt to parade erudition to the bewilderment of the reader. No colloquialisms such as "nigger," "darkey," "coon," etc. Plenty of dialogue, and language that is realistic.
>
> We will not accept any stories that are depressing, saddening, or gloomy. Our people have enough troubles without reading about any. We want them to be interested, cheered, and buoyed up; conforted, gladdened, and made to laugh.
>
> Nothing that casts the least reflection on contemporary moral or sex standards will be allowed. Keep away from the erotic! Contributions must be clean and wholesome.
>
> Everything must be written in that intimate manner that wins the reader's confidence at once and makes him or her feel that what is written is being spoken exclusively to that particular reader.
>
> No attempt should be made to be obviously artistic. Be artistic, of course, but "put it over" on the reader so he or she will be unaware of it.
>
> Stories must be swiftly moving, gripping the interest and sweeping on to a climax. The heroine should always be beautiful and desirable, sincere and virtuous. The hero should be of the he-man type, but not stiff, stereotyped, or vulgar. The villain should obviously be a villain and of the deepest-dyed variety: crafty, unscrupulous, suave, and resourceful.

Above all, however, these characters must live and breathe, and be just ordinary folks such as the reader has met. The heroine should be of the brown-skin type.

All matter should deal exclusively with Negro life. Nothing will be permitted that is likely to engender ill feelings between blacks and whites. The color problem is bad enough without adding any fuel to the fire.[17]

It is precisely these strictures, widely circulated in those very journals in which black authors could most readily publish, which, along with the extended controversy over black oral forms, enable us to begin to understand the black milieu against which Hurston would define herself as a writer of fiction. Here we can only recall, with some irony, W. S. Scarborough's 1899 plea for a great black novelist:

We are tired of vaudeville, of minstrelsy and of the Negro's pre-eminence in those lines. We want something higher, something more inspiring than that. We turn to the Negro for it. Shall we have it? The black novelist is like the white novelist, in too many instances swayed by the almighty dollar. . . . Like Esau he is ready to sell his birthright for a mess of pottage.

Let the Negro writer of fiction make of his pen and brain all-compelling forces to treat of that which he well knows, best knows, and give it to the world with all the imaginative power possible, with all the magic touch of an artist. Let him portray the Negro's loves and hates, his hopes and fears, his ambitions, his whole life, in such a way that the world will weep and laugh over the pages, finding the touch that makes all nature kin, forgetting completely that hero and heroine are God's bronze images, but knowing only that they are men and women with joys and sorrows that belong alike to the whole human family. Such is the novelist that the race desires. Who is he that will do it? Who is he that can do it?[18]

He that could do it, it seems, turned out to be a she, Zora Neale Hurston.

II

Zora Neale Hurston is the first writer that our generation of black and feminist critics has brought into the canon, or perhaps I should say the canons. For Hurston is now a cardinal figure in the Afro-American canon, the feminist canon, and the canon of American fiction, especially as our readings of her work become increasingly close readings, which Hurston's texts sustain delightfully. The curious aspect of the widespread critical attention being shown to Hurston's texts is that so many critics embracing such a diversity of theoretical approaches seem to find something new at which to marvel in her texts.

My own method of reading *Their Eyes Were Watching God* stems fundamentally from the debates over modes of representation, over theories of mimesis, which as I have suggested form such a crucial part of the history of Afro-American literature and its theory. Mimetic principles can be both implicitly and explicitly ideological, and the explication of Hurston's rhetorical strategy, which I shall attempt below, is no exception. I wish to read *Their Eyes* in such a way as to move from the broadest notion of *what* it thematizes through an ever-tighter spiral of *how* it thematizes, that is, its rhetorical strategies. I shall attempt to show that Hurston's text not only cleared a rhetorical space for the narrative strategies that Ralph Ellison would render so deftly in *Invisible Man,* but also that Hurston's text is the first example in our tradition of "the speakerly text," by which I mean a text whose rhetorical strategy is designed to represent an oral literary tradition, designed "to emulate the phonetic, grammatical, and lexical patterns of actual speech and produce the 'illusion of oral narration.' "[19] The speakerly text is that text in which all other structural elements seem to be devalued, as important as they remain to the telling of the tale, because the narrative strategy signals attention to its own importance, an importance which would seem to be the privileging of oral speech and its inherent linguistic features. Whereas Toomer's *Cane* draws upon the black oral voice essentially as a different voice from the narrator's, as a repository of socially distinct, contrapuntal meanings and beliefs, a speakerly text would seem primarily to be oriented toward imitating one of the numerous forms of oral narration to be found in classical Afro-American vernacular literature.

Obviously, I am concerned with what we traditionally think of as matters of voice. "Voice" here connotes not only traditional definitions of "point of view," a crucial matter in the reading of *Their Eyes*, but also the linguistic presence of a literary tradition that exists for us as a written text primarily because of the work of sociolinguists and anthropologists such as Hurston. I am concerned in this chapter to discuss the representation of what we might think of as the voice of the black oral tradition—represented here as direct speech—as well as with Hurston's use of free indirect discourse as the rhetorical analogue to the text's metaphors of inside and outside, so fundamental to the depiction of Janie's quest for consciousness, her very quest to become a speaking black subject. Just as we have begun to think of Hurston as an artist whose texts relate to those of Jean Toomer and Sterling A. Brown, let us round out our survey of the tradition by comparing Hurston's concept of voice with that of Richard Wright and Ralph Ellison.

In *American Hunger* (1977), which along with *Black Boy* (1945) comprises the full text of an autobiography he initially called "The Horror and the Glory," Richard Wright succinctly outlines his idea of the ironic relationship between the individual black talent and an Afro-American cultural tradition ravaged and laid waste to by an omnipresent and irresistible white racism:

> What could I dream of that had the barest possibility of coming true? I could think of nothing. And, slowly, it was upon exactly that nothing-ness that my mind began to dwell, that constant sense of wanting without having, of being hated without reason. A dim notion of what life meant to a Negro in America was coming to consciousness in me, not in terms

of external events, lynchings, Jim Crowism, and the endless brutalities, but in terms of crossed-up feelings, of psyche pain. I sensed that Negro life was a sprawling land of unconscious suffering, and that there were but few Negroes who knew the meaning of their lives, who could tell their [own] story.[20]

Wright, as both of his autobiographies seem intent on claiming, certainly counted himself among those few Negroes who could tell not only their own story but also the woeful tale of their pathetic, voiceless black countrymen. If they were signs of the "horror," then his articulated escape was meant to be our "glory."

In his autobiographies and novels, Wright evolved a curious and complex myth of origins of self and race. Whereas a large part of the black autobiographical tradition, as exemplified by Frederick Douglass's three autobiographies, generally depicts a resplendent self as representative of possibilities denied systematically to one's voiceless fellow blacks, Wright's class of ideal individual black selves seems to have included only Wright. *Black Boy*, for example, charts how the boy, Dick, through the key texts of naturalism, gave a shape and a purpose to an exceptional inherent nobility of spirit which emerges from within the chaotic depths of the black cultural maelstrom. Wright's humanity is achieved only at the expense of his fellow blacks, pitiable victims of the pathology of slavery and racial segregation who surround and suffocate him. Indeed, Wright wills this especial self into being through the agency of contrast: the sensitive, healthy part is foregrounded against a determined, defeated black whole. He is a noble black savage, in the ironic tradition of Oroonoko and film characters played by Sidney Poitier—the exception, not the rule.

For Ralph Ellison, Wright's notion of the self and its relation to black culture seemed unduly costly. Indeed, it is this dark and brooding fiction of black culture against which both Ellison and James Baldwin railed, drawing upon a rich body of tropes and rhetorical strategies prefigured, among other places, in Hurston's fictions and critical writings. It is this fiction of obliteration that created the great divide in black literature, a fissure first rendered apparent in the late thirties in an extended debate between Hurston and Wright.

The Hurston-Wright debate, staged not only in the lyrical shape of *Their Eyes Were Watching God* (1937) against the naturalism of *Native Son* (1940) but also in reviews of each other's books, turns between two poles of a problematic of representation—between what is represented and what represents, between the signifier and the signified. Theirs are diametrically opposed notions of the internal structure of the sign, the very sign of blackness.

Hurston rather self-consciously defined her theory of the novel against that received practice of realism which Wright would attempt to revitalize in *Native Son*. Hurston thought that Wright stood at the center of "the sobbing school of Negrohood who hold that nature somehow has given them a low down dirty deal."[21] Against Wright's idea of psychological destruction and chaos, Hurston framed a counternotion which the repressed and conservative maternal figure of *Their Eyes* articulates: "[It] wasn't for me to fulfill my dreams of whut a woman oughta be and to do. Dat's one of de hold-backs of slavery. But nothing can't stop you from wishin'. You can't beat nobody down so low till you can rob 'em of they will." The sign of this transcendent self would be the shaping of a strong, self-reflective voice: "Ah wanted to preach a great sermon about colored women sittin' on high, but they wasn't no pulpit for me. Freedom found me widh a baby daughter in mah arms, so Ah said Ah'd take a broom and a cook-pot and throw up a highway through de wilderness for her. She would expound what Ah felt. But somehow she got lost offa de highway and next thing Ah knowed here you was in de world. So whilst Ah was tendin' you of nights Ah said Ah'd save de text for you."[22] Hurston revoices this notion of the articulating subject in her autobiography, *Dust Tracks on the Road* (1942), in a curious account of her mother's few moments before death: "Her mouth was slightly open, but her breathing took up so much of her strength that she could not talk. But she looked at me, or so I felt, to speak for her. She depended on me for a voice."[23] We can begin to understand how far apart Hurston and Wright stand in the tradition if we compare Hurston's passage about her mother with the following passage from Wright's *Black Boy,* a deathbed revision of Hurston's passage:

> Once, in the night, my mother called me to her bed and told me that she could not endure the pain, that she wanted to die. I held her hand and begged her to be quiet. That night I ceased to react to my mother; my feelings were frozen.[24]

Wright explains that this event, and his mother's extended suffering, "grew into a symbol in my mind, gathering to itself all the poverty, the ignorance, the helplessness; . . . Her life set the emotional tone of my life, colored the men and women I was to meet in the future, conditioned my relation to events that had not happened, determined my attitude to situations and circumstances I had yet to face." If Hurston figures her final moments with her mother in terms of the search for a voice, then Wright, three years later, figures the significance of a similar scene as responsible for a certain "somberness of spirit that I was never to lose." No two authors in the tradition are more dissimilar than Hurston and Wright.

The narrative voice Hurston created, and her legacy to Afro-American fiction, is a lyrical and disembodied yet individual voice, from which emerges a singular longing and utterance, a transcendent, ultimately racial self, extending far beyond the merely individual. Hurston realized a resonant and authentic narrative voice that echoes and aspires to the status of the impersonality, anonymity, and authority of the black vernacular tradition, a nameless, selfless tradition, at once collective and compelling, true somehow to the unwritten text of a common blackness. For Hurston, the search for a telling form of language, indeed the search for a black literary language itself, defines the search for the self. Similarly, for Ellison, the self can emerge

only through the will, as signified by the problematical attempt to write itself into being, a unique black self consolidated and rendered integral within
a first-person narrative structure.

For Wright, nature was ruthless, irreducible, and ineffable. Unlike Hurston and Ellison, Wright sees fiction not as a model of reality but as a representative bit of it, a literal report of the real. Art, for Wright, always remains
referential. His blackness, therefore, can never be a mere sign; it is rather
the text of his great and terrible subject. Accordingly, Wright draws upon
the voice of the third-person, past-tense authorial mode and various tools of
empirical social science and naturalism to blend public with private experience, inner with outer history. Rarely does he relinquish what Roland Barthes
calls the "proprietary consciousness," the constant sign of his presence and
of some larger context, which the third-person voice inevitably entails. Rather
predictably, Wright found Hurston's great novel to be "counter-revolution-
ary," while Hurston replied that she wrote novels "and not treatises on
sociology."

Hurston, Wright, and Ellison's divergent theories of narrative structure
and voice, the cardinal points of a triangle of influence, with their attendant
ramifications upon the ideology of form and its relation to knowledge and
power, comprise a matrix of issues to which subsequent black fictions, by
definition, must respond. The rhetorical question that subsequent texts must
answer remained the question which the structure of *Their Eyes* answered for
Hurston: "In what voice would the Negro speak for her or himself in the
language of fiction?" By discussing *Their Eyes*' topoi and figures, its depiction of the relationship among character, consciousness, and setting, and its
engagement of shifting points of view, we can begin to understand how
primary Hurston's rhetorical strategies remain in this compelling text.

On the broadest level, *Their Eyes* depicts the search for identity and self-
understanding of an Afro-American woman. This quest for self-knowledge,
which the text thematizes through an opposition between the inside and the
outside of things, directs attention to itself as a central theme of the novel
by certain narrative strategies. I am thinking here especially of the use of the
narrative frame and of a special form of plot negation. The tale of Janie
Crawford-Killicks-Starks-Woods is narrated to her best friend, Phoeby, while
the two sit together on Janie's back porch. We, the readers, "overhear" the
tale that Janie narrates to her auditor, whose name we recall signifies the
poet. Phoeby, as we might suspect, is an ideal listener: to seduce Janie into
narrating her story, Phoeby confesses to her friend, "It's hard for me to
understand what you mean, de way you tell it. And then again Ah'm hard
of understandin' at times" (p. 19). Phoeby speaks as the true pupil; Janie
responds as the true pedagogue:

> "Naw, 'tain't nothin' lak you might think. So 'tain't no use in me tell-
> ing you somethin' unless Ah give you de understandin' to go 'long wid it.
> Unless you see de fur, a mink skin ain't no different from a coon hide.
> Looka heah, Phoeby, is Sam waitin' on you for his supper?" (p. 19)

At the end of the telling of Janie's tale, an interruption which the text signifies by ellipses and a broad white space (on p. 283), Phoeby, always the perfect pupil, responds to her teacher as each of us wishes the students to respond:

> "Lawd!" Phoeby breathed out heavily, "Ah done growed ten feet higher from jus' listenin' tuh you, Janie. Ah ain't satisfied wid mahself no mo'. Ah means tuh make Sam take me fishin' wid him after this. Nobody better not criticize yuh in mah hearin." (p. 284)

Such a powerfully transforming tale has effected an enhanced awareness even in Janie's transfixed pupil. And to narrate this tale, Hurston draws upon the framing device, which serves on the order of plot to interrupt the received narrative flow of linear narration of the realistic novel, and which serves on the order of theme to enable Janie to recapitulate, control, and narrate her own story of becoming, the key sign of sophisticated understanding of the self. Indeed, Janie develops from a nameless child, known only as "Alphabet," who cannot even recognize her own likeness as a "colored" person in a photograph, to the implied narrator of her own tale of self-consciousness. This is merely one of Hurston's devices to achieve thematic unity.

Hurston matches the use of the frame with the use of negation as a mode of narrating the separate elements of the plot. The text opens and ends in the third-person omniscient voice, which allows for a maximum of information giving. Its third paragraph commences: "So the beginning of this was a woman and she had come back from burying the dead" (p. 9). By introducing this evidence of the return from burying the dead, Hurston negates her text's themes of discovery, rebirth, and renewal, only to devote the remainder of her text to realizing these same themes. Hurston also draws upon negation to reveal, first, the series of self-images that Janie does not wish to be and, second, to define the matrix of obstacles that frustrate her desire to know herself. The realization of the full text of *Their Eyes* represents the fulfillment of the novel's positive potentialities, by which I mean Janie's discovery of self-knowledge.

How does this negated form of plot development unfold? Hurston rather cleverly develops her plot by depicting a series of intimate relationships in which Janie engages with a fantasy of sexual desire, then with her grandmother, with her first husband (Logan Killicks), her second husband (Joe Starks), and, finally, with her ideal lover, Vergible Woods, "Tea Cake." Her first three relationships are increasingly problematic and self-negating, complex matters which Hurston renders through an inverse relationship between character or consciousness on one hand and setting on the other. If we think about it, Janie comes to occupy progressively larger physical spaces—Nanny's cabin in the backyard of the Washburn's place, Logan Killick's "often-mentioned" sixty acres, and, finally, Joe Starks's big white wooden house, replete with banisters, and his centrally located general store. Indeed, it is fair to say that Mayor Starks owns the town. With each successive move to

a larger physical space, however, her housemate seeks to confine Janie's consciousness inversely, seemingly, by just as much. It is only when she eschews
what her grandmother had named the "protection" (p. 30) both of material
possessions and of rituals of entitlement (i.e., bourgeois marriage) and moves
to the swamp, to "the muck," with Vergible "Teacake" Woods that she, at
last, gains control of her understanding of herself. We can, in fact, conclude
that the text opposes bourgeois notions of progress (Killicks owns the only
organ "amongst colored folks"; Joe Starks is a man of "positions and possessions") and of the Protestant work ethic, to more creative and lyrical
notions of unity. Tea Cake's only possession is a guitar. The relationship
between character and setting, then, is ideal for the pedagogical purpose of
revealing that character and setting are merely aspects of narrative strategy,
and not things in the ordinary sense that we understand a thing to be.

One pleasant way to chart this relationship between consciousness and
setting is to examine briefly the metaphor of the tree, which Hurston repeats
throughout her text. The use of repetition is fundamental to the process of
narration, and Hurston repeats the figure of the tree both to expound her
theme of becoming and to render the action of the plot as simultaneous and
as unified as possible. In *Dust Tracks on a Road,* Hurston explains that:

> I was only happy in the woods. . . . I made particular friendship with
> one huge tree and always played about its roots. I named it "the loving
> pine," and my chums came to know it by that name. (p. 64)

In *Their Eyes,* Janie uses the metaphor of the tree to define her own desires
but also to mark the distance of those with whom she lives from these desires. There are well over two dozen repetitions of the figure of the tree in
this text. The representation of Janie's narrative to Phoeby commences with
the figure of the tree:

> Janie saw her life like a great tree in leaf with the things suffered, things
> enjoyed, things done and undone. Dawn and doom was in the branches.
> (p. 20)

"Dawn and doom," we are to learn so poignantly, are the true stuff of Janie's
tale. "Dawn and doom *was* in the branches," an example of free indirect
discourse, reveals precisely the point at which Janie's voice assumes control
over the text's narration, significantly in a metaphor of trees. The text describes her own, rather private dawning sexual awareness through lush and
compelling tree imagery. Janie longs for an identity with the tree in imagery
the text shall echo when she encounters Tea Cake:

> Oh to be a pear tree—*any* tree in bloom! With kissing bees singing of the
> beginning of the world! She was sixteen. She had glossy leaves and burst-
> ing buds and she wanted to struggle with life but it seemed to elude her.
> Where were the singing bees for her? Nothing on the place nor in her
> grandma's house answered her. (p. 25)

To "be a pear tree—*any* tree in bloom," which becomes Janie's master trope
on her road to becoming, is first stated as she fantasizes under a tree and

experiences her first orgasm. That this metaphor returns when she meets Tea Cake echoes the text's enigmatic statement in its second paragraph that, for women, "The dream is the truth." Thus transformed "through pollinated air" (p. 25), Janie experiences her first kiss with the figure she formerly knew as shiftless Johnny Taylor, now "beglamored" even in his rags in her eyes by the splendors of cross-pollination.

This crucial kiss "across the gatepost" establishes the text's opposition between the dream and the truth, already posited in the text's first two paragraphs which as I said earlier, revise Frederick Douglass's apostrophe to the ships.[25]

The ensuing action, moreover, posits a key opposition for us critics between theory and interpretation. Nanny's discovery of Johnny Taylor's "lacerating her Janie with a kiss" (p. 26) transforms both the event itself and Nanny's physical appearance. For Nanny's reading of the event, her "words," the text tells us, "made Janie's kiss across the gatepost seem like a manure pile after a rain." Nanny's perverse interpretation now transforms her in Janie's eyes into the dreaded figure of Medusa:

> Nanny's head and face looked like the standing roots of some old tree that had been torn away by storm. Foundation of ancient power that no longer mattered. The cooling palma christi leaves that Janie had bound about her grandma's head with a white rag had wilted down and become part and parcel of the woman. Her eyes didn't bore and pierce. They diffused and melted Janie, the room and the world into one comprehension. (p. 26)

When Nanny begins to narrate the story of her oppression in slavery, the narrator informs us that she "thrust back the leaves from her face" (p. 28). "Standing roots from some old tree" is, of course, the negation of the wonderfully lyrical imagery of blossoming pear trees. It is Nanny's "one comprehension" that suffocates, like the stench of the manure pile after a rain. Nanny is truly, as she later says to Janie in her own version of an oral slave narrative (pp. 31–32) delivered just after Janie's sexual experience under the pear tree, a branch without roots, at least the sort of roots that Janie is only just learning to extend.

Afraid that her grandchild will suffer an untimely defoliation, Nanny acts swiftly to gain for her the necessary "protection" to preserve her honor intact. While explaining her dreams for Janie, Nanny tells her that

> when you got big enough to understand things, Ah wanted you to look upon yo'self. Ah don't want yo' feathers always crumpled by folks throwin' up things in yo' face. And Ah can't die easy thinkin' maybe de menfolks white or black is makin' a spit cup outa you: Have some sympathy fuh me. Put me down easy, Janie, Ah'm a cracked plate." (p. 37)

So Nanny, the cracked plate, the Medusa figure, forces Janie to marry Logan Killicks.

As the text states, "The vision of Logan Killicks was desecrating the pear tree" (p. 28). Logan's famed sixty acres strike Janie as "a lonesome place like a stump in the middle of the woods where nobody had ever been" (p. 39), unlike her fecund pear tree. As she complains to Nanny, when after "the new moon had been up and down three times" and love had not yet begun, Janie "wants things sweet wid mah marriage lak when you sit under a pear tree and think. Ah . . ." (p. 43). Love, we learn, never quite finds its way to Logan Killicks's sixty acres. But even in this confined space, Janie comes, by negation, to a measure of knowledge, signified in the language of the trees:

> So Janie waited a bloom time, and a green time and an orange time. But when the pollen again gilded the sun and sifted down on the world she began to stand around the gate and expect things. What things? She didn't know exactly. Her breath was gusty and short. She knew things that nobody had ever told her. For instance, the words of the trees and the wind. (pp. 43–44)

Ultimately, Janie comes to know that "marriage did not make love." As the text concludes, "Janie's first dream was dead, so she became a woman," an echo of the text's opening paragraphs, which figure the opposition between women and men as that between the identity of dream and truth as a figure for desire (women) and the objectification and personification of desire onto objects over which one has no control (men).

Janie soon is "liberated" from Logan Killicks by the dashing Joe Starks. At their first encounter, at the water pump, Joe tells Janie, twice, that he wishes "to be a big voice" (p. 48) and shares with her his own dreams of dominance "under the tree [where they] talked" (p. 49). Jody is not yet the embodiment of Janie's tree, but he signifies the horizon.

> Every day after that they managed to meet in the scrub oaks across the road and talk about when he would be a big ruler of things with her reaping the benefits. Janie pulled back a long time because he did not represent sun-up and pollen and blooming trees, but he spoke for far horizon. (pp. 49–50)

To accept his proposals, Janie must exchange her own master metaphor for a new master's metaphor: "He spoke for change and chance. Still she hung back. The memory of Nanny was still powerful and strong" (p. 50). The horizon is not only a key figure in *Their Eyes,* serving to unify it by its repetition in the novel's final paragraph, but it has a central place as well in *Dust Tracks,* Hurston's autobiography:

> I had a stifled longing. I used to climb to the top of one of the huge chinaberry trees which guarded our front gate, and look out over the world. The most interesting thing that I saw was the horizon. Everyway I turned, it was there, and the same distance away. Our house then, was in the center of the world. It grew upon me that I ought to walk out to the horizon and see what the end of the world was like. (p. 44)

With Jody, Janie seeks the horizon. In a burst "of sudden newness and change," she heads south to find her freedom.

From now on until death she was going to have flower dust and spring-time sprinkled over everything. A bee for her bloom. Her old thoughts were going to come in handy now, but new words would have to be made and said to fit them. (pp. 54–55)

But Jody, we learn painfully, is a man of words, primarily, a man of "positions and possessions" (p. 79), a man who "talks tuh unlettered folks wid books in his jaws" (p. 79), "uh man dat changes everything, but nothin' don't change him" (p. 79). For him, Janie is merely a possession: the town's people, we are told, "stared at Joe's face, his clothes and his wife" (p. 57). Just before the lamp-lighting ceremony, where Joe, whose favorite parenthetical is "I god," brings light to the town (purchased from Sears and Roebuck), Tony Taylor welcomes "Brother Starks" to town "and all dat you have seen fit tuh bring amongst us—yo' belov-ed wife, yo' store, yo' land—" (p. 67). Joe, all voice and less and less substance, who had seduced Janie in part by telling her, in an echo of Nanny's desire for Janie to "sit on high," that "A pretty doll-baby lak you is made to sit on de front porch and rock and fan yo' self and eat p'taters dat other folks plant just special for you" (p. 49), not only serves to stifle Janie's potentially emerging voice but chops down the town's virgin trees to build his house and store, in which he keeps Janie imprisoned. That which, for Jody, represents the signs of progress, represents for Janie just another muted, fallen tree.

The text figures Janie's denial of a voice by substituting the metaphor of horizon for Janie's tree metaphor. Only with Tea Cake does Janie's lyrical trope of desire return. Metaphors of silence and the death of flora confirm Janie's sadness and oppression. Joe, having just been elected mayor by acclamation, denies Janie Tony Taylor's request that she address the crowd:

"Thank yuh fuh yo' compliments, but mah wife don't know nothin' 'bout no speech-makin'. Ah never married her for nothin' lak dat. She's uh woman and her place is in de home." (p. 69)

The text, in Janie's response, conflates the tree imagery with her reactions to Jody's silencing:

Janie made her face laugh after a short pause, but it wasn't too easy. She had never thought of making a speech, and didn't know if she cared to make one at all. It must have been the way Jody spoke out without giving her a chance to say anything one way or another that took the bloom off of things. (pp. 69–70)

This silencing leads, of course, to a disastrous degeneration; when Janie protests her absence of a voice, Joe responds predictably in a revealing exchange about who is privileged to "tell" what they "see":

[Joe]: "How come you can't do lak Ah tell yuh?"
[Janie]: "You sho loves to tell me whut to do, but Ah can't tell you nothin' Ah see!"
[Joe]: "Dat's 'cause you need tellin'," he rejoined hotly. "It would be

pitiful if Ah didn't. Somebody got to think for women and chillun and chickens and cows. I god, they sho don't think none theirselves."

[Janie]: "Ah knows uh few things, and womenfolks thinks sometimes too!"

[Joe]: "Aw naw they don't. They just think they's thinkin'. When Ah see one thing Ah understands ten. You see ten things and don't understand one." (pp. 110–11)

Their dying relationship soon does. As the narrator tells us, again through the negation of the flowering images:

The spirit of the marriage left the bedroom and took to living in the parlor. . . . The bed was no longer a daisy-field for her and Joe to play in. It was a place where she went and laid down when she was sleepy and tired.

She wasn't petal-open anymore with him. (p. 111)

And finally, after Joe slaps her:

She stood there until something fell off the shelf inside her. Then she went inside there to see what it was. It was her image of Jody tumbled down and shattered. But looking at it she saw that it never was the flesh and blood figure of her dreams. Just something she had grabbed up to drape her dreams over. In a way she turned her back upon the image where it lay and looked further. She had no more blossomy openings dusting pollen over her man, neither any glistening young fruit where the petals used to be. She found that she had a host of thoughts she had never expressed to him, and numerous emotions she had never let Jody know about. Things packed up and put away in parts of her heart where he could never find them. She was saving up feelings for some man she had never seen. She had an inside and an outside now and suddenly she knew how not to mix them. (pp. 112–13)

With this newly defined sense of her inside and her outside, Janie learns to cross deftly that narrow threshold between her two selves:

Then one day she sat and watched the shadow of herself going about tending store and prostrating itself before Jody, while all the time she herself sat under a shady tree with the wind blowing through her hair and her clothes. Somebody near about making summertime out of lonesomeness. (p. 119)

Jody finally dies, just after Janie gains her voice on the porch of the story by Signifyin(g) upon Jody. Jody leaves Janie a handsome legacy and frees her to love again. Eventually she meets Tea Cake, and the text's fecund imagery of desire returns:

He looked like the love thoughts of women. He could be a bee to a blossom—a pear tree blossom in the spring. He seemed to be crushing scent out of the world with his footsteps. Crushing aromatic herbs with every step he took. Spices hung about him. He was a glance from God. (p. 161)

Unlike Jody, who wanted to be seen as the deliverer of light, Tea Cake is the "glance from God" that reflects upon Janie, who in turn reflects her own inner light back upon him. "Nobody else on earth," Tea Cake tells her, "kin hold uh candle tuh you, baby" (p. 165). Tea Cake negates the terms of the material relationship of "marriage" ordained by Nanny and realized by Logan Killicks and Joe Starks. "Dis ain't no business proposition," Janie tells Phoeby, "and no race after property and titles. Dis is uh love game" (p. 171). Tea Cake not only embodies Janie's tree, he is the woods themselves, the delectable veritable woods, as his name connotes ("Vergible" being a vernacular term for "veritable"). Vergible Tea Cake Woods is a sign of verity, one who speaks the truth, one genuine and real, one not counterfeit or spurious, one not false or imaginary but the thing that in fact has been named. "Veritable," we know, also suggests the aptness of metaphor. Hurston now replaces the figure of the tree as the sign of desire with figures of play, rituals of play that cause Janie to "beam with light" (p. 153).

III

Let us "descend" to a more latent level of meaning by examining the figures of play that recur frequently in Janie's narrative of her life with Tea Cake. We can consider these figures of play along with the play of voices that, I wish to argue, make *Their Eyes* an especially rich and complex instance of a multiply vocal text. The mode of narration of *Their Eyes* consists, at either extreme, of narrative commentary (rendered in third-person omniscient and third-person restricted voices) and of characters' discourse (which manifests itself as a direct speech rendered in what Hurston called dialect). Hurston's innovation is to be found in the middle spaces between these two extremes of narration and discourse, in what we might think of as represented discourse, which as I am defining it includes both indirect discourse and free indirect discourse. It was Hurston who introduced free indirect discourse into Afro-American narration. It is this innovation, as I hope to demonstrate, which enables her to represent various traditional modes of Afro-American rhetorical play while simultaneously representing her protagonist's growth in self-consciousness through free indirect discourse. Curiously, Hurston's narrative strategy depends on the blending of the text's two most extreme and seemingly opposed modes of narration—that is, narrative commentary, which begins at least in the diction of standard English, and characters' discourse, which is always foregrounded by quotation marks and by its black diction. As the protagonist approaches self-consciousness, however, not only does the text use free indirect discourse to represent her development, but the diction of the black characters' discourse comes to inform the diction of the voice of narrative commentary such that, in several passages, it is extraodinarily difficult to distinguish the narrator's voice from the protagonist's. In other words, through the use of what Hurston called a highly "adorned" free indirect discourse, which we might think of as a third or mediating term between narrative commentary and direct discourse, *Their Eyes Were Watching God* resolves that implicit tension between standard English and black dialect, the two voices that function as verbal counterpoints in the text's opening paragraphs.

Let us return briefly to the triangle of influence that I have drawn to connect *Invisible Man, Native Son,* and *Their Eyes Were Watching God.* As I argued earlier in this chapter, for Hurston the search for a form of narration and discourse, indeed the search for a black formal language itself, both defines the search for the self and is its rhetorical or textual analogue. Not only would Ellison concur, but he would go farther. Ellison's is a literal morality of narration. As he writes in *Invisible Man,* "to remain unaware of one's form is to live death," an idea that Hurston prefigures in *Their Eyes,* from the moment when the child Janie, or "Alphabet," fails to recognize her own image in a group photograph, to the moment in the text when, first, Janie learns to distinguish between her inside and her outside, and when, second, the diction of the black characters' dialect comes to inform heavily the diction of the narrative commentary. We might think of Hurston's formal relation to Wright and Ellison in this way: whereas the narrative strategy of *Native Son* consists primarily of a disembodied, omniscient narrative commentary, similar to the voice that introduces *Their Eyes,* Ellison's first-person narrative strategy in *Invisible Man* revises the possibilities of representing the development of consciousness that Hurston rendered through a dialect-informed free indirect discourse. Wright uses free indirect discourse to some extent in *Native Son,* but its diction is not informed by Bigger's speech. The distinction between figures of speech and figures of thought is one useful way to distinguish between Wright's and Hurston's narrative strategies. The narrative strategies of *Native Son* and *Invisible Man,* then, define the extremes of narrative mode in the tradition, while the narrative strategy of *Their Eyes* partakes of these as well as of a subtle blend of the two. Rhetorically, at least, *Native Son* and *Invisible Man* Signify upon the rhetorical strategies of *Their Eyes Were Watching God.*

Even more curiously, the marvelous potential that *Their Eyes'* mode of narration holds for the representation of black oral forms of storytelling would seem to be remarkably akin to that which Ellison says he is using in his next novel. In an interview with John Hersey, Ellison says that he too has turned away from first-person toward third-person narration "to discover [the text's] most expressive possibilities." As Ellison argues, "I've come to believe that one of the challenges facing a writer who tries to handle the type of materials I'm working with is that of allowing his characters to speak for themselves in whatever artistic way they can." The third person, Ellison concludes, makes it "possible to draw upon broader and deeper resources of American vernacular speech," including multiple narrators and a wide variety of characters.[26] There can be little doubt that this sort of narration, so concerned to represent the sheer multiplicity of American oral narrative forms and voices, is more closely related to the speakerly strategies of *Their Eyes* than it is to most other texts in the Afro-American canon. These are rather large claims to make, but they are firmly supported by the Signifyin(g) strategies of the text itself.

Hurston, whose definition of *signify* in *Mules and Men* is one of the earliest in the linguistic literature, has made *Their Eyes Were Watching God* into a paradigmatic Signifyin(g) text. Its narrative strategies resolve that implicit tension between the literal and the figurative, between the semantic and the rhetorical, contained in standard usages of the term *signifying*. *Their Eyes* draws upon the trope of Signifyin(g) both as thematic matter and as a rhetorical strategy. Janie, as we shall see, gains her voice within her husband's store not only by daring to speak aloud where others might hear, but by engaging in that ritual of Signifyin(g) (which her husband had expressly disallowed) and by openly Signifyin(g) upon the impotency of her husband, Joe, Mayor, "I god," himself. Janie kills her husband, rhetorically, by publicly naming his impotence (with her voice) in a public ritual of Signifyin(g). His image fatally wounded, he soon succumbs to a displaced "kidney" failure.

Their Eyes Signifies upon Toomer's *Cane* in several ways. First, its plot reverses the movement of *Cane*'s plot. Whereas the settings of *Cane* move from broad open fields, through ever-diminishing physical spaces, to a circle of light in a dark and damp cellar (corresponding to the levels of self-consciousness of the central characters), *Their Eyes*' settings within its embedded narrative move from the confines of Nanny's tiny cabin in the Washburn's backyard, through increasingly larger physical structures, finally ending "on the Muck" in the Everglades, where she and her lover, Tea Cake, realize the male-female relationship for which Janie had longed so very urgently. Similarly, whereas *Cane* represents painfully unconsummated relationships, the agony of which seems to intensify in direct proportion to the diminishment of physical setting, true consummation occurs in *Their Eyes* once Janie eschews the values implied by material possessions (such as middle-class houses, especially those on which sit idle women who rock their lives away), learns to play with Tea Cake, and then moves to the swamp. The trope of the swamp, furthermore, in *Their Eyes* signifies exactly the opposite of what it does in Du Bois's *Quest for the Silver Fleece*. Whereas the swamp in Du Bois's text figures an uncontrolled chaos that must be plowed under and controlled, for Hurston the swamp is the trope of the freedom of erotic love, the antithesis of the bourgeois life and order that her protagonist flees but to which Du Bois's protagonists aspire. Whereas Du Bois's characters gain economic security by plowing up and cultivating cotton in the swamp, Janie flees the bourgeois life that Du Bois's characters realize, precisely by abandoning traditional values for the uncertainties and the potential chaos of the uncultivated, untamed swamp, where love and death linger side by side. Du Bois's shadowy figure who seems to dwell in the swamp, we recall, is oddly enough named Zora.

But *Their Eyes* is also a paradigmatic Signifyin(g) text because of its representations, through several subtexts or embedded narratives presented as the characters' discourse, of traditional black rhetorical games or rituals. It is the text's imitation of these examples of traditionally black rhetorical rituals and modes of storytelling that allows us to think of it as a speakerly text. For in a speakerly text certain rhetorical structures seem to exist primarily as representations of oral narration, rather than as integral aspects of plot or character development. These verbal rituals signify the sheer play of black language which *Their Eyes* seems to celebrate. These virtuoso displays of verbal play constitute Hurston's complex response to the New Negro poets' strictures of the use of dialect as a poetic diction. *Their Eyes Were Watching God*'s narrative Signifies upon James Weldon Johnson's arguments against dialect just as surely as Sterling A. Brown's *Southern Road* did. Indeed, we are free to think of these two texts as discursive analogues. Moreover, Hurston's masterful use of free indirect discourse (*style indirect libre*) allows her to Signify upon the tension between the two voices of Toomer's *Cane* by adding to direct and indirect speech a strategy through which she can privilege the black oral tradition, which Toomer found to be problematical and dying.

As I stated earlier, figures of play are the dominant repeated figures in the second half of *Their Eyes,* replacing the text's figures of flowering vegetation, which as we have seen repeat at least two dozen times in the first half of the text. After Janie meets Tea Cake, figures of play supplant those floral figures that appeared each time Janie dreamed of consummated love. Moreover, it is the rhetorical play that occurs regularly on the porch of his store that Janie's husband Jody prevents Janie from enjoying. As the text reads:

> Janie loved the conversation and sometimes she thought up good stories on the mule, but Joe had forbidden her to indulge. He didn't want her talking after such trashy people. "You'se Mrs. Mayor Starks, Janie. I god, Ah can't see what uh woman uh yo' sability would want tuh be treasurin' all dat gum-grease from folks dat don't even own de house dey sleep in. 'Tain't no earthly use. They's jus' some puny humans playin' round de toes uh Time." (p. 85)

When the Signifyin(g) rituals commence—rituals that the text describes as created by "big picture talkers [who] were using a side of the world for a canvas"—Jody forces Janie to retreat inside the store, much against her will.

Eventually, however, this friction ignites a heated argument between the two, the key terms of which shall be repeated, in reverse, when Janie later falls in love with Tea Cake. Their exchange follows:

> "Ah had tuh laugh at de people out dere in de woods dis mornin', Janie. You can't help but laugh at de capers they cuts. But all the same, Ah wish mah people would git mo' business in 'em and not spend so much time on foolishness."
> "Everybody can't be lak you, Jody. Somebody is bound tuh want tuh laugh and play."
> "Who don't love tuh laugh and play?"
> "You make out like you don't, anyhow." (p. 98)

It is this tension between work and play, between maintaining appearances of respectability and control against the seemingly idle, nonquantifiable verbal maneuvers that "produce" nothing, which becomes the central sign of the distance between Janie's unarticulated aspirations and the material aspirations signified by Jody's desire to "be a big voice," a self-designation that Jody repeats with alacrity almost as much as he repeats his favorite parenthetical, "I god."

"Play" is also the text's word for the Signifyin(g) rituals that imitate "courtship," such as the symbolic action executed by Sam Watson, Lige Moss, and Charlie Jones, which the text describes in this way: "They know it's not courtship. It's acting out courtship and everybody is in the play" (p. 105). Play, finally, is the irresistible love potion that Tea Cake administers to Janie. Tea Cake, an apparently unlikely suitor of Joe Starks's widow, since he is a drifter and is generally thought to be "irresponsible," seduces Janie by teaching her to play checkers. Responding to his challenge of a game with "Ah can't play uh lick," Tea Cake proceeds to set up the board and teach Janie the rules. Janie "found herself glowing inside. Somebody wanted her to play. Somebody thought it natural for her to play. That was even nice. She looked him over and got little thrills from every one of his good points" (p. 146). No one had taught her to play in her adulthood. The text repeats Joe's prohibition as Tea Cake's perceptive mode of seduction. As Tea Cake concludes prophetically, "You gointuh be uh good player too, after while." And "after while," Janie and Tea Cake teach each other to become "good players" in what the text depicts as a game of love.

This repeated figure of play is only the thematic analogue to the text's rhetorical play, plays of language that seem to be present essentially to reveal the complexity of black oral forms of narration. For *Their Eyes Were Watching God* is replete with storytellers, or Signifiers as the black tradition has named them. These Signifiers are granted a remarkable amount of space in this text to reveal their talents. These imitations of oral narrations, it is crucial to recall, unfold within what the text represents as Janie's framed tale, the tale of her quests with Tea Cake to the far horizon and her lonely return home. This oral narrative commences in chapter 2, while Janie and her friend, Phoeby, sit on Janie's back porch, and "the kissing, young darkness became a monstropolous old thing while Janie talked" (p. 19). Then follow almost three full pages of Janie's direct speech, "while all around the house, the night time put on flesh and blackness" (p. 23). Two paragraphs of narrative commentary follow Janie's narration; then, curiously, the narrative "fades" into "a spring-time afternoon in West Florida," the springtime of Janie's adolescence.

Without ever releasing its proprietary consciousness, the disembodied narrative voice reassumes control over the telling of Janie's story after nine paragraphs of direct discourse. We can characterize this narrative shift as from third person, to "no-person" (that is, the seemingly unmediated representation of Janie's direct speech), back to the third person of an embedded or framed narrative. This device we encounter most frequently in the storytelling devices of film, in which a first-person narrative yields, as it were, to the form of narration that we associate with the cinema. ("Kabnis," we remember, imitates the drama.) *Their Eyes Were Watching God* would seem to be imitating this mode of narration, with this fundamental difference: the bracketed tale, in the novel, is told by an omniscient, third-person narrator who reports thoughts, feelings, and events that Janie could not possibly have heard or seen. This framed narrative continues for the next eighteen chapters, until in chapter 20 the text indicates the end of Janie's storytelling to Phoeby, which we have overheard, by the broad white space and a series of widely spaced ellipses that I mentioned earlier.

This rather unusual form of narration of the tale-within-a-tale has been the subject of some controversy about the success or failure of Janie's depiction as a dynamic character who comes to know herself. Rather than retread that fruitless terrain, I would suggest that the subtleness of this narrative strategy allows for, as would no other mode of narration, the representation of the forms of oral narration that *Their Eyes* imitates so often—so often, in fact, that the very subject of this text would appear to be not primarily Janie's quest but the emulation of the phonetic, grammatical, and lexical structures of actual speech, an emulation designed to produce the illusion of oral narration. Indeed, each of the oral rhetorical structures emulated within Janie's bracketed tale functions to remind the reader that he or she is overhearing Janie's narrative to Phoeby, which unfolds on her porch, that crucial place of storytelling both in this text and in the black community. Each of these playful narratives is, by definition, a tale-within-the-bracketed-tale, and most exist as Significations of rhetorical play rather than events that develop the text's plot. Indeed, these embedded narratives, consisting as they do of long exchanges of direct discourse, often serve as plot impediments but simultaneously enable a multiplicity of narrative voices to assume control of the text, if only for a few paragraphs on a few pages, as Ellison explained his new narrative strategy to John Hersey.

Hurston is one of the few authors of our tradition who both theorized about her narrative process and defended it against the severe critiques of contemporaries such as Wright. Hurston's theory allows us to read *Their Eyes* through her own terms of critical order. It is useful to recount her theory of black oral narration, if only in summary, and then to use this to explicate the various rhetorical strategies that, collectively, comprise the narrative strategy of *Their Eyes Were Watching God*.

Hurston seems to be not only the first scholar to have defined the trope of Signifyin(g) but also the first to represent the ritual itself. Hurston represents a Signifyin(g) ritual in *Mules and Men,* then glosses the word *signify* as a means of "showing off," rhetorically. The exchange is an appropriate one to repeat, because it demonstrates that women most certainly can, and do, Signify upon men, and because it prefigures the scene of Signification in *Their Eyes* that proves to be a verbal sign of such importance to Janie's quest for consciousness:

"Talkin' 'bout dogs," put in Gene Oliver, "they got plenty sense. Nobody can't fool dogs much."

"And speakin' 'bout hams," cut in Big Sweet meaningly, "if Joe Willard don't stay out of dat bunk he was in last night, Ah'm gonter springle some salt down his back and sugar-cure *his* hams."

Joe snatched his pole out of the water with a jerk and glared at Big Sweet, who stood sidewise looking at him most pointedly.

"Aw, woman, quit tryin' to signify."

"Ah kin signify all Ah please, Mr. Nappy-Chin, so long as Ah know what Ah'm talkin' about."[27]

This is a classic Signification, an exchange of meaning and intention of some urgency between two lovers.

I use the word *exchange* here to echo Hurston's use in her essay, "Characteristics of Negro Expression." In this essay Hurston argues that "language is like money," and its development can be equated metaphorically with the development in the marketplace of the means of exchange from bartered "actual goods," which "evolve into coin" (coins symbolizing wealth). Coins evolve into legal tender, and legal tender evolves into "cheques for certain usages." Hurston's illustrations are especially instructive. People "with highly developed languages," she writes, "have words for detached ideas. That is legal tender." The linguistic equivalent of legal tender consists of words such as "chair," which comes to stand for "that-which-we-squat-on." "Groan-causers" evolves into "spear," and so on. "Cheque words" include those such as "ideation" and "pleonastic." *Paradise Lost* and *Sartor Resartus,* she continues, "are written in cheque words!" But "the primitive man," she argues, eschews legal tender and cheque words; he "exchanges descriptive words," describing "one act . . . in terms of another." More specifically, she concludes, black expression turns upon both the "interpretation of the English language in terms of pictures" and the supplement of what she calls "action words," such as "chop-axe," "sitting-chair," and "cook pot." It is the supplement of action, she maintains, which underscores her use of the word "exchange."

Such an exchange, as we have seen, is that between Big Sweet and Joe Willard. As the exchange continues, not only does the characters' language exemplify Hurston's theory, but the definitions of Signifyin(g) that I have been drawing upon throughout this book are also exemplified:

"See dat?" Joe appealed to the other men. "We git a day off and figger we kin ketch some fish and enjoy ourselves, but naw, some wimmins got to drag behind us, even to de lake."

"You didn't figger Ah was draggin' behind you when you was bringin' dat Sears and Roebuck catalogue over to my house and beggin' me to choose my ruthers. Lemme tell *you* something, *any* time Ah shack up wid any man Ah gives myself de privilege to go wherever he might be, night or day. Ah got de law in my mouth."

"Lawd, ain't she specifyin'!" sniggered Wiley.

> "Oh, Big Sweet does dat," agreed Richardson. "Ah knewed she had somethin' up her sleeve when she got Lucy and come along."
>
> "Lawd," Willard said bitterly. " 'My people, my people,' as de monkey said. You fool with Aunt Hagar's chillun and they'll sho discriminate you and put yo'name in de streets." (pp. 161–62)

Specifying, putting one's name in the streets, and "as de monkey said" are all figures for Signifyin(g). In *Dust Tracks on a Road,* Hurston even defines specifying as "giving a reading" in the following passage:

> The bookless may have difficulty in reading a paragraph in a newspaper, but when they get down to "playing the dozens" [Signifyin(g)] they have no equal in America, and, I'd risk a sizable bet, in the whole world. Starting off in the first by calling you a seven-sided son-of-a-bitch, and pausing to name the sides, they proceed to "specify" until the tip-top branch of your family tree has been "given a reading." (p. 217)

The sort of close reading that I am attempting here is also an act of specifying.

Let me return briefly to Hurston's theory of "Negro Expression" before turning to explicate rhetorical strategies at work in *Their Eyes Were Watching God.* Her typology of black oral narration, in addition to "picture" and "action" words, consists of what she calls "the will to adorn," by which she means the use of densely figurative language, the presence of "revision," which she defines as "[making] over a great part of the [English] tongue," and the use of "metaphor and simile," "the double-descriptive," and "verbal nouns." It is Hurston's sense of revision, defined as "originality [in] the modification of ideas" and "of language," as well as "reinterpretation," which I have defined in Chapter 2 as the ultimate meaning of the trope of Signifyin(g). By "revision," she also means "imitation" and "mimicry," for which she says "The Negro, the world over, is famous" and which she defines as "an art in itself." The Negro, she claims, imitates and revises, not "from a feeling of inferiority," rather "for the love of it." This notion of imitation, repetition, and revision, she maintains, is fundamental to "all art," indeed is the nature of art itself, even Shakespeare's.

Near the end of her compelling essay, Hurston argues that dialect is "Negro speech," and Negro speech, she contends throughout the essay, is quite capable of expressing the most subtle nuances of meaning, despite "the majority of writers of Negro dialect and the burnt-cork artists." "Fortunately," she concludes, "we don't have to believe them. We may go directly to the Negro and let him speak for himself." Using in large part Hurston's own theory of black oral narration, we can gain some understanding of the modes of narration at work in *Their Eyes* and thereby demonstrate why I have chosen to call it a speakerly text, a phrase that I derive both from Roland Barthes's opposition between the "readerly" and the "writerly" texts—the binarism of which I am here Signifyin(g) upon—as well as from the trope of the Talking Book, which not only is the Afro-American tradition's fundamental repeated trope but also is a phrase used by both Hurston and Ishmael Reed to define their own narrative strategies.

The "white man thinks in a written language," Hurston claims, while "the Negro thinks in hieroglyphics." By hieroglyphics, she means the "word-pictures" or the "thought pictures" as she defines these in *Their Eyes* (p. 81). It is a fairly straightforward matter to list just a few of what we might think of as Hurston's "figures of adornment," the specifically black examples of figurative language that she labels "simile and metaphor," "double-descriptives," and "verbal-nouns." Karla Holloway lists these as expressed in *Their Eyes:*

1. An envious heart makes a treacherous ear.
2. Us colored folks is branches without roots.
3. They's a lost ball in high grass.
4. She . . . left her wintertime wid me.
5. Ah wanted yuh to pick from a higher bush.
6. You got uh willin' mind, but youse too light behind.
7. . . . he's de wind and we'se de grass.
8. He was a man wid salt in him.
9. . . . what dat multiplied cockroach told you.
10. still-bait
11. big-bellies
12. gentlemanfied man
13. cemetary-dead
14. black-dark
15. duskin-down-dark[28]

This list certainly could be extended. Suffice it to say that the diction of both the characters' discourse and the free indirect discourse are replete with the three types of adornment that Hurston argued were fundamental to black oral narration.

In addition to these sorts of figures of adornment, *Their Eyes* is comprised of several long exchanges of direct discourse, which seem to be present in the text more for their own sake than to develop the plot. *Their Eyes* consists of a remarkable percentage of direct speech, rendered in black dialect, as if to display the capacity of black language itself to convey an extraordinarily wide variety of ideas and feelings. Frequently, these exchanges between characters extend for two or three pages, with little or no interruption from the text's narrator. When such narrative commentary does surface, it often serves to function as stage direction rather than as a traditional omniscient voice, as if to underscore Hurston's contention that it is "drama" that "permeates [the Negro's] entire self," and it is the dramatic to which black oral narration aspires. Because, as Hurston writes, "an audience is a necessary part of any drama," these Signifyin(g) rituals tend to occur outdoors, at the communal scene of oral instruction, on the porches of homes and stores.

From the novel's earliest scenes, the porch is both personified and then represented through a series of synecdoches as the undifferentiated "eyes," "mouth," and "ears" of the community. Of these three senses, however, it is the communal speaking voice—"Mouth-Almighty," as the text has it—which emerges early on as the most significant. Indeed, the first time the porch "speaks," the text represents its discourse in one paragraph of "direct quota-

tion" consisting of ten sentences separated only by dashes, as if to emphasize
the anonymous if collective voice of the community that the text proceeds to
represent in several ways. Against this sort of communal narration the text
pits Jody Starks, Janie's second husband, who repeatedly states that he wishes
to become "a big voice." This voice, however, is the individual voice of domination. The figure of Jody's big voice comes to stand as a synecdoche of oppression, in opposition to the speech community of which Janie longs to become an integral part.

The representation of modes of black narration begins, as we have seen,
with Janie's narration of her story to Phoeby, the framed tale in which most
of the novel's action unfolds. Throughout this narrative, the word *voice* recurs with great frequency. Who speaks, indeed, proves to be of crucial import
to Janie's quest for freedom, but who sees and who hears at all points in the
text remain fundamental as well. Phoeby's "hungry listening," we recall,
"helped Janie to tell her story." Almost as soon as Janie's narrative begins,
however, Nanny assumes control of the text and narrates the story of Janie's
genealogy, from slavery to the present, as Janie listens painfully. This quasi-
slave narrative, rendered as a tale-within-a-tale, is one of the few instances of
direct speech that serve as a function of the plot. Subsequent speaking narrators assume control of the narrative primarily to demonstrate forms of traditional oral narration.

These double narratives-within-the-narrative begin as soon as Janie and
Jody move to Eatonville. Amos Hicks and Joe Coker engage in a brief and
amusing exchange about the nature of storytelling generally and about the nature of figurative language specifically, a discussion to which we shall return.
Tony Taylor next demonstrates the ironies of speech-making on the day of
dedication of Jody's store, a speech that ends with requests that Janie address
the community, only to be thwarted by her husband who says that "mah wife
don't know nothin' 'bout no speech-makin.' " Jody's harsh actions, the narrator tell us ominously, "took the bloom off of things" for Janie. Subsequent
forms of oral narration include "a traditional prayer-poem," a series of
speeches, the sung communal poetry of the spirituals, but especially the front-
porch Signifyin(g) rituals that serve to impede the plot. The porch is dominated by three narrators. Sam, Lige, and Walter are known as "the ring-
leaders of the mule-talkers," who sit for hours on the storefront porch and
Signify upon Matt Bonner's yellow mule. These exchanges about the mule extend for pages (pp. 81–85, 87–96) and would seem to be present primarily
to display the nature of storytelling, allowing a full range of characters' discourse to be heard.

At the end of the second mule Signification, still another tale-within-a-tale-
within-a-tale unfolds, which we might think of as the allegory of the buzzards
(pp. 96–97). After the second mule tale concludes with his mock funeral and
mock eulogy, the disembodied narrator relates the narrative of "the already
impatient buzzards," who proceed in ritual fashion to examine and disem-
bowel the mule's carcass. This allegory, of course, serves to mock the pre-
ceding mock eulogy, complete with the speaking characters and a patterned

oral ritual. This allegory, more especially, shatters completely any illusion the reader might have had that this was meant to be a realistic fiction, even though the text has naturalized the possiblity of such an event occurring, if only by representing storytelling in direct speech as its principal mode of narration. Once the reader encounters the allegory of the buzzards, his or her generic expectations have been severely interrupted.

Two pages later, the text returns to more Signifyin(g) rituals, defined by the narrator as "eternal arguments," which "never ended because there was no end to reach. It was a contest in hyperbole," the narrator concludes, "carried on for no other reason" (p. 99). Sam Watson and Lige Moss then proceed to debate, for six pages, the nature of the subject and whether or not "you got to have a subjick tuh talk from, do yuh can't talk" (p. 100), and whether or not these sorts of "readings" have "points" (p. 102). Just as the two Signifiers are about to commence still another oral narration of High John de Conquer tales, three women come walking down the street and thereby generate three pages of rhetorical courtship rituals. At this point in the narrative, as at the beginning of the first mule tale, the omniscient narrator establishes the context by shifting from the past tense to the present tense, then disappears for pages and pages while the characters narrate, underscoring thereby the illusion of overhearing an event.

The most crucial of these scenes of represented speech is the devastating exchange in which Janie first speaks in public against her husband. This exchange is a Signifyin(g) ritual of the first order because Janie Signifies upon Jody's manhood, thereby ending his dominance over her and over the community, and thereby killing Jody's will to live. The exchange is marvelous. Jody begins the fatal confrontation by insulting Janie for improperly cutting a plug of tobacco:

> "I god almighty! A woman stay round uh store till she get old as
> Methusalem and still can't cut a little thing like a plug of tobacco! Don't
> stand dere rollin' yo' pop eyes at me wid yo' rump hangin' nearly to yo'
> knees!" (p. 121)

After a short, quick "big laugh," the crowd assembled in the store, "got to thinking and stopped. It was like somebody," the narrative continues, "snatched off part of a woman's clothes while she wasn't looking and the streets were crowded." But most remarkably of all, "Janie took the middle of the floor to talk right into Jody's face, and that was something that hadn't been done before."

Janie, as a startled Jody says, is speaking a new language, "Talkin' any such language as dat." "You de one started talkin' under people's clothes," she retorts. "Not me." Then, indeed, Janie proceeds to talk under clothes, after Jody says:

> " 'T'ain't no use in gettin' all mad, Janie, 'cause Ah mention you ain't
> no young gal no mo'. Nobody in heah ain't lookin' for no wife outa yuh.
> Old as you is." (p. 122)

Janie responds:

> "Naw, Ah ain't no young gal no mo' but den Ah ain't no old woman
> neither. Ah reckon Ah looks mah age too. But Ah'm uh woman every inch
> of me, and Ah know it. Dat's uh whole lot more'n *you* kin say. You big-
> bellies round here and put out a lot of brag, but 'tain't nothin' to it but
> yo' big voice. Humph! Talkin' 'bout *me* lookin' old! When you pull down
> yo' britches, you look lak de change uh life." (pp. 122–23)

"Great God from Zion!" Sam Watson gasped. "Y'all really playin' de dozens
tuhnight," the text reads, naming the sort of Signifyin(g) ritual that has occurred. "Wha-whut's dat you said?" Joe challenged, hoping that his ears had
fooled him, to which lame retort "Walter taunted" in a synesthesia that the
text has just naturalized for us: "You heard her, you ain't blind." Jody, we
well know, now thoroughly shattered by the force of Janie's voice, soon succumbs to acute humiliation and his displaced kidney disorder. As he lies dying, Janie contemplates "what had happened in the making of a voice out of
a man," the devastating synecdoche that names both Jody's deepest aspiration
and his subsequent great fall.

It is striking that Janie gains her voice and becomes a speaking subject inside her husband's store. Not only does she, by speaking, defy his expressed
prohibition, but the scene itself is a key repetition of the metaphors of inside
and outside, which repeat frequently throughout the text and which, as I hope
to show, serve as a thematic, if metaphorical, counterpart to the most striking
innovation of *Their Eyes'* narrative strategy, the presence of free indirect discourse.

The repeated metaphors of inside and outside begin in the text's first chapter. Janie narrates her tale, as Phoeby listens, outside on her back porch.
Janie's metaphorical and densely lyrical "outside observations," the narrator
tells us, "buried themselves in her flesh." After she experiences her first orgasm, then kisses Johnny Taylor, she extends "herself outside of her dream"
and goes "inside of the house." As we have seen, it is inside houses in which
a series of people (first her grandmother, Nanny; then her first husband, Logan Killicks; then her second husband, Joe Starks) attempt to oppress her
and prevent her from speaking and asserting herself. Janie dreams outdoors,
in metaphors of flowering springtime, often under pear trees. When Logan insults her, the narrator says that "she turned wrongside out just standing there
and feeling." Jody seduces her with dreams of "far horizons," "under the
tree" and outdoors "in the scrub oaks." What Jody speaks out loud and what
Janie thinks inside come to represent an opposition of such dimensions that
we are not at all surprised when their final confrontation occurs. Janie, we recall, is forced to retreat inside the store when the storytelling rituals commence.

The text represents Janie's crucial if ironic scene of self-discovery rather
subtly in this figurative framework of inside and outside. This coming to consciousness is not represented by a speaking scene, however; rather, it is rep-

resented in these inside-outside figures. When she finally does speak, therefore, by Signifyin(g) in the store upon Jody's impotence, the gaining of her own voice is a sign of her authority, but not a sign of a newly found unified identity. Janie's speaking voice, rather, is an outcome of her consciousness of division.[29] Indeed, hers is a rhetoric of division.

The text represents this consciousness of division in two scenes that transpire in the chapter that precedes the chapter in which she Signifies upon Jody. The text reads:

> The spirit of the marriage left the bedroom and took to living in the parlor. It was there to shake hands whenever company came to visit, but it never went back inside the bedroom again. So she put something in there to represent the spirit like a Virgin Mary image in a church. The bed was no longer a daisy-field for her and Joe to play in. It was a place where she went and laid down when she was sleepy and tired. (p. 111)

In this passage, Janie's inner feelings, "the spirit of the marriage," are projected onto outer contiguous physical spaces (the bedroom and the parlor). Her inside, in other words, is figured as an outside, in the rooms. Her bed, moreover, ceases to be a place for lovemaking, as signified by both the daisy-field metaphor and the metaphor of play (reminding us, through the repetition, of her central metaphors of dream and aspiration that repeat so often in the novel's first half). The contiguous relation of the bedroom and the parlor, both physical spaces, through which the metaphorical spirit of the marriage now moves, reveals two modes of figuration overlapping in Janie's indirectly reported thoughts for the first time—that is, one mode dependent upon substitution, the other on contiguity.[30] Clearly, the rhetorical relation among "sex" and "spirit of the marriage," and "spirit of the marriage," "bedroom," and "parlor" is a complex one.

Until this moment in the text, Janie's literacy was represented only as a metaphorical literacy. Janie's "conscious life," the text tells us, "had commenced at Nanny's gate," across which she had kissed Johnny Taylor just after experiencing her first orgasm under her "blossoming pear tree in the back-yard." In the moving passage that precedes the event but prepares us for it by describing her increasing awareness of her own sexuality, rendered in free indirect discourse, Janie names her feelings in her first metaphor: "The rose of the world was breathing out smell. It followed her through all her waking moments and caressed her in her sleep" (pp. 23–24). Janie's first language, the language of her own desire, is registered in a lyrical and metaphorical diction found in these passages of free indirect discourse. Janie has mastered, the text tells us early on, "the words of the trees and the wind" (p. 44). In this metaphorical language, "she spoke to falling seeds," as they speak to her, in lyrical metaphors, renaming "the world," for example, "a stallion rolling in the blue pasture of ether." Whereas she speaks, thinks, and dreams in metaphors, the communal voice of the porch describes her in a string of synecdoches, naming parts of her body—such as her "great rope of

black hair," "her pugnacious breasts," her "faded shirt and muddy overalls"—
as parts standing for the whole (p. 11).

One paragraph later, as a sign that she can name her division, the direction of her figuration reverses itself. Whereas in the first scene she projects her
inner feelings onto outer physical space, in this scene she internalizes an outer
physical space, her scene of oppression, the store:

> Janie stood where he left her for unmeasured time and thought. She
> stood there until something fell off the shelf inside her. Then she went
> inside there to see what it was. It was her image of Jody tumbled down
> and shattered. But looking at it she saw that it never was the flesh and
> blood figure of her dreams. Just something she had grabbed up to drape
> her dreams over. (p. 112)

Janie has internalized the store through the synecdoche of the shelf.[31] As Barbara Johnson summarizes the rhetorical import of this scene: "These two figural mini-narratives [represent] a kind of chiasmus, or crossover, in which the
first paragraph presents an externalization of the inner, a metaphorically
grounded metonymy, while the second paragraph presents an internalization
of the outer, or a metonymically grounded metaphor. . . . The reversals op-
erated by the chiasmus map out a reversal of the power relations between
Janie and Joe."[32] When she soon speaks aloud in public against Jody and
thereby redefines their relationship, it is the awareness of this willed figurative
division of which her speaking voice is the sign. As the text reads, Janie
"found that she had a host of thoughts she had never expressed to him, and
numerous emotions she had never let Jody know about. Things packed up
and put away in parts of her heart where he could never find them" (p. 112).

Janie is now truly fluent in the language of the figurative: "She had an inside and an outside now and suddenly knew how not to mix them." Three
pages before she Signifies upon Jody, the text represents this fluency as follows:

> Then one day she sat and watched the shadow of herself going about
> tending the store and prostrating itself before Jody, while all the time
> she herself sat under a shady tree with the wind blowing through her hair
> and her clothes. Somebody near about making summertime out of lone-
> someness. (p. 119)

Janie's ability to name her own division and move the parts simultaneously
through contiguous spaces, her newly found and apparently exhilarating double-consciousness, is that crucial event that enables her to speak and assert
herself, after decades of being defined almost exclusively by others.

The text prefigures this event. The sign that this consciousness of her own
division liberates her speaking voice is Janie's first instance of voicing her
feelings within the store, which occurs in the text midway between the slap-
ping scene in which she first internally names her outside and inside (p. 112)
and the scene in which she so tellingly Signifies upon Joe (pp. 121–22). Janie
speaks after listening in a painful silence as Coker and Joe Lindsay discuss
the merits of beating women:

". . . Tony love her too good," said Coker. "Ah could break her if she wuz mine. Ah'd break her or kill her. Makin' uh fool outa me in front of everybody."

"Tony won't never hit her. He says beatin' women is just like steppin' on baby chickens. He claims 'tain't no place on uh woman tuh hit," Joe Lindsay said with scornful disapproval, "but Ah'd kill uh baby just born dis mawnin' fuh uh thing like dat. 'Taint nothin' but low-down spiteful- ness 'ginst her husband make her do it." (p. 116)

This exchange, of course, refigures the crucial scene in which Joe slaps Janie because her meal was not well prepared. Joe Lindsay's comparison in this pas- sage of "beatin' women" and "steppin' on baby chickens" echoes Joe's procla- mation to Janie that "somebody got to think for women and chillun and chickens and cows," made in their argument about who has the right "to tell" (pp. 110–11). After Joe Lindsay finishes speaking, and after his sexist re- marks are affirmed as gospel by Jim Stone, Janie—for the first time—speaks out against the men's opinion about the merits of beatings. As the text states, "Janie did what she had never done before, that is, thrust herself into the conversation":

> "Sometimes God gits familiar wid us womenfolks too and talks His inside business. He told me how surprised He was 'bout y'all turning out so smart after Him makin' yuh different; and how surprised y'all is goin' tuh be if you ever find out you don't know half as much 'bout us as you think you do. It's so easy to make yo'self out God Almighty when you ain't got nothin' tuh strain against but *women and chickens.*" (p. 117, emphasis added)

Janie reveals God's "inside business" to the superficial store-talkers, warning all who can hear her voice that a "surprise" lay in waiting for those who see only appearances and never penetrate to the tenor of things. Joe, we learn just four pages later, is in for the surprise of his life: the killing timbre of Janie's true inner voice. Joe's only response to this first scene of speaking is to tell his wife, "You gettin' too moufy, Janie," a veritable literalizing of the metaphor of mouth, followed by the ultimate sign of ignoring and circum- venting Janie's domain, an order to her to "Go fetch me de checker-board *and* de checkers." Joe's turn to the male world of play, at Janie's expense, leads Janie to play the dozens on his sexuality and thus to his death. These metaphorical echoes and exchanges are deadly serious in Hurston's text.

Earlier in the narrative, Hicks defined the metaphorical as "co-talkin' " and says that his is "too deep" for women to understand, which explains, he says, why "Dey love to hear me talk" precisely "because dey can't understand it. . . . Too much co to it," he concludes (p. 59). As soon as Janie learns to name her inside and outside and to move between them, as we have seen, Jody argues that women "need tellin' " because "somebody got to think for women and chillun and chickens and cows" because a man sees "one thing" and "understands ten," while a woman sees "ten things and don't understand one" (pp. 110–11). Jody ironically accuses Janie of failing to understand how one thing can imply or be substituted for ten, thereby arguing that Janie does not understand metaphor, whereas Janie is a master of metaphor whose self-liberation awaits only the knowledge of how to narrate her figures contiguously. It is Jody who has failed to read the situation properly. As a character in *Mules and Men* argues, most people do not understand the nature of the figurative, which he characterizes as expression that "got a hidden meanin', jus' like de Bible. Everybody can't understand what they mean," he continues. "Most people is thin-brained. They's born wid they feet under the moon. Some folks is born wid they feet on de sun and they kin seek out de inside meanin' of words" (pp. 162–63). Jody, it turns out, is both thin-brained and thin-skinned, and proves to have been born with his feet under the moon. He is all vehicle, no tenor. The "inside meanings of words," of course, we think of as the tenor, or inside meaning of a rhetorical figure, while the outside corresponds to its "vehicle." Janie, as the text repeats again and again in its central metaphor for her character, is a child of the sun.

Hurston's use of free indirect discourse is central to her larger strategy of critiquing what we might think of as a "male writing." Joe Starks, we remember, fondly and unconsciously refers to himself as "I god." During the lamp-lighting ceremony (pp. 71–74), as I have suggested earlier, Joe is represented as the creator (or at least the purchaser) of light. Joe is the text's figure of authority and voice, indeed the authority *of* voice:

> "Naw, Jody, it jus' looks lak it keeps us in some way we ain't natural wid one 'nother. You'se always off talkin' and fixin' things, and Ah feels lak Ah'm jus' markin' time. Hope it soon gits over."
>
> "Over, Janie? I god, Ah ain't even started good. Ah told you in de very first beginnin' dat Ah aimed tuh be uh big voice. You oughta be glad, 'cause dat makes uh big woman outa you." (p. 74)

Joe says that "in de very first beginnin' " he "aimed tuh be uh big voice," an echo of the first verse of the Gospel of John: "In the beginning was the Word, and the Word was with God, and the Word was God." Joe, we know, sees himself, and wishes to be seen as the God-figure of his community. The text tells us that when speakers on formal occasions prefaced their remarks with the phrase "Our beloved Mayor," the phrase was equivalent to "one of those statements that everybody says but nobody believes like 'God is everywhere' " (p. 77). Joe is the figure of the male author, he who has authored both Eatonville and Janie's existences. We remember that when Joe lights the town's newly acquired lamp, Mrs. Bogle's alto voice sings "Jesus, the light of the world":

> We'll walk in de light, de beautiful light
> Come where the dew drops of mercy shine bright
> Shine all around us by day and by night
> Jesus, the light of the world. (p. 73)

So, when Janie Signifies upon Joe, she strips him of his hubristic claim to the godhead and exposes him, through the simile of the "change of life," as impotent and de/masculated. The revelation of the truth kills him. Janie, in effect, has rewritten Joe's text of himself, and liberated herself in the process. Janie writes herself into being by naming, by speaking herself free. As we shall see in Chapter 7, Alice Walker takes this moment in Hurston's text as the moment of revision and creates a character whom we witness literally writing herself into being, but writing herself into being in a language that imitates that idiom spoken by Janie and Hurston's black community generally. This scene, this transformation or reversal of status, is truly the first feminist critique of the fiction of the authority of the male voice, and its sexism, in the Afro-American tradition.

This opposition between metaphor and metonym appears in another form as well, that of strategies of tale-telling. Nanny narrates her slave narrative in a linear, or metonymic, manner, with one event following another in chronological order. Janie, by contrast, narrates her tale in a circular, or framed, narrative replete with vivid, startling metaphors. Janie only liberates herself by selecting alternatives exactly opposed to those advocated by Nanny, eschewing the sort of "protection" afforded by Logan Killicks and so graphically figured for Janie in her grandmother's fantasy of preaching "a great sermon about colored women sittin' on high." Only after Janie satisfies Nanny's desire, "sittin' on high" on Joe Starks's front porch, then rejecting it, will she in turn "preach" her own sermon by narrating her tale to Phoeby in a circular, framed narrative that merges her voice with an omniscient narrator's in free indirect discourse.

IV

If *Their Eyes* makes impressive use of the figures of outside and inside, as well as the metaphor of double-consciousness as the prequisite to becoming a speaking subject, then the text's mode of narration, especially its "speakerliness," serves as the rhetorical analogue to this theme. I use the word *double* here intentionally, to echo W. E. B. Du Bois's metaphor for the Afro-American's peculiar psychology of citizenship and also to avoid the limited description of free indirect discourse as a "dual voice," in Roy Pascal's term.[33] Rather than a dual voice, free indirect discourse, as manifested in *Their Eyes Were Watching God,* is a dramatic way of expressing a divided self. Janie's self, as we have seen, is a divided self. Long before she becomes aware of her division, of her inside and outside, free indirect discourse communicates this division to the reader. After she becomes aware of her own division, free indirect discourse functions to represent, rhetorically, her interrupted passage from outside to inside. Free indirect discourse in *Their Eyes* reflects both the text's theme of the doubling of Janie's self and that of the problematic relationship between Janie as a speaking subject and spoken language. Free indirect discourse, furthermore, is a central aspect of the rhetoric of the text and serves to disrupt the reader's expectation of the necessity of the shift in point of view from third person to first within Janie's framed nar-

rative. Free indirect discourse is not the voice of both a character and a narrator; rather, it is a bivocal utterance, containing elements of both direct and
indirect speech. It is an utterance that no one could have spoken, yet which
we recognize because of its characteristic "speakerliness," its paradoxically
written manifestation of the aspiration to the oral.

I shall not enter into the terminological controversy over free indirect discourse, except to refer the reader to the controversy itself.[34] My concern with
free indirect discourse, for the purposes of this chapter, is limited to its use
in *Their Eyes*.[35] I am especially interested in its presence in this text as an
implicit critique of that ancient opposition in narrative theory between showing and telling, between mimesis and diegesis. The tension between diegesis,
understood here as that which can be represented, and mimesis, that which
Hurston repeats in direct quotations, strikes the reader early on as a fundamental opposition in *Their Eyes*. Only actions or events can be represented,
in this sense, while discourse here would seem to be overheard or repeated.
Hurston's use of this form of repetition creates the illusion of a direct relationship between her text and a black "real world" (which has led some of
her most vocal critics to call this an anthropological text), while representation of the sort found in narrative commentary preserves, even insists upon,
the difference and the very distance between them.

Free indirect discourse, on the other hand, is a third, mediating term. As
Michal Ginsberg argues perceptively, "it is a *mimesis* which tries to pass for
a *diegesis*."[36] But it is also, I contend, a diegesis that tries to pass for a mimesis. Indeed, it is precisely this understanding of free indirect discourse that
derives from its usages in *Their Eyes Were Watching God,* simply because we
are unable to characterize it either as the representation of an action (diegesis) or as the repetition of a character's words (mimesis). When we recall
Hurston's insistence that the fundamental indicator of traditional black oral
narration is its aspiration to the "dramatic," we can see clearly that her use of
free indirect discourse is a profound attempt to remove the distinction between repeated speech and represented events. Here discourse "is not distinct
from events." As Ginsberg argues, "Subject and object dissolve into each
other. Representation which guaranteed the distance between them is in danger."[37] For Hurston, free indirect discourse is an equation: direct speech
equals narrative commentary; representation of an action equals repetition of
that action; therefore, narrative commentary aspires to the immediacy of the
drama. Janie's quest for consciousness, however, always remains that for the
consciousness of her own division, which the dialogical rhetoric of the text—
especially as expressed in free indirect discourse—underscores, preserves, and
seems to celebrate. It is this theme, and this rhetoric of division, which together comprise the modernism of this text.

A convenient way to think about free indirect discourse is that it appears
initially to be indirect discourse (by which I mean that its signals of time and
person correspond to a third-person narrator's discourse), "but it is pene-
trated, in its syntactic and semantic structures, by enunciative properties, thus
by the discourse of a character,"[38] and even in Hurston's case by that of char-

acters. In other words, free indirect discourse attempts to represent "consciousness without the apparent intrusion of a narrative voice," thereby "presenting the illusion of a character's acting out his [or her] mental state in an immediate relationship with the reader." Graham Hough defines free indirect discourse as one extreme of "coloured narrative," or narrative-cum-dialogue as in Jane Austen's fictions.[39] Hurston's use of free indirect discourse, we are free to say, is indeed a kind of "coloured narrative"! But Hurston allows us to rename free indirect discourse; near the beginning of her book, the narrator describes the communal, undifferentiated voice of "the porch" as "A mood come alive. Words walking without masters; walking altogether like harmony in a song." Since the narrator attributes these words to "the bander log" (p. 11), or the place where Kipling's monkeys sit, Hurston here gives one more, coded, reference to Signifyin(g): that which the porch (monkeys) has just done is to Signify upon Janie. If Signifyin(g) is "a mood come alive," "words walking without masters," then we can also think of free indirect discourse in this way.

There are numerous indices whereby we identify free indirect discourse in general, among these grammar, intonation, context, idiom, register, and content; it is naturalized in a text by stream of consciousness, irony, empathy, and polyvocality.[40] The principal indices of free indirect discourse in *Their Eyes* include those which "evoke a 'voice' or presence" that supplements the narrator's, especially when one or more sentences of free indirect discourse follow a sentence of indirect discourse. Idiom and register, particularly, Hurston uses as markers of black colloquialism, of the quality of the speakerly informed by the dialect of the direct discourse of the characters. In *Their Eyes,* naturalization would seem to function as part of the theme of the developing but discontinuous self. This function is naturalized primarily by irony, empathy, and polyvocality. When it is used in conjunction with Joe Starks, irony obtains and distancing results; when it is used in conjunction with Janie, empathy obtains and an illusory identification results, an identity we might call lyric fusion between the narrator and Janie. Bivocalism, finally, or the double-voiced utterance, in which two voices co-occur, is this text's central device of naturalization, again serving to reinforce both Janie's division and paradoxically the narrator's distance from Janie. As Ginsberg concludes so perceptively, "Free indirect discourse is a way of expression of a divided self."[41]

Their Eyes employs three modes of narration to render the words or thoughts of a character. The first is direct discourse:

> "Jody," she smiled up at him, "but s'posin—"
> "Leave de s'posin' and everything else to me."

The next is indirect discourse:

> "The vision of Logan Killicks was desecrating the pear tree, but Janie didn't know how to tell Nanny that."

The third example is free indirect discourse. Significantly, this example occurs when Joe Starks enters the narrative:

> Joe Starks was the name, yeah Joe Starks from in and through Georgy.
> Been workin' for white folks all his life. Saved up some money—round
> three hundred dollars, yes indeed, right here in his pocket. Kept hearin'
> 'bout them buildin' a new state down heah in Floridy and sort of wanted
> to come. But he was makin' money where he was. But when he heard all
> about 'em makin' a town all outa colored folks, he knowed dat was de
> place he wanted to be. He had always wanted to be a big voice, but de
> white folks had all de sayso where he come from and everywhere else,
> exceptin' dis place dat colored folks was buildin' theirselves. Dat was
> right too. De man dat built things oughta boss it. Let colored folks build
> things too if dey wants to crow over somethin'. He was glad he had his
> money all saved up. He meant to git dere whilst de town wuz yet a baby.
> He meant to buy in big. (pp. 47–48)

I selected this example because it includes a number of standard indices of
free indirect speech. Although when read aloud it sounds as if entire sections
are in, or should be in, direct quotation, none of the sentences in this paragraph is direct discourse. There are no quotation marks here. The character's
idiom, interspersed and contrasted colorfully with the narrator's voice, indicates nevertheless that this is an account of the words that Joe spoke to Janie.
The sentences imitating dialect clearly are not those of the narrator alone;
they are those of Joe Starks and the narrator. Moreover, the presence of the
adverb *here* ("yes, indeed, right here in his pocket") as opposed to *there,*
which would be required in normal indirect speech because one source would
be describing another, informs us that the assertion originates within and reflects the character's sensibilities, not the narrator's. The interspersion of indirect discourse with free indirect discourse, even in the same sentence, serves
as another index to its presence, precisely by underscoring Joe's characteristic
idiom, whereas the indirect discourse obliterates it. Despite the third person
and the past tense, then, of which both indirect and free indirect discourse
consist, several sentences in this paragraph appear to report Joe's speech,
without the text resorting to either dialogue or direct discourse. The principal
indices of free indirect discourse direct the reader to the subjective source of
the statement, rendered through a fusion of narrator and a silent but speaking character.

Exclamations and exclamatory questions often introduce free indirect discourse. The text's first few examples occur when Janie experiences the longing for love, and then her first orgasm:

> She saw a dust-bearing bee sink into the sanctum of a bloom; the thou-
> sand sister-calyxes arch to meet the love embrace and the ecstatic shiver
> of the tree from root to tiniest branch creaming in every blossom and
> frothing with delight. So this was a marriage! . . . Then Janie felt a
> pain remorseless sweet that left her limp and languid. (p. 24)

Then in the next paragraph:

> She was lying across the bed asleep so Janie tipped on out of the front
> door. Oh to be a pear tree—*any* tree in bloom! With kissing bees singing
> of the beginning of the world! She was sixteen. (p. 25)

Unlike the free indirect discourse that introduces Joe, these three sentences retain the narrator's level of diction, her idiom, as if to emphasize on one hand that Janie represents the potentially lyrical self, but on the other hand that the narrator is interpreting Janie's inarticulate thoughts to the reader on her behalf.

This usage remains fairly consistent until Janie begins to challenge, if only in her thoughts, Joe's authority:

> Janie noted that while he didn't talk the mule himself [Signify], he sat and laughed at it. Laughed his big heh, hey laugh too. But then when Lige or Sam or Walter or some of the other big picture talkers were using a side of the world for a canvas, Joe would hustle her off inside the store to sell something. Look like he took pleasure in doing it. Why couldn't he go himself sometimes? She had come to hate the inside of that store anyway. (p. 85)

Here we see Janie's idiom entering, if only in two sentences, the free indirect speech. After she has "slain" Jody, however, her idiom, more and more, informs the free indirect discourse, in sentences such as "Poor Jody! He ought not to have to wrassle in there by himself" (p. 129). Once Janie meets Tea Cake, the reader comes to expect to encounter Janie's doubts and dreams in free indirect discourse, almost always introduced by the narrator explicitly as being Janie's thoughts. Almost never, however, curiously enough, does Janie's free indirect discourse unfold in a strictly black idiom, as does Joe's; rather, it is represented in an idiom informed by the black idiom but translated into what we might think of as a colloquial form of standard English, which always stands in contrast to Janie's direct speech, which is foregrounded in dialect.

This difference between the representations of the level of diction of Janie's direct discourse and the free indirect discourse that the text asks us to accept as the figure of Janie's thoughts reinforces for the reader both Janie's divided consciousness and the double-voiced nature of free indirect discourse, as if the narrative commentary cannot relinquish its proprietary consciousness over Janie as freely as it does for other characters. Nevertheless, after Janie falls in love with Tea Cake, we learn of her feelings through a remarkable amount of free indirect discourse, almost always rendered in what I wish to call idiomatic, but standard, English.

It is this same voice, eventually, which we also come to associate with that of the text's narrator; through empathy and irony, the narrator begins to read Janie's world and everyone in it, through this same rhetorical device, rendered in this identical diction, even when the observation clearly is not Janie's. The effect is as if the lyrical language created by the indeterminate merging of the narrator's voice and Janie's almost totally silences the initial level of diction of the narrator's voice. Let us recall the narrator's voice in the text's opening paragraph:

> Ships at a distance have every man's wish on board. For some they come in with the tide. For others they sail forever on the horizon, never

out of sight, never landing until the Watcher turns his eyes away in resignation, his dreams mocked to death by Time. That is the life of men.
(p. 1)

Compare that voice with the following:

> So Janie began to think of Death. Death, that strange being with the
> huge square toes who lived way in the West. The great one who lived in
> the straight house like a platform without sides to it, and without a roof.
> What need has Death for a cover, and what winds can blow against him?
> (p. 129)

Ostensibly, these are Janie's thoughts. But compare this sentence, which is
part of the narrator's commentary: "But, don't care how firm your determination is, you can't keep turning round in one place like a horse grinding
sugar cane" (p. 177).

This idiomatic voice narrates almost completely the dramatic scene of the
hurricane, where "six eyes were questioning *God.*" One such passage serves
as an excellent example of a communal free indirect discourse, of a narrative
voice that is not fused with Janie's but which describes events in the idiom of
Janie's free indirect discourse:

> They looked back. Saw people trying to run in raging waters and scream-
> ing when they found they couldn't. A huge barrier of the makings of the
> dike to which the cabins had been added was rolling and tumbling for-
> ward. . . . The monstropolous beast had left his bed. . . . The sea was
> walking the earth with a heavy heel. (p. 239)

At several passages after this narration of the hurricane, the interspersed
indirect discourse and free indirect discourse become extraordinarily difficult
to isolate because of this similarity in idiom:

> Janie fooled around outside awhile to try and think it wasn't so.
> . . . Well, she thought, that big old dawg with the hatred in his eyes had
> killed her after all. She wished she had slipped off that cow-tail and
> drowned then and there and been done. But to kill her through Tea Cake
> was too much to bear. Tea Cake, the son of the Evening Sun, had to die
> for loving her. She looked hard at the sky for a long time. Somewhere up
> there beyond blue ether's bottom sat He. Was He noticing what was
> going on around here? . . . Did He *mean* to do this thing to Tea Cake
> and her? . . . Maybe it was some big tease and when He saw it had gone
> far enough He'd give her a sign. (pp. 263–64)

Narrative commentary and free indirect discourse, in passages such as this,
move toward the indistinguishable. The final instance of free indirect discourse
occurs, appropriately enough, in the novel's ultimate paragraph, in which
Janie's true figurative synthesis occurs:

> The day of the gun, and the bloody body, and the courthouse came
> and commenced to sing a sobbing sigh out of every corner in the room;
> out of each and every chair and thing. Commenced to sing, commenced
> to sob and sigh, singing and sobbing. Then Tea Cake came prancing

around her where she was and the song of the sigh flew out of the window and lit in the top of the pine trees. Tea Cake, with the sun for a shawl. Of course he wasn't dead. He could never be dead until she herself had finished feeling and thinking. The kiss of his memory made pictures of love and light against the wall. Here was peace. She pulled in her horizon like a great fish-net. Pulled it from around the waist of the world and draped it over her shoulder. So much of life in its meshes! She called in her soul to come and see. (p. 286)

Ephi Paul, in a subtle reading of various tropes in *Their Eyes* (in an unpublished essay, "My Tongue Is in My Friend's Mouth"), argues that this "final moment of transcendence" is also a final moment of control and synthesis of the opposed male and female paradigmatic tropes defined in the novel's first two paragraphs:

> The horizon that she learns about from Joe, that helps her rediscover how to "play" again with Tea Cake, has been transformed from the object of a longing gaze to a figurative "fish-net" which an active subject can pull in. While Joe's desires are, like the men of the first paragraph, "mocked to death by Time," Janie's are still alive and thriving: "The kiss of his memory made pictures of love and light against the wall." Janie finds "peace" in "his memory," just as she has always privileged her inward contemplative self over the outer active one. Yet in its own way, Janie's thriving survival of hard times has been an active process of finding a language to name her desire. The horizon as a fish-net seems to signify the synthesis of "men" and "women's" figuration, because the fish-net's "meshes" seem so like the sifting of women's memories—remembering and forgetting all that they want. So Janie has cast her horizon into a sea of possibilities and sorted out her catch of loves, naming them with an even more accurate figuration of desire. She opens her arms to "the waist of the world" and gathers in her satisfactions, rooted in her power of "feeling and thinking" for herself. (pp. 44–45)

This merging of the opposed modes of figuration in the novel's first two paragraphs stands as an analogue of Janie's transcendent moment because of, as Paul argues,

> the male and female modes of figuration (as established in the "paradigm" of its first two paragraphs)—bringing together the horizon of change and the fish-net of memory. In her search for desire and its naming, Janie shifts back and forth between the alienation of the gazing "Watcher" and the empowerment of women believing that "the dream is the truth." She finds her satisfaction only after using Joe's horizon of "change and chance" to transform the desire she experiences alone under the pear tree; she retains the horizon long after she has dismissed Joe, because she can re-figure it to have meaning for herself. (p. 71)

To this I would only add that both the pulling in of her horizon and the calling in of her soul reveal not a unity of self but a maximum of self-control over the division between self and other. Whereas before Tea Cake Janie was forced to send a mask of herself outward, now, at novel's end, she can invite both her horizon (the figure for her desires after meeting Jody) and her soul inside herself "to come and see." She has internalized her metaphors, and brought them home, across a threshold heretofore impenetrable. This self-willed, active, subjective synthesis is a remarkable trope of self-knowledge. And the numerous sentences of free indirect discourse in this paragraph serve to stress this fact of Janie's self-knowledge and self-control. Her invitation to her soul to come see the horizon that had always before been a figure for external desire, the desire of the other, is the novel's sign of Janie's synthesis.

It is because of these dramatic shifts in the idiom in which the voice of the narrator appears that we might think of *Their Eyes* as a speakerly text. For it is clear that the resonant dialect of the character's discourse has come to color the narrator's idiom such that it resembles rather closely the idiom in which Janie's free indirect discourse is rendered. But *Their Eyes* would seem to be a speakerly text for still another reason. Hurston uses free indirect discourse not only to represent an individual character's speech and thought but also to represent the collective black community's speech and thoughts, as in the hurricane passage. This sort of anonymous, collective, free indirect discourse is not only unusual but quite possibly was Hurston's innovation, as if to emphasize both the immense potential of this literary diction, one dialect-informed as it were, for the tradition, as well as the text's apparent aspiration to imitate oral narration. One example follows:

> Most of the great flame-throwers were there and naturally, handling Big John de Conquer and his works. How he had done everything big on earth, then went up tuh heben without dying atall. Went up there picking a guitar and got all de angels doing the ring-shout round and round de throne . . . that brought them back to Tea Cake. How come he couldn't hit that box a lick or two? Well, all right now, make us know it. (p. 232)

Still another example is even more telling:

> Everybody was talking about it that night. But nobody was worried. The fire dance kept up till nearly dawn. The next day, more Indians moved east, unhurried but steady. Still a blue sky and fair weather. Beans running fine and prices good, so the Indians could be, *must* be, wrong. You couldn't have a hurricane when you're making seven and eight dollars a day picking beans. Indians are dumb anyhow, always were. Another night of Stew Beef making dynamic subtleties with his drum and living, sculptural, grotesques in the dance. (p. 229)

These instances of free indirect discourse are followed in the text by straight diegesis, which retains the dialect-informed echoes of the previous passage:

> Morning came without motion. The winds, to the tiniest, lisping baby breath had left the earth. Even before the sun gave light, dead day was creeping from bush to bush watching man. (p. 229)

There are many other examples of this curious voice (see pp. 75–76, 276). Hurston, in this innovation, is asserting that an entire narration could be rendered, if not in dialect, then in a dialect-informed discourse. This form of collective, impersonal free indirect discourse echoes Hurston's definition of "a mood come alive. Words walking without masters; walking altogether like harmony in a song." The ultimate sign of the dignity and strength of the black voice is this use of a dialect-informed free indirect discourse as narrative commentary beyond that which represents Janie's thoughts and feelings alone.

There are paradoxes and ironies in speakerly texts. The irony of this dialect-informed diction, of course, is that it is not a repetition of a language that anyone speaks; indeed, it can never be spoken. As several other scholars of free indirect discourse have argued, free indirect discourse is speakerless, by which they mean "the presentation of a perspective outside the normal communication paradigm that usually characterizes language."[42] It is literary language, meant to be read in a text. Its paradox is that it comes into use by Hurston so that discourse rendered through direct, indirect, or free indirect means may partake of Hurston's "word-pictures" and "thought-pictures," as we recall she defined the nature of Afro-American spoken language. "The white man thinks in a written language," she argued, "and the Negro thinks in hieroglyphics." The speakerly diction of *Their Eyes* attempts to render these pictures through the imitation of the extensively metaphorical medium of black speech, in an oxymoronic oral hieroglyphic that is meant only for the printed page. Its obvious oral base, nevertheless, suggests that Hurston conceived of it as a third language, as a mediating third term that aspires to resolve the tension between standard English and black vernacular, just as the narrative device of free indirect discourse aspires to define the traditional opposition between mimesis and diegesis as a false opposition. And perhaps this dialogical diction, and this dialogical narrative device, can serve as a metaphor for the critic of black comparative literature whose theoretical endeavor is intentionally double-voiced as well.

If Esu's double voice is figured in *Their Eyes Were Watching God* in the dialogical basis of free indirect discourse, it manifests itself in the fiction of Ishmael Reed in the sustained attempt to critique the strategies of narration central to certain canonical Afro-American texts through parody and pastiche. Like Hurston's text, we may think of Reed's novel as double-voiced, but in an essentially different way. Reed's relation to these authors in the tradition is at all points double-voiced, since he seems to be especially concerned with employing satire to utilize literature in what Frye calls "a special function of analysis, of breaking up the lumber of stereotypes, fossilized beliefs, superstitious terrors, crank theories, pedantic dogmatisms, oppressive fashions, and all other things that impede the free movement . . . of society."[43] Reed, of course, seems to be most concerned with the "free movement" of writing itself. In Reed's work, parody and hidden polemic overlap, in a process Bakhtin describes as follows: "When parody becomes aware of substantial resistance, a certain forcefulness and profundity in the speech act it parodies, it takes on a new dimension of complexity via the tones of the hidden polemic. . . . [A] process of inner dialogization takes place within the parodic speech act."[44] This "internal dialogization" can have curious implications, the most interesting of which perhaps is what Bakhtin describes as "the splitting of double-voice discourse into two speech acts, into two entirely separate and autonomous voices." The clearest evidence that Reed in *Mumbo Jumbo* is Signifyin(g) through parody as hidden polemic is his use of the two autonomous narrative voices in *Mumbo Jumbo,* which Reed employs in the manner of and renders through foregrounding, to parody the two simultaneous stories of detective narration, that of the present and that of the past, in a narrative flow that moves hurriedly from cause to effect. In *Mumbo Jumbo,* however, the second narrative, that of the past, bears an ironic relation to the first narrative, that of the present, because it comments on the other narrative as well as on the nature of its writing itself, in what Frye describes, in another context, as "the constant tendency to self-parody in satiric rhetoric which prevents even the process of writing itself from becoming an oversimplified convention or idea."[45] Reed's rhetorical strategy assumes the form of the relationship between the text and the criticism of that text, which "serves as discourse on that text." If Hurston's novel is a Signifyin(g) structure because it seems to be so concerned to represent Signifyin(g) rituals for their own sake, then Reed's text is a Signifyin(g) structure because he Signifies upon the tradition's convention of representation.

6

On "The Blackness of Blackness": Ishmael Reed and a Critique of the Sign

Amongst the Mandingoes there is a cant language, entirely unknown to the women, being only spoken by the men, and is seldom us'd by them in any other discourse than concerning a dreadful bugbear to the Women, call'd mumbo jumbo, which is what keeps the women in awe: And tho' they should chance to understand this language, yet were the men to know it, they would certainly murder them.

I was visited by mumbo jumbo, an idol, which is among the Mandingoes a kind of cunning mystery.

Frances Moore, *Travels into the Inland Part of Africa,* 1732

Be careful what you do,
Or Mumbo-Jumbo, God of the Congo,
And all of the other
Gods of the Congo,
Mumbo-Jumbo will hoo-doo you,
Mumbo-Jumbo will hoo-doo you,
Mumbo-Jumbo will hoo-doo you,
        Vachel Lindsay, "The Congo"

I. Talking Texts: The Signifyin(g) Revision

If Zora Neale Hurston's *Their Eyes Were Watching God* is a paradigmatic Signifyin(g) text because it figures Signifyin(g) both as theme and as rhetorical strategy, then Ishmael Reed's *Mumbo Jumbo* is a Signifyin(g) text for still another reason. *Mumbo Jumbo* seems to be concerned to critique and to revise the modes of representation fundamental to the canonical texts that comprise the tradition of the Afro-American novel. *Mumbo Jumbo* attempts this critique by Signifyin(g), by repeating received tropes and narrative strategies with a difference. In Reed's differences lie an extended commentary on the history of the black novel. It is fair to say that *The Signifying Monkey,* as a theory of criticism and as the shape it has assumed in this book, at the very least began with (and at most was shaped by) my explication of Reed's difficult novel. If anything, Reed's text is the text-specific element from which my theory arose, from his characterization of *Esu-Elegbara* as Pa Pa La Bas to his explicit splitting of the narrative voices of showing (mimesis) and telling (diegesis). *The Signifying Monkey* and *Mumbo Jumbo* bear something of a symbiotic relationship. In this chapter, I attempt to employ the definitions of narrative parody and critical Signification, set out earlier in this book, as a frame within which to read *Mumbo Jumbo*.

A close reading of Reed's work suggests strongly his concerns with the received form of the novel, with the precise rhetorical shape of the Afro-American literary tradition, and with the relation that the Afro-American tradition bears to the Western tradition.[1] Reed's concerns, as exemplified in his narrative forms, seem to be twofold: (1) the relation his own art bears to his black literary precursors, including Hurston, Wright, Ellison, and Baldwin; and (2) the process of willing into being a rhetorical structure, a literary language, replete with its own figures and tropes, but one that allows the black writer to posit a structure of feeling that simultaneously critiques both the metaphysical presuppositions inherent in Western ideas and forms of writing and the metaphorical system in which the blackness of the writer and his experience have been valorized as a "natural" absence. In six demanding novels, Reed has criticized, through Signifyin(g), what he perceives to be the conventional structures of feeling that he has received from the Afro-American tradition. He has proceeded almost as if the sheer process of the analysis can clear a narrative space for the next generation of writers as decidedly as Ellison's narrative response to Wright and naturalism cleared a space for Leon Forrest, Ernest Gaines, Toni Morrison, Alice Walker, James Alan McPherson, John Wideman, and especially for Reed himself.

By undertaking the difficult and subtle art of pastiche, Reed criticizes the Afro-American idealism of a transcendent black subject, integral and whole, self-sufficient, and plentiful, the "always already" black signified, available for literary representation in received Western forms as would be the water dippered from a deep and dark well. Water can be poured into glasses or cups or canisters, but it remains water just the same. Put simply, Reed's fictions argue that the so-called black experience cannot be thought of as a fluid content to be poured into received and static containers. For Reed, it is the signifier that both shapes and defines any discrete signified—and it is the signifiers of the Afro-American tradition with whom Reed is concerned.

Reed's first novel lends credence to this sort of reading and also serves to create a set of generic expectations for reading the rest of his works. *The Free-Lance Pallbearers* is, above all else, a parody of the confessional mode which is the fundamental, undergirding convention of Afro-American narrative, received, elaborated upon, and transmitted in a chartable heritage from Briton Hammon's captivity narrative of 1760, through the antebellum slave narratives, to black autobiography, and into black fiction, especially that of Hurston, Wright, Baldwin, and Ellison.[2] The narrative of Reed's Bukka

Doopeyduk is a pastiche of the classic black narrative of the questing protagonist's "journey into the heart of whiteness"; but it parodies that narrative form by turning it inside out, exposing the character of the originals
and thereby defining their formulaic closures and disclosures. Doopeyduk's
tale ends with his own crucifixion; as the narrator of his own story, therefore, Doopeyduk articulates, literally, from among the dead, an irony implicit in all confessional and autobiographical modes, in which any author
is forced by definition to imagine himself or herself to be dead. More specifically, Reed Signifies upon *Black Boy* and *Go Tell It on the Mountain* in
a foregrounded critique which can be read as an epigraph to the novel: "read
growing up in soulsville first of three installments—or what it means to be
a backstage darkey."[3] Reed foregrounds the "scat-singing voice" that introduces the novel against the "other" voice of Doopeyduk, whose "second"
voice narrates the novel's plot. Here Reed parodies both Hurston's use of
free indirect discourse in *Their Eyes Were Watching God* and Ellison's use
in *Invisible Man* of the foregrounded voice in the prologue and epilogue
that frame his nameless protagonist's picaresque account of his own narrative. As Neil Schmitz concludes of Reed's device, "In killing off that latter
Doopeyduk, Reed murders a style, the Black writer's appropriation of what
D. H. Lawrence . . . called 'art-speech.' Doopeyduk's attempt to fashion
his discourse in formal English "only reveals his stupidity, an ignorance not
of correct grammar or proper diction, but of his world. For the language in
which he invests his feelings and perceptions is a dead language."

Other examples of this, such as the parody of the allegorical significance
of the degradation of Tod Clifton when Cipher X incarcerates and humili-
ates Doopeyduk, are too numerous to analyze here. (Schmitz reads a few
of these extremely carefully.) What is relevant to our reading of *Mumbo
Jumbo* is not only that Reed parodies and deflates his precursors' rhetorical
strategies as essentially complex attempts to render the black experience (the
transcendent signified), but also that Reed employs a self-referential language, at all points directing attention to itself as rhetoric, to do so. Reed's
burlesques of events in other black novels, cast frequently in vulgarity and
hyperbole, critiquing "The writers's credentials as bona fide explicator [of
the black experience which] are manifest in the finish of his language, his
mastery of the European tradition."[4] What's more, the text's self-references
to literary devices (such as "a cloud moved above sagging with rain. It
seemed as if it had eyes, nose, lips. It did, my eyes, nose, and lips. Get it?
Clouds"[5]) are meant both to expose the nature of conventions and to insist
on new and black structures of feeling. As Schmitz concludes, "The rites
of passage established by Wright, Ellison, and Baldwin in their fiction are
stripped of their dramatic force and reduced to the pratfalls of a burlesque
routine. Doopeyduk's award for promising service is a bedpan, not a brief-
case and a scholarship, and SAM, both as place and person, holds no mysteries. . . . In HARRY SAM, simply put, there are no mythic labyrinths
for the Black hero to explore,"[6] as there are in the fictions of Wright, Baldwin, and Ellison.

In his second novel, *Yellow Back Radio Broke-Down,* Reed more fully and successfully critiques both realism and modernism. The exchange between Bo Shmo and the Loop Garoo Kid is telling:

> It was Bo Shmo and the neo-social realist gant. They rode to this spot from their hideout in the hills. Bo Shmo leaned in his saddle and scowled at Loop, whom he considered a deliberate attempt to be obscure. A buffoon an outsider and frequenter of sideshows. . . .
>
> The trouble with you Loop is that you're too abstract, the part time autocrat monarchist and guru finally said. Crazy dada nigger that's what you are. You are given to fantasy and are off in matters of detail. Far out esoteric bullshit is where you're at. Why in those suffering books that I write about my old neighborhood and how hard it was every gumdrop machine is in place while your work is a blur and a doodle. I'll bet you can't create the difference between a German and a redskin.
>
> What's your beef with me Bo Shmo, what if I write circuses? No one says a novel has to be one thing. It can be anything it wants to be, a vaudeville show, the six o'clock news, the mumblings of old men saddled by demons.
>
> All art must be for the end of liberating the masses. A landscape is only good when it shows the oppressor hanging from a tree.
>
> Right on! Right on, Bo, the henchmen chorused.
>
> Did you receive that in a vision or was it revealed to you?[7]

At several points in his first two novels, then, Reed deliberately reflects on the history of the black tradition's debate over the nature and purpose of art.

Reed's third novel, *Mumbo Jumbo,* is a novel about writing itself—not only in the figurative sense of the postmodern, self-reflexive text but also in a literal sense: "So Jes Grew is seeking its words. Its text. For what good is a liturgy without a text?"[8] *Mumbo Jumbo* is both a book about texts and a book of texts, a composite narrative composed of subtexts, pretexts, posttexts, and narratives-within-narratives. It is both a definition of Afro-American culture and its deflation. "The Big Lie concerning Afro-American culture," *Mumbo Jumbo*'s dust jacket states, "is that it lacks a tradition." The "Big Truth" of the novel, on the other hand, is that this very tradition is as rife with hardened convention and presupposition as is the rest of the Western tradition. Even this cryptic riddle of Jes Grew and its text parodies Ellison: *Invisible Man*'s plot is set in motion with a riddle, while the themes of the relationship between words and texts echo a key passage from Ellison's short story "And Hickman Arrives": "Good. Don't talk like I talk; talk like I *say* talk. Words are your business, boy. Not just *the* Word. Words are everything. The key to the Rock, the answer to the Question."[9]

Reed's Signifyin(g) on tradition begins with his book's title. *Mumbo jumbo* is the received and ethnocentric Western designation for the rituals of black religions as well as for black languages themselves. According to *Webster's Third New International Dictionary, mumbo jumbo,* connotes "language that is unnecessarily involved and difficult to understand: GIBBERISH." *The Oxford English Dictionary* cites its etymology as "of unknown origin," implicitly serving here as the signified on which Reed's title Signifies, recalling the myth of Topsy in *Uncle Tom's Cabin,* who, with no antecedents, "jes' grew"—a phrase with which James Weldon Johnson characterizes the creative process of black sacred music. *Mumbo Jumbo,* then, Signifies upon Western etymology, abusive Western practices of deflation through misnaming, and Johnson's specious, albeit persistent, designation of black creativity as anonymous.

But there is even more parody in this title. Whereas Ellison tropes the myth of presence in Wright's title of *Native Son* and *Black Boy* through his title of *Invisible Man,* Reed parodies all three titles by employing as his title the English-language parody of black language itself. Although the etymology of *mumbo jumbo* has been problematic for Western lexicographers, any Swahili speaker knows that the phrase derives from the common greeting *jambo* and its plural, *mambo,* which loosely translated mean "What's happening?" Reed is also echoing, and Signifying upon, Vachel Lindsay's ironic poem, "The Congo," which so (fatally) influenced the Harlem Renaissance poets, as Charles T. Davis has shown.[10] From its title on, *Mumbo Jumbo* serves as a critique of black and Western literary forms and conventions, and of the complex relationships between the two.

On the book's cover, which Reed designed (with Allen Weinbert), repeated and reversed images of a crouching, sensuous Josephine Baker are superimposed upon a rose.[11] Counterposed to this image is a medallion depicting a horse with two riders. These signs—the rose and the medallion—adumbrate the two central oppositions of the novel's complicated plot. The rose and the double image of Baker together form a cryptic *vé vé.* A *vé vé* is a key sign in Haitian Vaudou, a sign drawn on the ground with sand, cornmeal, flour, and coffee to represent the *loas.* The *loas* are the deities comprising the pantheon of Vaudou gods. The rose is a sign of Erzulie, goddess of love, as are the images of Baker, who became the French goddess of love in the late 1920s in the Parisian version of the Jazz Age. The doubled image, as if mirrored, is meant to suggest the divine crossroads, where human beings meet their fate. At its center presides the *loa,* Legba (Esu), guardian of the divine crossroads, messenger of the gods, the figure representing the interpreter and interpreter itself, the muse or *loa* of the critic. Legba is master of that mystical barrier separating the divine from the profane world. This complex yet cryptic *vé vé* is meant both to placate Legba himself and to summon his attention and integrity in a double act of criticism and interpretation: that of Reed in the process of his representation of the tradition, to be found between the covers of the book, and of the critic's interpretation of Reed's figured interpretation.

Located outside the *vé vé,* as counterpoint, placed almost off the cover itself, is the medallion, the sign of the Knights Templar, representing the heart of the Western tradition. The opposition between the *vé vé* and the medallion represents two distinct warring forces, two mutually exclusive modes of reading. Already we are in the realm of doubles, but not the binary realm; rather, we are in the realm of doubled doubles. (Doubled doubles are central to Yoruba mythology, and to Esu.) Not only are two distinct and conflicting metaphysical systems here represented and invoked, but Reed's cover also serves as an overture to the critique of dualism and binary opposition which gives a major thrust to the text of *Mumbo Jumbo*. Reed parodies this dualism, which he thinks is exemplified in Ellison's *Invisible Man,* not just in *Mumbo Jumbo* but also in another text, his poem "Dualism: in ralph ellison's invisible man," to which I shall return at the end of this chapter.

Reed's critique of dualism would appear on a first reading to be a polemic for tertiary relations, for the triad, as Robert Eliot Fox persuasively argues in "The Mirrors of Caliban." After all, *Mumbo Jumbo* informs us that this, Reed's third novel, was "finished" at three p.m. (p. 249). America, the narrative states, was "born" at 3:03 on July 4 (p. 17). The Center of Art Detention houses 30,000 items (p. 97). Berbelang and Thor are charged 3 cents for a cup of coffee (p. 102), and Hinkle Von Vampton gives W. W. Jefferson 3 cents to buy an "August Ham" (p. 114). Pa Pa La Bas owns a dog called "Hoodoo 3¢" (p. 23). Ancient Egypt had 30 dynasties (p. 204). Julian the Apostate was assassinated in A.D. 363 (p. 195). The case for the triad would seem to be convincing. On the other hand, however, in a key image which parodies a scene in Rudolph Fisher's black detective novel, *The Conjure-Man Dies,* Reed compares "Western History" to a three-story building, undermining thereby the case for the triad. The passage reads:

> The *Mu'tafikah* are holding a meeting in the basement of a 3-story building located at the edge of 'Chinatown.' Upstairs is a store which deals in religious articles. Above this is a gun store; at the top, an advertising firm which deals in soap accounts. If Western History were a 3-story building located in downtown Manhattan during the 1920s it would resemble this little architectural number." (*MJ,* 82)

It is the critique of dualism through the play of doubles which Reed employs in his text, simultaneously as thematic devices and as underlying structuring principles; Reed underscores the play of doubles by a narrative strategy of double voices, double plot lines, and most especially by the repetition of the "double-double" figure itself, "22," which reappears frequently throughout the novel, as James A. Snead pointed out to me.

This critique of dualism is implicit in *Mumbo Jumbo*'s central speaking character, Pa Pa La Bas. I emphasize speaking here because the novel's central character, of course, is Jes Grew itself, which never speaks and is never seen in its "abstract essence," only in discrete manifestations, or "outbreaks." Jes Grew is the supraforce which sets the text of *Mumbo Jumbo* in motion, as Jes Grew and Reed seek their texts, as all characters and events define themselves against this omnipresent, compelling force. Jes Grew here is a clever and subtle parody of similar forces invoked in the black novel of naturalism, most notably in Wright's *Native Son.*

Unlike Jes Grew, Pa Pa La Bas does indeed speak. He is the chief detective in hard and fast pursuit of both Jes Grew and its text. Pa Pa La Bas's name is a conflation of two of the several names of Esu, our Pan-African trickster. Called Papa Legba as his Haitian honorific and invoked through the phrase "eh là-bas" in New Orleans jazz recordings of the 1920s and 1930s, Pa Pa La Bas is the Afro-American trickster figure from black sacred tradition. His surname, of course, is French for "down" or "over there," and his presence unites "over there" (Africa) with "right here." He is indeed the messenger of the gods, the divine Pan-African interpreter, pursuing, in the language of the text, "The Work," which is not only Vaudou but also the very work (and play) of art itself. Pa Pa La Bas is the figure of the critic, in search of the text, decoding its telltale signs in the process. Even the four syllables of his name recall *Mumbo Jumbo*'s play of doubles. Chief sign reader, La Bas also in a sense is a sign himself. Indeed, Pa Pa La Bas's incessant and ingenious search for the text of Jes Grew, culminating as it does in his recitation and revision of the myth of Thoth's gift of writing to civilization, constitutes an argument against the privileging in black discourse of what Reed elsewhere terms "the so-called oral tradition" in favor of the primacy and priority of the written text. It is a brief for the permanence of the written text, for the need of criticism, for which La Bas's myth of origins also accounts: "Guides were initiated into the Book of Thoth, the 1st anthology written by the 1st choreographer" (p. 164).

Let us examine the text of *Mumbo Jumbo* as a textbook, complete with illustrations, footnotes, and a bibliography. A prologue, an epilogue, and an appended "Partial Bibliography" frame the text proper, again in a parody of Ellison's framing devices in *Invisible Man*. (Reed supplements Ellison's epilogue with the bibliography, parodying the device both by its repeated presence and by the subsequent asymmetry of *Mumbo Jumbo*.) This documentary scheme of notes, illustrations, and bibliography parodies the documentary conventions of black realism and naturalism, as does Reed's recurrent use of lists and catalogues. These "separate" items Reed fails to separate with any sort of punctuation, thereby directing attention to their presence as literary conventions rather than as sources of information, particularly about the black experience. Reed's text also includes dictionary definitions, epigraphs, epigrams, anagrams, photoduplicated type from other texts, newspaper clippings and headlines, signs (such as those that hang on doors), invitations to parties, telegrams, "Situation Reports" (which come from "the 8-tubed Radio," p. 32), yin-yang symbols, quotations from other texts, poems, cartoons, drawings of mythic beasts, handbills, photographs, dust-jacket copy, charts and graphs, playing cards, a representation of a Greek vase, and a four-page handwritten letter, among still other items. Just as our word *satire* derives from *satura,* "hash," so Reed's form of satire is a version of "gumbo," a parody of form itself.[12]

Reed here parodies and underscores our notions of intertextuality, present in all texts. *Mumbo Jumbo* is the great black intertext, replete with intratexts referring to one another within the text of *Mumbo Jumbo* and also referring outside themselves to all those other named texts, as well as to those texts unnamed but invoked through concealed reference, repetition, and reversal.

The "Partial Bibliography" is Reed's most brilliant stroke, since its uncon-cealed presence (along with the text's other undigested texts) parodies both the scholar's appeal to authority and all studied attempts to conceal literary antecedents and influence. All texts, claims *Mumbo Jumbo,* are intertexts, full of intratexts. Our notions of originality, Reed's critique suggests, are more related to convention and material relationships than to some supposedly transcendent truth. Reed lays bare that mode of concealment and the illusion of unity which characterize modernist texts. Coming as it does after the epi-logue, Reed's "Partial Bibliography" is an implicit parody of Ellison's ideas of craft and technique in the novel and suggests an image of Ellison's name-less protagonist, buried in his well-lighted hole, eating vanilla ice cream smothered by sloe gin, making annotations for his sequel to *Invisible Man.* The device, moreover, mimics the fictions of documentation and history which claim to order the ways societies live. The presence of the bibliography also recalls Ellison's remarks about the complex relationship between the "writer's experience" and the writer's experience with books.

Reed's parodic use of intertextuality demonstrates that *Mumbo Jumbo* is a postmodern text. But what is its parody of the Jazz Age and the Harlem Renaissance about, and for whom do the characters stand? Reed's novel is situated in the 1920s because, as the text explains, the Harlem Renaissance was the first full-scale, patronized attempt to capture the essence of Jes Grew in discrete literary texts. Jes Grew had made its first appearance in the 1890s, when "the Dance" swept the country. Indeed, James Weldon Johnson appro-priated the phrase "jes' grew" to refer to the composition of the musical texts of Ragtime, which depended on signifying riffs to transform black secular, and often vulgar, songs into formal, repeatable compositions. Ellison makes es-sentially the same statement about the 1890s by suggesting that Signifyin(g) is implicit in the common designation of this music as "Ethiopian Airs." Elli-son's pun could well serve as still another signified upon which *Mumbo Jumbo* Signifies. The power of Jes Grew was allowed to peter out in the 1890s, Reed argues, because it found no literary texts to contain, define, interpret, and thereby will it to subsequent black cultures.

Although the Harlem Renaissance did succeed in the creation of numer-ous texts of art and criticism, most critics agree that it failed to find its voice, which lay muffled beneath the dead weight of Romantic convention, which most black writers seemed not to question but to adopt eagerly. This is es-sentially the same critique rendered by Wallace Thurman in his *Infants of the Spring* (1932), a satirical novel about the Harlem Renaissance written by one of its most thoughtful literary critics. Few of Reed's characters stand for historical personages; most are figures for types. Hinckle Von Vampton, however, suggests Carl Van Vechten, but his first name, from the German *hinken* ("to limp"), could suggest the German engraver Hermann Knackfuss, whose name translates as "a person with a clubfoot."[13] Abdul Sufi Hamid recalls a host of Black Muslims, most notably Duse Mohamed Ali, editor of the *African Times and Orient Review,* as well as Elijah Muhammad's shad-owy mentor, W. D. Fard. The key figures in the action of the plot, however, are the Atonist Path and its military wing, the Wallflower Order, on one hand, and the neo-HooDoo detectives, headed by Pa Pa La Bas and its "military" wing, the *Mu'tafikah,* on the other. "Wallflower Order" is a two-term pun on "Ivy League,"* while *Mu'tafikah* puns on "motherfucker," which signifies chaos. Also, as Robert Eliot Fox suggests, "mu" is the twelfth letter of the Greek alphabet, suggesting the dozens, which forms a subdivision of Signifyin(g); the *Mu'tafikah* play the dozens on Western art museums. The painter Knackfuss created a heliogravure from Wilhelm II's allegorical drawing of the European authority to go to war against the Chinese. This heliogravure, *Völker Europas, wahrt eure heiligsten Güter* ("People of Europe, protect that which is most holy to you"), was completed in 1895. It appears in *Mumbo Jumbo* as part of a chapter in which members of the Wallflower Order plot against the *Mu'tafikah* (see p. 155). The pun on Knackfuss and *hinken* is wonderfully consistent with Reed's multiple puns on the Wallflower Order and Atonist.

"Atonist" signifies multiply here. "One who atones" is an Atonist; a follower of Aton, Pharaoh Akhnaton's Supreme Being who reappears as Jehovah, is an Atonist; but also one who lacks physiological tone, especially of a contractile organ, is an Atonist. On a wall at Atonist headquarters are the order's symbols:

> the Flaming Disc, the #1 and the creed—*Look at them! Just look at them! throwing their hips this way, that way* while I, my muscles, stone, the marrow of my spine, plaster, *my back supported by decorated paper, stand here as goofy as a Dumb Dora, Lord, if I can't dance, no one shall.*
> (p. 65; emphasis added)

The Atonists and the Jes Grew Carriers ("J.G.C.s") reenact allegorically a primal, recurring battle between the forces of light and the forces of darkness, between forces of the left hand and forces of the right hand, between the descendants of Set and the descendants of Osiris, all symbolized in Knackfuss's heliogravure.

We learn of this war in *Mumbo Jumbo*'s marvelous parody of the scene of recognition so fundamental to the structure of detective fiction, which occurs in the library of a black-owned villa at Irvington-on-Hudson, called Villa Lewaro, "an anagram," the text tells us, "upon the Hostess' name, by famed tenor Enrico Caruso" (p. 156). Actually, "Lewaro" is an anagram for "we oral." This recognition scene, in which Pa Pa La Bas and his sidekick, Black Herman, arrest Hinckle Von Vampton and his sidekick, Hubert "Safecracker" Gould, parodies its counterpart in the detective novel by its exaggerated frame. When forced to explain the charges against Von Vampton and Gould, La Bas replies, "Well, if you must know, it all began 1000s of years ago in Egypt, according to a high up member in the Haitian aristocracy" (p. 160). He then proceeds to narrate, before an assembled company of hundreds, the myth of Set and Osiris and its key subtext, the myth of the introduction of writing in Egypt by the god Thoth. The parody involved

* Catherine Mursofsky suggested this to me.

here is the length of the recapitulation of facts—of the decoded signs—which La Bas narrates in a thirty-one-page chapter, the longest in the book (see pp. 161–91). The myth, of course, recapitulates the action of the novel up to this point of the narrative, but by an allegorical representation through mythic discourse. By fits and turns, we realize that Von Vampton and the Wallflower Order are the descendants of Set, by way of the story of Moses and Jethro and the birth of the Knights Templar in A.D. 1118. Von Vampton, we learn, was the Templar librarian, who found the sacred Book of Thoth, "the 1st anthology written by the 1st choreographer," which is Jes Grew's sacred text (p. 164). In the twentieth century, Von Vampton subdivided the Book of Thoth into fourteen sections, just as Set had dismembered his brother Osiris's body into fourteen segments. The fourteen sections of the anthology he mailed anonymously to fourteen black people, who are manipulated into mailing its parts to each other in a repeating circle, in the manner of a "chain book" (p. 69). Abdul Sufi Hamid, one of these fourteen who, we learn, are unwitting Jes Grew Carriers, calls in the other thirteen chapters of the anthology, reassembles the text, and even translates the Book of Thoth from the hieroglyphics. Sensing its restored text, Jes Grew surfaces in New Orleans, as it had in the 1890s with the birth of Ragtime, and heads toward New York. Ignorant of the existence or nature of Jes Grew and of the true nature of the sacred text, Abdul destroys the book, and then, when he refuses to reveal its location, is murdered by the Wallflower Order. La Bas, Von Vampton's arch foe, master of HooDoo, devout follower of Jes Grew—"Pa Pa La Bas carries Jes Grew in him like most other folk carry genes" (p. 23)—chief decoder of signs, recapitulates this complex story in elaborate detail to the assembled guests at Villa Lewaro, thereby repeating, through the recited myth, the figures of *Mumbo Jumbo*'s own plot, functioning as what Reed calls "the shim-ering Etheric Double of the 1920s. The thing that gives it its summary" (p. 20). Despite numerous murders and even the arrests of Von Vampton and Gould and their repatriation to Haiti for trial by the *loas* of *Vaudou,* neither the mystery of the nature of Jes Grew nor the identity of its text is ever resolved. The epilogue presents Pa Pa La Bas in the 1960s, delivering his annual lecture to a college audience on the Harlem Renaissance and its unconsummated Jes Grew passion.

But just as we can define orders of multiple substitution and signification for Reed's types and caricatures, as is true of allegory generally (e.g., Von Vampton/Van Vechten, *hinken*/Knackfuss), so too can we find many levels of meaning which could provide a closure to the text. The first decade of readers of *Mumbo Jumbo* have attempted, with great energy, to find one-to-one correlations, decoding its allegorical structure by finding analogues between, for example, the Harlem Renaissance and the Black Arts movement. As interesting as such parallel universes are, however, I am more concerned here with *Mumbo Jumbo*'s status as a rhetorical structure, as a mode of narration, and with relating this mode of narration to a critique of traditional notions of closure in interpretation. Reed's most subtle achievement in *Mumbo Jumbo* is to parody, to Signify upon, the notions of closure implicit in the key texts of the Afro-American canon. *Mumbo Jumbo,* in contrast to that canon, is a novel that figures and glorifies indeterminacy. In this sense, *Mumbo Jumbo* stands as a profound critique and elaboration upon the convention of closure, and its metaphysical implications, in the black novel. In its stead, Reed posits the notion of aesthetic play: the play of tradition, the play on the tradition, the sheer play of indeterminacy itself.

II. Indeterminacy and the Text of Blackness

The text of *Mumbo Jumbo* is framed by devices characteristic of film narration, an apparent echo of the fade out, fade in frame of *Their Eyes Were Watching God.* The prologue, situated in New Orleans, functions as a false start of the action: five pages of narration are followed by a second title page, a second copyright and acknowledgment page, and a second set of epigraphs, the first of which concludes the prologue. This prologue functions like the prologue of a film, with the title and credits appearing next, before the action continues. The novel's final words are "Freeze frame" (p. 218). The relative fluidity of the narrative structure of film, compared with that of conventional prose narrative, announces here an emphasis on figural multiplicity rather than singular referential correspondence, an emphasis that Reed recapitulates throughout the text by an imaginative play of doubles. The play of doubles extends from the title and the double-Erzulie image of Baker on the novel's cover (*Erzulie* means "love of mirrors," p. 162) to the double beginning implicit in every prologue, through all sorts of double images scattered in the text, such as the "two heads" of Pa Pa La Bas (see pp. 25, 45) and the frequently repeated arabic numerals 4 and 22, all the way to the double ending of the novel implied by its epilogue and "Partial Bibliography." The double beginning and double ending frame the text of *Mumbo Jumbo,* a book of doubles, from its title on.

These thematic aspects of doubleness represent only its most obvious form of doubling; the novel's narrative structure, a brilliant elaboration upon that of the detective novel, is itself a rather complex doubling. Reed refers to this principle of "structuration" as "a doubleness, not just of language, but the idea of a double-image on form. A mystery-mystery, *Erzulie-Erzulie.*"[14] In *Mumbo Jumbo,* form and content, theme and structure, all are ordered upon this figure of the double; doubling is Reed's "figure in the carpet." The form the narration takes in *Mumbo Jumbo* replicates the tension of the two stories which grounds the form of the detective novel, defined by Tzvetan Todorov as "the missing story of the crime, and the presented story of the investigation, the role justification of which is to make us discover the first story." Todorov describes three forms of detective fiction—the whodunit, the *série noire* (the thriller, exemplified by Chester Himes's *For Love of Imabelle*), and the suspense novel, which combines the narrative features of the first two.[15] Let us consider Todorov's typology in relation to the narrative structure of *Mumbo Jumbo.*

The whodunit comprises two stories: the story of the crime and the story of the investigation. The first story has ended by the time the second story begins. In the story of the investigation, the characters "do not act, they learn." The whodunit's structure, as in Agatha Christie's *Murder on the Orient Express,* is often framed by a prologue and an epilogue, "that is, the discovery of the crime and the discovery of the killer," according to Todorov (p. 45). The second story functions as an explanation not just of the investigation but also of how the book came to be written; indeed, "it is precisely the story of that very book" (p. 45). As Todorov concludes, these two stories are the same as those which the Russian Formalists isolated in every narrative, that of the fable (story) and that of the subject (or plot): "The story is what has happened in life, the plot is the way the author presents it to us" (p. 45). "Story" here describes the reality represented, while "plot" describes the mode of narration, the literary convention and devices, used to represent. A detective novel merely renders these two principles of narrative present simultaneously. The story of the crime is a story of an absence since the crime of the whodunit has occurred before the narrative begins; the second story, therefore, "serves only as mediator between the reader and the story of the crime" (p. 46). This second story, the plot, generally depends on temporal inversions and subjective, shifting points of view. These two conventions figure prominently in the narrative structure of *Mumbo Jumbo.*

Todorov's second type of detective fiction, the *série noire,* or thriller, combines the two stories into one, suppressing the first and vitalizing the second. Whereas the whodunit proceeds from effect to cause, the thriller proceeds from cause to effect: the novel reveals at its outset the causes of the crime, the *données* (in *Mumbo Jumbo,* the Wallflower Order, the dialogue of whose members occupies sixty percent of the prologue), and the narration sustains itself through sheer suspense, through the reader's expectation of what will happen next. Although *Mumbo Jumbo*'s narrative strategy proceeds through the use of suspense, its two stories are not fused; accordingly, neither of these categories fully describes it.

Mumbo Jumbo imitates and Signifies upon the narrative strategy of the third type of detective novel, the suspense novel. According to Todorov, its defining principles are these: "It keeps the mystery of the whodunit and also the two stories, that of the past and that of the present; but it refuses to reduce the second to a simple detection of the truth" (p. 50). What has happened is only just as important to sustaining interest as what will happen; the second story, then, the story of the present, is the focus of interest. Reed draws upon this type of narrative as his rhetorical structure in *Mumbo Jumbo,* with one important exception. We do find the two-story structure intact. What's more, the mystery presented at the outset of the text, the double mystery of the suppression of both Jes Grew and its text (neither of which is ever revealed nor their mysteries solved in the standard sense of the genre) is relayed through the dialogue of the *données.* This means that the movement of the narration is from cause to effect, from the New Orleans branch of the Wallflower Order and their plans to "decode this coon mumbo jumbo" (*Mumbo Jumbo,* p. 4) through their attempts to kill its text and thereby dissipate its force. The detective of the tale, Pa Pa La Bas, moreover, is integrated solidly into the action and universe of the other characters, risking his life and systematically discovering the murdered corpses of his friends and colleagues as he proceeds to decode the signs leading to mystery's solution, in the manner of "the vulnerable detective," which Todorov identifies as a subtype of the suspense novel (Todorov, p. 51).

In these ways, the structure of *Mumbo Jumbo* conforms to that of the suspense novel. The crucial exception to the typology, however, whereby Reed is able to parody even the mode of the two stories themselves and transform the structure into a self-reflecting text or allegory on the nature of writing itself, is *Mumbo Jumbo*'s device of drawing upon the story of the past to reflect upon, analyze, and philosophize about the story of the present. The story of the present is narrated from the limited but multiple points of view of the characters who people its subplots and submysteries; the story of the past, however, is narrated in an omniscient voice, which reads the story of the present, in the manner of a literary critic's close reading of a primary text. *Mumbo Jumbo*'s double narrative, then, its narrative-within-a-narrative, is an allegory of the act of reading itself. Reed uses this second mode of ironic omniscient narration to Signify upon the nature of the novel in general but especially upon Afro-American naturalism and modernism.

The mystery type of narrative discourse is characterized by plot inversions, which, of course, function as temporal inversions. Before discussing Reed's use of the narrative-within-a-narrative and its relation to the sort of indeterminacy the text seems to be upholding, it would be useful to chart his use of inversion as impediment. The summary of the fable, the essential causal-temporal relationships of the work which I have sketched above, is somewhat misleading, for the novel can be related in summary fashion only after we have read it. In the reading process we confront a collection of mysteries, mysteries within mysteries, all of which are resolved eventually except for the first two. We can list the following mysteries which unfold in this order as the subject, or the plot:[16]

1. The mystery of Jes Grew ("the Thing").	These are basic mysteries. They frame the plot and remain unsolved.
2. The mystery of its text.	
3. The mystery of the Wallflower Order's history and its relation to that of the Knights Templar.	The mystery of the identity of these medieval orders, Jes Grew's antagonists, runs the length of the novel and is resolved only in the recognition scene at Villa Lewaro. Figured as antithetical dance metaphors.
4. The *Mu'tafikahs'* raids on American art museums, especially the North Wing of the Center of Art Detention.	This partial mystery is resolved, but disastrously for La Bas's forces. It creates a series of imbalances between Earline and Berbelang, and between Berbelang

and Pa Pa La Bas, which function as structural parts to the tension between the Wallflower Order and the Knights Templar.

5. Installation of the anti-Jes Grew President Warren Harding and mystery of his complex racial heritage.

Plot impediments.

6. The mystery of the Talking Android.

7. Gang wars between Buddy Jackson and Schlitz, "the Sarge of Yorktown."

8. Mystery of the U.S. Marine invasion of Haiti.

Resolved midway; allows for ironic denouement.

9. Mystery of Pa Pa La Bas's identity and Mumbo Jumbo Kathedral.

Resolved in epilogue.

10. Woodrow Wilson Jefferson and the mystery of the Talking Android.

Plot impediments; resolved, but ambiguously. Explanations resort to fantastic element.

11. Staged mystery of "Charlotte's (Isis) Pick" (Doctor Peter Pick).

12. Hinckle Von Vampton's identity.

This mystery is resolved and in the process resolves the mysteries of the Wallflower Order and the Atonist Path.

13. Mystery of the fourteen J. G. C.s and the sacred anthology.

This resolves mystery 3, but only partially, superficially.

14. The mystery of Abdul Sufi Hamid's murder and his riddle, "Epigram on American-Egyptian Cotton."

These mysteries function in a curious way, seemingly to resolve the mystery of Jes Grew's text.

15. Berbelang's murder and betrayal of the *Mu'tafikah* by Thor Wintergreen; Charlotte's murder.

Plot impediments.

16. Earline's possession by Erzulie and Yemanjá *loas;* Doctor Peter Pick's disappearance.

17. Mystery of *The Black Plume* and Benoit Battraville, and the ring of the Dark Tower.

VooDoo/HooDoo exposition. Resolves Knights Templar mystery. Leads to capture of Von Vampton.

Most of these interwoven mysteries impede the plot in the manner of detective fiction by depicting, as does jazz, several simultaneous actions whose relationship is not apparent. These mysteries run parallel throughout the novel, only to be resolved in the scene of recognition in the library at the Villa Lewaro, where Pa Pa La Bas presents his decoded evidence through his elaborate recasting of the myth of Osiris and Set. This allegory recapitulates, combines, and decodes the novel's several simultaneous subplots, and also traces the novel's complex character interrelationships from ancient Egypt up to the very moment of La Bas's narration. The narration leads to the arrest of Gould and Von Vampton, but also to the antidiscovery of the sacred Book of Thoth, the would-be text of Jes Grew. Recast myths serve the same function of plot impediment for the purpose of repeating the novel's events through metaphorical substitution in two other places: these are the allegories of Faust and the *houngan,* Ti Bouton (see pp. 90–92, 132–39). These recast myths serve as the play of doubles, consistent with the "double-image on form" which Reed sought to realize, and are implicit in the nature of allegory itself.

Plot impediment can be created in ways other than through temporal inversion; local-color description does as well. Local color, of course, came to be a standard feature in the social realist novel; in the Afro-American narrative, realism as local color is perhaps the most consistent aspect of black rhetorical strategy from the slave narratives to *Invisible Man.* Reed uses and simultaneously parodies the convention of local color as plot impediment by employing unpunctuated lists and categories throughout the text, as seen in the novel's first paragraph:

> A True Sport, the Mayor of New Orleans, spiffy in his patent-leather brown and white shoes, his plaid suit, the Rudolph Valentino parted-down-the-middle hair style, sits in his office. Sprawled upon his knees is Zuzu, local doo-wack-a-doo and voo-do-dee-odo-fizgig. A slatternly floozy, her green, sequined dress quivers. (p. 3)

The following sentence exemplifies Reed's undifferentiated catalogues: "The dazzling parodying punning mischievous pre-Joycean style-play of your Cakewalking your Calinda your Minstrelsy give-and-take of the ultra-absurd" (p. 152). Viktor Sklovskij says that the mystery novel was drawn upon formally by the social novel; Reed's use of devices from the detective novel, then, to parody the black social novel reverses this process, appropriately and ironically enough.[17]

I have discussed how the tension of the two stories generally operates in the types of detective fiction. Reed's play of doubles assumes its most subtle form in his clever rhetorical strategy of using these two narratives, the story of the past and the story of the present. It is useful to think of these two as the narrative of understanding and the narrative of truth. The narrative of understanding is the presented narrative of the investigation of a mystery, in which a detective (reader) interprets or decodes clues. Once these signs are sufficiently decoded, this narrative of understanding reconstitutes the missing story of the crime, which we can think of as the narrative of truth. The presented narrative, then, is implicitly a story of another, absent story and hence functions as an internal allegory.

The nature of this narrative of the investigation in *Mumbo Jumbo* can be easily characterized: the narrative remains close to the action with local-color description and dialogue as its two central aspects; character as description and extensive catalogues propel the narrative forward; the narrative remains essentially in the present tense, and the point of view is both in the third person and limited, as it must be if the reader's understanding of the nature of the mystery is to remain impeded until the novel's detective decodes all the clues, assembles all the suspects, interprets the signs, and reveals the truth of the mystery. The detective makes his arrests, and then everyone left eats dinner.

Mumbo Jumbo's prologue opens in this narrative mode of the story of the present. Near the end of the prologue, however, a second narrative mode intrudes. It is separated from the first narrative by spacing and is further foregrounded by italic type (see p. 6). It not only interprets and comments on characters and actions in the first story but does so in a third-person omniscient mode. In other words, it reads its counterpart narrative, of which it is a negation. Following its italic type are three other sorts of subtexts which comprise crucial aspects of this second, antithetical narration of past, present, and future: a black-and-white photograph of people dancing; an epigraph on the nature of the "second line," written by Louis Armstrong; and an etymology of *mumbo jumbo* taken from the *American Heritage Dictionary*. What the characters ponder or misunderstand this foregrounded antithetical narration reads correctly for the reader.

> *But they did not understand that the Jes Grew epidemic was unlike physical plagues. Actually Jes Grew was an anti-plague. Some plagues caused the body to waste away; Jes Grew enlivened the host. . . . So Jes Grew is seeking its words. Its text. For what good is a liturgy without a text? In the 1890s the text was not available and Jes Grew was out there all alone. Perhaps the 1920s will also be a false alarm and Jes Grew will evaporate as quickly as it appeared again broken-hearted and double-crossed (++). (p. 6)*

This second, anti-, narration consists of all of *Mumbo Jumbo*'s motley subtexts which are not included in its first narration. Whereas the first story adheres to the present, the second roams remarkably freely through space and time, between myth and history, humorously employing the device of anachronism. It is discontinuous and fragmentary, not linear like its counterpart; it never contains dialogue; rather, it contains all of the text's abstractions.

All of the novel's subtexts (illustrations, excerpts from other texts, "Situation Reports," etc.) are parts of this second narration, which we might think of as an extended discourse on the history of Jes Grew. The only mysteries this antithetical narration does not address are the text's first two mysteries: what exactly Jes Grew is and what precisely its text is. After chapter 8, the foregrounding of italics tends to disappear, for the narration manages to bracket or frame itself, functioning almost as the interior monologue of the first narrative mode. While the first story remains firmly in the tradition of the presented detective story, the second turns that convention inside out, functioning as an ironic double, a reversed mirror image like the cryptic *vé vé* on the novel's cover.

This second mode of narration allows for the allegorical double of *Mumbo Jumbo*. As many critics have gone to great lengths to demonstrate, *Mumbo Jumbo* is a thematic allegory of the Black Arts movement of the 1960s rendered through causal connections with the Harlem Renaissance of the 1920s. A more interesting allegory, however, is found in the antithetical narrative, which is a discourse on the history and nature of writing itself, especially that of the Afro-American literary tradition. *Mumbo Jumbo,* then, is a text that directs attention to its own writing, to its status as a text, related to other texts which it Signifies upon. Its second narration reads its first, as does discourse upon a text. It is Reed reading Reed and the tradition. A formal metaphor for Reed's mode of writing is perhaps the bebop mode of jazz, as exemplified in that great reedist, Charlie Parker, who sometimes played a chord on the alto saxophone, then repeated and reversed the same chord to hear, if I understand him correctly, what he had just played. Parker is a recurring figure in Reed's works: "Parker, the houngan (a word derived from *n'gana gana*) for whom there was no master adept enough to award him the Asson, is born" (p. 16).[18] Just as Jes Grew, the novel's central character, in searching for its text is seeking to actualize a desire, to "find its Speaking or strangle upon its own ineloquence," so too is the search for a text replicated and referred to throughout the second, Signifin(g) narration (p. 34).

What is the status of this desired text? How are we to read Reed? Jes Grew's desire would be actualized only by finding its text. *Mumbo Jumbo's* parodic use of the presented story of the detective novel states this desire; the solution of the novel's central mystery would be for Jes Grew to find its text. This text, Pa Pa La Bas's allegorical narrative at the Villa Lewaro tells us, is in fact the vast and terrible Text of Blackness itself, "always already" there: "the Book of Thoth, the sacred Work . . . of the Black Bird-man, as assistant to Osiris. (If anyone thinks this is 'mystifying the past' [the narrative intrudes] kindly check out your local bird book and you will find the sacred Ibis' Ornithological name to be *Threskiornis aethiopicus*)" (p. 188). The irony of the mystery structure evident in *Mumbo Jumbo* is that this text, Jes Grew's object of desire, is defined only by its absence; it is never seen or found. At the climax of La Bas's amusingly detailed and long recapitulation of his process of reading the signs of the mystery (as well as the history of the dissemination of the text itself), La Bas instructs his assistant, T. Malice, to unveil the text:

> Go get the Book T!
> T Malice goes out to the car and returns with a huge gleaming box covered with snakes and scorpions shaped or sparkling gems.
> The ladies intake their breath at such a gorgeous display. On the top can be seen the Knights Templar seal; 2 Knights riding Beaseauh, the Templars' piebald horse. T. Malice places the box down in the center of the floor and removes the 1st box, an iron box, and the 2nd box, which is bronze and shines so that they have to turn the ceiling lights down. And within this box is a sycamore box and under the sycamore, ebony, and under this ivory, then silver and finally gold and then . . . empty!!
> (p. 196)

The nature of the text remains undetermined and, indeed, indeterminate, as it was at the novel's beginning. Once the signs of its presence have been

read, the text disappears, in what must be the most humorous anticlimax in
the whole of Afro-American fiction.

We can read this anticlimax against the notion of indeterminacy. Geoffrey H. Hartman defines the function of indeterminacy as "a bar separating
understanding and truth."[19] The bar in *Mumbo Jumbo* is signified by that
unbridgeable white space that separates the first narrative mode from the
second, the narrative of truth. *Mumbo Jumbo* is a novel about indeterminacy
in interpretation itself. The text repeats this theme again and again; its two
narrative voices, moreover, the Atonist Path and its Wallflower Order, are
criticized severely for a foolish emphasis on unity, on the number 1, on
what the novel calls "point." One of the three symbols of the Atonist Order is "the #1" (p. 65). Their leader is called "Hierophant 1" (p. 63). A
hierophant, of course, is an expositor. The Atonists are defined in the antithetical narrative as they who seek to interpret the world through one interpretation: "To some if you owned your own mind you were indeed sick
but when you possessed an Atonist mind you were healthy. A mind which
sought to interpret the world by using a single loa. Somewhat like filling a
milk bottle with an ocean" (p. 24). The novel defines the nature of this urge
for the reduction to unity:

> 1st they intimidate the intellectuals by condemning work arising out
> of their own experience as being 1-dimensional, enraged, non-objective,
> preoccupied with hate and not universal, universal being a word co-opted
> by the Catholic Church when the Atonists took over Rome, as a way of
> measuring every 1 by their deals. (p. 133)

One is an Atonist, the novel maintains consistently, who attempts to tie the
sheer plurality of signification to one determinate meaning.

In contrast is the spirit of Jes Grew and Pa Pa La Bas. As I have shown,
the name "La Bas" is derived from Esu-Elegbara. The Yoruba call Esu the
god of indeterminacy (*ariyemuye*) and of uncertainty. Pa Pa La Bas, in
contradistinction to Hierophant 1, has not one but two heads, like the face
of the sign: "Pa Pa La Bas, noonday HooDoo, fugitive-hermit, obeah-man,
botanist, animal impersonator, 2-headed man, You-Name-It" (p. 45). Moreover, he functions as the detective of Jes Grew, as a decoder, as a sign reader,
the man who cracked *de* code, by using his two heads: "Evidence? Woman,
I dream about it, I feel about it, I feel it, I use my 2 heads. My Knockings"
(p. 25). La Bas is the critic, engaged in the Work, the work of art, refusing
to reduce it to a "point":

> People in the 60s said they couldn't follow him. (In Santa Cruz the
> students walked out.) What's your point? they asked in Seattle whose
> central point, the Space Needle, is invisible from time to time. What are
> you driving at? they would say in Detroit in the 1950s. In the 40s he
> haunted the stacks of a ghost library. (p. 218)

While arguing ironically with Abdul Sufi Hamid, the Black Muslim who
subsequently burns the Book of Thoth, La Bas critiques Abdul's "black aesthetic" in terms identical to his critique of the Atonists:

Where does that leave the ancient Vodun aesthetic: pantheistic, becoming, I which bountifully permits 1000s of spirits, as many as the imagination can hold. Infinite Spirits and Gods. So many that it would take a book larger than the Koran and the Bible, the Tibetan Book of the Dead and all of the holy books in the world to list, and still room would have to be made for more. (p. 35; see also Abdul's letter to La Bas, pp. 200–203)

It is indeterminacy, the sheer plurality of meaning, the very play of the signifier itself, which *Mumbo Jumbo* celebrates. *Mumbo Jumbo* addresses the play of the black literary tradition and, as a parody, is a play upon that same tradition. Its central character, Jes Grew, cannot be reduced by the Atonists, as they complain: "It's nothing we can bring into focus or categorize; once we call it 1 thing it forms into something else" (p. 4). Just as La Bas the detective is the text's figure for indeterminacy (paradoxically because he is a detective), so too is Jes Grew's "nature" indeterminate: its text is never a presence, and it disappears when its text disappears, as surely as does Charlotte when Doctor Peter Pick recites, during his reverse-minstrel plantation routine, an incantation from Pa Pa La Bas's *Blue Back: A Speller* (see pp. 104–5, 199).

Even the idea of one transcendent subject, Jes Grew's text, the Text of Blackness itself, *Mumbo Jumbo* criticizes. When the poet, Nathan Brown, asks the Haitian *houngan* Benoit Battraville how to catch Jes Grew, Benoit replies: "Don't ask me how to catch Jes Grew. Ask Louis Armstrong, Bessie Smith, your poets, your painters, your musicians, ask them how to catch it" (p. 152). Jes Grew also manifests itself in more curious forms:

> The Rhyming Fool who sits in Rē'-mote Mississippi and talks "crazy" for hours. The dazzling parodying punning mischievous pre-Joycean style-play of your Cakewalking your Calinda your Minstrelsy give-and-take of the ultra-absurd. Ask the people who put wax paper over combs and breathe through them. In other words, Nathan, I am saying Open-Up-To-Right-Here and then you will have something coming from your experience that the whole world will admire and need. (p. 152)

Jes Grew's text, in other words, is not a transcendent signified but must be produced in a dynamic process and manifested in discrete forms, as in black music and black speech acts: "The Blues is a Jes Grew, as James Weldon Johnson surmised. Jazz was a Jes Grew which followed the Jes Grew of Ragtime. Slang is Jes Grew too," Pa Pa La Bas tells his 1960s audience in his annual lecture on the Harlem Renaissance (p. 214).

"Is this the end of Jes Grew?" the narrative questions when we learn that its text does not exist. "Jes Grew has no end and no beginning," the text replies (p. 204). The echoes here are intentional: Reed echoes Ellison or, rather, Ellison's echo of T. S. Eliot. "In my end is my beginning," writes Eliot in "East Coker." "In my beginning is my end." The "end," writes Ellison, "is in the beginning and lies far ahead."[20] Reed signifies upon Ellison's gesture of closure here, and that of the entire Afro-American literary tradition, by positing an open-endedness of interpretation, of the play of signifiers, just as his and Ellison's works both signify upon the idea of the transcendent signified of the black tradition, the Text of Blackness itself.

The tradition's classic text on the "Blackness of Blackness" is found in the prologue of *Invisible Man:*

> "Brothers and sisters, my text this morning is the 'Blackness of Blackness.' "
>
> And a congregation of voices answered: "That blackness is most black, brother, most black . . ."
>
> "In the beginning . . ."
>
> "At the very start," they cried.
>
> ". . . there was blackness . . ."
>
> "Preach it . . ."
>
> ". . . and the sun . . ."
>
> "The sun, Lawd . . ."
>
> ". . . was bloody red . . ."
>
> "Red . . ."
>
> "Now black . . ." the preacher shouted.
>
> "Bloody . . ."
>
> "I said black is . . ."
>
> "Preach it, brother . . ."
>
> ". . . an' black ain't . . ."
>
> "Red, Lawd, red: He said it's red!"
>
> "Amen, brother . . ."
>
> "Black will git you . . ."
>
> "Yes, it will . . ."
>
> ". . . an' black won't . . ."
>
> "Naw, it won't!"
>
> "It do . . ."
>
> "It do, Lawd . . ."
>
> ". . . an' it don't."
>
> "Halleluiah . . ."
>
> ". . . It'll put you, glory, glory, Oh my Lawd, in the WHALE'S BELLY."
>
> "Preach it, dear brother . . ."
>
> ". . . an' make you tempt . . ."
>
> "Good God a-mighty!"
>
> "Old Aunt Nelly!"
>
> "Black will make you . . ."
>
> "Black . . ."
>
> ". . . or black will un-make you."
>
> "Ain't it the truth, Lawd?" (*Invisible Man,* pp. 12–13)

This sermon Signifies upon Melville's passage in *Moby-Dick* on "the blackness of darkness" and on the sign of blackness, as represented by the algorithm *signified/signifier.*[21] As Ellison's text states, "black is" and "black ain't," "It do, Lawd," "an' it don't." Ellison parodies here the notion of essence, of the supposedly natural relationship between the symbol and the symbolized. The vast and terrible Text of Blackness, we realize, has no essence; rather, it is signified into being by a signifier. The trope of blackness in Western discourse has signified absence at least since Plato. Plato, in the *Phaedrus,* recounts the myth of Theuth (*Mumbo Jumbo*'s "Thoth") and the introduction of writing into Egypt. Along the way, Plato has Socrates draw upon the figure of blackness as a metaphor for one of the three divisions of the soul, that of "badness": "The other is crooked of frame, a massive jumble of a creature, with thick short neck, snub nose, black skin, and gray eyes; hot-blooded, consorting with wantonness and vainglory; shaggy of ear, deaf, and hard to control with whip and goad."[22] Reed's use of the myth of Thoth is, of course, not accidental or arbitrary: he repeats and inverts Plato's dialogue, salient point for salient point, even down to Socrates' discourse on the excesss of the dance, which is a theme of *Mumbo Jumbo.*[23] It is not too much to say that *Mumbo Jumbo* is one grand Signifyin(g) riff on the *Phaedrus,* parodying it through the hidden polemic.

Both Ellison and Reed, then, critique the received idea of blackness as a negative essence, as a natural, transcendent signified; but implicit in such a critique is an equally thorough critique of blackness as a presence, which is merely another transcendent signified. Such a critique, therefore, is a critique of the structure of the sign itself and constitutes a profound critique. The Black Arts movement's grand gesture was to make of the trope of blackness a trope of presence. That movement willed it to be, however, a transcendent presence. Ellison's "text for today," "the 'Blackness of Blackness,' " analyzes this gesture, just as surely as does Reed's Text of Blackness, the "sacred Book of Thoth." In literature, blackness is produced in the text only through a complex process of signification. There can be no transcendent blackness, for it cannot and does not exist beyond manifestations of it in specific figures. Put simply, Jes Grew cannot conjure its texts: texts, in the broadest sense of the term (Parker's music, Ellison's fictions, Romare Bearden's collages, etc.), conjure Jes Grew.

Reed has, in *Mumbo Jumbo,* Signified upon Ellison's critique of the central presupposition of the Afro-American literary tradition, by drawing upon Ellison's trope as a central theme of the plot of *Mumbo Jumbo* and by making explicit Ellison's implicit critique of the nature of the sign itself, of a transcendent signified, an essence, which supposedly exists prior to its figuration. Their formal relationship can only be suggested by the relation of modernism to postmodernism, two overworked terms. Blackness exists, but "only" as a function of its signifiers. Reed's open-ended structure, and his stress on the indeterminacy of the text, demands that critics, in the act of reading, produce a text's signifying structure. For Reed, as for his great precursor, Ellison, figuration is indeed the "nigger's occupation."

III. Coda: The Warp and the Woof

Reed's Signifying relation to Ellison is exemplified in his poem "Dualism: in ralph ellison's invisible man":

                    i am outside of
                    history. i wish
                    i had some peanuts, it
                    looks hungry there in
                    its cage.

                    i am inside of
                    history. its
                    hungrier than i
                    thot.[24]

The figure of history here is the Signifying Monkey; the poem Signifies upon that repeated trope of dualism that figures initially in black discourse in Du Bois's essay "Of Our Spiritual Strivings," which forms the first chapter of *The Souls of Black Folk*. The dualism parodied by Reed's poem is that represented in the epilogue of *Invisible Man*: "Now I know men are different and that all life is divided and that only in division is there true health" (p. 499). For Reed, this belief in the reality of dualism spells death. Ellison here had refigured Du Bois's trope:

> After the Egyptian and Indian, the Greek and Roman, the Teuton and Mongolian, the Negro is a sort of seventh son, born with a veil, and gifted with second-sight in this American world,—a world which yields him no true self-consciousness, but only lets him see himself through the revelation of the other world. It is a peculiar sensation, this double-consciousness, this sense of always looking at one's self through the eyes of others, of measuring one's soul by the tape of a world that looks on in amused contempt and pity. One ever feels his two-ness,—an American, a Negro; two souls, two thoughts, two unreconciled strivings; two warring ideals in one dark body, whose dogged strength alone keeps it from being torn asunder.
>
> The history of the American Negro is the history of this strife,—this longing to attain self-conscious manhood, to merge his double self into a better and truer self. In this merging he wishes neither of the older selves to be lost.[25]

Reed's poem parodies, profoundly, both the figure of the black as outsider and the figure of the divided self. For, he tells us, even these are only tropes, figures of speech, rhetorical constructs like "double-consciousness," and not some preordained reality or thing. To read these figures literally, Reed tells us, is to be duped by figuration, just like the Signified Lion. Ellison, we know, fully understands the nature of this figure, even if some of his less imaginative readers have not done so. Reed has secured his place in the canon precisely by his critique of the received, repeated tropes peculiar to that very canon. His works are the grand works of critical Signification.

7

Color Me Zora:
Alice Walker's (Re)Writing of the Speakerly Text

> O, write my name, O write my name:
>   O write my name . . .
> Write my name when-a you get home . . .
> Yes, write my name in the book of life . . .
> The Angels in the heav'n going-to write my name.
>   Spiritual Underground Railroad

> My spirit leans in joyousness tow'rd thine,
> My gifted sister, as with gladdened heart
> My vision flies along thy "speaking pages."
>   Ada, "A Young Woman of Color," 1836

> I am only a pen in His hand.
>   Rebecca Cox Jackson

> I'm just a link in a chain.
>   Aretha Franklin, "Chain of Fools"

For just over two hundred years, the concern to depict the quest of the black speaking subject to find his or her voice has been a repeated topos of the black tradition, and perhaps has been its most central trope. As theme, as revised trope, as a double-voiced narrative strategy, the representation of characters and texts finding a voice has functioned as a sign both of the formal unity of the Afro-American literary tradition and of the integrity of the black subjects depicted in this literature.

Esu's double voice and the language of Signifyin(g) have served through-out this book as unifying metaphors, indigenous to the tradition, both for patterns of revision from text to text and for modes of figuration at work within the text. The Anglo-African narrators published between 1770 and 1815 placed themselves in a line of descent through the successive revision of one trope, of a sacred text that refuses to speak to its would-be black auditor. In *Their Eyes Were Watching God,* Zora Neale Hurston depicts her protagonist's ultimate moment of self-awareness in her ability to name her own divided consciousness. As an element of theme and as a highly accomplished rhetorical strategy that depends for its effect on the bivocality of free indirect discourse, this voicing of a divided consciousness (another topos of the tradition) has been transformed in Ishmael Reed's *Mumbo Jumbo* into a remarkably self-reflexive representation of the ironies of writing a text in which two foregrounded voices compete with each other for control of narration itself. Whereas the development of the tradition to the publication of *Their Eyes Were Watching God* seems to have been preoccupied with the mimetic possibilities of the speaking voice, black fiction after *Their Eyes* would seem even more concerned to explore the implications of doubled voices upon strategies of writing.

Strategies as effective as Hurston's innovative use of free indirect discourse and Reed's bifurcated narrative voice lead one to wonder how a rhetorical strategy could possibly extend, or Signify upon, the notions of voice at play in these major texts of the black tradition. How could a text possibly trope the extended strategies of voicing which we have seen to be in evidence in *Their Eyes* and in *Mumbo Jumbo?* To Signify upon both Hurston's and Reed's strategies of narration would seem to demand a form of the novel that, at once, breaks with tradition yet revises the most salient features through which I have been defining the formal unity of this tradition.

Just as Hurston's and Reed's texts present seemingly immovable obstacles to an equally telling revision of the tradition's trope of voicing, so too does *Invisible Man,* the tradition's text of blackness and, in my opinion, its most profound achievement in the novel. The first-person narration of *Invisible Man,* the valorization of oral narration in *Their Eyes,* and the italicized interface of showing and telling in *Mumbo Jumbo,* taken together, would seem to leave rather little space in which narrative innovation could even possibly be attempted. Alice Walker's revisions of *Their Eyes Were Watching God* and of Rebecca Cox Jackson's *Gifts of Power,* however, have defined an entirely new mode of representation of the black quest to make the text speak.

To begin to account for the Signifyin(g) revisions at work in Walker's *The Color Purple,* it is useful to recall the dream of literacy figured in John Jea's autobiography. In Chapter 4, I maintained that Jea's odd revision of the scene of the Talking Book served to erase the figurative potential of this trope for the slave narrators who followed him. After Jea, slave narrators refigured a repeated scene of instruction in terms of reading and writing rather than in terms of making the text speak. While these two tropes are obviously related, it seems equally obvious that the latter represents a key reworking of the former, in terms more conducive to the directly polemical role in which the slave narratives were engaged in an antebellum America seemingly preoccupied with the future of human slavery.

While the trope of the Talking Book disappeared from the male slave narratives after Jea literalized it it is refigured in the mystical writings of Rebecca Cox Jackson, an Afro-American visionary and Shaker eldress who was a contemporary of Jea's. Jackson was a free black woman who lived between 1795 and 1871. She was a fascinating religious leader and feminist, who founded a Shaker sisterhood in Philadelphia in 1857, after a difficult struggle with her family, with her initial religious denomination, and even with the Shakers. Her extensive autobiographical writings (1830–1864) were collected and edited by Jean McMahon Humez, published in 1981, and reviewed by Alice Walker in that same year.[1] The reconstitution of Jackson's texts is one of the major scholarly achievements in Afro-American literature, both because of the richness of her texts and because the writings of black women in antebellum America are painfully scarce, especially when compared to the large body of writings by black men.

Jackson, like her contemporary black ex-slave writers, gives a prominent place in her texts to her own literacy training. Hers is a divinely inspired literacy training even more remarkable than Jea's. Writing between 1830 and 1832, just fifteen-odd years after Jea, Jackson—with or without Jea's text in mind—refigures Jea's divine scene of instruction. Jackson's refiguration of this supernatural event, however, is cast within a sexual opposition between male and female. Whereas her antecedents used the trope to define the initial sense of difference between slave and free, African and European, Jackson's revision charts the liberation of a (black) woman from a (black) man over the letter of the text. I bracket *black* because, as we shall see, Jackson freed herself of her brother's domination of her literacy and her ability to interpret, but supplanted him with a mythical white male interpreter.

Jackson, recalling Jea, writes, "After I received the blessing of God, I had a great desire to read the Bible." Lamenting the fact that "I am the only child of my mother that had not learning," she seeks out her brother to "give me one hour's lesson at night after supper or before we went to bed."[2] Her brother, a prominent clergyman in the Bethel African Methodist Episcopal Church, was often "so tired when he would come home that he had not [the] power so to do," a situation, Jackson tells us, which would "grieve" her. But the situation that grieved Jackson even more was her brother's penchant to "rewrite" her words, to revise her dictation, one supposes, to make them more "presentable." Jackson takes great care to describe her frustration in the fight with her brother to control her flow of words:

> So I went to get my brother to write my letters and to read them. . . . I told him what to put in. Then I asked him to read. He did. I said, "Thee has put in more than I told thee." This he done several times. I then said, "I don't want thee to *word* my letter. In only want thee to *write* it." Then he said, "Sister, thee is the hardest one I ever wrote for!" These words, together with the manner that he had wrote my letter, pierced my soul like a sword. . . . I could not keep from crying.[3]

This scene is an uncanny prefigurement of the battle over her public speaking voice that Janie wages with Joe Starks in *Their Eyes Were Watching God*, as we have seen in Chapter 5. Jackson's brother, "tired" from his arduous work for the Lord, cannot be relied on to train his sister to read. When she compromises by asking him to serve as her amanuensis, he "words" her letters, as Jackson puts it, rather than simply translating her words (in their correct order, as narrated) from spoken to written form. This contest over her wording is not merely the anxiety the author experiences when edited or rewritten; rather, we eventually learn that Rebecca's rather individual mode of belief not only comes to threaten the minister-brother but also leads ultimately to a severance of the kinship bond. The brother-sister conflict over the "word" of the letter, then, prefigures an even more profound conflict over the word and letter of God's will.

God, however, takes sides. He comforts the grieving Rebecca with a divine message: "And these words were spoken in my heart, 'Be faithful, and the time shall come when you can write.' These words were spoken in my heart as though a tender father spoke them. My tears were gone in a moment."[4] God was as good as his promise. Just as he had done for his servant, John Jea, the Lord taught Jackson how to read:

> One day I was sitting finishing a dress in haste and in prayer. [Jackson sustained herself by dressmaking.] This word was spoken in my mind, "Who learned the first man on earth?" "Why, God." "He is unchangeable, and if He learned the first man to read, He can learn you." I laid down my dress, picked up my Bible, ran upstairs, opened it, and kneeled down with it pressed to my breast, prayed earnestly to Almighty God if it was consisting to His holy will, to learn me to read His holy word. And when I looked on the word, I began to read. And when I found I was reading, I was frightened—then I could not read one word. I closed my eyes again in prayer and then opened my eyes, began to read. So I done, until I read the chapter. . . . So I tried, took my Bible daily and praying and read until I could read anywhere. The first chapter that I read I never could know it after that day. I only knowed it was in James, but what chapter I can never tell.[5]

When confronted with the news, Jackson's incredulous husband challenged her claim: "Woman, you are agoing crazy!" Jackson, undaunted, read to him. "Down I sat and read through. And it was in James. So Samuel praised the Lord with me." Similarly, her brother accused her merely of memorizing passages overheard being read by his children: "Once thee has heard the children read, till thee has got it by heart." Once convinced by Jackson's husband, Jackson tells us with an air of triumph, "He sat down very sorrowful."

When challenged by her doubting brother, Jackson tells us, "I did not speak," allowing her husband, Samuel, to speak in her defense. At the end of her long description of this miracle of literacy, this "gift of power," she summarizes the event as "this unspeakable gift of Almighty God to me." It is this double representation of unspeakability which connects Jackson's miracle of literacy to Alice Walker's strategies of narration in *The Color Purple*.

Despite the parallel in Jackson's mini-narrative of her fight to control her words and Janie's fight to control hers (resolved, for Jackson, by the divine discourse of God, and for Janie by the black vernacular discourse of Signifyin(g), we know that Hurston did not have access to Jackson's texts. Walker, however, makes much of this scene in her essay on Jackson, underscoring the fact that "Jackson *was* taught to read and write by the spirit within her."[6] When Walker dedicates *The Color Purple* "To the Spirit," it is to this spirit which taught Rebecca Jackson to read. It is the representation of the unfolding of this gift of the "spirit within her," an "unspeakable gift," through which Walker represents the thoroughly dynamic development of her protagonist's consciousness, within the "unspeakable" medium of an epistolary novel comprised of letters written but never said, indeed written but never read. Celie's only reader, and Rebecca's only literacy teacher, is God.

Rather than representing the name of God as unspeakable, Walker represents Celie's words, her letters addressed to "God," as unspeakable. God is Celie's silent auditor, the addressee of most of her letters, written but never sent. This device, as Robert Stepto has suggested to me, is an echo of the first line of W. E. B. Du Bois's well-known "After-Thought" to *The Souls of Black Folk:* "Hear my cry, O God the Reader." But more important to our analysis of Walker's revisions of *Their Eyes Were Watching God,* Celie's written voice to God, her reader, tropes the written yet never uttered voice of free indirect discourse which is the predominant vehicle of narrative commentary in Hurston's novel.

As I have attempted to show in Chapter 5, Hurston draws upon free indirect discourse as a written voice masked as a speakerly voice, as an "oral hieroglyphic," as Hurston put it. Celie's voice in *The Color Purple,* on the other hand, is a spoken or mimetic voice, cast in dialect, yet marked as a written one—a mimetic voice masking as a diegetic voice, but also a diegetic voice masking as a mimetic one. If mimesis is a showing of the fact of telling, then Celie's letters are visual representations that attempt to tell the fact of showing. Whereas Hurston represents Janie's discovery of her voice as the enunciation of her own doubled self through a free indirect "narrative of division," Walker represents Celie's growth of self-consciousness as an act of writing. Janie and her narrator speak themselves into being; Celie, in her letters, writes herself into being. Walker Signifies upon Hurston by troping the concept of voice that unfolds in *Their Eyes Were Watching God.* Whereas Janie's movement from object to subject begins with her failure to recognize an image of her colored self in a photograph, precisely at a point in her childhood when she is known merely as "Alphabet" (a figure for all names and none), Celie's ultimate movement of self-negation is her self-description in her first letter to God: "~~I am~~." Celie, like Janie, is an absence, an erased presence, an empty set. Celie, moreover, writes in "Janie's voice," in a level of diction and within an idiom similar to that which Janie speaks. Celie, on the other hand, never speaks; rather, she writes her speaking voice and that of everyone who speaks to her.

This remarkably self-conscious Signifyin(g) strategy places *The Color*

Purple in a direct line of descent from *Their Eyes Were Watching God,* in an act of literary bonding quite unlike anything that has ever happened within the Afro-American tradition. Walker, we well know, has written at length about her relationship to Zora Neale Hurston. I have always found it difficult to identify this bond textually, by which I mean that I have not found Hurston's presence in Walker's texts. In *The Color Purple,* however, Walker rewrites Hurston's narrative strategy, in an act of ancestral bonding that is especially rare in black letters, since, as we saw in Chapter 3, black writers have tended to trace their origins to white male parents.[7]

Walker, in effect, has written a letter of love to her authority figure, Hurston. While I am not aware of another epistolary novel in the Afro-American tradition, there is ample precedent in the tradition for the publication of letters. Ignatius Sancho's *Letters* were published at London in 1782. As we saw in Chapter 3, Phillis Wheatley's letters to Arbour Tanner were so well known by 1830 that they could be parodied in a broadside. Even the device of locating Celie's sister in Africa, writing letters home to her troubled sister, has a precedent in the tradition in Amanda Berry Smith's diarylike entries about her African missionary work, published in her *Autobiography* (1893).[8] But we do not have, before *The Color Purple,* an example of the epistolary novel in the black tradition of which I am aware.

Why does Walker turn to the novel of letters to revise *Their Eyes Were Watching God?* As a way of concluding this study of voices in texts, and texts that somehow talk to other texts, I would like to discuss some of the implications of Walker's Signification upon Hurston's text by examining, if only briefly, a few of the more startling aspects of the rhetorical strategies at work in *The Color Purple* and its use of the epistolary form of narration.[9]

The Color Purple is comprised of letters written by two sisters, Celie and Nettie. Celie addresses her letters first to God and then to Nettie, while Nettie, off in the wilds of Africa as a missionary, writes her letters to Celie— letters intercepted by Celie's husband, stashed away in a trunk, and finally read by Celie and Shug Avery, her friend, companion, and lover. Nettie's unreceived letters to Celie appear, suddenly, almost at the center of the text (p. 107) and continue in what we might think of as the text's middle passage (to p. 150) with interruptions of three letters of Celie's addressed to God. Then Celie's addressee is Nettie, until she writes her final letter (pp. 242–44), which is addressed to God (twice) and to the stars, trees, the sky, to "peoples," and to "Everything." While I do not wish to diminish the importance of the novel's plot or its several echoes of moments in Hurston's novel, I am more interested here in suggesting the formal relationship that obtains between the strategies of narration of *Their Eyes* and of *The Color Purple.* Like Janie, Celie is married to a man who would imprison her, indeed brutalize her. Unlike Janie, however, Celie is liberated by her love for Shug Avery, the "bodaciously" strong singer with whom she shares the love that Janie shared with Tea Cake. It is Shug Avery, I shall argue, who stands in this text as Walker's figure for Hurston herself. Perhaps it will suffice to note

that this is Celie's text, a text of becoming as is *Their Eyes,* but a becoming
with a signal difference.

The most obvious difference between the two texts is that Celie writes
herself into being, before our very eyes. Whereas Janie's moment of consciousness is figured as a ritual speech act, for Celie it is the written voice which
is her vehicle for self-expression and self-revelation. We read the letters of
the text, as it were, over Celie's shoulder, just as we overhear Janie telling
her story to Phoeby as they sit on Janie's back porch. Whereas Janie and the
narrator do most of Janie's speaking (in an idiomatic free indirect discourse),
in *The Color Purple* two of the novel's three principal characters do all of
the writing. Celie is her own author, in a manner that Janie could not possibly be, given the third-person form of narration of *Their Eyes.* To remind
the reader that we are rereading letters, the lower border of each page of
The Color Purple is demarcated by a solid black line, an imitation of how
the border of a photoduplicated letter might look if bound in hardcover.

What is the text's motivation for the writing of letters? Nettie writes to
Celie because she is far away in Africa. Celie writes to God for reasons that
Nettie recapitulates in one of her letters:

> I remember one time you said your life made you feel so ashamed
> you couldn't even talk about it to God, you had to write it, bad as you
> thought your writing was. Well, now I know what you meant. And
> whether God will read letters or no, I know you will go on writing them;
> which is guidance enough for me. Anyway, when I don't write to you I
> feel as bad as I do when I don't pray, locked up in myself and choking
> on my own heart. I am so *lonely, Celie.* (p. 110)

The italicized command that opens the novel—*"You better not never tell
nobody but God. It'd kill your mammy."*—which we assume has been uttered
by Celie's stepfather, is responded to literally by Celie. Celie writes to God
for the same reason that Nettie writes to Celie, so that each may read the
text of her life, almost exactly or simultaneously as events unfold.

This is the text's justification of its own representation of writing. But
what are Walker's motivations? As I suggested above, Celie writes herself
into being as a text, a text we are privileged to read over her shoulder.
Whereas we are free to wonder aloud about the ironies of self-presentation
in a double-voiced free indirect discourse, the epistolary strategy eliminates
this aspect of reader response from the start. Celie writes her own story, and
writes everyone else's tale in the text except Nettie's. Celie writes her text,
and is a text, standing in discrete and episodic letters, which we, like voyeurs,
hurriedly read before the addressees (God and Nettie) interrupt our stolen
pleasures. Celie is a text in the same way in which Langston Hughes wrote
(in *The Big Sea*) that Hurston was a book—"a perfect book of entertainment
in herself."[10] We read Celie reading her world and writing it into being, in
one subtle discursive act. There is no battle of voices here, as we saw in
Their Eyes, between a disembodied narrator and a protagonist; Celie

speaks—or writes—for Celie and, of course, to survive for Nettie, then for Shug, and finally for Celie.

Ironically, one of the well-known effects of the epistolary narrative is to underscore the illusion of the real, but also of the spontaneous.[11] The form allows for a maximum of identification with a character, precisely because the devices of empathy and distance, standard in third-person narration, no longer obtain. There is no apparent proprietary consciousness in the epistle, so readers must supply any coherence of interpretation of the text themselves. Samuel Richardson understood this well:

> It is impossible that readers the most attentive, can always enter into the views of the writer of a piece, written, as hoped, to Nature and the moment. A species of writing, too, that may be called new; and every one putting him and herself into the character they read, and judging of it by their own sensations.[12]

Celie recounts events, seemingly as they unfold; her readers decide their meaning. Her readers piece together a text from the fragmented letters which Celie never mails and which Celie, almost all at once, receives. But Walker escapes the lack of control over how we read Celie precisely by calling before us a writing style of such innocence with which only the most hardened would not initially sympathize, then eventually *empathize*. By showing Celie as the most utterly dynamic of characters, who comes to know her world and to trust her readings of her world, and by enabling Celie to compel from us compassion for the brutalities she is forced to suffer, followed triumphantly by Celie's assertion of control (experiential control that we learn of through her ever-increasing written control of her letters), Walker manipulates our responses to Celie without even once revealing a voice in the text that Celie or Nettie does not narrate or repeat or edit.

How is this different from first-person narration in a fluid, or linear, narrative? Again, a remarkably self-conscious Richardson tells us in *Clarissa:*

> Such a sweetness of temper, so much patience and resignation, as she seems to be mistress of; yet writing of and in the midst of *present* distresses! How *much more* lively and affecting, for that reason, must her style be; her mind tortured by the pangs of uncertainty (the events then hidden in the womb of fate) *than* the dry, narrative, unanimated style of persons, relating difficulties and dangers surmounted; the relator perfectly at ease; and if himself unmoved by his own story, not likely greatly to affect the reader![13]

Unlike the framed tales of Janie in *Their Eyes* or of the nameless protagonist of *Invisible Man,* the reader of a novel of letters does not, indeed cannot, know the outcome of Celie's tale until its writing ceases. The two voices that narrate Ishmael Reed's "anti-detective" novel, for instance, are troped in *The Color Purple* almost by a pun that turns upon this fact: whereas a topos of *Mumbo Jumbo* is a supraforce searching for its text, for its "writing," as Reed puts it, Celie emerges as a force, as a presence, by writing all-too-short leters which, taken together, her readers weave or stitch together as both the text of *The Color Purple* and the autobiographical text of Celie's life and times, her bondage and her freedom. Celie charts her growth of consciousness day to day, or letter to letter. By the end of the novel, we know that Celie, like Reed's silent character, "jes' grew." Celie, moreover, "jes' grew" by writing her text of herself. Whereas Reed's Jes Grew disappears, at the end of *The Color Purple* we are holding Celie's text of herself in our hands. It is we who complete or close the circle or chain of Jes Grew Carriers, in an act of closure that Jes Grew's enemies disrupt in *Mumbo Jumbo*. When Nettie inevitably gets around to asking Celie how she managed to change so much, Celie quite probably could respond, "I jes' grew, I 'spose," precisely because the tyranny of the narrative present can only be overthrown by a linear reading of her letters, from first to last. Celie does not recapitulate her growth, as does Ellison's narrator or Hurston's Janie; only her readers have the leisure to reread Celie's text of development, the text of her becoming. Celie exists letter to letter; her readers supply the coherence necessary to speak of a precisely chartable growth, one measured by comparing or compiling all of the fragments of experience and feeling that Celie has selected to write.

Let us consider this matter of what I have called the tyranny of the narrative present. Celie, as narrator or author, presents herself to us, letter to letter, in a continuous written present. The time of writing is Celie's narrative present. We see this even more clearly when Celie introduces Nettie's first letter, the first letter that Celie and Shug recover from the attic trunk:

> Dear God,
>   This the letter I been holding in my hand. (p. 100)

The text of Nettie's letter follows, as an embedded narrative. This narrative present is comprised of (indeed, *can* be compromised of) only one event: the process of writing itself. All other events in *The Color Purple* are in the narrative past: no matter how near to the event Celie's account might be, the event is past, and it is this past about which Celie is writing.

We can see this clearly in Celie's first letter. The letter's first paragraph both underscores the moment of writing and provides a frame for the past events that Celie is about to share with her addressee, God:

> Dear God,
>   I am fourteen years old. ~~I am~~ I have always been a good girl.

Celie places her present self ("I am") under erasure, a device that reminds us that she is writing, and searching for her voice by selecting, then rejecting, word choice or word order, but also that there is some reason why Celie was once "a good girl" but no longer feels that she can make this claim before God. Because "a good girl" connotes the avoidance of sex, especially at the age of fourteen, we expect her fall from grace to be a fall of sensual pleasure. Celie tells us that we were right in this suspicion, but also wrong: there has been no pleasure involved in her "fall." Her account of the recent past explains:

Last spring after little Lucious come I heard them fussing. He was pulling on her arm. She say It too soon, Fonso, I ain't well. Finally he leave her alone. A week go by, he pulling on her arm again. She says Naw, I ain't gonna. Can't you see I'm already half dead, an all of these chilren.

She went to visit her sister doctor over Macon. Left me to see after the others. He never had a kine word to say to me. Just say You gonna do what your mammy wouldn't. First he put his thing up gainst my hip and sort of wiggle it around. Then he grab hold my titties. Then he push his thing inside my pussy. When that hurt, I cry. He start to choke me, saying You better shut up and git used to it.

But I don't never git used to it. And now I feels sick every time I be the one to cook. My mama she fuss at me an look at me. She happy, cause he good to her *now*. But too sick to last long. (p. 3; emphasis added)

Celie has been raped by the man she knows as her father. Her tale of woe has begun. Celie's first letter commences in a narrative present, shifts to a narrative past, then, in the letter's penultimate sentence, returns to a narrative present signified by "now." Prophetically, she even predicts the future, her mother's imminent death. In the narrative past, Celie develops, in fact controls, the representation of character and event. In the narrative present, Celie reveals to us that hers is the proprietary consciousness that we encounter in third-person narration, rendered in an epistle in a first-person narrative present. Celie, as author of her letters to God, might not be able to know what course events shall take, but the past belongs to her, salient detail by salient detail. We only know of Celie's life and times by her recounting of their significance and meaning, rendered in Celie's own word order. In this epistolary novel, the narrator of Celie's tale is identical with the author of Celie's letters. Because there is no gap here, as we saw in *Their Eyes* between the text's narrator and Janie, there would seem to be no need to bridge this gap through free indirect discourse.

This, however, is not the case in *The Color Purple*. While the gap between past and present is not obliterated, the gap between who sees and who speaks *is* obliterated by Celie's curious method of reporting discourse. The epistolary form's necessary shift between the narrative present and the narrative past creates the very space in which free indirect discourse dwells in Celie's narrative. It is in her representation of free indirect discourse that Walker undertakes her most remarkable revision of *Their Eyes Were Watching God*.

The Color Purple is replete with free indirect discourse. The double-voiced discourse of *Their Eyes* returns in the text of Celie's letters. Celie, as I have said, is the narrator and author of her letters. The narrator's voice, accordingly, is the voice of the protagonist. This protagonist, moreover, is divided into two parts: Celie, the character whose past actions we see represented in letters (an active but initially dominated and undereducated adolescent), and that other Celie, who—despite her use of written dialect—we soon understand is a remarkably reflective and sensitive teller, or writer, of a tale, or her own tale. Because of the curious interplay of the narrative past (in which Celie is a character) and a narrative present (in which Celie is the author), Celie emerges as both the subject and the object of narration. The subject-object split, or reconciliation, which we have seen in Hurston's use of free indirect discourse, in *The Color Purple* appears as the central rhetorical device by which Celie's self-consciousness is represented, in her own capacity to write a progressively better-structured story of herself.

Whereas Hurston represents Janie's emergent self in the shifting level of diction in the narrator's commentary and in the black-speech-informed indirect discourse, Walker represents Celie's dynamism in her ability to control her own narrative voice (that is, her own style of writing) but also in her remarkable ability to control all other voices spoken to Celie, which we encounter only in Celie's representation of them. Celie represents these voices, this spoken discourse, through the rhetorical device of free indirect discourse. It is Celie's voice that is always a presence whenever anyone in her world is represented as having spoken. We can, therefore, never be certain whether a would-be report, or mimesis, of dialogue is Celie's or the character's whose words we are overhearing or, more precisely, reading over Celie's shoulder.

Let me be clear: no one speaks in this novel. Rather, two sisters correspond to each other, through letters which one never receives (Celie's) and which the other receives almost all at once (Nettie's). There is no true mimesis, then, in *The Color Purple,* only diegesis. But, through Celie's mode of apparently reporting speech, underscored dramatically by her written dialect voice of narration, we logically assume that we are being shown discourse, when all along we never actually are. Celie only tells us what people have said to her. She never shows us their words in direct quotation. Precisely because her written dialect voice is identical in diction and idiom to the supposedly spoken words that pepper her letters, we believe that we are overhearing people speak, just as Celie did when the words were in fact uttered. We are not, however; indeed, we can never be certain whether or not Celie is showing us a telling or telling us a showing, as awkward as this sounds. In the speeches of her characters, Celie's voice and a character's merge into one, almost exactly as we saw happen in *Their Eyes* when Janie and her narrator speak in the merged voice of free indirect discourse. In these passages from *The Color Purple,* the distinction between mimesis and diegesis is apparently obliterated: the opposition between them has collapsed.

This innovation, it seems to me, is Walker's most brilliant stroke, her most telling Signifyin(g) move on Hurston's text. Let us examine just a few of scores of examples. The first is Celie's account of Mr. _____'s sisters, named Carrie and Kate, as one of Walker's Signifyin(g) gestures toward Jean Toomer's *Cane,* where Carrie Kate appears as a central character in "Kabnis."[14] (Walker, incidentally, loves *Cane* almost as much as she does *Their Eyes,* as she writes in "Zora Neale Hurston: A Cautionary Tale and a Partisan View."[15]) Celie's depiction of Carrie and Kate's discourse follows:

> Well that's no excuse, say the first one, Her name Carrie, other one
> name Kate. When a woman marry she spose to keep a decent house and
> a clean family. Why, wasn't nothing to come here in the winter time and
> all these children have colds, they have flue, they have direar, they have
> newmonya, they have worms, they have the chill and fever. They hungry.
> They hair ain't comb. They too nasty to touch. (p. 19)

Who is speaking in these passages: Carrie and Kate, or Celie, or all three?
All three are speaking, or, more properly, no one is speaking, because Celie
has merged whatever was actually said with her own voice and has written
it out for us in a narrative form that aspires to the spoken but never represents or reports anyone else's speech but Celie's on one hand, and Celie-
cum-characters' on the other. Celie is in control of her narration, even to the
point of controlling everyone else's speech, which her readers cannot encounter without hearing their words merged with Celie's.

We can see Celie's free indirect discourse in another example, which
reveals how sophisticated an editor Celie becomes, precisely as she grows in
self-awareness.[16] Celie is introducing, or framing, one of Nettie's letters, in a
narrative present:

> It's hot, here, Celie, she write. Hotter than July. Hotter than August
> *and* July. Hot like cooking dinner on a big stove in a little kitchen in
> August and July. Hot. (p. 126)

Who said, or wrote, these words, words which echo both the Southern expression "a cold day in August" and Stevie Wonder's album *Hotter Than
July?* Stevie Wonder? Nettie? Celie? All three, and no one. These are Celie's
words, merged with Nettie's, in a written imitation of the merged voices of
free indirect discourse, an exceptionally rare form in that here even the
illusion of mimesis is dispelled.

I could cite several more examples, but one more shall suffice. This
moving scene appears just as Celie and Shug are beginning to cement their
bond, a bond that bespeaks a sisterly, and later a sexual, bonding:

> Shug saying Celie. Miss Celie. And I look up where she at.
> She say my name again. She say this song I'm bout to sing is call
> Miss Celie's song. Cause she scratched it out of my head when I was
> sick. . . .
> First time somebody made something and name it after me. (p. 65)

Once again, Celie's voice and Shug's are merged together into one, one we
think is Shug's but which can only be Celie's-and-Shug's, simultaneous, in-
separable, bonded.

What are we to make of Walker's remarkable innovation in Hurston's
free indirect discourse? We can assume safely that one of Hurston's purposes
in the narrative strategies at play in *Their Eyes* was to show James Weldon
Johnson and Countee Cullen, and just about everyone else in the New Negro
Renaissance that dialect not only was not limited to two stops—humor and

pathos—but was fully capable of being used as a literary language even to write a novel. Dialect, black English vernacular and its idiom, as a literary device was not merely a figure of spoken speech; rather, for Hurston, it was a storehouse of figures. As if in a coda to the writing of *Their Eyes,* Hurston even published a short story entirely in the vernacular, entitled "Story in Harlem Slang" (1942), complete with a "Glossary."[17] Yet, just as Johnson had edited or interpreted the language of the black vernacular in his rendition of the "Seven Sermons in Verse" that comprise *God's Trombones* (1927), so too had Hurston merged dialect and standard English in the idiom of the free indirect discourse that gradually overtakes the narrative commentary in *Their Eyes.* Hurston showed the tradition just how dialect could blend with standard English to create a new voice, a voice exactly as black as it is white. (Johnson, of course, had "translated" from the vernacular into standard English.) Walker's Signifyin(g) riff on Hurston was to seize upon the device of free indirect discourse as practiced in *Their Eyes* but to avoid standard English almost totally in Celie's narration. Walker has written a novel in dialect, in the black vernacular. The initial impression that we have of Celie's naiveté slowly reveals how one can write an entire novel in dialect. This, we must realize, is as important a troping of *Their Eyes* as is the page-by-page representation of Celie's writing of her own tale. If Hurston's writing aspired to the speakerly, then Walker's apparently speaking characters turn out to have been written.

There are other parallels between the two texts which provide evidence of their Signifyin(g) relationship. Whereas Janie's sign of self-awareness is represented as her ability to tell Phoeby her own version of events, Walker matches this gesture by having Celie first write her own texts, discover her sister's purloined letters, arrange them with Shug in "some kind of order," as Shug says to Celie, then read them so that a second narrative unfolds which both completes and implicitly comments on Celie's narrative which has preceded it by 106 of the text's pages. This newly recovered narrative is a parallel text. This initial cache of unreceived letters functions as a framed tale within Celie's tale, as do Nettie's subsequently received letters, recapitulating events and providing key details absent from Celie's story. Nettie's letters are written in standard English, not only to contrast her character to Celie's but also to provide some relief from Celie's language. But even this narrative Celie controls, by ordering their reading but especially by introducing them, within her letters, with her own commentary. Nettie's letters function as a second narrative of the past, echoing the shift from present to past that we see within the time shifts of Celie's letters. But Nettie's discovered letters are *The Color Purple*'s structural revision of Janie's bracketed tale. We recognize a new Celie once Nettie's letters have been read. Celie's last letter to God reads:

Dear God,
    That's it, say Shug. Pack your stuff. You coming back to Tennessee with me.
    But I feels daze.

> My daddy lynch. My mama crazy. All my little half-brothers and
> sisters no kin to me. My children not my sister and brother. Pa not pa.
> You must be sleep. (p. 151)

Order has been restored, the incest taboo has not been violated, Celie is confused but free and moving.

Janie's Signifyin(g) declaration of independence read in the starkest of
terms to her husband, Joe, in *Their Eyes* is repeated in *The Color Purple*. As
Celie is about to leave with Shug, this exchange occurs between her and her
husband:

> Celie is coming with us, say Shug.
> Mr. _____'s head swivel back straight. Say what? he ast.
> Celie is coming to Memphis with me.
> Over my dead body, Mr. _____ say,
> . . . what wrong now?
> You a lowdown dog is what's wrong, I say. It's time to leave you and
> enter into the Creation. And your dead body just the welcome mat I need.
> Say what? he ast. Shock.
> All round the table folkses mouths be dropping open. . . .
> Mr. _____ start to sputter. ButButButButBut. Sound like some
> kind of motor. (p. 170)

This marvelous exchange refigures that between Janie and Joe. Celie's newly
found voice makes "folkses mouths" drop open, and Mr. _____'s voice inarticulate and dehumanized, "like some kind of motor." A bit later, Celie
continues, in triumph, to curse her oppressor:

> Any more letters come? I ast.
> He say, What?
> You heard me, I say. Any more letters from Nettie come?
> If they did, he say, I wouldn't give 'em to you. You two of a kind, he
> say. A man try to be nice to you, you fly in his face.
> I curse you, I say.
> What that mean? he say.
> I say, Until you do right by me, everything you touch will crumble.
> (pp. 175–76)

This quasi-Hoodoo curse reads like one of Hurston's recipes for revenge that
she published in her classic work on Vaudou, entitled *Tell My Horse* (1938).
Significantly, these exchanges—Celie's first open defiance of her husband, Albert—are repeated or written in Celie's first two letters addressed to Nettie
rather than to God. Celie's husband's desparate response follows:

> He laugh. Who you think you is? he say. You can't curse nobody.
> Look at you. You black, you pore, you ugly, you a woman. Goddam, he
> say, you nothing at all. (p. 176)

But Albert no longer has the power of the word over Celie, just as in Hurston
Joe cannot recoup from Janie's Signifyin(g) on his manhood in public. This
exchange continues:

Until you do right by me, I say, everything you even dream about will fail. I give it to him straight, just like it come to me. And it seem to come to me from the trees.

Whoever heard of such a thing, say Mr. _____. I probably didn't whup your ass enough.

Every lick you hit me you will suffer twice, I say. Then I say, You better stop talking because all I'm telling you ain't coming just from me. Look like when I open my mouth the air rush in and shape words.

Shit, he say. I should have lock you up. Just let you out to work.

The jail you plan for me is the one in which you will rot, I say. . . .

I'll fix her wagon! say Mr. _____, and spring toward me.

A dust devil flew up on the porch between us, fill my mouth with dirt. The dirt say, Anything you do to me, already done to you.

Then I feel Shug shake me. Celie, she say. And I come to myself.

I'm pore, I'm black, I may be ugly and can't cook, a voice say to everything listening. But I'm here.

Amen, say Shug. Amen, amen. (p. 176)

Celie has at last issued her liberating (and liberated) call, while her friend Shug, like any black audience, provides the proper ritual response to a masterful performance: "Amen, say Shug. Amen, amen." Celie speaks herself free, as did Janie, but in a speaking we know only by its writing, in a letter to Nettie. Celie has conquered her foe, Albert, and the silences in her self, by representing an act of speech in the written word, in which she turns Albert's harsh curses back on him, masterfully.

Just as this scene of instruction echoes Janie's, so too is *The Color Purple* full of other thematic echoes of *Their Eyes Were Watching God.* Houses confine in *The Color Purple* just as they do in *Their Eyes,* but Celie, Nettie, Shug, and Janie all find a form of freedom in houses in which there are no men: Nettie's hut in Africa, Shug's mansion in Tennessee, and Janie's empty home in Eatonville. The home that Nettie and Celie inherit will include men, but men respectful of the inherent strength and equality of women. Celie and Nettie own this home, and the possession of property seems to preclude the domination of men.

Shug would seem to be a refugee from *Their Eyes.* It is Shug who teaches Celie that God is not an "old white man," that God is nature and love and even sex, that God is a sublime feeling:

Here's the thing, say Shug. The thing I believe. God is inside you and inside everybody else. You come into the world with God. But only them that search for it inside find it. And sometimes it just manifest itself even if you not looking, or don't know what you looking for. Trouble do it for most folks, I think. Sorrow, lord. Feeling like shit.

It? I ast.

Yeah, It. God ain't a he or a she, but a It.

But what do it look like? I ast.

Don't look like nothing, she say. It ain't a picture show. It ain't something you can look at apart from anything else, including yourself. I believe God is everything, say Shug. Everything that is or ever was or

ever will be. And when you can feel that, and be happy to feel that,
you've found It. (pp. 166–67)

But it is also Shug who teaches Celie about Janie's lyrical language of the
trees, a language of nature in which God speaks in the same metaphors in
which he spoke to Janie, a divine utterance which led Janie to enjoy her first
orgasm, an experience that Shug tells Celie is God's ultimate sign of presence:

> She say, My first step from the old white man was trees. Then air.
> Then birds. Then other people. But one day when I was sitting quiet and
> feeling like a motherless child, which I was, it come to me: that feeling
> of being part of everything, not separate at all. I knew that if I cut a tree,
> my arm would bleed. And I laughed and I cried and I run all round the
> house. I knew just what it was. In fact, when it happen, you can't miss it.
> It sort of like you know what, she say, grinning and rubbing high up on
> my thigh.
> *Shug!* I say.
> Oh, she say. God love all them feelings. That's some of the best stuff
> God did. And when you know God loves 'em you enjoys 'em a lot more.
> You can just relax, go with everything that's going, and praise God by
> liking what you like.
> God don't think it dirty? I ast. (p. 167)

God don't think it dirty? I ast. (p. 167) And if we miss Shug's connection
with Janie, Walker first describes Shug in terms in which she has described
Hurston:

> She do more then that. She git a picture. The first one of a real person
> I ever seen. She say Mr. _____ was taking something out his bill-
> fold to show Pa an it fell out an slid under the table. Shug Avery was
> a woman. The most beautiful woman I ever saw. She more pretty then
> my mama. She bout ten thousand times more prettier then me. I see her
> there in furs. Her face rouge. Her hair like somethin tail. She grinning
> with her foot up on somebody motocar. Her eyes serious tho. Sad some.
> (p. 8)

Compare that description with Walker's description of Hurston:

> [She] loved to wear hats, tilted over one eye, and pants and boots. (I
> have a photograph of [Hurston] in pants, boots, and broadbrim that was
> given to me by her brother, Everette. She has her foot up on the running
> board of a car—presumably hers, and bright red—and looks racy.)[18]

There are several other echoes, to which I shall allude only briefly. Celie's
voice, when she first speaks out against the will of Mr. _____, "seem to
come to me from the trees" (p. 176) just as Janie's inner voice manifests itself under the pear tree. Celie, like Janie, describes herself as a "motherless
child" (p. 167). Key metaphors repeat: Hurston's figure of nature mirroring
Janie's emotions—"the rose of the world was breathing out smell" (*Their
Eyes,* p. 23)—becomes Shug and Celie's scene in which Shug teaches Celie to
masturbate, using a mirror to watch herself:

> I stand there with the mirror.
> She say, What, too shame even to go off and look at yourself? And you look so cute too, she say, laughing. All dressed up for Harpo's, smelling good and everything, but scared to look at your own pussy. . . .
> I lie back on the bed and haul up my dress. Yank down my bloomers. Stick the looking glass tween my legs. Ugh. All that hair. Then my pussy lips be black. Then inside look like a wet rose.
> It a lot prettier than you thought, ain't it? she say from the door. (p. 69)

Later, in her first letter to Nettie, Celie uses the figure of the rose again in a simile: "Shug a beautiful something, let me tell you. She frown a little, look out cross the yard, lean back in her chair, look like a big rose" (p. 167).

In the same way that Walker's extends to the literal Hurston's figure of the rose of the world breathing out smell, she also erases the figurative aspect of Janie's metaphor for her narration to Phoeby ("mah tongue is in mah friend's mouf") by making Shug and Celie literal "kissin-friends," or lovers. That which is implicit in Hurston's figures Walker makes explicit. Walker, in addition, often reverses Hurston's tropes: whereas *Their Eyes* accounts for the orgasm Janie experiences under the pear tree by saying, in free indirect discourse, "So this was a marriage!" (p. 24), Celie writes that when Mr. _____ beats her, she turns herself into a tree:

> He beat me like he beat the children. Cept he don't never hardly beat them. He say, Celie, git the belt. The children be outside the room peeking through the cracks. It all I can do not to cry. I make myself wood. I say to myself, Celie, you a tree. That's how come I know trees fear man. (p. 22)

Their Eyes' circular narration, in which the end is the beginning and the beginning the end, *The Color Purple* tropes with a linear narration. There are several other examples of these Signifyin(g) riffs.

Walker has Signified upon Hurston in what must stand to be the most loving revision, and claim to title, that we have seen in the tradition. Walker has turned to a black antecedent text to claim literary ancestry, or motherhood, not only for content but for structure. Walker's turn to Hurston for form (and to, of all things, the topoi of medieval romance known as "The Incestuous Father" and "The Exchanged Letter" for plot structure),[19] openly disrupts the patterns of revision (white form, black content) that we have discussed in Chapter 3. Even Walker's representation of Celie's writing in dialect echoes Hurston's definition of an "oral hieroglyphic," and her ironic use of speakerly language which no person can ever speak, because it exists only in a written text. This, too, Walker tropes, by a trick of figuration, one so clever that only Esu's female principle could have inspired it: people who speak dialect *think* that they are saying standard English words; when they write the words that they speak as "dis" or "dat," therefore, they spell "this" and "that." Walker, like Hurston, masters the illusion of the black vernacular by its writing, in a masterful exemplification of the black trope of Stylin' out.

Walker's revision of Hurston stands at the end of a chain of narration. Walker's text, like those by Toni Morrison, James Baldwin, Ann Petry, Paule Marshall, Leon Forrest, Ernest Gaines, John Wideman, and others, afford subsequent writers tropes and topoi to be revised. Endings, then, imply beginnings. Increasingly, however, after Walker and Reed, black authors could even more explicitly turn to black antecedent texts for both form and content. The tradition of Afro-American literature, a tradition of grounded repetition and difference, is characterized by its urge to start over, to begin again, but always to begin on a well-structured foundation. Our narrators, our Signifiers, are links in an extended ebony chain of discourse, which we, as critics, protect and explicate. As Martin Buber puts the relation in *The Legend of Baal-Shem:*

> I have told it anew as one who was born later. I bear in me the blood and spirit of those who created it, and out of my blood and spirit it has become new. I stand in the chain of narrators, a link between links; I tell once again the old stories, and if they sound new it is because the new already lay dormant in them when they were told for the first time.

While the principal silent second text is *Their Eyes Were Watching God,* Walker's critique of Celie's initial conception of God, and especially its anthropomorphism, revises a key figure in Rebecca Cox Jackson's narrative and perhaps surfaces as a parable for the so-called noncanonical critic.

Just after Celie and Shug have discovered, arranged, and read Nettie's purloined letters, Celie writes this to Nettie:

> Dear Nettie,
>   I don't write to God no more, I write to you.
>   What happen to God? ast Shug.
>   Who that? I say.
>   . . . what God do for me? I ast.
>   She say, Celie! Like she shock. He gave you life, good health, and a good woman that love you to death.
>   Yeah, I say, and he give me a lynched daddy, a crazy mama, a lowdown dog of a step pa and a sister I probably won't ever see again. Anyhow, I say, the God I been praying and writing to is a man. And act just like all the other mens I know. Trifling, forgitful, and lowdown. (p. 164)

A few pages later, Shug describes to Celie the necessity of escaping the boundaries caused by the anthropomorphism of God and calls this concept that of "the old white man" (p. 167). This, Celie confesses, is difficult: "Well, us talk and talk bout God, but I'm still adrift. Trying to chase that old white man out of my head" (p. 168). Shug responds that the problem is not only "the old white man," but all men:

> Still, it is like Shug say, You have got to git man off your eyeball, before you can see anything a'tall.
>   Man corrup everything, say Shug. He on your box of grits, in your

hand, and all over the road. He try to make you think he everywhere. Soon as you think he everywhere, you think he God. But he ain't. Whenever you trying to pray, and man plop himself on the other end of it, tell him to git lost, say Shug. Conjure up flowers, wind, water, a big rock. (p. 168)

This passage, most certainly, constitutes an important feminist critique of the complex fiction of male domination. But it also recalls a curious scene in Rebecca Cox Jackson's text. Indeed, Walker's text Signifies upon it. Earlier, I discussed Jackson's supernatural mastery of literacy. Jackson was careful to show that God's gracious act of instruction freed her from the domination and determination of her words (their order, their meaning) by her minister-brother, who by rearranging her words sought to control their sense. Jackson indeed became free, and freely interprets the Word of God in her own, often idiosyncratic way. But is Jackson's a truly liberating gesture, a fundamental gesture of a nascent feminism?

Jackson substitutes a mystical "white man," the image of whom Shug and Celie seek to dispel, for the interpretive role of the male, the relation of truth to understanding, of sound and sense. Jackson's account is strikingly vivid:

A white man took me by my right hand and led me on the north side of the room, where sat a square table. On it lay a book open. And he said to me, "Thou shall be instructed in this book, from Genesis to Revelations." And then he took me on the west side, where stood a table. And it looked like the first. And said, "Yea, thou shall be instructed from the beginning of creation to the end of time." And then he took me on the east side of the room also, where stood a table and book like the two first, and said, "I will instruct thee—yea, thou shall be instructed from the beginning of all things to the end of all things. Yea, thou shall be well instructed. I will instruct."

When Samuel handed me to this man at my own back door, he turned away. I never saw him any more. When this man took me by the hand, his hand was soft like down. He was dressed all in light drab. He was bareheaded. His countenance was serene and solemn and divine. There was a father and a brother's countenance to be seen in his face.

And then I awoke, and I saw him as plain as I did in my dream. And after that he taught me daily. And when I would be reading and come to a hard word, I would see him standing by my side and he would teach me the word right. And often, when I would be in meditation and looking into things which was hard to understand, I would find him by me, teaching and giving me understanding. And oh, his labor and care which he had with me often caused me to weep bitterly, when I would see my great ignorance and the great trouble he had to make me understand eternal things. For I was so buried in the depth of the tradition of my forefathers, that it did seem as if I never could be dug up.[20]

Jackson opposes the "white man" who would "teach me the word right," he who would stand "by me, teaching and giving me understanding," with the delineation of understanding imposed by her brother and, curiously enough, by "the depth of the tradition of my forefathers." So oppressive was the latter that, she admits, "it did seem as if I never could be dug up."

Shug and Celie's conception of God Signifies upon these passages from Jackson. Jackson's "white man" and Celie's, the speaking interpreter and the silent reader, are identical until Celie, with Shug's help, manages to "git man off your eyeball." Whereas Jackson suffocates under the burden of tradition, "buried in the depth" as she puts it, Walker's text points to a bold new model for a self-defined, or internally defined, notion of tradition, one black and female. The first step toward such an end, she tells us, was to eliminate the "white man" to whom we turn for "teaching" and the "giving [of] understanding." This parable of interpretation is Walker's boldest claim about the nature and function of the black tradition and its interpretation. To turn away from, to step outside the white hermeneutical circle and into the black is the challenge issued by Walker's critique of Jackson's vision.

Notes

Chapter 1

1. *Oriki Esu*, quoted by Ayodele Ogundipe, *Esu Elegbara, the Yoruba God of Chance and Uncertainty: A Study in Yoruba Mythology*, 2 vols. Ph.D. dissertation, Indiana University, 1978, Vol. II, p. 135.

2. *Oriki Esu*, quoted by Leo Frobenius, *The Voice of Africa* (New York: Benjamin Blom, 1913), Vol. I, p. 229.

3. Larry Neal, "Malcolm X—An Autobiography," in *Black Fire: An Anthology of Afro-American Writing* (New York: William Morrow, 1968), p. 316.

4. The literature on "African survivals" is extensive. The following sources are helpful: Okon E. Uya, "The Culture of Slavery: Black Experience Through a Filter," *Afro-American Studies* 1 (1971): 209; Robert Farris Thompson, *Flash of the Spirit* (New York: Random House, 1983); William Bascom, *Shango in the New World* (Austin: African and Afro-American Institute, University of Texas, 1972); Melville J. Herskovits, ed., *The Interdisciplinary Aspects of Negro Studies* (Washington: American Council of Learned Societies *Bulletin* No. 32, 1941); M. G. Smith, "The African Heritage in the Caribbean," in *Caribbean Studies: A Symposium*, ed. Vera Rubin (Seattle: University of Washington Press, 1960); George E. Simpson and Peter B. Hammond, "Discussion," in *Caribbean Studies*, ed. Rubin; Robert Farris Thompson, "African Influence on the Art of the United States," in *Black Studies in the University: A Symposium*, ed. Armstead L. Robinson et al. (New Haven: Yale University Press, 1969), pp. 122–70; and Roger D. Abrahams and John F. Szwed, *After Africa: Extracts from British Travel Accounts and Journals of the Seventeenth, Eighteenth, and Nineteenth Centuries Concerning the Slaves, Their Manners, and Customs in the British West Indies* (New Haven: Yale University Press, 1983), esp. pp. 4–22.

5. For a brilliant parallel study to this book, see Houston A. Baker, Jr., *Blues, Ideology, and Afro-American Literature: A Vernacular Theory* (Chicago: University of Chicago Press, 1984). Baker explores another side of the Afro-American vernacular—the blues—as his trope for a theory of criticism based on the black vernacular music tradition, whereas I am exploring here a theory of criticism based on the linguistic and poetic traditions of the vernacular encoded in the ritual of Signifyin(g). My great indebtedness to Baker's work is obvious and is acknowledged here (especially his readings of the liminality of the trickster figure).

6. To supplement my explication of hundreds of *Oriki Esu* and myths of Esu still in use today among the Yoruba of Nigeria, the Fon of Benin, the Nago of Brazil, and the Lucumi of Cuba, I have explored systematically the extensive secondary literature on Esu and his or her variants. Some sources especially useful to this study of the nature of interpretation are: Juana Elbein dos Santos and

Deoscoredes M. dos Santos, *Esu Bara Laroye: A Comparative Study* (Ibadan: Institute of African Studies, 1971); idem, "Esu Bara, Principle of Individual Life in the Nago System," *Colloque International sur la Notion de Personne en Afrique Noire* (Paris: Centre National de la Recherche Scientifique, Colloque Internationaux, No. 544, 1971); Juana Elbein dos Santos, *Os Nàgô e a Morte: Pàde, Àsèsè e o Culto Ègun na Bahia* (Paris: Editoria Vozes, Petropolis, 1976); Robert Farris Thompson, *Black Gods and Kings: Yoruba Art at UCLA* (1971; Bloomington: Indiana University Press, 1976); idem, *Flash of the Spirit;* Ogundipe, *Esu Elegbara;* Melville J. Herskovits, *Dahomey, An Ancient West African Kingdom,* 2 vols. (Evanston: Northwestern University Press, 1967); idem and Frances S. Herskovits, *Dahomean Narrative: A Cross-Cultural Analysis* (Evanston: Northwestern University Press, 1958); Bernard Maupoil, *La Géomancie à l'ancienne Côte des Esclaves,* Travaux et Memoires de l'Institut d'Ethnologie, Vol. 42 (Paris: Institut d'Ethnologie, 1943); Wande Abimbola, "An Exposition of Ifa Literary Corpus," Ph.D. dissertation, University of Lagos, 1970; idem, *Sixteen Great Poems of Ifa* (New York: UNESCO, 1975); idem, *Ifa Divination Poetry* (New York: Nok, 1977); E. Bolaji Idowu, *Olodumare: God in Yoruba Belief* (London: Longman, 1962); William Bascom, *Ifa Divination: Communication Between Gods and Men in West Africa* (Bloomington: Indiana University Press, 1969); Lydia Cabrera, *El Monte: Igbo Fina Ewe Orisha, Vititinfinda* (Havana: Ediciones C.R., 1954); Pierre Verger, *Notes sur le culte des Orisha et Voudoun à Bahia, la Baie de tous les saint au Brésil et à l'ancienne Côtes des esclaves, en Afrique.* Memoria 51 du Institut Francais pour l'Afrique Noir (Dakar: Ifan, 1957); Roger Bastide, *Le Candomblé de Bahia, Rite Nagô* (Paris: Mouton, 1958); Robert D. Pelton, *The Trickster in West Africa: A Study of Mythic Irony and Sacred Delight* (Los Angeles: University of California Press, 1980); Peter M. Morton-Williams, "An Outline of the Cosmology and Cult Organization of Oyo Yoruba," *Africa* 32 (1962): 336–53; and Hans Witte, *Ifa and Esu: Iconography of Order and Disorder* (Soest, Holland: Kunsthandel Luttik, 1984).

7. Because the variations of Esu are topoi and because I wish to underscore the literary (rather than the anthropological) discourse unfolding in this chapter, I use the words *Esu* and *Yoruba* interchangeably with Esu's bynames in the Yoruba-informed cultures in Dahomey, Brazil, and Cuba. *Esu* and *Yoruba* for me are signs of shared hermeneutical principles that transcend mere national boundaries.

8. *Ase* has plural signification. See Juana Elbein and D. M. dos Santos, "La Religion Nago Generatrice et Reserve de Valeurs culturelles au Bresil," Colloquium on African Traditional Religions, UNESCO and SAC, Cotonou, 1970; idem, "Esu Bara"; dos Santos, *Os Nago e a Morte,* pp. 171–81; and Thompson, *Flash of the Spirit,* Chap. 1. I refer to "Esu Ebitan lo Riwa." I was taught this *Oriki Esu* by my Yoruba instructor, Professor Michael O. Afolayan, whose understanding of Yoruba poetics and linguistics is unsurpassed. My understanding of the nature and function of the Ifa oracle is a direct result of my instruction by Afolayan and by Wole Soyinka.

9. Dos Santos and dos Santos, *Esu Bara Laroye,* p. 80.

10. Ibid., pp. 28, 26, and 2.

11. Wole Soyinka coined this neologism for this book.

12. *Oriki Esu,* cited by Michael O. Afolayan. See also Abimbola, "An Exposition of Ifa Literary Corpus," pp. 388, 394, for a slightly different version.

13. Bascom, *Ifa Divination,* pp. 109–10. Bascom writes that the myth was said

to be based on a verse from Ofun Ogunda. For a full analysis of Bosman's myth, see my *Black Letters in the Enlightenment: On Race, Writing, and Difference* (New York: Oxford University Press, forthcoming).

14. For other myths of origin of Ifa that underscore Esu's role as teacher of the system of Ifa to his friend, see Rev. P. Baudin, *Fetichism and Fetich Worshippers*, trans. M. McMahon (New York: Benziger Brothers, 1885), pp. 32–35. See also A. B. Ellis, *The Yoruba-Speaking Peoples of the Slave Coast of West Africa* (London: Chapman and Hall, 1894), pp. 56–64; James Johnson, *Yoruba Heathenism* (Exeter: James Townsend and Son, 1899); R. E. Dennett, *At the Back of the Black Man's Mind* (London: Macmillan, 1906), pp. 243–69; Frobenius, *The Voice of Africa*, Vol. I, pp. 229–32; Stephen S. Farrow, *Faith, Fancies and Fetich, or Yoruba Paganism* (London: Society for Promoting Christian Knowledge, 1926), pp. 36–37; J. Olumide Lucas, *The Religion of the Yorubas: Being an Account of the Religious Beliefs and Practices of the Yoruba Peoples of Southern Nigeria, Especially in Relation to the Religion of Ancient Egypt* (Lagos: C.M.S. Bookshop, 1948), pp. 73–74; and Ogundipe, *Esu Elegbara*, Vol. II, pp. 100–101, 128–32. See esp. Bascom, *Ifa Divination*, pp. 105–7, 156–61, 221–27, 553–55.

15. Frobenius, *The Voice of Africa*, Vol. I, pp. 229–32.

16. Ogundipe, *Esu Elegbara*, Vol. II, pp. 100–101, 128. See also Baudin, *Fetichism*, p. 34; Frobenius, *The Voice of Africa*, Vol. I, pp. 229–32; Farrow, *Faith, Fancies and Fetich*, p. 37; and Lucas, *The Religion of the Yoruba*, pp. 73–74. See esp. Herskovits and Herskovits, *Dahomean Narrative*, pp. 173–83.

17. Herskovits, *Dahomey*, Vol. II, pp. 295–96.

18. Cabrera, *El Monte*, p. 87. Alberto del Pozo graciously located this source for me. The translation published here is by José Piedra. See also Alberto del Pozo, *Oricha* (Miami: 1982), p. 1. Piedra's work on the Yoruba-KiKongo-Cuban cultural matrix is superb. See his "Money Tales and Cuban Songs," *Modern Language Notes* 100 (1985): 361–90.

19. Herskovits and Herskovits, *Dahomean Narrative*, pp. 151–52, 193–94.

20. Ogundipe, *Esu Elegbara*, Vol. II, p. 42.

21. Herskovits and Herskovits, *Dahomean Narrative*, pp. 150–51.

22. I am profoundly indebted to José Piedra, whose reading of an earlier draft of this chapter led him to the Cuban myth of the *guije* and the *jigue* as analogues of the Signifying Monkey. I am delighted to discover the *jigue* to be another dense encoding of Esu. See "El guije de la Bajada," in Salvador Bueno, *Leyendas Cubanas* (Havana: Editorial Arte y Literatura, 1978), pp. 257–61; Teofilo Radillo, "Canción del jigue," ("The Song of the Jigue") in Enrique Noble, *Literatura afrohispano-americana. Poesía y prose de ficción.* (Lexington, Mass., and Toronto: Xerox College Publishing, 1973), pp. 49–52; and Facundo Ramos, "El mito del guije cubano," in Samuel Feijoo, *El negro en la literatura folklórica cubana* (Havana: Editorial Letras Cubanas, 1980), pp. 322–59. The translation of Radillo's poem is by José Piedra. See Appendix. The *Oriki Esu* are replete with descriptions of Esu as "little man."

23. *Guije* or *jigue*, from the Efik-Ejagham word *jiwe* ("monkey"), as verified by Fernando Ortiz, *Nuevo Catauro de Cubanismos*, reedited version of his own *Un catauro de cubanismo. Apuntes lexicográficos* (Havana: Colección Cubana de Libros y Documentos Inéditos y Raros, Vol. 4, 1923), published posthumously (Havana: Editorial de Ciencias Sociales, 1974), p. 305; Pierre Alexandre, *Languages and Language in Black Africa* (Evanston: Northwestern University Press, 1972), pp. 56, 39.

24. In Swahili, *nganga* would be *mganga,* a traditional African doctor cum philosopher. The KiKongo alternative is more likely because of the large numbers of people who were stolen from Congo and enslaved in the Western Hemisphere. *Nganga-Nganga,* in English transliteration from KiKongo, is applied in compound words to the concept of expert on a particular subject. Its early colonial translation as "fetish-maker" clearly conveys a biased misconception and should be substituted by other terms such as *faiseur* ("maker" or "producer"), as it was called in French by J. Van Wing, according to his etymological study of the word, in his *Études BaKongo. Sociologie–Religion et Magie,* 2d ed. (1921, 1938; rpt. Leopoldville: Museum Lessianum, Section Missiologique No. 39, 1959), pp. 418–19. The most complete study on this subject is by Buakasa, who suggests the essential function of the *nganga* to be the interpretation of *kindoki* (a language of obscure forces ruling communication, which includes acts, words, objects, and dreams). See Tulu Kia Mpansu Buakasa, *L'Impense du Discours: "Kindoki" et "nkisi" en pays kongo du Zaire* (Kinshasa: Presse Universitaire, 1973). See also Germain de Granada, *De la Matrice Africaine de la "Langue Congo" de Cuba (Recherche preliminaires)* (Dakar: Centre de Hautes Etudes Afro-Ibero-Americaines, 1973).

25. Del Pozo, *Oricha,* p. 1.

26. Pelton, *The Trickster in West Africa,* p. 162. See esp. Chaps. 3 and 4 for a brilliant analysis of Esu's relation to discourse, as a "kind of reconciliation of opposites of discourse" (p. 79).

27. Ogundipe, *Esu Elegbara,* Vol. II, p. 18.

28. Ibid., Vol. II, pp. 66–67. Herskovits, *Dahomey,* Vol. II, p. 296.

29. Herskovits, *Dahomey,* Vol. II, p. 130.

30. Ibid., p. 131.

31. R. E. Dennett, *At the Back of the Black Man's Mind* (London: Macmillan, 1906), pp. 246–47. See Bascom, *Ifa Divination,* p. 17.

32. Morton-Williams, "An Outline of the Cosmology," pp. 254–55. See also Pelton, *The Trickster in West Africa,* p. 162; Maupoil, *La Geomancie,* p. 17; trans. Paul Mercier, "The Fon of Dahomey," in *African Worlds: Studies in the Cosmological Ideas and Social Values of African Peoples* (London: Oxford University Press, 1954), p. 228; Pelton, *The Trickster in West Africa,* p. 94.

33. Herskovits, *Dahomey,* Vol. II, p. 203.

34. Geoffrey H. Hartman, *Criticism in the Wilderness: The Study of Literature Today* (New Haven: Yale University Press, 1980), p. 272.

35. Ibid., p. 270.

36. Walter J. Ong, *Orality and Literacy: The Technologizing of the Word* (London: Methuen, 1982), pp. 13, 53.

37. On the presence of archaic form, see dos Santos and dos Santos, *Esu Bara Laroye,* p. 15.

38. See Herskovits, *Dahomey,* Vol. II, p. 205; and Pelton, *The Trickster in West Africa,* pp. 88, 102, 108–9, 119. See also Herskovits and Herskovits, *Dahomean Narrative,* p. 147.

39. Herskovits, *Dahomey,* Vol. II, pp. 205–6.

40. Ibid., pp. 225, 229. See Pelton, *The Trickster in West Africa,* pp. 108–9, also pp. 88–89, 102.

41. Herskovits, *Dahomey,* Vol. II, pp. 207–8.

42. Ibid., p. 222.

43. Ibid., pp. 229–30, 225.

44. Ogundipe, *Esu Elegbara,* Vol. I, p. 119. See also W. J. Argyle, *The Fon*

of Dahomey: A History and Ethnography of the Old Kingdom (Oxford: Clarendon Press, 1966), p. 64; Pelton, *The Trickster in West Africa,* p. 105; dos Santos and dos Santos, *Esu Bara Laroye,* p. 91.

45. Ogundipe, *Esu Elegbara,* Vol. I, p. 148.

46. See Thompson, *Black Gods and Kings,* Chap. 4; and Ogundipe, *Esu Elegbara,* Vol. I, pp. 163–64, 172–73.

47. Pelton, *The Trickster in West Africa,* pp. 79, 149.

48. Dos Santos and dos Santos, *Esu Bara Laroye,* p. 91.

49. Mercier, "The Fon of Dahomey," p. 232; cited in Pelton, *The Trickster in West Africa,* p. 105.

50. See Pelton, *The Trickster in West Africa,* pp. 104, 146, 156.

51. Ogundipe, *Esu Elegbara,* Vol. I, p. 134; Vol. II, p. 20.

52. Ibid., Vol. I, p. 147.

53. Ibid., Vol. I, pp. 198, 133.

54. E. Bolaji Idowu, *Olodumare: God in Yoruba Belief* (London: Longman, Green, 1962), p. 74.

55. Ogundipe, *Esu Elegbara,* Vol. I, p. 234.

56. Dos Santos and dos Santos, *Esu Bara Laroye,* pp. 91, 93–94; and Pelton, *The Trickster in West Africa,* pp. 71–113.

57. Dos Santos and dos Santos, *Esu Bara Laroye,* pp. 93–94.

58. Cabrera, *El Monte,* p. 87. See also Argeliers Leon, "Elebwa: Una Divinidad de la Santaria Cubana," in *Abhandlungen und Berichte des Staatlichen Museums für Völkerkunde,* Dresden, Band 21 (Berlin: Akademie Verlag, 1962), pp. 57–61.

59. Roger Bastide, *Les Religions Africaines au Brésil: vers une Sociologie des Interpénétrations de Civilisations* (Paris: Une Presse Universitaire de France, 1960), pp. 350–52. For representations of Esu in formal literature, see Aime Cesaire, *Une tempête* (Paris: Editions du Sevil, 1969), pp. 67–71; Wale Ogunyemi, *Eshu Elegbara* (Ibadan: Orisun Acting Editions, 1970); and Wole Soyinka, *Death and the King's Horseman* (New York: Norton, 1975).

60. Ogundipe, *Esu Elegbara,* Vol. I, p. 207.

61. See ibid., Vol. I, pp. 196–97; Vol. II, pp. 132, 133–35, 311; Pelton, *The Trickster in West Africa,* p. 141; Frobenius, *The Voice of Africa,* Vol. I, pp. 240–42; and Bascom, *Ifa Divination,* p. 105.

62. Ogundipe, *Esu Elegbara,* Vol. II, pp. 133–35.

63. Dos Santos and dos Santos, *Esu Bara Laroye,* p. 90.

64. Ibid., p. 119.

65. Ibid., p. 29.

66. Thompson, *Flash of the Spirit,* Chap. 1.

67. Dos Santos and dos Santos, *Esu Bara Laroye,* p. 85.

68. Ibid., p. 8.

69. Ibid., pp. 27, 101.

70. Ibid., pp. 26–27.

71. Ibid., pp. 110, 91.

72. Peter Morton-Williams, "The Yoruba Ogboni Cult in Oyo," *Africa* 30: 373. See also John Pemberton III, "Descriptive Catalogue," *Yoruba: Sculpture of West Africa,* ed. Bryce Holcomb (New York: Knopf, 1982), p. 186.

73. See dos Santos and dos Santos, *Esu Bara Laroye,* pp. 88–89, 83–84.

74. Ibid., pp. 48–49.

75. Ibid., pp. 84, 91–92.

76. Abimbola, "An Exposition of Ifa Literary Corpus," pp. 388, 394; dos Santos and dos Santos, *Esu Bara Laroye,* pp. 2, 93–94; Ogundipe, *Esu Elegbara,* Vol. II, p. 2; see also Pelton, *The Trickster in West Africa,* p. 104.

77. Jacques Derrida, *Of Grammatology,* trans. Gayatri Chakravorty Spivak (Baltimore: Johns Hopkins University Press, 1976), pp. 34–43; cf. Jonathan Culler, *On Deconstruction: Theory and Criticism After Structuralism* (Ithaca: Cornell University Press, 1982), p. 101. See Culler, *On Deconstruction,* p. 109.

78. Pelton, *The Trickster in West Africa,* pp. 163, 143. See Derrida, "Linguistics and Grammatology," in *Of Grammatology,* pp. 27–73.

79. Christopher Norris, *Deconstruction: Theory and Practice* (London: Methuen, 1982), p. 33.

80. For a lucid exposition of these aspects of poststructural theory, see Norris, *Deconstruction,* pp. 39, 28, 29, 32, 24, 16, 13.

81. Ogundipe, *Esu Elegbara,* Vol. II, pp. 38–39.

82. Nicolas Guillen, "Balada del guije" ("Ballad of the Guije"), in *West Indies, Ltd.,* 1934. See *Songoro Cosongo, Motivos de son, West Indies Lt., España,* 4th ed. (1952; Buenos Aires: Losada, 1967), pp. 62–64. Translation by José Piedra.

83. Ogundipe, *Esu Elegbara,* p. 18.

Chapter 2

1. Ferdinand de Saussure, *Course in General Linguistics,* ed. Charles Bally and Albert Sechehaye, trans. Wade Baskin (New York: McGraw-Hill, 1966), p. 66ff.

2. For a superbly lucid discussion, see Christopher Norris, *Deconstruction: Theory and Practice* (New York: Methuen, 1982), p. 32.

3. See my discussion of the word "down" in *Figures in Black: Words, Signs, and the Racial Self* (New York: Oxford University Press, 1986).

4. Saussure, *Course,* p. 71.

5. Jacques Lacan, *Ecrits: A Selection,* trans. Alan Sheridan (New York: Norton, 1977), p. 154.

6. Anthony Easthope, *Poetry as Discourse* (New York: Methuen, 1983), p. 37.

7. Quoted in Gary Saul Morson, *The Boundaries of Genre: Dostoevsky's "Diary of a Writer" and the Traditions of Literary Utopia* (Austin: University of Texas Press, 1981), p. 108.

8. Saussure, *Course,* p. 71.

9. Ibid., pp. 75, 72.

10. See, for example, Claudia Mitchell-Kernan, *Language Behavior in a Black Urban Community* (Monographs of the Language-Behavior Laboratory, University of California, Berkeley, No. 2), pp. 88–90; and Roger D. Abrahams, *Talking Black* (Rowley, Mass.: Newbury House Publishers, 1976), pp. 50–51.

11. On Tar Baby, see Ralph Ellison, "Hidden Name and Complex Fate: A Writer's Experience in the United States," *Shadow and Act* (New York: Random House, 1964), p. 147; and Toni Morrison, *Tar Baby* (New York: Knopf, 1981).

12. Geneva Smitherman defines these and other black tropes, then traces their use in several black texts. Smitherman's work, like that of Mitchell-Kernan and Abrahams, is especially significant for literary theory. See Geneva Smitherman, *Talkin and Testifyin: The Language of Black America* (Boston: Houghton Mifflin, 1977), pp. 101–67. And on signifying as a rhetorical trope, see Smitherman,

Talkin' and Testifyin', pp. 101–67; Thomas Kochman, *Rappin' and Stylin' Out: Communication in Urban Black America* (Urbana: University of Illinois Press, 1972); Thomas Kochman, " 'Rappin' in the Black Ghetto," *Trans-Action* 6 (February 1969): 32; Alan Dundes, *Mother Wit from the Laughing Barrel: Readings in the Interpretation of Afro-American Folklore* (Englewood Cliffs: Prentice-Hall, 1973), p. 310; Ethen M. Albert, " 'Rhetoric,' 'Logic,' and 'Poetics' in Burundi: Culture Patterning of Speech Behavior," in John J. Gumperz and Dell Hymes, eds., *The Ethnography of Communication, American Anthropologist* 66 (1964): 35–54. One example of signifying can be gleaned from the following anecdote. While writing this essay, I asked a colleague, Dwight Andrews, if he had heard of the Signifying Monkey as a child. "Why, no," he replied intently. "I never heard of the Signifying Monkey until I came to Yale and read about him in a book." I had been signified upon. If I had responded to Andrews, "I know what you mean; your Mama read to me from that same book the last time I was in Detroit," I would have signified upon him in return.

13. Julia Kristeva, *Desire in Language: A Semiotic Approach to Literature and Art* (New York: Columbia University Press, 1980), p. 31; Dundes, editor's note, *Mother Wit from the Laughing Barrel*, p. 310.

14. Roger D. Abrahams, *Deep Down in the Jungle: Negro Narrative Folklore from the Streets of Philadelphia* (Chicago: Aldine Publishing, 1970), pp. 51–52, 66–67, 264. Abrahams's awareness of the need to define uniquely black significations is exemplary. As early as 1964, when he published the first edition of *Deep Down in the Jungle,* he saw fit to add a glossary, as an appendix of "Unusual Terms and Expressions," a title which unfortunately suggests the social scientist's apologia.

15. Ibid., pp. 66–67, 264. (Emphasis added.)

16. Ibid., p. 113. In the second line of the stanza, "motherfucker" is often substituted for "monkey."

17. "The Signifying Monkey," *Book of Negro Folklore,* ed. Langston Hughes and Arna Bontemps (New York: Dodd, Mead, 1958), pp. 365–66.

18. See Bruce Jackson, *"Get Your Ass in the Water and Swim Like Me": Narrative Poetry from the Black Oral Tradition* (Cambridge: Harvard University Press, 1974), esp. pp. 164–65. Subsequent references to tales collected by Jackson will be given in the text. Jackson's collection of "Toasts" is definitive.

19. A clear example of paradigmatic contiguity is the addition of the metonym "hairy" as an adjective for "ass" in the second quoted line.

20. J. L. Dillard, *Lexicon of Black English* (New York: Continuum, 1977), pp. 130–41; Zora Neale Hurston, *Mules and Men* (Philadelphia: J. B. Lippincott, 1935), p. 37; Sterling A. Brown, "Folk Literature," in *The Negro Caravan* (1941; New York: Arno, 1969), p. 433.

21. Sigmund Freud, *The Interpretation of Dreams,* trans. James Strachey (1953; New York: Avon, 1965), p. 386.

22. Quoted in Easthope, *Poetry as Discourse,* p. 82.

23. Ibid., pp. 82–83, 42.

24. Ibid., pp. 84–86.

25. Quoted in Easthope, *Poetry as Discourse,* p. 90. For a nineteenth-century commentary on black rhyme schemes in music, see James Hungerford, *The Old Plantation and What I Gathered There in an Autumn Month [of 1832]* (New York, 1859), reprinted in Eileen Southern, ed., *Readings in Black American Music* (New York: Norton, 1971), pp. 71–81, esp. p. 73.

26. Easthope, *Poetry as Discourse,* pp. 90–91.

27. Ibid., pp. 89–90, 93. (Emphasis added.)

28. Ralph Ellison, "The Little Man at Chehaw Station," *The American Scholar* (Winter 1977–78): 26.

29. *Oriki Esu*, quoted by Ayodele Ogundipe, *Esu Elegbara, the Yoruba God of Chance and Uncertainty: A Study in Yoruba Mythology*, 2 vols. Ph.D. dissertation, Indiana University, 1978, Vol. II, pp. 12, 77.

30. "Test on Street Language Says It's Not Grant in That Tomb," *New York Times*, April 17, 1983, p. 30.

31. Langston Hughes, *Ask Your Mama: 12 Moods for Jazz* (New York: Knopf, 1971), p. 8; "Test on Street Language," p. 30. (Emphasis added.)

32. *Journal of Nicholas Cresswell, 1774–1777*, ed. L. MacVeigh (New York: Dial Press, 1924), pp. 17–19.

33. Frederick Douglass, *Narrative of the Life of Frederick Douglass, An American Slave, Written by Himself* (1845; New York: Doubleday, 1963), pp. 13–14. (Emphasis added.)

34. Ibid., pp. 13, 15.

35. Frederick Douglass, *My Bondage and My Freedom* (New York: Orton & Mulligan, 1855), p. 253.

36. William Faux, *Memorable Days in America* (London: W. Simpkins and R. Marshall, 1823), pp. 77–78. See also John Dixon Long, *Pictures of Slavery in Church and State* (Philadelphia: the author, 1857), pp. 197–98.

37. George P. Rawick, ed., *The American Slave: A Composite Autobiography*, Vol. 5, Part 4, p. 198.

38. Clarence Major, *Dictionary of Afro-American Slang* (New York: International Publisher, 1970), pp. 104, 46, 34.

39. Hermese E. Roberts, *The Third Ear: A Black Glossary*, entry on signifying.

40. Mezz Mezzrow and Bernard Wolfe, *Really the Blues* (New York: Random House, 1946), pp. 378, 230.

41. Ibid., pp. 230–31.

42. Malachi Andrews and Paul T. Owens, *Black Language* (West Los Angeles: Seymour-Smith, 1973), p. 95. (Emphasis added.) See also their entry on "Wolf," p. 106.

43. Dillard, *Lexicon of Black English*, pp. 154, 177.

44. Hurston, *Mules and Men*, p. 161. See also C. Merton Babcock, "A Word List from Zora Neale Hurston," *Publications of the American Dialect Society*, No. 40 (University, Ala.: University of Alabama Press, 1963), pp. 1–12. I analyze Hurston's uses of Signifyin(g) in Chapter 5 herein.

45. Dillard, *Lexicon of Black English*, p. 134.

46. See Jackson, *Get Your Ass in the Water*, esp. pp. 161–80.

47. Jim Haskins and Hugh F. Butts, *The Psychology of Black Language* (New York: Barnes & Noble, 1973), p. 86.

48. Ibid., p. 51.

49. Harold Wentworth and Stuart Berg Flexner, comp. and ed., *Dictionary of American Slang*, Second Supplemental Edition (New York: Thomas Y. Crowell, 1975), p. 477.

50. Peter Tamary, quoted in Robert S. Gold, *Jazz Talk* (New York: Bobbs-Merrill, 1975), p. 76.

51. H. Rap Brown, *Die Nigger Die!* (New York: Dial Pres, 1969), pp. 25–26.

52. Ibid., pp. 26–29.

53. Ibid., pp. 29–30.

54. Ibid.

55. See Roger D. Abrahams, "The Changing Concept of the Negro Hero," in *The Golden Log,* ed. Mody C. Boatright, Wilson M. Hudson, and Allen Maxwell (Dallas: Southern Methodist University Press, 1962), pp. 119–34; Abrahams, *Deep Down in the Jungle,* esp. "Introduction to the Second Edition" (1970).

56. Abrahams, "The Changing Concept," p. 125.

57. Abrahams, *Deep Down in the Jungle,* pp. 51–53, 66–70, 113–19, 142–47, 153–56, 264.

58. Richard A. Lanham, *The Motives of Eloquence: Literary Rhetoric in the Renaissance* (New Haven: Yale University Press, 1976), pp. 2–3. See also Abrahams, *Deep Down in the Jungle,* p. 17; and Edith A. Folb, *Runnin' Down Some Lines: The Language and Culture of Black Teenagers* (Cambridge: Harvard University Press, 1980), p. 90: "Young people growing up in the black community play endless verbal games with one another, much as their mainstream white counterparts play games of war, cops and robbers, or cowboys and Indians. Like skilled musicians, children early on learn to refine their verbal skills, to develop their instrument so that it can play a variety of songs."

59. Lanham, *The Motives of Eloquence,* pp. 2–3.

60. Roger D. Abrahams, *Talking Black* (Rawley, Mass. Newbury House, 1976), p. 19.

61. Ibid., p. 33.

62. Ibid., p. 51.

63. Ibid., pp. 49, 46, 53, 56, 73–76, 50. See also Roger D. Abrahams, *The Man-of-Words in the West Indies: Performance and the Emergence of Creole Culture* (Baltimore: Johns Hopkins University Press, 1983), p. 56–57.

64. Abrahams, *Talking Black,* p. 52. (Emphasis added.) "Duke Ellington and John Coltrane," Impulse Records, AS-30.

65. Thomas Kochman, "Towards an Ethnography of Black American Speech Behavior," in *Rappin' and Stylin' Out: Communication in Urban Black America* (Urbana: University of Illinois Press, 1972), p. 257. See also Kochman's " 'Rapping' in the Black Ghetto," *Trans-action* 6 (February 1969): 26–35. Kochman's "Towards an Ethnography" was originally published in *Afro-American Anthropology: Contemporary Perspectives,* ed. Norman E. Whitten, Jr., and John F. Szwed (New York: Free Press, 1970), pp. 145–63.

66. Kochman, "Ethnography," p. 257.

67. Ibid., p. 258.

68. See also Herbert L. Foster, *Ribbin', Jivin', and Playin' the Dozens: The Unrecognized Dilemma of Inner City Schools* (Cambridge: Ballinger, 1974), pp. 203–10; and Edith A. Folb, *Runnin' Down Some Lines; The Language and Culture of Black Teenagers* (Cambridge: Harvard University Press, 1980), esp. pp. 69–131.

69. See Claudia Mitchell-Kernan, *Language Behavior in a Black Urban Community,* Monographs of the Language-Behavior Laboratory, University of California, Berkeley, No. 2 (February 1971), esp. pp. 87–129, reprinted as "Signifying as a Form of Verbal Art" in *Mother Wit from the Laughing Barrel: Readings in the Interpretation of Afro-American Folklore,* ed. Alan Dundes (Englewood Cliffs: Prentice-Hall, 1973), pp. 310–28; and Kochman, *Rappin' and Stylin' Out,* pp. 315–36. These quotations appear on p. 311 of the Dundes reprint. All subsequent page numbers refer to this volume.

70. Mitchell-Kernan, "Signifying," p. 311.

71. Ibid., pp. 312–13, 311–12, 322–23.

72. Ibid., p. 313. See Richard A. Lanham, *A Handlist of Rhetorical Terms* (Berkeley: University of California Press, 1969), pp. 101–3, 52.

73. Mitchell-Kernan, "Signifying," p. 313.

74. Ibid., p. 314.

75. Ibid.

76. Ibid., pp. 314–15.

77. Ibid.

78. Ibid., p. 316.

79. Ibid., pp. 316–21.

80. Ibid., p. 318.

81. Harold Bloom, *A Map of Misreading* (New York: Oxford University Press, 1975), p. 93, esp. pp. 83–105; Mitchell-Kernan, "Signifying," p. 319.

82. Mitchell-Kernan, "Signifying," pp. 318–19.

83. Ibid., pp. 320–21.

84. Ibid., pp. 321–22.

85. Ibid., p. 322.

86. See ibid., pp. 322–23.

87. Ibid., p. 325. (Emphasis added.)

88. Ibid. For an excellent summary of the literature of Signifyin(g), see Lawrence W. Levine, *Black Culture and Black Consciousness: Afro-American Folk Thought from Slavery to Freedom* (New York: Oxford University Press, 1977), pp. 346, 378–80, 483, 498–99.

89. Harold Bloom, *A Map of Misreading,* p. 84.

90. The source for this riff and its analysis is a personal conversation with Kimberly W. Benston.

91. Montaigne, "Of the Vanity of Words," in *The Complete Essays of Montaigne,* trans. Donald M. Frame (Stanford: Stanford University Press, 1965), p. 223.

Chapter 3

1. For a full discussion of Juan Latino's life and works, see V. B. Spratlin, *Juan Latino, Slave and Humanist* (New York: Spinner Press, 1938); and Henry Louis Gates, Jr. ed., *The Poetry of Juan Latino,* trans. by Jack Winkler, forthcoming).

2. Spratlin, *Juan Latino,* p. 41.

3. Ibid., pp. 41–42.

4. Ibid., p. 42.

5. See Nathaniel Shurtleff, "Phillis Wheatley, the Negro Slave Poet," in *Proceedings of the Massachusetts Historical Society* VII (1863–64): 273–74; and Julian D. Mason, Jr., ed., *The Poems of Phillis Wheatley* (Chapel Hill: University of North Carolina Press, 1966), pp. 103–9. On "Dreadful Riot on Negro Hill," see William H. Robinson, *Phillis Wheatley in the Black American Beginnings* (Detroit: Broadside Press, 1975), pp. 25–26.

6. See note 5 above.

7. Anonymous, "A Black Lecture on Language" (London: William Follit, [1846]).

8. These lectures are located at the Lewis Walpole Library in Farmington, Connecticut.

9. Ethiop, "What Shall We Do with the White People?" *Anglo-African Magazine* II, no. 2 (February 1860): 41–45.

10. For a full analysis of this statement, see Henry Louis Gates, Jr., *Black Letters in the Enlightenment: Race, Writing, and Difference* (New York: Oxford University Press, forthcoming).

11. Ethiop, "What Shall We Do," p. 45.

12. Geneva Smitherman, *Talkin and Testifyin: The Language of Black America* (Boston: Houghton Mifflin, 1977), pp. 118–34. See also Roger D. Abrahams, *Talking Black* (Rowley, Mass.: Newbury House, 1976), p. 77.

13. Smitherman, *Talkin and Testifyin,* p. 118.

14. Ibid., p. 121.

15. Ibid.

16. Quoted in ibid., pp. 121–22.

17. Ibid., p. 122.

18. Quoted in ibid.

19. Quoted in ibid., pp. 122–23.

20. Quoted in ibid., p. 123.

21. Michel Fabre, *The Unfinished Quest of Richard Wright,* trans. by Isabel Barzun (New York: William Morrow, 1973), p. 135.

22. See Chapter 5, herein.

23. Quoted in Smitherman, *Talkin and Testifyin,* pp. 126–28.

24. Ibid., p. 128.

25. Ibid., p. 131.

26. Ibid., p. 132.

27. Ibid., p. 132–33.

28. Langston Hughes, *Ask Your Mama: 12 Moods for Jazz* (New York: Knopf, 1971).

29. Ibid., p. 43.

30. Alston Anderson, *Lover Man* (Garden City, N.Y.: Doubleday, 1959), pp. 19–27.

31. Ibid., pp. 20–21.

32. Ibid., p. 26.

33. See Chapter 2 herein; John Edgar Wideman, "Charles Chesnutt and the WPA Narratives," in *The Slave's Narrative,* ed. by Charles T. Davis and Henry Louis Gates, Jr. (New York: Oxford University Press, 1985); Toni Cade Bambara, "The Johnson Girls," in *Gorilla, My Love* (New York: Vintage Books, 1981), pp. 163–77; Roger D. Abrahams, *Talking Black,* p. 77, for a discussion of this story; John Edgar Wideman, "The Watermelon Story," in *Damballah* (New York: Avon, 1981), p. 104; Carolyn Rodgers, "Black Poetry—Where It's At," in *Rappin' and Stylin' Out,* ed. by Thomas Kochman, pp. 336–45.

34. Quoted in Roger D. Abrahams, *Positively Black,* p. 2.

35. Ralph Ellison, "And Hickman Arrives," in *Black Writers of America,* ed. by Richard Barksdale and Keneth Kinnamon (New York: Macmillan, 1972), p. 704.

36. Ralph Ellison, "On Bird, Bird-Watching, and Jazz," *Saturday Review,* July 20, 1962, reprinted in *Shadow and Act* (New York: Random House, 1964), p. 231. Ellison uses a stanza of this verse in *Invisible Man:*

> O well they picked poor Robin clean
> O well they picked poor Robin clean
> Well they tied poor Robin to a stump
> Lawd, they picked all the feathers round from Robin's rump
> Well they picked poor Robin clean.

Ralph Ellison, *Invisible Man* (New York: Random House, 1982), p. 147.

37. Library of Congress conversations with Alan Lomax, recorded on *Discourse on Jazz*, Riverside RLP9003, side 1. Quoted in J. L. Dillard, *Lexicon of Black English* (New York: Seabury Press, 1977), p. 70 (emphasis added).

38. Ralph Ellison, "Blues People," in *Shadow and Act*, pp. 249, 250. The essay was first printed in *The New York Review of Books*, February 6, 1964.

39. Ralph Ellison, "The World and Jug," in *Shadow and Act*, p. 117. The essay appeared first in *The New Leader*, December 9, 1963.

40. For a fascinating and extended reading of this passage from Wright, see Houston A. Baker, Jr., *Blues, Ideology, and Afro-American Literature: A Vernacular Theory* (Chicago: University of Chicago Press, 1985).

41. Ellison, *Shadow and Act*, p. 137.

42. Wole Soyinka, *The Lion and the Jewel*, in *Collected Plays*, Vol. 2 (New York: Oxford University Press, 1974), p. 21. Robert Elliot Fox makes this point in *The Mirrors of Caliban: The Fiction of LeRoi Jones, Ishmael Reed, and Samuel R. Delany*. Ph.D. dissertation, SUNY at Buffalo, 1976, p. 157.

43. O. O. Gabugah, "The Old O.O. Blues," *Yardbird Reader*, Vol. 2 (Berkeley: Yardbird Publishing Cooperative, 1973), pp. 219–20. See also O. O. Gabugah, "What You Seize Is What You Git," *Yardbird Reader*, Vol. 1 (1971), pp. 117–19.

44. See Jean Bodin, *Method for the Easy Comprehension of History*, trans. by Beatrice Reynolds (1945; New York: Octagon Books, 1966), p. 105; Aristotle, *Historia Animalum*, trans. by D'Arch W. Thompson, in J. A. Smith and W. D. Ross, eds., *The Works of Aristotle*, Vol. IV (Oxford: Oxford University Press, 1910), p. 606b; Thomas Herbert, *Some Years Travels* (London: R. Everingham (1677), pp. 16–17; John Locke, *An Essay Concerning Human Understanding*, Vol. II (London: Churchill and Manship, 1721), p. 53 (bk. III, chap. 6, sec. 23).

45. Ellison, *Shadow and Act*, p. 100.

46. See David Worchester, *The Art of Satire* (New York: Russell and Russell, 1960), p. 42; and Mikhail Bakhtin, "Discourse Typology in Prose," in *Readings in Russian Poetics: Formalist and Structuralist Views*, ed. by Ladislav Matejka and Krystyna Pomorska (Cambridge: MIT Press, 1971), pp. 176–96.

47. Bakhtin, "Discourse Typology in Prose," pp. 185–86.

48. Bakhtin, "Discouse Typology in Prose," p. 87.

49. The use of interlocking triangles as a metaphor for the intertextual relationships of the tradition is not meant to suggest any form of concrete, inflexible reality. On the contrary, as René Girard says:

> The triangle is no *Gestalt*. The real structures are intersubjective. They cannot be localized anywhere; *the triangle has no reality whatever; it is a systematic metaphor, systematically pursued*. Because changes in size and shape do not destroy the identity of this figure, . . . the diversity as well as the unity of the works can be simultaneously illustrated. The purpose and limitations of this structural geometry may become clearer through a reference to structural models. The triangle is a model of a sort, or rather a whole family of models. But these models are not mechanical like those of Claude Lévi-Strauss. They always allude to the mystery, transparent yet opaque, of human relations. All types of structural thinking assume that human reality is intelligible; it is a *logos* and, as such, *it is an incipient logic, or it degrades itself into a logic*. It can thus be systematized, at least up to a point, however unsystematic, irrational, and chaotic it may appear even to those, or rather especially to those who operate the system.

Rene Girard, *Deceit, Desire and the Novel: Self and Other in Literary Structure* (Baltimore: Johns Hopkins University Press, 1965), pp. 2–3 (emphasis added).

50. For Ishmael Reed on "a talking book," see "Ishmael Reed: A Self Interview," *Black World,* June 1974, p. 25. For the slave narratives in which this figure appears, see James Albert Ukawsaw Gronniosaw, *A Narrative of the Most Remarkable Particulars of the Life of James Albert Ukawsaw Gronniosaw, An African Prince* (Bath: n.p., 1770); John Marrant, *Narrative of the Lord's Wonderful Dealings with John Marrant, A Black* (London: Gilbert and Plummer, 1785); Ottabah Cugoano, *Thoughts and Sentiments on the Evil and Wicked Traffic of the Slavery and Commerce of the Human Species* (London: n.p., 1787); Olaudah Equiano, *The Interesting Narrative of the Life of Olaudah Equiano, or Gustavus Vassa, the African. Written by Himself.* (London: for the author, 1789); and John Jea, *The Life History, and Unparalleled Sufferings of John Jea, the African Preacher* (Portsea, Eng.: for the author, 1815?).

51. Northrop Frye, *Anatomy of Criticism: Four Essays* (Princeton: Princeton University Press, 1971), p. 233.

52. Bakhtin, "Discourse Typology in Prose," p. 190.

53. Frye, *Anatomy of Criticism,* p. 233.

54. David Hume, "Of National Characters," in *Essays: Moral, Political, and Literary,* 2 vols. ed. by T. H. Green and T. H. Grose (London: Longmans, 1895), Vol. I, p. 252, n. 1. See Vernon Loggins, *The Negro Author: His Development in America to 1900* (New York: Columbia University Press, 1931), p. 341; and Sterling A. Brown, *Negro Poetry and Drama* (1937; New York: Atheneum, 1972), pp. 11, 13.

55. W. E. B. Du Bois, *The Negro* (New York: Henry Holt, 1915), p. 231.

56. W. E. B. Du Bois, *The Crisis* 41 (June 1934): 182. For two excellent discussions of this aspect of Du Bois's thought, see Vincent Harding, "W. E. B. Du Bois and the Black Messianic Vision," in *Black Titan: W. E. B. Du Bois,* ed. by John Henrik Clarke, Esther Jackson, Ernest Kaiser, and J. H. O'Dell (Boston: Beacon Press, 1970), pp. 52–69; and Arnold Rampersad, *The Art and Imagination of W. E. B. Du Bois* (Cambridge: Harvard University Press, 1976), p. 81.

57. John H. Smythe, *The Bee,* June 25, 1887, cited in August Meier, *Negro Thought in America, 1880–1915: Racial Ideologies in the Age of Booker T. Washington* (Ann Arbor: University of Michigan Press, 1966), p. 54.

58. Paul Laurence Dunbar, "Prometheus," in *The Complete Poems of Paul Laurence Dunbar* (New York: Dodd, Mead, 1976), pp. 188–89.

59. Quoted in Virginia Cunningham, *Paul Laurence Dunbar and His Song* (New York: Dodd, Mead, 1947), p. 160.

60. Quoted in Benjamin Brawley, *Paul Laurence Dunbar: Poet of His People* (Chapel Hill: University of North Carolina Press, 1936), pp. 76–77.

61. Carlin T. Kindilien, *American Poetry in the Eighteen Nineties* (Providence: Brown University Press, 1956), p. 62.

62. Helen M. Chesnutt, *Charles Waddell Chesnutt: Pioneer of the Color Line* (Chapel Hill: University of North Carolina Press, 1952), pp. 88, 20.

63. Ibid., p. 21.

64. Ibid.

65. Ibid.

66. Ibid.

67. Ibid., p. 28.

68. Ibid.

69. See Richard O. Lewis, "Sources of Charles W. Chesnutt's 'The Passing of Grandison,' *Studies in American Fiction,* forthcoming.

70. Ralph Ellison, "Remarks at the American Academy Conference on the Negro American, 1965," *Daedelus* 95, no. 1 (Winter 1966): 408.

71. Nancy Cunard, ed., *Negro* (1934; New York: Negro Universities Press, 1969), pp. 39–62. Reprinted in Zora Neale Hurston, *The Sanctified Church,* ed. by Toni Cade Bambara (Berkeley: Turtle Island, 1981), pp. 41–78.

72. Zora Neale Hurston, "Originality," in Cunard, *Negro,* p. 42.

73. Ibid., p. 43.

74. Zora Neale Hurston, "Imitation," in Cunard, *Negro,* p. 43.

75. Richard Wright, "How 'Bigger' Was Born," in *Native Son* (1940; New York: Harper & Row, 1966), p. xvi (emphasis added).

76. Ibid.

77. Richard Wright, "Blueprint for Negro Writing," in Addison Gayle, Jr., ed., *The Black Aesthetic* (Garden City, N.Y.: Doubleday-Anchor, 1972), p. 315.

78. Ibid.

79. Ibid., p. 322.

80. Richard Wright, *White Man, Listen!* (Garden City, N.Y.: Doubleday, 1957). This essay is reprinted in Addison Gayle, Jr., ed., *Black Expression* (New York: Weybright and Talley, 1969), pp. 198–229, from which all subsequent citations are taken. This quotation is from p. 212 (emphasis added).

81. Ellison, *Shadow and Act,* pp. 127, 134.

82. Ibid., p. 140.

83. Ibid., p. 131 (emphasis added).

84. See Ibid., pp. 121, 130.

85. In John O'Brien, ed., *Interviews with Black Writers* (New York: Liveright, 1973), p. 56.

86. Kimberly W. Benston, "I Yam What I Am": Naming and Unnaming in Afro-American Literature," in *Black Literature and Literary Theory,* ed. by H. L. Gates, Jr. (New York: Methuen, 1984), pp. 151–72.

87. See Benston's *Afro-American Modernism,* forthcoming.

88. This analysis of Basie's composition is the result of listening sessions with two remarkably articulate jazz musicians, Dwight Andrews and Anthony Davis. My debt to them is a large one.

Chapter 4

1. Morgan Godwyn, *The Negro's and Indians' Advocate . . . in Our Plantation* (1680), cited in Frances Smith Foster, *Witnessing Slavery: The Development of Antebellum Slave Narratives* (Westport, Conn.: Greenwood, 1979), pp. 7–9.

2. James W. C. Pennington, "To the Reader," in Ann Plato, *Essays; Including Biographies and Miscellaneous Pieces, in Prose and Poetry* (Hartford: for the author, 1841), pp. xviii, xx.

3. On April 30, 1773, Mrs. Susanna Wheatley wrote to the Countess of Huntington to thank her for granting permission to her slave, Phillis, to dedicate her forthcoming volume of poems to this distinguished humanitarian. Since Phillis Wheatley sailed to England in May of 1773, and because the book was published in London before she returned to Boston in late July, we must conclude that the

certificate of attestation was signed well before Susanna Wheatley sent the manuscript to the countess. See Sarah D. Jackson, "Letters of Phillis Wheatley and Susanna Wheatley," *Journal of Negro History* LVII, no. 2 (April 1972): 214–15; and William H. Robinson, *Phillis Wheatley in the Black American Beginnings* (Detroit: Broadside Press, 1975), pp. 15–18. See also "To the Publick," in *Poems on Various Subjects, Religious and Moral,* by Phillis Wheatley, Negro Servant to Mr. John Wheatley, of Boston, in New England (London: A. Bell, 1773).

4. For a full list of this book's editions, see Janheinz Jahn and Claus Peter Dressler, *Bibliography of Creative African Writing* (Millwood, N.Y.: Kraus-Thomson Organization, 1975), p. 135. The 1770 edition was published by S. Hazard, with an introduction by W. Shirley. The 1770 edition consists of forty-nine pages, but the 1840 edition that I am using has twenty-nine pages.

5. Briton Hammon, *Narrative . . .* (Boston: Green & Russell, 1760), p. 14; Gronniosaw, p. 17.

6. See Wylie Sypher, *Guinea's Captive Kings: British Anti-Slavery Literature of the XVIIIth Century* (Chapel Hill: University of North Carolina Press, 1942), pp. 103–55.

7. Gronniosaw, p. 11.

8. Ibid., p. 3.

9. Ibid., pp. 4–5.

10. Ibid., pp. 3, 5, 9.

11. Ibid., p. 14.

12. Ibid., pp. 10, 11, 13.

13. Ibid., p. 15.

14. Ibid., pp. 17, 21. George Whitefield, a central figure of the Protestant Great Awakening of the eighteenth century, appears frequently in black texts published before 1800. Gronniosaw, Wheatley, and Equiano, among others, refer to him or depict him as a character in their narratives.

15. Ibid., pp. 8, 9, 19.

16. Ibid., p. 8 (emphasis added).

17. Ralph Ellison, *Invisible Man* (New York: Random House, 1982), p. 293. See the epigraph to Chapter 3.

18. Gronniosaw, p. 8.

19. I say forty-five years later because W. Shirley, the author of the "Preface" to Gronniosaw's *Narrative,* deduces that he was "about fifteen years old" when "James Albert left his native country," and that at the time of publication, "He now appears to be turned of sixty."

20. See Gronniosaw, pp. 8, 10, 11, 14, 15, 19, 21.

21. Willem Bosman, *A New and Accurate Description of the Coast of Guinea* (1705; New York: Barnes and Noble, 1967). These facts, as well as the biographical description that follows, are taken from Robert D. Richardson's headnote to his reprinting of "Letter X" in *The Rise of Modern Mythology, 1680–1860,* ed. by Burton Feldman and Robert D. Richardson (Bloomington: Indiana University Press, 1972), pp. 41–42. All subsequent citations refer to this edition.

22. Elmira Fort (or "Castle") was the site of Jacobus Capitein's departure from Africa and his subsequent return. Capitein was one of the African children chosen to be educated in Europe as an experiment to ascertain the black's "capacity" for "progress" and "elevation." Feldman and Richardson, *The Rise of Modern Mythology,* p. 42.

23. Margaret T. Hodgen, *Early Anthropology in the Sixteenth and Seventeenth Centuries* (Philadelphia: University of Pennsylvania Press, 1964), p. 491; Feldman and Richardson, *The Rise of Modern Mythology*, p. 42.

24. Feldman and Richardson, *The Rise of Modern Mythology*, p. 44.

25. Ibid., pp. 44–45.

26. Immanuel Kant, *Observations on the Feelings of the Beautiful and the Sublime*, trans. by John T. Goldthwait (Berkeley: University of California Press, 1960), pp. 111, 113.

27. For a full discussion of the Indian captivity tales, and a selection of some of the most gripping of the genre, see Richard Van Der Beets, *Held Captive by Indians* (Knoxville: University of Tennessee Press, 1973). See Van Der Beets, p. 177; and Dorothy B. Porter, "Early American Negro Writings: A Bibliographical Study," *Papers of the Bibliographical Society of America* 39 (Fourth Quarter 1945): 247–51. Throughout I am citing a reprinting of the London edition of 1788. John Marrant, *A Narrative of the Lord's Wonderful Dealings with John Marrant, A Black (Now Gone to Preach the Gospel in Nova-Scotia) Born in New-York, North-America, Taken Down from his own Relation, arranged, corrected and published by the Rev. Mr. Aldridge* (London: Gilbert and Plummer, 1788), reprinted in Van Der Beets, *Held Captive by Indians*, pp. 178–201.

28. Van Der Beets, p. 185.

29. Ibid., p. 190.

30. Ibid., pp. 191–92.

31. Ibid., p. 193.

32. Marrant tells us in the third sentence of the *Narrative's* first paragraph that he "went to school" in St. Augustine, where he learned "to read and spell." Ibid., p. 180.

33. Ibid., p. 193.

34. Ibid.

35. Ibid., pp. 181, 185.

36. These letters are reprinted in Paul Edwards's edition of *Thoughts and Sentiments on the Evil and Wicked Traffic of the Slavery and Commerce of the Human Species, Humbly Submitted to the Inhabitants of Great-Britain, by Ottobah Cugoano, a Native of Africa* (1787; London: Dawsons of Pall Mall, 1969), pp. xix–xxiii. This prefatory matter is hereafter referred to as Edwards, while Cugoano's text is referred to as Cugoano.

37. Cugoano used his full name in his edited and revised 1791 edition. See Edwards, pp. xi-xii.

38. Cugoano, p. 6. All biographical details come from Edwards's "Introduction" to the 1969 edition of Cugoano's *Thoughts and Sentiments* and from Cugoano's biographical note printed on p. iv of his text. See Cugoano, p. 12, and Edwards, p. iv.

39. Edwards, pp. v–vii.

40. Cugoano, pp. 12–13.

41. On the relationship between freedom and literacy, see Robert Burns Stepto, *From Behind the Veil: A Study of Afro-American Narrative* (Urbana: University of Illinois Press, 1979), pp. 3–32. On Job Ben Solomon, see Douglass Grant, *The Fortunate Slave: An Illustration of African Slavery in the Early Eighteenth Century* (London: Oxford University Press, 1968).

42. Cugoano, p. 13.

43. Ibid., p. 22.

44. Ibid., p. 23.

45. Ibid., pp. 77, 78.

46. Ibid., pp. 78–81.

47. Jean Toomer, *Cane* (New York: Harper & Row, 1969), p. 237.

48. Cugoano, p. 81.

49. Gracilasso de la Vega, *The Royal Commentaries of Peru*, Part II, *General History of Peru*, trans. by Sir Paul Rycaut (London: Miles Flesher, 1688), pp. 456–57. The Spanish edition is entitled El Ynca Gracilasso de la Vega, *Historia General del Perú* (Córdoba, 1617), p. 20. José Piedra located this source, and I am especially indebted to him for sharing it with me.

50. Gracilasso, *General History of Peru*, pp. 456–57.

51. Olaudah Equiano, *The Interesting Narrative of the Life of Olaudah Equiano, or Gustavus Vassa, the African. Written by Himself*, 2 vols. (London: the author, 1789). I shall be using Paul Edwards's 1969 edition of Equiano's first edition, published at London by Dawsons and hereafter referred to as Equiano.

52. Paul Edwards's excellent "Introduction" to the 1969 edition is the source of these data on Equiano's editions as well as Equiano's place of origins, hereafter referred to as Edwards. See Edwards, pp. v, vii–ix.

53. Edwards, p. v.

54. Ibid., pp. xlv–liii.

55. See ibid., pp. lxvii–lxix.

56. Equiano, Vol. I, pp. 98, 109.

57. Ibid., pp. 132–33.

58. Ibid., pp. 151–52.

59. *Monthly Review* (June 1789): 551.

60. Equiano, Vol. I, pp. 92–93.

61. Ibid., pp. 104, 106.

62. Ibid., pp. 106–7.

63. John Jea, *The Life, History, and Unparalleled Sufferings of John Jea, the African Preacher. Compiled and Written by Himself* (Portsea, Eng.: for the author, 1815?). Jea wrote a number of religious poems, which he called hymns. In 1816, he collected these and published them in a volume that also includes hymns written by other authors. This extraordinarily rare and interesting volume was discovered in the summer of 1983. See Henry Louis Gates, Jr., *The Collected Works of John Jea, African Preacher* (New York: Oxford University Press, forthcoming).

64. See *Periodical Accounts, Relative to the Baptist Missionary Society* (Dunstable, 1806), Vol. 3; and the silhouettes of Petumber Singee and Krishno Presaud, Indian preachers of the Gospel. David Dabydeen pointed out this reference to me.

65. Jea, *The Life*, p. 39.

66. Ibid., pp. 33–38.

67. Ibid., p. 9 (emphasis added).

68. See Stepto, *From Behind the Veil*, chapter 1.

Chapter 5

1. Hurston's revision of Douglass's apostrophe to the sails was suggested to me by Kimberly W. Benston. On chiasmus in *Their Eyes*, see Ephi Paul, "Mah Tongue is in Mah Friend's Mouf," unpublished essay, pp. 10–12.

2. Thomas Hamilton, "Apology," *The Anglo-African Magazine* I, no. 1 (January 1859): 1.

3. W. J. Wilson, "The Coming Man," *The Anglo-African Magazine* I, no. 2 (February 1859): 58.

4. Frances E. W. Harper, letter to Thomas Hamilton, dated 1861.

5. A Lady from Philadelphia, "The Coming American Novelist," *Lippincott's Monthly Magazine* xxxvii (April 1886): 440–43.

6. Ibid., p. 441.

7. Ibid., p. 443.

8. Ibid. On Scarborough's citation, see note 12 below.

9. W. H. A. Moore, "A Void in Our Literature," *New York Age* III, no. 4 (July 5, 1890): 3.

10. *Recorder,* August 1, 1893; *A.M.E. Church Review* xv (October 1898): 629–30. On Scarborough, see note 11 below. For an excellent discussion of these positions, see August Meier, *Negro Thought in America, 1880–1915: Racial Ideologies in the Age of Booker T. Washington* (Ann Arbor: University of Michigan Press, 1969), pp. 265–66.

11. W. S. Scarborough, "The Negro in Fiction as Portrayer and Portrayed," *Hampton Negro Conference,* No. 3 (Hampton, Va.: Hampton Institute, 1899), pp. 65–66.

12. Ibid., p. 67.

13. See "Dis and Dat: Dialect and the Descent," in Henry Louis Gates, Jr., *Figures in Black* (New York: Oxford University Press, 1986), pp. 167–95.

14. Ibid., p. 22.

15. Johnson's 1932 comments are found in his "Preface" to Brown's *Southern Road,* reprinted in *The Collected Poems of Sterling A. Brown* (New York: Harper & Row, 1980), p. 16–17.

16. Jean Toomer, *Cane* (1923; New York: Harper & Row, 1969), pp. 171–72. All subsequent references are to this edition and will be given parenthetically in the text.

17. George Schuyler, "Instructions for Contributors," reprinted in Eugene Gordon, "Negro Fictionist in America," *The Saturday Evening Quill* (April 1929): 20.

18. Scarborough, "The Negro in Fiction," p. 67.

19. I cite a definition of *skaz* deliberately, for this concept of Russian Formalism is similar to what I am calling the speakerly. See Victor Erlich, *Russian Formalism: History-Doctrine* (Mouton: The Hague, 1969), p. 238.

20. Richard Wright, *American Hunger* (New York: Harper & Row, 1979), p. 7.

21. Zora Neale Hurston, "How It Feels to Be Colored Me," *The World Tomorrow* (1928).

22. Zora Neale Hurston, *Their Eyes Were Watching God* (1937; Urbana: University of Illinois, 1978), pp. 31–32. All subsequent references are to this edition and will be given parenthetically in the text.

23. Zora Neale Hurston, *Dust Tracks on a Road: An Autobiography* (Philadelphia: J. D. Lippincott, 1942), pp. 94–95. Subsequent references will be given parenthetically.

24. Richard Wright, *Black Boy* (1945; New York: Harper & Row, 1966), p. 111.

25. See the epigraphs to this chapter.

26. John Hersey, "Interview with Ralph Ellison," in *The Language of Blackness,* ed. by Kimberly W. Benston and Henry Louis Gates, Jr., forthcoming.

27. Zora Neale Hurston, *Mules and Men: Negro Folktales and Voodoo Practices in the South* (1935; New York: Harper & Row, 1970), p. 161. Subsequent references will be given parenthetically.

28. The best discussion of the representation of black speech in Hurston's work is Karla Francesca Holloway, *A Critical Investigation of Literary and Linguistic Structures in the Fiction of Zora Neale Hurston,* Ph.D. dissertation, Michigan State University, 1978. See esp. pp. 93–94, and 101.

29. I wish to thank Barbara Johnson of Harvard University for calling my attention to this ironic mode of self-consciousness.

30. In a brilliant analysis of this scene of the novel, Barbara Johnson writes that "The entire paragraph is an externalization of Janie's feelings onto the outer surroundings in the form of a narrative of movement from private to public space. While the whole figure relates metaphorically, analogically, to the marital situation it is designed to express, it reveals the marriage space to be metonymical, a movement through a series of contiguous rooms. It is a narrative not of union but of separation centered on an image not of conjugality but of virginity." See Barbara Johnson, "Metaphor, Metonymy, and Voice in Zora Neale Hurston's *Their Eyes Were Watching God,*" in *Black Literature and Literary Theory,* ed. by H. L. Gates, Jr. (New York: Methuen, 1984), pp. 205–19.

31. Cf. Johnson: "Janie's 'inside' is here represented as a store that she then goes in to inspect. While the former paragraph was an externalization of the inner, here we find an internalization of the outer; Janie's inner self *resembles* a store. The material for this metaphor is drawn from the narrative world of contiguity; the store is the place where Joe has set himself up as lord, master, and proprietor. But here, Jody's image is broken, and reveals itself never to have been a metaphor, but only a metonymy, of Janie's dream: 'Looking at it she saw that it never was the flesh and blood *figure* of her dreams. Just something to drape her dreams over.' " Ibid.

32. Ibid.

33. See Roy Pascal, *The Dual Voice: Free Indirect Discourse and Its Functioning in the Nineteenth-Century European Novel* (Totowa, N.J.: Rowman and Littlefield, 1977), pp. 1–33.

34. See Brian McHale, "Free Indirect Discourse: A Survey of Recent Accounts," *PTL* 3 (1978): 249–87, for an excellent account of the controversy. I think the most lucid study is Michel Peled Ginsberg, "Free Indirect Discourse: Theme and Narrative Voice in Flaubert, George Eliot, and Verga," Ph.D. dissertation, Yale University, 1977. See also Stephen Ullmann, *Style in the French Novel* (Cambridge: Cambridge University Press, 1957).

35. In a sequel to this book, I would like to compare Hurston's use of free indirect discourse to that of other writers, especially Virginia Woolf.

36. Ginsberg, "Free Indirect Discourse," p. 34.

37. Ibid., p. 35.

38. Oswald Ducrot and Tzvetan Todorov, *Encyclopedic Dictionary of the Sciences of Language,* trans. by Catherine Porter (Baltimore: Johns Hopkins University Press, 1979), p. 303.

39. See Graham Hough, "Narration and Dialogue in Jane Austen," *The Critical Quarterly* xii (1970); and Pascal, *The Dual Voice,* p. 52.

40. McHale, "Free Indirect Discourse," pp. 264–80.

41. Ginsberg, "Free Indirect Discourse," p. 23.

42. Janet Holmgren McKay, *Narration and Discourse in American Realistic Fiction* (Philadelphia: University of Pennsylvania Press, 1982), p. 19.

43. Northrop Frye, *Anatomy of Criticism: Four Essays* (Princeton, N.J., 1957), p. 233.

44. Mikhail Bakhtin, "Discourse Typology in Prose," p. 190.

45. Frye, *Anatomy of Criticism*, p. 234.

Chapter 6

1. See Ishmael Reed, *The Free-Lance Pallbearers* (Garden City, N.Y., 1967), *Yellow Back Radio Broke-Down* (Garden City, N.Y., 1969), *Mumbo Jumbo* (Garden City, N.Y., 1972), *The Last Days of Louisiana Red* (New York, 1974), *Flight to Canada* (New York, 1976), and *The Terrible Twos* (New York, 1982).

2. See Neil Schmitz, "Neo-HooDoo: The Experimental Fiction of Ishmael Reed," *Twentieth Century Literature* 20 (April 1974): 126–28. Schmitz's splendid reading is, I believe, the first to discuss this salient aspect of Reed's rhetorical strategy. This paragraph is heavily indebted to Schmitz's essay.

3. Reed, *The Free-Lance Pallbearers*, p. 107.

4. Schmitz, "Neo-HooDoo," p. 127.

5. Reed, *The Free-Lance Pallbearers*, p. 93.

6. Ibid., pp. 125, 129.

7. Reed, *Yellow Back Radio Broke-Down*, pp. 34–36. For an excellent close reading of *Yellow Back Radio Broke-Down*, see Michel Fabre, "Postmodern Rhetoric in Ishmael Reed's *Yellow Back Radio Broke-Down*," in *The Afro-American Novel Since 1960*, ed. by Peter Bruck and Wolfgang Karrer (Amsterdam, 1982), pp. 167–88.

8. Reed, *Mumbo Jumbo*, p. 6. All further references to this work will be included parenthetically in the text.

9. Ralph Ellison, "And Hickman Arrives," p. 701.

10. See Charles T. Davis, *Black Is the Color of the Cosmos: Essays on Black Literature and Culture, 1942–1981*, ed. by Henry Louis Gates, Jr. (New York, 1982), pp. 167–233. See also David Dalby, "The African Element in American English," in *Rappin' and Stylin' Out*, p. 173.

11. My reading of the imagery on Reed's cover was inspired by a conversation with Robert Farris Thompson.

12. On Reed's definition of *gombo* (gumbo), see his "The Neo-HooDoo Aesthetic," *Conjure: Selected Poems, 1963–1970* (Amherst, Mass., 1972), p. 26.

13. This clever observation is James A. Snead's, for whose Yale seminar on parody I wrote the first draft of this essay.

14. Ishmael Reed, interview by Calvin Curtis, January 29, 1979.

15. Tzvetan Todorov, "The Two Principles of Narrative," trans. by Philip E. Lewis, *Diacritics* 1 (Fall 1971): 41. See his *The Poetics of Prose*, trans. by Richard Howard (Ithaca, N.Y., 1977), pp. 42–52. All further references to this work will be included parenthetically in the text.

16. For a wonderfully useful discussion of *fabula* ("fable") and *sjuzet* ("subject"), see Victor Sklovskij, "The Mystery Novel: Dickens's *Little Dorrit*," in *Readings in Russian Poetics*, pp. 220–26. On use of typology, see p. 222.

17. See Sklovskij, "The Mystery Novel," pp. 222, 226.

18. A *houngan* is a priest of Vaudou. On Vaudou, see Jean Price-Mars, *Ainsi parla l'Oncle* (Port-au-Prince, 1928); and Alfred Metraux, *Le Vodou haitien* (Paris, 1958). See my gloss on *nganga* in Chapter 2.

19. Geoffrey H. Hartman, *Criticism in the Wilderness: The Study of Literature Today* (New Haven, Conn., 1980), p. 272.

20. Ralph Ellison, *Invisible Man* (New York, 1952), p. 9. All further references to this work will be included parenthetically in the text.

21. Melville's passage from *Moby-Dick* reads: "It seemed the great Black Parliament sitting Tophet. A hundred black faces turned round in their rows to peer; and beyond, a black Angel of Doom was beating a book in a pulpit. It was a negro church; and the preacher's text was about the blackness of darkness, and the weeping and wailing and teeth-gnashing there. Ha, Ishmael, muttered I, backing out, Wretched entertainment at the sign of 'The Trap.' " *Moby-Dick* (1851; New York, 1967), p. 18. This curious figure also appears in James Pike's *The Prostrate State: South Carolina Under Negro Government* (New York, 1874), p. 62.

22. Plato, *Phaedrus*, 253d–254a. For the myth of Theuth, see 274c–275b.

23. See ibid., 259b–259e.

24. Ishmael Reed, "Dualism: in ralph ellison's invisible man," *Conjure*, p. 50.

25. W. E. B. Du Bois, *The Souls of Black Folk: Essays and Sketches* (1903; New York, 1961), p. 16–17.

Chapter 7

1. Rebecca Cox Jackson, *Gifts of Power: The Writings of Rebecca Jackson, Black Visionary, Shaker Eldress,* ed. by Jean McMahon Humez (Amherst: University of Massachusetts Press, 1981). See Alice Walker, "Gifts of Power: The Writings of Rebecca Jackson," in *In Search of Our Mothers' Gardens: Womanist Prose by Alice Walker* (New York: Harcourt Brace Jovanovich, 1983), pp. 71–82. The review first appeared in the November–December 1981 issue of *Black Scholar*. In a letter, Walker has informed me that Jackson's book "was the first book I read (I read almost nothing while writing *The Color Purple*) and reviewed *after* I finished. I took it as a sign that I was on the right track." The uncanny resemblances between key figures in Jackson's and Walker's texts suggest that forms of tradition and patterns of revision can be remarkably complex, indeed cultural.

2. Jackson, *Gifts of Power,* p. 107.

3. Ibid.

4. Ibid., pp. 107–8.

5. Ibid., p. 108.

6. Walker, "Gifts of Power," p. 73.

7. For Walker's explicit comments on Hurston, see *In Search of Our Mothers' Gardens,* pp. 83–116.

8. Amanda Smith, *An Autobiography: The Story of the Lord's Dealings with Mrs. Amanda Smith, the Colored Evangelist; Containing an Account of her Life Work of Faith, and her Travels in America, England, Ireland, Scotland, India and Africa, as an Independent Missionary* (1893; Chicago: Christian Witness Co., 1921). I wish to thank Mary Helen Washington for pointing this out to me.

9. Alice Walker, *The Color Purple* (New York: Harcourt Brace Jovanovich, 1982).

10. Quoted in Walker, *In Search of Our Mothers' Gardens*, p. 100.

11. Terry Eagleton discusses these aspects of epistolary fiction in *The Rape of Clarissa: Writing, Sexuality and Class Struggle in Samuel Richardson* (Minneapolis: University of Minnesota Press, 1982), p. 25.

12. Cited in ibid., p. 25.

13. Ibid., p. 26.

14. Jean Toomer, *Cane*, p. 204. Walker informs me that "All names in *Purple* are *family* or Eatonton, Georgia, community names. Kate was my father's mother. In real life she was the model for Annie Julia (in the novel), my grandfather's 'illegitimate' daughter (who in the novel is the wife, but who in real life was the granddaughter of Albert who in the novel is her father). It was *she,* Kate, my grandmother, who was murdered by her lover (he shot her) when my dad was eleven. Carrie was an aunt. But your version is nice, too, and my version is so confusing. For instance, the germ for Celie is Rachel, my step-grandmother: she of the poem 'Burial' in *Revolutionary Petunias."*

15. Walker writes, *"There is no book more important to me than this one* (including Toomer's *Cane,* which comes close, but from what I recognize is a more perilous direction)." *In Search of Our Mothers' Gardens,* p. 86. See also "The Divided Life of Jean Toomer," pp. 60–65.

16. Kate Nickerson points this out in an unpublished essay, " 'From Listening to the Rest': On Literary Discourse Between Zora Neale Hurston and Alice Walker," p. 57.

17. Zora Neale Hurston, "Story in Harlem Slang," *The American Mercury* 45 (July 1942): 84–96.

18. Walker, "Zora Neale Hurston," p. 88.

19. See Margaret Schlauch, *Chaucer's Constance and Accused Queens* (New York: New York University Press, 1927), pp. 63–69. I am deeply appreciative of Dr. Elizabeth Archibald for pointing this out to me.

20. Jackson, *Gifts of Power,* pp. 146–47.

Index